MITCHELL
BEAZLEY
WINE
GUIDES

# WINES OF
# Australia

JAMES HALLIDAY

**Wines of Australia**
by James Halliday

Published in Great Britain in 2005 by Mitchell Beazley,
an imprint of Octopus Publishing Group Limited,
2–4 Heron Quays, London E14 4JP

Revised editions 2003, 2005

A CIP catalogue record for this book is available from the British Library.

ISBN: 1 84533 057 9

Commissioning Editor: Hilary Lumsden
Executive Art Editor: Yasia Williams
Senior Editor: Julie Sheppard
Editor: Adrian Tempany
Design: Peter Gerrish
Production: Seyhan Esen
Index: Hilary Bird

Typeset in Versailles by Cyber Media Services
Printed and bound by Toppan Printing Company in China

# Contents

# Key to Symbols

☆☆☆☆☆   Outstanding winery regularly producing exemplary wines
☆☆☆☆⅟   Extremely good; virtually on a par with a five-star winery
☆☆☆☆   Consistently producing high-quality wines
☆☆☆⅟   A solid, reliable producer of good wine
☆☆☆   Typically good, but may have a few lesser wines
☆☆⅟   Adequate

☎   Telephone number
Ⓕ   Fax number
*est*   Established in
⚱   Production (cases)
🍷   Tastings
A$   Cellar-door sales
🍽   Restaurant
🛏   Accommodation
🚶   Guided tours

# Abbreviations

**NR**   Not Rated; used in a number of situations. Mostly for a
  new winery which has not released enough wine for a
  proper judgement to be made. Also for small, perhaps
  remote, wineries that rely solely on cellar-door trade
  and are reluctant to submit wines for critical review.
**V**   Denotes a winery whose wines are particularly well
  priced in the context of their quality.
**NA**   Not Available
**NFP**   Not for Publication
**GI**   Geographic Indication
**NSW**   New South Wales
**SA**   South Australia
**WA**   Western Australia
**EU**   European Union

# Key to Maps

·—·—·—·   State border
— — — —   Zone boundary
————   Official regional boundary
- - - - -   Interim regional boundary
·············   Probable regional boundary

Letters indicate Zones
Numbers indicate regions (excludes map on facing page)

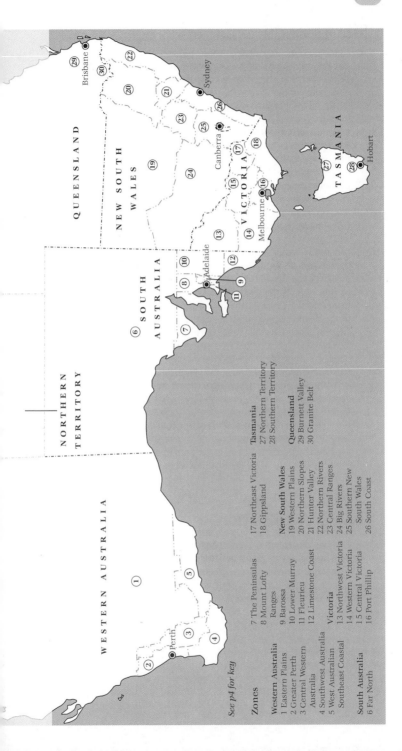

WESTERN AUSTRALIA

NORTHERN
TERRITORY

SOUTH
AUSTRALIA

QUEENSLAND

NEW SOUTH
WALES

VICTORIA

TASMANIA

Perth

Adelaide

Canberra

Melbourne

Sydney

Brisbane

Hobart

See p4 for key

## Zones

**Western Australia**
1 Eastern Plains
2 Greater Perth
3 Central Western
   Australia
4 Southwest Australia
5 West Australian
   Southeast Coastal

**South Australia**
6 Far North

7 The Peninsulas
8 Mount Lofty
   Ranges
9 Barossa
10 Lower Murray
11 Fleurieu
12 Limestone Coast

**Victoria**
13 Northwest Victoria
14 Western Victoria
15 Central Victoria
16 Port Phillip

17 Northeast Victoria
18 Gippsland

**New South Wales**
19 Western Plains
20 Northern Slopes
21 Hunter Valley
22 Northern Rivers
23 Central Ranges
24 Big Rivers
25 Southern New
   South Wales
26 South Coast

**Tasmania**
27 Northern Territory
28 Southern Territory

**Queensland**
29 Burnett Valley
30 Granite Belt

# Introduction

The new millennium arrived at what is likely to be regarded as the height of a period of unprecedented growth (and change) in the Australian wine industry.

There are many measures of this development, some of which are explained on page 7. The impact is most directly reflected in the number of wineries, which was around a little over 1,300 when the previous (2003) edition of this book was written, and at the corresponding point for this edition was 1,865. Moreover, in the last twelve months, 377 new wineries came on stream, lifting the birth rate to one every day of the year. To complicate matters, Australia has no mechanism for registration of new vineyard plantings, and no central register of new wineries. Some sensibly (and proudly) announce their arrival; others seem determined to hide their wine under a bushel.

However, this should not obscure the fundamental reality. Over the past twenty years Australian wine has permanently altered international perceptions of, and tastes in, wine and wine styles. It has dared to challenge the citadels of fine wine in France and Italy. It has edged ahead of France as the dominant supplier in the ever-competitive UK market. The United States is now Australia's largest and most profitable market in terms of value. There, only Californian wines can command a higher average retail price than those of Australia.

This demonstrates that while Australian wine is seen internationally as offering exceptional value for money, its principal focus is on quality and style rather than price. The industry has deliberately sought the views and requirements of the principal export markets, and endeavoured to accommodate these wherever feasible. It has been possible for Australia to do this for several reasons. Australia is not constrained by the European system of *appellation contrôlée*, and there is the sheer size and striking climatic and topographic diversity of the continent, exploited by the free but tenacious spirit of Australia's winemakers.

We may be the lucky country, but we have made the most of that luck.

## How to Use This Book

This book is arranged geographically. The first division is by state and then by region (*see* pages 9–10 for an explanation of these terms). Once in a region, the wineries are arranged alphabetically. There is no official classification or hierarchy of producers in Australia, but the author has used the following rating system:

| | |
|---|---|
| ☆☆☆☆☆ | Outstanding winery regularly producing exemplary wines |
| ☆☆☆☆⯪ | Extremely good; virtually on a par with a five-star winery |
| ☆☆☆☆ | Consistently producing high-quality wines |
| ☆☆☆⯪ | A solid, reliable producer of good wine |
| ☆☆☆ | Typically good, but may have a few lesser wines |
| ☆☆⯪ | Adequate |

Then there are the following symbols and abbreviations:

**NR**   Not Rated; this is used on far fewer occasions than in the previous
edition, simply because space constraints have meant the exclusion
of over 500 wineries (the size of the book could not be increased).
I have by and large elected to omit those wineries which are either
of unknown quality (they have not provided wines for review) or are
so small they are of academic interest only. Finally, some have been
omitted owing to the indifferent quality of their wines. Thus the
two-star rating has also become redundant.

**V**   Denotes a winery whose wines are particularly well priced in the
context of their quality.

**NA**   Not Available

**NFP**  Not for Publication

# History and The Future

A potted history of the Australian wine industry between 1820 and 2004
neatly divides it into four periods. The first period ran from 1820 to 1900, as
winemaking spread through New South Wales (NSW), Tasmania, Western
Australia (WA), Victoria and South Australia (SA). By 1870, production had
risen to 8.7 million litres; twenty years later Victoria alone was producing
twice that amount. Both fine table wines and fortified wines were made for
domestic and export markets.

Between 1900 and 1955, Australia became an exporter of low-cost
sweet "sherry" and "tawny port", sourced largely from South Australia's
Riverlands and around Griffith on the Murrumbidgee River. The third
period, from 1955 to 1985, saw the transition back from fortified wine to
table wine. This was also a time of declining exports and of increasing
domestic consumption of table wine; per capita, it rose from two litres
per annum in 1960 to twenty-one litres in 1985. The engine driving this
consumption was the development of the bag-in-box, which introduced
cheap table wine to all socio-economic sections of the community,
combined with a massive shift from red to white wine consumption
between 1975 and 1985.

The golden era of wine exports, 1985 to 2004, followed. This fourth
period also marked a fundamental shift in the make-up (and size) of the
nation's vineyards. In 1984/5, Australian exports were 8.7 million litres,
worth A$17 million; by June 2004, annual exports of 581 million litres were
valued in excess of A$2.55 billion.

Underlying this most recent development were three phases of change
in the vineyards. Firstly, the plantings of premium grapes increased from
33.3 per cent to over eighty per cent of the total. The other two phases are
interlinked: a complete reversal of the earlier red/white consumption ratio,
and a massive explosion in the rate and amount of new vineyard plantings.
Between 1995 and 2003, vineyard plantings increased by over 250 per cent,
from a little over 60,000 hectares to 157,000 hectares.

As has repeatedly been the case over the past twenty years, industry-wide
forecasts of export increases have become redundant the moment the ink
dried on the paper. The most recent, spanning 2000 to 2010, saw exports
increasing from 288 million litres in 2000 to 537 million litres by 2005, and

676 million litres by 2010. By 2003 exports had already reached 519 million litres (not far short of the 2005 target) and by 2004 (all these are financial-year figures) were 581 million litres. The very large 2004 vintage will drive the volume up even more steeply, but much of the increase will be at low prices.

## Climate and Soils

Rightly or wrongly, the Australian view is that climate has a far greater influence on wine quality and style than does soil. Linked with that proposition is the belief that it is far easier to modify soil structure and chemical composition than it is to mediate the effect of climate (with one major exception: irrigation).

Australia has a bewildering number of soil types, many reflecting the extreme age of the continent. Even within a small, fifteen-hectare vineyard there may be three or four different soil types. Overall, however, these are likely to be the so-called "duplex soils", marked by a sudden change from sandy or loamy surface soils to a clay subsoil. If there is no hard pan between the soil and clay, and no significant increase in acidity (*i.e.* no drop in pH), these are excellent soils for grape-growing. Australia's most celebrated soil is the terra rossa of Coonawarra (also found elsewhere in that corner of South Australia). It is a uniform limestone-derived soil with no major structural change; its red colour comes from oxidized iron traces.

The majority of Australia's wine regions are coastal, and enjoy a Mediterranean climate. Rain falls predominantly in winter and spring; the day-to-night temperature range is not great, and the risk of spring frost is much reduced. Yet there is great diversity in the comparative warmth (measured in heat-degree days: average daily temperature multiplied by the number of days in the growing season) of these maritime regions. The Swan and Hunter valleys are hotter than the Midi of France; Margaret River is (deceptively) distinctly warmer than Bordeaux; Langhorne Creek and Coonawarra are on a par with it; the Yarra Valley is cooler than Bordeaux but warmer than Burgundy; and Geelong is cooler than Burgundy.

If you look at the map of Australia on page 5, you will see just how close to the coast most of the continent's wine regions are, and how vast and empty the centre and north are. There are, of course, inland regions, with what are called Continental climates. These are unaffected by the moderating influences of oceans, and have considerable day/night (and seasonal) temperature shifts. The coldest are to be found in the mountain areas of southern NSW, Central and Southern Victoria, and Tasmania.

## Grape Varieties

Thanks largely to the extraordinary efforts of James Busby (a Scottish gardener by birth and training) and William MacArthur (best known as the founder of Australia's sheep industry), all the classic grape varieties came to Australia between 1800 and 1850. James Busby's *Journal of a Tour* makes it clear that the varieties came from impeccable vineyards. They were also brought over before phylloxera (a virulent vine pest) appeared in Europe.

Nonetheless, by 1955 there were just a handful of premium varieties in significant production. This was due to the total domination of the market by fortified wines, and the shrinking of the viticultural map to irrigated areas and to production centres in the Barossa and Hunter valleys. Only a few outposts remained.

White wines were restricted to Semillon (spelled here without the é; notably from the Hunter Valley, NSW) and Riesling (the Barossa, Clare, and Eden valleys, SA). There was only one classic red variety, Shiraz, although the winemakers of today would include Grenache and Mourvèdre (or Mataro) of which there was plenty used – mind you, in fortified winemaking. The most obvious absentees were Chardonnay (not to mention a raft of other white grapes), Cabernet Sauvignon, Merlot, and Pinot Noir. The massive changes that then took place between 1956 and 2003 are best understood from the tables that follow.

## WHITE GRAPE VARIETIES (TONNES)

|  | 1956 | 1966 | 1979 | 1989 | 2004 |
|---|---|---|---|---|---|
| Chardonnay | Nil | Nil | 1,471 | 28,419 | 328,969 |
| Riesling | 2,500 | 1,958 | 21,464 | 41,176 | 36,585 |
| Semillon | 3,000 | 11,987 | 28,457 | 40,232 | 103,171 |
| Sauvignon Blanc | Nil | Nil | 939 | 7,315 | 43,107 |

## RED GRAPE VARIETIES (TONNES)

|  | 1956 | 1966 | 1979 | 1989 | 2004 |
|---|---|---|---|---|---|
| Shiraz | 12,410 | 14,529 | 62,595 | 57,823 | 442,102 |
| Cabernet Sauvignon | 500* | 621 | 20,504 | 31,207 | 317,472 |
| Pinot Noir | 142 | 150 | 631 | 6,007 | 42,427 |
| Merlot | Nil | Nil | Nil | 2,334 | 125,179 |
| Grenache | 21,000 | 32,000 | 52,000 | 33,656 | 25,935 |
| Mourvèdre | 3,800 | 4,000 | 12,500 | 10,106 | 13,583 |

* Estimate

# Labels and Laws

Laws of the kind one expects under some form of *appellation contrôlée* system were first introduced by each of the states in 1963. While the regulations were adequate, the states refused to supply the financial and human resources needed to police compliance, so their impact was minimal.

In 1989, the industry took the matter into its own hands. The regulations were embodied in the federal government's Food Standards Code, and the industry voted for a compulsory levy to provide funds for policing the Label Integrity Programme. The core of the legislation covers the control of label claims. If a vintage, single variety, and/or single region is claimed on a label, eighty-five per cent of the wine must be of that stated vintage, variety, and region. If more than one region or variety is claimed, they must be named in the order of importance (*i.e.* percentage). There are also lists of permitted additives. Any substance not on the list is banned. Sugar is the most notorious.

In October 1994, the Australian Wine & Brandy Corporation Act was amended to provide for the registration of defined place-names. There is now a multi-tiered hierarchy of what are called Geographic Indications (GI). The most general is simply "Product of Australia". Next comes "Southeast Australia", which takes in all the principal regions of the eastern states (NSW, SA, and Victoria). Then come each of the states, a self-explanatory concept. The states are in turn divided into Zones, and next, regions, which is where the fun (or is it tragi-comedy?) starts.

To qualify, a region must produce at least 500 tonnes of wine grapes a year from at least five individually owned vineyards of at least five hectares each. The region must also be a single tract of land that is discrete and homogeneous in its grape-growing attributes to a degree that is measurable but less substantial than in a sub-region. A sub-region has similar requirements, except that it must be "homogeneous in its grape-growing attributes to a degree that is substantial". Sophisticated indeed, and small wonder the registration pace has been painfully slow. It also explains why this book is divided into regions that are in part legally defined, and in part simply reflect existing practice.

# AUSTRALIAN WINES VINTAGE CHART

1–Worst Vintage 10–Best Vintage

| Vintage | 93 | 94 | 95 | 96 | 97 | 98 | 99 | 00 | 01 | 02 | 03 |
|---|---|---|---|---|---|---|---|---|---|---|---|
| **NEW SOUTH WALES** | | | | | | | | | | | |
| **Lower Hunter Valley** | | | | | | | | | | | |
| red | 5 | 7 | 5 | 6 | 5 | 8 | 8 | 9 | 4 | 8 | 8 |
| white | 5 | 6 | 7 | 8 | 4 | 8 | 8 | 9 | 8 | 7 | 7 |
| **Upper Hunter Valley** | | | | | | | | | | | |
| red | 6 | 7 | 8 | 9 | 7 | 9 | 7 | 9 | 5 | 7 | 8 |
| white | 7 | 7 | 8 | 9 | 7 | 9 | 9 | 9 | 8 | 7 | 8 |
| **Mudgee** | | | | | | | | | | | |
| red | 5 | 8 | 6 | 8 | 8 | 8 | 5 | 3 | 5 | 9 | 6 |
| white | 7 | 8 | 7 | 8 | 7 | 9 | 5 | 5 | 6 | 7 | 6 |
| **Orange** | | | | | | | | | | | |
| red | 6 | 8 | 7 | 9 | 8 | 8 | 6 | 4 | 6 | 9 | 10 |
| white | 7 | 7 | 8 | 8 | 9 | 8 | 7 | 5 | 5 | 9 | 9 |
| **Riverina** | | | | | | | | | | | |
| red | 7 | 6 | 8 | 9 | 8 | 8 | 7 | 5 | 5 | 10 | 7 |
| white | 8 | 7 | 8 | 8 | 8 | 7 | 8 | 6 | 4 | 8 | 7 |
| **Canberra District** | | | | | | | | | | | |
| red | 8 | 8 | 9 | 8 | 8 | 9 | 6 | 5 | 8 | 9 | 8 |
| white | 7 | 6 | 8 | 8 | 8 | 7 | 7 | 6 | 8 | 8 | 7 |
| **Hastings River** | | | | | | | | | | | |
| red | 8 | 6 | 7 | 5 | 5 | 7 | 6 | 8 | 5 | 9 | 6 |
| white | 8 | 7 | 8 | 6 | 8 | 9 | 6 | 9 | 7 | 9 | 6 |
| **VICTORIA** | | | | | | | | | | | |
| **Yarra Valley** | | | | | | | | | | | |
| red | 7 | 9 | 7 | 8 | 9 | 9 | 6 | 9 | 7 | 10 | 9 |
| white | 8 | 9 | 5 | 7 | 8 | 8 | 6 | 9 | 6 | 9 | 9 |
| **Mornington Peninsula** | | | | | | | | | | | |
| red | 10 | 8 | 7 | 5 | 10 | 9 | 7 | 9 | 8 | 8 | 9 |
| white | 9 | 9 | 8 | 7 | 8 | 9 | 7 | 8 | 8 | 9 | 8 |
| **Geelong** | | | | | | | | | | | |
| red | 6 | 8 | 9 | 8 | 8 | 9 | 8 | 9 | 6 | 9 | 8 |
| white | 8 | 9 | 9 | 8 | 8 | 8 | 6 | 8 | 6 | 9 | 9 |
| **Macedon** | | | | | | | | | | | |
| red | 8 | 8 | 8 | 7 | 8 | 10 | 9 | 8 | 7 | 9 | 10 |
| white | 8 | 8 | 8 | 6 | 7 | 8 | 9 | 8 | 7 | 8 | 9 |
| **Grampians** | | | | | | | | | | | |
| red | 9 | 9 | 10 | 9 | 10 | 9 | 10 | 8 | 8 | 7 | 9 |
| white | 7 | 7 | 9 | 7 | 9 | 7 | 8 | 9 | 7 | 7 | 8 |
| **Pyrenees** | | | | | | | | | | | |
| red | 8 | 8 | 8 | 10 | 7 | 8 | 8 | 8 | 9 | 8 | 8 |
| white | 8 | 7 | 8 | 10 | 7 | 8 | 9 | 8 | 7 | 8 | 6 |
| **Henty** | | | | | | | | | | | |
| red | 9 | 8 | 7 | 8 | 8 | 8 | 5 | 6 | 6 | 8 | 7 |
| white | 7 | 9 | 8 | 9 | 8 | 8 | 6 | 5 | 5 | 8 | 10 |

| Vintage | 93 | 94 | 95 | 96 | 97 | 98 | 99 | 00 | 01 | 02 | 03 |
|---|---|---|---|---|---|---|---|---|---|---|---|
| **VICTORIA** *continued* | | | | | | | | | | | |
| **Bendigo** | | | | | | | | | | | |
| red | 6 | 8 | 7 | 9 | 10 | 9 | 9 | 8 | 9 | 9 | 7 |
| white | 5 | 7 | 6 | 8 | 9 | 9 | 6 | 5 | 6 | 7 | 6 |
| **Goulburn Valley** | | | | | | | | | | | |
| red | 6 | 7 | 8 | 7 | 9 | 10 | 7 | 8 | 8 | 9 | 8 |
| white | 6 | 8 | 7 | 8 | 6 | 9 | 9 | 8 | 7 | 8 | 6 |
| **Glenrowan and Rutherglen** | | | | | | | | | | | |
| red | 5 | 7 | 5 | 8 | 5 | 9 | 5 | 4 | 7 | 10 | 9 |
| white | 6 | 7 | 6 | 5 | 5 | 9 | 5 | 5 | 6 | 9 | 7 |
| **King Valley** | | | | | | | | | | | |
| red | 5 | 7 | 5 | 6 | 5 | 9 | 8 | 7 | 6 | 10 | 7 |
| white | 6 | 7 | 6 | 5 | 5 | 9 | 9 | 7 | 7 | 9 | 8 |
| **Gippsland** | | | | | | | | | | | |
| red | 6 | 9 | 8 | 7 | 9 | 9 | 6 | 8 | 8 | 5 | 7 |
| white | 7 | 8 | 8 | 6 | 8 | 8 | 7 | 8 | 7 | 5 | 6 |
| **SOUTH AUSTRALIA** | | | | | | | | | | | |
| **Barossa Valley** | | | | | | | | | | | |
| red | 8 | 8 | 7 | 9 | 8 | 9 | 5 | 4 | 8 | 10 | 7 |
| white | 7 | 8 | 8 | 9 | 7 | 7 | 6 | 5 | 5 | 8 | 7 |
| **Eden Valley** | | | | | | | | | | | |
| red | 8 | 9 | 7 | 9 | 7 | 8 | 7 | 6 | 9 | 9 | 7 |
| white | 7 | 7 | 8 | 8 | 9 | 8 | 6 | 6 | 8 | 10 | 9 |
| **Clare Valley** | | | | | | | | | | | |
| red | 7 | 8 | 7 | 7 | 8 | 10 | 9 | 5 | 7 | 10 | 8 |
| white | 8 | 9 | 8 | 7 | 10 | 8 | 8 | 4 | 9 | 10 | 10 |
| **Adelaide Hills** | | | | | | | | | | | |
| red | 6 | 8 | 8 | 9 | 7 | 8 | 7 | 5 | 8 | 9 | 8 |
| white | 6 | 7 | 8 | 9 | 7 | 8 | 6 | 6 | 8 | 9 | 8 |
| **Adelaide Plains** | | | | | | | | | | | |
| red | 7 | 8 | 9 | 8 | 9 | 9 | 8 | 7 | 8 | 9 | 6 |
| white | 8 | 8 | 8 | 9 | 9 | 9 | 7 | 6 | 7 | 8 | 7 |
| **Coonawarra** | | | | | | | | | | | |
| red | 8 | 9 | 6 | 9 | 7 | 10 | 9 | 8 | 8 | 9 | 9 |
| white | 8 | 9 | 7 | 9 | 6 | 8 | 7 | 7 | 7 | 8 | 8 |
| **Padthaway** | | | | | | | | | | | |
| red | 6 | 9 | 6 | 8 | 6 | 10 | 9 | 7 | 8 | 9 | 8 |
| white | 8 | 10 | 8 | 9 | 8 | 8 | 8 | 9 | 7 | 9 | 9 |
| **McLaren Vale** | | | | | | | | | | | |
| red | 8 | 9 | 8 | 9 | 7 | 10 | 7 | 7 | 7 | 9 | 8 |
| white | 8 | 9 | 8 | 9 | 7 | 8 | 7 | 5 | 5 | 8 | 7 |

| Vintage | 93 | 94 | 95 | 96 | 97 | 98 | 99 | 00 | 01 | 02 | 03 |
|---|---|---|---|---|---|---|---|---|---|---|---|
| **WESTERN AUSTRALIA** | | | | | | | | | | | |
| **Margaret River** | | | | | | | | | | | |
| red | 7 | 9 | 9 | 8 | 8 | 7 | 10 | 9 | 8 | 8 | 8 |
| white | 9 | 8 | 9 | 8 | 6 | 7 | 8 | 8 | 8 | 8 | 8 |
| **Great Southern** | | | | | | | | | | | |
| red | 7 | 10 | 9 | 8 | 7 | 6 | 7 | 7 | 9 | 8 | 7 |
| white | 7 | 9 | 8 | 8 | 9 | 7 | 8 | 7 | 8 | 8 | 6 |
| **Swan District** | | | | | | | | | | | |
| red | 7 | 6 | 6 | 6 | 7 | 9 | 9 | 7 | 9 | 10 | 7 |
| white | 10 | 7 | 7 | 6 | 5 | 9 | 7 | 6 | 6 | 9 | 6 |
| **TASMANIA** | | | | | | | | | | | |
| **Northern Tasmania** | | | | | | | | | | | |
| red | 5 | 8 | 9 | 7 | 8 | 10 | 9 | 10 | 8 | 9 | 7 |
| white | 8 | 9 | 9 | 7 | 9 | 9 | 9 | 9 | 8 | 9 | 7 |
| **Southern Tasmania** | | | | | | | | | | | |
| red | 9 | 9 | 8 | 5 | 8 | 9 | 8 | 10 | 8 | 9 | 8 |
| white | 9 | 8 | 9 | 6 | 8 | 8 | 7 | 9 | 8 | 9 | 7 |
| **QUEENSLAND** | | | | | | | | | | | |
| red | 10 | 10 | 9 | 9 | 7 | 9 | 8 | 10 | 8 | 9 | 8 |
| white | 9 | 9 | 9 | 10 | 6 | 5 | 6 | 9 | 7 | 8 | 7 |

# New South Wales

1994    14,332 hectares    21.37 per cent of total plantings
2003    37,039 hectares    23.51 per cent of total plantings
NSW has slightly exceeded the national growth rate in plantings.
A significant contributor has been the increase in the number and size of
the vineyards on the western side of the Great Dividing Range.

## Lower Hunter Valley

The chief reason for the birth in 1825 and consequent survival of the
Hunter Valley is its proximity to Sydney. In best parochial fashion, the
city has come to regard the region as its own. Theoretically, however, the
Hunter is by no means a natural winemaking area. The Lower Hunter
surely has to be one of the most capricious and vexatious wine regions in
the world. It produces one of Australia's greatest – and unique – wines,

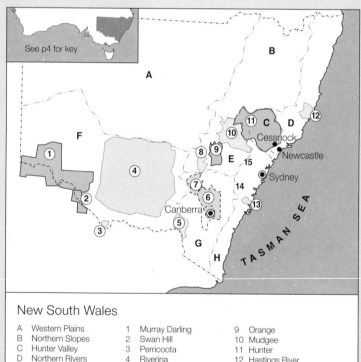

## New South Wales

| | | |
|---|---|---|
| A | Western Plains | 1 Murray Darling | 9 Orange |
| B | Northern Slopes | 2 Swan Hill | 10 Mudgee |
| C | Hunter Valley | 3 Perricoota | 11 Hunter |
| D | Northern Rivers | 4 Riverina | 12 Hastings River |
| E | Central Ranges | 5 Tumbarumba | 13 Shoalhaven Coast |
| F | Big Rivers | 6 Canberra District | 14 Sydney Basin |
| G | Southern New | 7 Hilltops | 15 Southern Highlands |
|   | South Wales | 8 Cowra | |
| H | South Coast | | |

the long-lived Semillon, and some very fine Shiraz. It can even be cajoled into making excellent Chardonnay (Tyrrell's, Lake's Folly) and Cabernet Sauvignon (Lake's Folly). It can do all this in spite of the fact that it is (or ought to be) far too warm for fine table wine; only small patches of its soils are truly suitable for grape-growing; and – most of all – rainfall tends to be concentrated during vintage time, when the tail-ends of summer monsoons sweep down the coast from Queensland. Yet none of this deters the winemakers – or wine-lovers, for the Lower Hunter is, of course, a Mecca for wine tourists.

Tourism began in a tentative way in the early 1970s, grew strongly in the '80s, and became a gale in the '90s. There are now luxury hotels, vineyard cottages, restaurants of every variety. Visitors are also drawn by the peculiarly Australian beauty of the gently undulating valley. The smoky blue of the Brokenback Range is a significant part of the landscape, wherever in the valley you are. Its stark outline rises threateningly above the nearest vineyards along the Broke Road, and is distantly though clearly etched as you look back from Allandale and Wilderness Roads. All this, and only one-and-a-half hours' drive north of Sydney. There are 148 wineries in the region.

**Allandale** ☆☆☆☆ **V**

*Lovedale Road, Lovedale, NSW 2320, ☎ (02) 4990 4526, Ⓕ (02) 4990 1714; est 1978; ❖ 25,000 cases; 🍷; A$; Mon-Sat 9-5, Sun 10-5*

Winemaker Bill Sneddon presides over an unpretentious and very reliable, good-quality winery using both Hunter Valley and Central Ranges (Mudgee, Hilltops) grapes. Riesling, Semillon, and Chardonnay are all good. Exports to the UK and elsewhere.

**Audrey Wilkinson** ☆☆☆½

*Oakdale, De Beyers Road, Pokolbin, NSW 2320, ☎ (02) 4998 7411, Ⓕ (02) 4998 7303; est 1999; ❖ 15,000 cases; 🍷; A$; Mon-Fri 9-5, wkds 9.30-5*

A historic vineyard rehabilitated by the James Fairfax/Pepper Tree Wine Group, with a new cellar door and great views. Semillon, Shiraz and (uniquely for the region) Malbec are the best.

**Batchelor's Terrace Vale** ☆☆☆☆

*Deasey's Lane, Pokolbin, NSW 2321, ☎ (02) 4998 7517, Ⓕ (02) 4998 7814; est 1971; ❖ 9,000 cases; 🍷; A$; 7 days 10–4*

In April 2001, the Batchelor family acquired Terrace Vale, but little else has changed. Alain Leprince remains as winemaker, and the wines still come from the 30-year-old estate plantings.

**Belgenny Vineyard** ☆☆☆½

*92 De Beyers Road, Pokolbin, NSW 2320, ☎ (02) 9247 5300, Ⓕ (02) 9247 7273; est 1990; ❖ 7,000 cases; no visitors*

Established by Norman Seckold and Dudley Leitch with a carefully thought out business plan; seventeen hectares of vines, with a cellar door and restaurant planned; exports to the UK and elsewhere.

**Bimbadgen Estate** ☆☆☆½

*Lot 21, McDonalds Road, Pokolbin, NSW 2321, ☎ (02) 4998 7585, Ⓕ (02) 4998 7732; est 1968; ❖ 70,000 cases; 🍷; A$; 7 days 9.30-5; 🍽; 🛏*

Five owners (and name changes) since 1968 say much. The forty-five hectares of estate vineyards provide the base for substantial production, an on-site restaurant an added bonus. Exports to the UK and elsewhere.

**Briar Ridge** ☆☆☆☆
*Mount View Road, Mount View, NSW 2325, ☎ (02) 4990 3670, ⓕ (02) 4990 7802;*
*est 1972; ◊ 27,000 cases; ☗; A$; 7 days 10-5; ⛻*
Draws on forty-eight hectares of estate vineyards, with a winemaking team
of Karl Stockhausen and Steven Dodd. Crisp, minerally, lemony Semillon,
generous but not flabby Chardonnay, and bright, earthy/cherry Shiraz
are all very good. Exports to the UK and elsewhere.

**Broke's Promise Wines** ☆☆☆☆
*725 Milbrodale Road, Broke, NSW 2330, ☎ (02) 6579 1165, ⓕ (02) 9438 4985;*
*est 1996; ◊ 2,000 cases; ☗; A$; by appt*
Jane Marquard and Dennis Karp have followed tradition by planting
Shiraz, Chardonnay and Semillon, and broken it by planting Barbera and
olive trees. Exports to the UK and elsewhere.

**Brokenwood** ☆☆☆☆☆
*McDonalds Road, Pokolbin, NSW 2321, ☎ (02) 4998 7559, ⓕ (02) 4998 7893; est*
*1970; ◊ 70,000 cases; ☗; A$; 7 days 10-5*
A deservedly fashionable winery producing consistently excellent wines,
partly from estate-grown grapes (notably Graveyard Shiraz, in the top
Australian league), as well as from fruit purchased in the Hunter (Semillon)
and across Southeast Australia (Cricket Pitch). For the record, I was one of
the founders, but cut my ties in 1983. Exports to the UK and elsewhere.

**Calais Estate** ☆☆☆
*Palmers Lane, Pokolbin, NSW 2321, ☎ (02) 4998 7654, ⓕ (02) 4998 7813; est*
*1987; ◊ 11,000 cases; ☗; A$; 7 days 9-5; ⛻*
Richard and Susan Bradley purchased the substantial Calais Estate winery
in April 2000. Long-serving winemaker Adrian Sheridan continues in his
role, and the estate offers a wide range of facilities for visitors, ranging
from private function rooms to picnic spots, to an undercover outdoor
entertaining area.

**Capercaillie** ☆☆☆☆
*Londons Road, Lovedale, NSW 2325, ☎ (02) 4990 2904, ⓕ (02) 4991 1886;*
*est 1995; ◊ 6,000 cases; ☗; A$; Mon-Sat 9-5, Sun 10-5; art gallery*
Run by veteran Alasdair Sutherland. Draws on a fruit salad of estate-
grown Chardonnay (rich, peachy) and a range of varieties and regions
elsewhere across Australia; reds consistently good. Exports to the UK
and elsewhere.

**Catherine Vale Vineyard** ☆☆☆☆
*656 Milbrodale Road, Bulga, NSW 2330, ☎ (02) 6579 1334, ⓕ (02) 6579 1334;*
*est 1994; ◊ 1,500 cases; ☗; A$; wkds & hols 10-5, or by appt*
Former schoolteachers Bill and Wendy Lawson run the 5.6-hectare
vineyard, selling grapes to contract winemaker John Hordern, and taking
back wine in part payment.

**Chateau Francois** NR
*Broke Road, Pokolbin, NSW 2321, ☎ (02) 4998 7548, ⓕ (02) 4998 7805; est*
*1969; ◊ 700 cases; ☗; A$; wkds 9-5, or by appt*
A former fisheries director-turned-winemaker, Don Francois is an old
friend who sells his strongly regional and absurdly cheap wines from his
lovely hillside house-cum-winery.

**Chateau Pâto** ☆☆☆☆☆
*Thompson's Road, Pokolbin, NSW 2321, ☎ (02) 4998 7634, ⓕ (02) 4998 7860;*
*est 1980; ◊ 300 cases; ☗; A$; by appt*

Nicholas Paterson is in charge of this tiny estate operation, producing superbly rich, velvety Shiraz. Most of the grapes are sold (doubtless at prices reflecting their quality).

**Chatto Wines** ☆☆☆☆

*McDonalds Road, Pokolbin, NSW 2325, ☎ (04) 1710 9794, Ⓕ (02) 4998 7294; est 2000; ♦ 750 cases; ♀; A$; 7 days 9-5; K*

Owner/winemaker Jim Chatto moved from the Hunter to Tasmania and back again. He is now using Tasmanian Pinot and Hunter Semillon to great effect.

**Colvin Wines** ☆☆☆↓

*19 Boyle Street, Mosman, NSW 2088 (postal), ☎ (02) 9908 7886, Ⓕ (02) 9908 7885; est 1999; ♦ 6,500 cases; no visitors*

Sydney lawyer John Colvin and wife Robyn own the historic De Beyer Vineyard, with contract-made Semillon and Sangiovese to the fore.

**Constable & Hershon** ☆☆☆↓

*1 Gillards Road, Pokolbin, NSW 2320, ☎ (02) 4998 7887, Ⓕ (02) 4998 6555; est 1981; ♦ 3,000 cases; ♀; A$; 7 days 10-5; K; gardens*

Features four spectacular formal gardens: the Rose, Knot and Herb, Secret, and Sculpture. Offers a range of several vintages of buttery/toasty Chardonnay.

**De Bortoli** ☆☆☆↓ V

*Lot 1, Branxton Road, Pokolbin, NSW 2320, ☎ (02) 4993 8800, Ⓕ (02) 4993 8899; est 2002; ♦ 40,000 cases; ♀; A$; 7 days 10-5*

The most recent arm of the expanding De Bortoli empire, formerly known as the Wilderness Estate. Sixty-six hectares of vineyards, complemented by grapes and wines from other regions, underlie varietals at three quality and price levels. Worldwide distribution.

**De Iuliis** ☆☆☆↓

*21 Broke Road, Pokolbin, NSW 2320, ☎ (02) 4993 8000, Ⓕ (02) 4998 7168; est 1990; ♦ 9,000 cases; ♀; A$; 7 days 10-5; ♜; K*

Three generations of the De Iuliis family have been involved in the establishment of this twenty-hectare vineyard at Keinbah. Under Michael de Iuliis, they have moved from contract grape-growing into winemaking. Exports to the UK, Switzerland.

**Drayton's Family Wines** ☆☆☆

*Oakey Creek Road, Cessnock, NSW 2321, ☎ (02) 4998 7513, Ⓕ (02) 4998 7743; est 1853; ♦ 90,000 cases; ♀; A$; Mon-Fri 8-5, wkds & public hols 10-5; K*

Approaching its 150th birthday in direct family ownership. The flinty Semillon and Bin 5555 Hermitage are both good, mid-range wines; William Shiraz and Joseph Shiraz, from very old vines, are stylish, gently oaked flagships. Exports to the UK and elsewhere.

**Elysium Vineyard** ☆☆☆☆↓

*393 Milbrodale Road, Broke, NSW 2330, ☎ (02) 9664 2368, Ⓕ (02) 9664 2368; est 1990; ♦ 450 cases; ♀; A$; wkds 10-5, or by appt; ⊨; K; wine education wkds*

Victoria Foster has one hectare of Verdelho, and runs weekend wine and food courses at her award-winning (tourism) cottage that sleeps six. The Verdelho ages well.

**Evans Family** ☆☆☆☆

*151 Palmers Lane, Pokolbin, NSW 2321, ☎ (02) 4998 7237, Ⓕ (02) 4998 7201; est 1979; ♦ 2,600 cases; ♀; A$; 7 days 10-5*

Centred on the plantings of Gamay (which is rare in Australia) and

Chardonnay grown around the ancestral mansion of Leonard Paul Evans AO, OBE. The Chardonnay is voluptuous, the Gamay flirtatious.

**Fairview Wines** ☆☆☆⁄

*422 Elderslie Road, Branxton, NSW 2335, ☏ (02) 4938 1116, Ⓕ (02) 4938 1116; est 1997; ⏶ 2,000 cases; ⏼; A$; Fri-Mon 10-5, or by appt; ⏺; Ⲕ*

Greg and Elaine Searles grow Shiraz, Barbera, Semillon, Verdelho, and Chambourcin using organic techniques wherever possible, and will greet you in person at the cellar door. Exports to the UK.

**First Creek Wines** ☆☆☆☆

*Corner McDonalds Road and Gillards Road, Pokolbin, NSW 2321, ☏ (02) 4998 7293, Ⓕ (02) 4998 7294; est 1984; ⏶ 25,000 cases; ⏼; A$; 7 days 9.30-5; ⏗*

First Creek is the shop-front of Monarch Winemaking Services, which has acquired the former Allanmere wine business and offers a complex range of wines, under both the First Creek and Allanmere labels. The quality is very reliable. Exports to the UK and elsewhere.

**Gartlemann Hunter Estate** ☆☆☆☆

*Lovedale Road, Lovedale, NSW 2321, ☏ (02) 4930 7113, Ⓕ (02) 4930 7114; est 1970; ⏶ 10,000; ⏼; A$; 7 days 10-5; Ⲕ*

In 1996, Jan and Jorg Gartlemann purchased what was previously the sixteen-hectare George Hunter Estate, established by Sydney restaurateur Oliver Shaul in 1970. Chardonnay, Semillon, and Shiraz are contract-made. Exports to the UK and elsewhere.

**Glenguin** ☆☆☆☆

*Milbrodale Road, Broke, NSW 2330, ☏ (02) 6579 1009, Ⓕ (02) 6579 1009; est 1993; ⏶ 9,000 cases; ⏼; A$; at Boutique Wine Centre, Broke Road, Pokolbin*

Named for the Scottish distillery and Barony of WWII Air Chief Marshall Sir Arthur Tedder, grandfather of current owner Lord Robin Tedder. Robin also happens to be a Master of Wine, and oversees the making of wines from fifteen hectares of estate plantings at Broke and four hectares of Pinot Gris and Sangiovese at Orange. Exports to the UK and elsewhere.

**Heartland Vineyard** ☆☆☆⁄

*PO Box 78, Greta, NSW 2334, ☏ (02) 4938 6272, Ⓕ (02) 4938 6004; est 1998; ⏶ 1,500 cases; no visitors*

Cleverly named vineyard of cardiac surgeon and cardiac scrub nurse Duncan and Libby Thomson. Plantings of Shiraz, Semillon, Merlot, Barbera and Viognier, the wines competently contract-made.

**Honeytree Estate** ☆☆☆⁄

*16 Gillards Road, Pokolbin, NSW 2321, ☏ (02) 4998 7693, Ⓕ (02) 4998 7693; est 1970; ⏶ 3,600 cases; ⏼; A$; Wed-Fri 11-4, wkds 10-5; ⏗*

Honeytree was set up in 1970, then lapsed into obscurity before a change of ownership and revitalization by Henk and Robyn Strengers. Produces a trophy-winning Semillon via competent contract winemaking. Also specializes in Clairette. Exports to the UK and Netherlands.

**Hope Estate NR**

*Cobcroft Road, Broke, NSW 2330, ☏ (02) 6579 1161, Ⓕ (02) 6579 1373; est 1996; ⏶ 30,000 cases; ⏼; A$; 7 days 10-4*

Now the head of a wine empire established by pharmacist Michael Hope extending to Donnybrook in Western Australia and the distinguished Virgin Hills in Victoria. Exports to the UK and elsewhere.

**House of Certain Views** ☆☆☆☆
*1238 Milbrodale Road, Broke, NSW 2330, ☎ (02) 6579 1317, Ⓕ (02) 6579 1317; est 2001; ⏻ 1,500 cases; no visitors*
A stand-alone venture of Margan Family Wines using contract-grown grapes from pioneering vineyard sites high on the western slopes of the Great Dividing Range to make striking Shiraz, Cabernet, and Merlot. Exports to the UK and elsewhere.

**Hungerford Hill** ☆☆☆☆
*1 Broke Road, Pokolbin, NSW 2321, ☎ 1800 187 666, Ⓕ (02) 4998 7375; est 1967; ⏻ 20,000 cases; ⏰; A$; 7 days 10-5; ⏹*
Reborn under Cassegrain Wines' ownership, producing a kaleidoscopic array of over thirty varietal wines from seven regions at many different price points, all identified by variety/varietal blend.

**Iron Gate Estate** ☆☆☆
*Oakey Creek Road, Pokolbin, NSW 2320, ☎ (02) 4998 6570, Ⓕ (02) 4998 6571; est 2001; ⏻ 5,000 cases; ⏰; A$; 7 days 10-4*
Iron Gate Estate would not be out of place in the Napa Valley, which favours bold architectural statements made without regard to cost. No expense has been spared in equipping the winery and its lavish cellar-door facilities. Has eight hectares of estate plantings; Semillon by far the best.

**Ivanhoe Wines** ☆☆☆⏺
*Marrowbone Road, Pokolbin, NSW 2320, ☎ (02) 4998 7325, Ⓕ (02) 4998 7848; est 1995; ⏻ 7,000; ⏰; A$; 7 days 10-5; ⏹; wine school*
Stephen Drayton is the third branch of the family to be actively involved in this winery, with twenty-five hectares of thirty-year-old vines providing a first-class base. The Ivanhoe property has been so-called since 1840.

**Jackson's Hill** ☆☆☆⏺
*Mount View Road, Mount View, NSW 2321, ☎ 1300 720 098, Ⓕ 1300 130 220; est 1983; ⏻ 1,600 cases; ⏰; A$; by appt*
A resident of the spectacularly scenic Mount View Road quixotically specializing in Cabernet Franc and Semillon in various guises. The quality of the homemade chocolates is another good reason to visit.

**Keith Tulloch Wine** ☆☆☆☆☆
*Lilywood Farm, O'Connors Road, Pokolbin, NSW 2320, ☎ (02) 4990 7867, Ⓕ (02) 4990 7171; est 1997; ⏻ 6,500 cases; no visitors*
Born and bred in the Hunter, and with a distinguished career behind him, Keith Tulloch began the development of his own label in 1997, producing superbly textured Semillon, Chardonnay, Shiraz, and Merlot from day one. Exports to the UK.

**Krinklewood** ☆☆☆
*712 Wollombi Road, Broke, NSW 2330, ☎ (02) 9969 1311, Ⓕ (02) 9968 3435; est 1981; ⏻ 5,000 cases; ⏰; A$; wkds, long wkds, or by appt*
Rod and Suzanne Windrim moved from Pokolbin to Broke-Fordwich in 1996, establishing 17.5 hectares of vineyards. Semillon and Verdelho are best.

**Kulkunbulla** ☆☆☆☆
*Brokenback Estate, Lot 1, Broke Road, Pokolbin, NSW 2320, ☎ (02) 4998 7140, Ⓕ (02) 4998 7142; est 1996; ⏻ 5,000 cases; ⏰; A$; by appt*
A reincarnation of part of the former Rothbury Brokenback Estate. This smoothly run owner-syndicate has produced cleverly packaged Semillon and Chardonnay with excellent flavour, concentration, and style.

**Lake's Folly** ☆☆☆☆☆

*Broke Road, Pokolbin, NSW 2320, ☎ (02) 4998 7507, Ⓕ (02) 4998 7322; est 1963; ❀ 4,500 cases; ⚑; A$; Mon-Sat 10-4*

Dr Max Lake pioneered the concept of "weekend winemaking" by untrained winemakers in Australia (hence the name). Now owned by Perth businessman Peter Fogarty, still producing superb, complex stone-fruit/tangy Chardonnay and finely structured Cabernets. If you can find it, enjoy! Exports to the UK and elsewhere.

**Lindemans** ☆☆☆☆

*McDonalds Road, Pokolbin, NSW 2320, ☎ (02) 4998 7684, Ⓕ (02) 4998 7324; est 1843; ❀ NFP; ⚑; A$; 7 days 10-5*

The historic Ben Ean winery was completely restored in 1999 as an Olympic showplace, and is well worth the visit; some aged classic releases keep the flame alive (just); all winemaking activity in the Lower Hunter has ceased.

**Little Wine Company** ☆☆☆

*824 Milbrodale Road, Broke, NSW 2330, ☎ (02) 6579 1111, Ⓕ (02) 6579 1440; est 1984; ❀ 15,000 cases; ⚑; A$; Fri-Mon 10-4.30, Wed 12.30-4*

Incorporates the Olivine range of Viognier, Sangiovese Rosé, Sangiovese/Shiraz, Merlot, and the Canberra-District-sourced Talga range of Chardonnay and Shiraz, all neatly made. Exports to the UK and elsewhere.

**Margan Family Winegrowers** ☆☆☆☆

*1238 Milbrodale Road, Broke, NSW 2330, ☎ (02) 6579 1317, Ⓕ (02) 6579 1317; est 1997; ❀ 30,000 cases; ⚑; A$; 7 days 10-5; ⏏*

Flying winemaker Andrew Margan has returned to the roost with hospitality and marketing wife Lisa. A new 700-tonne winery is producing excellent wine from ten hectares of estate vineyards and thirteen under lease. The Chardonnay and Shiraz in particular stand out. Exports to the UK and elsewhere.

**Marsh Estate** ☆☆☆ V

*Deasey Road, Pokolbin, NSW 2321, ☎ (02) 4998 7587, Ⓕ (02) 4998 7884; est 1971; ❀ 7,000 cases; ⚑; A$; Mon-Fri 10-4.30, wkds 10-5*

A long-established family company; the winemaking reins have now passed from father Peter to son Andrew Marsh. Sales all via cellar door and mail order.

**McGuigan Wines** ☆☆☆☆ V

*Corner Broke Road and McDonalds Road, Pokolbin, NSW 2321, ☎ (02) 4998 7700, Ⓕ (02) 4998 7401; est 1992; ❀ 400,000 cases; ⚑; A$; 7 days 9.30-5; ⏏; ⚓*

A highly successful public company, relentlessly driven by the awesome energy and peerless marketing skills of Brian McGuigan, and more recently by the winemaking skills of Peter Hall. In February 2002, it engineered a reverse take-over of the giant Simeon Wines. Also owns Yaldara and Miranda (*q.v.*). Exports to the UK and elsewhere.

**McLeish Estate** ☆☆☆☆

*Lot 3, De Beyers Road, Pokolbin, NSW 2320, ☎ & Ⓕ (02) 4998 7754; est 1985; ❀ 3,000 cases; ⚑; A$; 7 days 10-5, or by appt*

Bob and Marion McLeish have progressively planted over ten hectares of vines since 1985, more recently opening a cellar door; competent contract winemaking by Andrew Thomas. Exports to the UK and elsewhere.

**McWilliam's Mount Pleasant** ☆☆☆☆☆ V

*Marrowbone Road, Pokolbin, NSW 2320, ☎ (02) 4998 7505, Ⓕ (02) 4998 7761; est 1921; ❀ NFP; ⚑; A$; 7 days 10-5; ⏏; ⚓; gift shop*

One of the Hunter Valley's treasures. The Elizabeth Semillon, released for a song when five years old, is the best-value white in Australia. Old Paddock and Old Hill Shiraz and O'Shea Shiraz are silky classics, too. Exports to the UK and elsewhere.

**Meerea Park** ☆☆☆☆

*Lot 3, Palmers Lane, Pokolbin, NSW 2320, ☎ (02) 4998 7474, Ⓕ (02) 4930 7100; est 1991; ◈ 10,000 cases; ♟; A$; at Boutique Wine Centre, Broke Road, Pokolbin*

This is a particularly interesting venture and the brainchild of Rhys Eather, great-grandson of Alexander Munro, a famous local vigneron. Eather buys grapes from here, there, and everywhere, and makes the wine at the former Little Winery on Palmers Lane. Exports to the UK and elsewhere.

**Millfield** ☆☆♦

*Lot 341, Mount View Road, Millfield, NSW 2325, ☎ (02) 4998 1571, Ⓕ (02) 4998 0172; est 1997; ◈ 500 cases; ♟; A$; wkds 10-4*

Situated on the Mount View Road, its neatly labelled and packaged Semillon, Chardonnay, and Shiraz have won gold medals from the first vintage in 1998. Mail order (worldwide).

**Mistletoe Wines** ☆☆☆♦

*771 Hermitage Road, Pokolbin, NSW 2320, ☎ (02) 4998 7770, Ⓕ (02) 4998 7792; est 1989; ◈ 3,000 cases; ♟; A$; 7 days 10-6; sculpture garden*

A name that has come and gone at various times since 1909 has been revived by the Sloan family. The pleasant wines are made by contract winemaker John Cassegrain and sold exclusively through cellar door and mail order.

**Molly Morgan Vineyard** ☆☆☆☆

*Talga Road, Lovedale, NSW 2321, ☎ (02) 9816 4088, Ⓕ (02) 9816 2680; est 1963; ◈ 5,500 cases; ♟; A$; by appt; ⇐*

Ownership by powerful former wine retailers, thirty-year-old vines, skilled winemaking, and the history of convict Molly Morgan have revitalized this picturesque vineyard. Powerful, lemony Semillon is setting the pace.

**Monahan Estate** ☆☆☆☆

*Lot 1, Wilderness Road, Rothbury, NSW 2320, ☎ (02) 4930 9070, Ⓕ (02) 4930 7679; est 1997; ◈ 2,000 cases; ♟; A$; Thurs-Sun 10-5*

Now owned by John and Patricia Graham, and situated in a sub-district long known for the quality of its Semillon. Skilled contract winemaking delivers the goods.

**Mount Eyre Vineyard** ☆☆☆♦

*1325 Broke Road, Broke, NSW 2330, ☎ 0438 683973, Ⓕ (02) 9744 3508; est 1996; ◈ 9,000 cases; ♟; A$; by appt*

Dr Aniello Inannuzzi's estate is planted with Semillon, Chardonnay, Shiraz, Cabernet Franc, and Cabernet Sauvignon. Blind winemaker CP Lin commutes between Christchurch, NZ (making Pinot Noir) and the Hunter Valley each vintage; he has also translated *The Oxford Companion to Wine* into Braille.

**Mount View Estate** ☆☆☆♦

*Mount View Road, Mount View, NSW 2325, ☎ (02) 4990 3307, Ⓕ (02) 4991 1289; est 1971; ◈ 3,100 cases; ♟; A$; 7 days 10-5*

Changes of ownership have led to changes in focus, with excellent red wines sourced from as far afield as McLaren Vale.

**Nightingale Wines** ☆☆☆☆

*1239 Milbrodale Road, Broke, NSW 2330, ☎ (02) 6579 1499, Ⓕ (02) 6579 1477; est 1997; ✦ 10,000 cases; ⛆; A$; 7 days 10-4; ▯*

Paul and Gail Nightingale have wasted no time in establishing twelve hectares of Verdelho, Merlot, Shiraz, Chardonnay, Cabernet Sauvignon, and Chambourcin; the wines are contract-made and sold through cellar door, a wine club, and exports to the UK and elsewhere.

**Oakvale** ☆☆☆☆

*Broke Road, Pokolbin, NSW 2320, ☎ (02) 4998 7088, Ⓕ (02) 4998 7077; est 1893; ✦ 17,000 cases; ⛆; A$; 7 days 10-5; coffee shop; museum*

Oakvale is the front-of-house for the several-million-dollar Hunter Valley investments of Richard and Mary Owens, who have retained a hundred years of history along with golden-hued, buttery/toasty Sauvignon and Chardonnay. Exports to the UK and US.

**Outram Estate** ☆☆☆☆

*PO Box 621, Broadway, NSW 2007, ☎ (02) 9481 7576, Ⓕ (02) 9481 7879; est 1995; ✦ 1,150 cases; no visitors*

Dr Geoff Cutter has established five hectares of Merlot on rich red volcanic basalt, and thirteen hectares of Verdelho and Chardonnay on the sandy grey soils of Wollombi Creek. The first wines show much promise; exports already established to the UK and elsewhere.

**Peacock Hill Vineyard** ☆☆☆

*Corner Branxton Road and Palmers Lane, Pokolbin, NSW 2320, ☎ (02) 4998 7661, Ⓕ (02) 4998 7661; est 1969; ✦ 1,500 cases; ⛆; A$; Thurs-Mon, public & school hols 10-5, or by appt; ⊨*

The Peacock Hill Vineyard was first planted in 1969 as part of the Rothbury Estate; it was acquired by George Tsiros and Silvi Laumets in '95; they have rejuvenated the vineyard and established a small lodge. The wines are contract-made.

**Pendarves Estate** ☆☆☆

*110 Old North Road, Belford, NSW 2335, ☎ (02) 6574 7222, Ⓕ (02) 9970 6152; est 1986; ✦ 12,000 cases; ⛆; A$; wkds 11-5, Mon-Fri by appt; ⊨*

Wine and health activist, wine historian, and general practitioner Dr Philip Norrie also finds time to grow grapes and (via contract) make worthwhile wines of assorted variety and hue, especially Chardonnay. Exports to the UK and elsewhere.

**Pepper Tree Wines** ☆☆☆☆

*Halls Road, Pokolbin, NSW 2321, ☎ (02) 4998 7539, Ⓕ (02) 4998 7746; est 1993; ✦ 60,000 cases; ⛆; A$; Mon-Fri 9-5, wkds 9.30-5; ▯; ⊨; ✗*

With access to vineyards in both the Hunter Valley and Coonawarra, Pepper Tree winemaker Chris Cameron has made a determined and quite successful effort to establish Pepper Tree as one of Australia's leading producers of Merlot. Exports to the UK and elsewhere.

**Petersons** ☆☆☆☆

*Mount View Road, Mount View, NSW 2325, ☎ (02) 4990 1704, Ⓕ (02) 4991 1344; est 1971; ✦ 15,000 cases; ⛆; A$; Mon-Sat 9-5, Sun 10-5*

One of the older wineries of this region, established by Newcastle pharmacist Colin Peterson, with twenty hectares of beautifully located vineyards. It has had various moments of glory along the way, with rich Semillon, Chardonnay, and powerful, earthy/cherryish Back Block Shiraz.

**Piggs Peake** ☆☆☆✓
*697 Hermitage Road, Pokolbin, NSW 2335, ☎ (02) 6574 7000, ⑤ (02) 6574 7070;
est 1998; ♦ 1,500 cases; ⚑; A$; 7 days 10-5, 10-6 during daylight savings; gallery; ✗*
The derivation of the name remains a mystery to me. It is one of the newer
wineries to be constructed in the Hunter Valley, sourcing most of its grapes
from other growers to complement the one hectare of estate Shiraz.

**Poole's Rock** ☆☆☆☆
*De Beyers Road, Pokolbin, NSW 2321, ☎ (02) 9563 2500, ⑤ (02) 9563 2555;
est 1988; ♦ 42,000 cases; ⚑; A$; 7 days 10-5*
Now the rock on which the burgeoning wine empire of leading investment
banker and wine man David Clarke is based. The seventy-four-hectare
Glen Elgin Estate vineyard operates in tandem with eighteen hectares of
Chardonnay at Broke, with additional grapes sourced throughout
Australia for the Poole's Rock and Cockfighters Ghost labels. Exports to
the UK and elsewhere.

**Pothana** ☆☆☆☆
*Pothana Lane, Belford, NSW 2335, ☎ (02) 6574 7164, ⑤ (02) 6574 7209;
est 1984; ♦ 5,000 cases; ⚑; A$; by appt*
Former flying winemaker David Hook is making splendid estate-grown
Semillon, Chardonnay, and Shiraz under The Gorge and Pothana labels.

**Reg Drayton Wines** ☆☆☆✓ V
*Corner Pokolbin Mountain and McDonalds Roads, Pokolbin, NSW 2321, ☎ (02)
4998 7523, ⑤ (02) 4998 7523; est 1989; ♦ 5,500 cases; ⚑; A$; 7 days 10-5;
museum*
Fifth-generation Robyn Drayton (billed as the Hunter's first female
vigneron) and husband Craig inherited the business after her parents
were killed in an air crash. Very good vineyards and skilled contract
winemaking by Tyrrell's help produce good Chardonnay, Shiraz, and
solidly built Semillon.

**Roche Wines** ☆☆☆✓
*Broke Road, Pokolbin, NSW 2320, ☎ (02) 4998 7600, ⑤ (02) 4998 7706; est 1999;
♦ 8,500 cases; ⚑; A$; 7 days 10-5; ⑩; ⊨*
The tip of the massive investment made by Bill Roche in the Pokolbin
sub-region, transforming the old Hungerford Hill development, building a
luxury resort hotel and an Irish pub on the old Tallawanta Vineyard, which
has been resuscitated.

**Rosebrook Estate** ☆☆✓
*1090 Maitlandvale Road, Rosebrook, NSW 2320, ☎ (02) 4930 1114, ⑤ (02) 4930
1690; ♦ 1,200 cases; ⚑; A$; by appt; ⊨*
Graeme and Tania Levick run Rosebrook Estate and Hunter River Retreat
as parallel operations. These include self-contained cottages, horse-riding,
tennis, canoeing, swimming, bush walking, fishing, riverside picnic area,
recreation room, and mini-bus for winery tours and transport to functions
or events in the area.

**The Rothbury Estate** ☆☆☆
*Broke Road, Pokolbin, NSW 2321, ☎ (02) 4998 7363, ⑤ (02) 4998 3559; est 1968;
♦ 82,500 cases; ⚑; A$; 7 days 9.30-4.30; ⑩*
Rothbury was wrestled from the hands of Len Evans by Fosters/Mildara-
Blass in a bitterly contested takeover battle in 1998, but it is still a Hunter
landmark. Unashamedly commercial, its wine quality has slipped in recent
years. Exports to the UK and elsewhere.

### Rothbury Ridge NR
*Talga Road, Rothbury, NSW 2320, ☎ (02) 4930 7122, ⓕ (02) 4930 7198; est 1988; ⚘ 10,000 cases; ♟; A$; Mon-Sat 9-5, Sun 10-5*

Not related to Rothbury Estate; a public company with seventeen hectares of an eclectic range of varieties, including Durif and Chambourcin.

### Rothvale Vineyard ☆☆☆☆
*Deasy's Road, Pokolbin, NSW 2321, ☎ (02) 4998 7290, ⓕ (02) 4998 7296; est 1978; ⚘ 8,000 cases; ♟; A$; 7 days 10-5; ⇔; pool & spa*

Owned and operated by the Patton family, headed by Max Patton with the unique academic qualifications of BVSc, MSc London, and BA Hons Canterbury, the scientific part of which does no doubt come in useful for his winemaking of a rich and powerful array of wines. Exports to the UK and US.

### Saddlers Creek ☆☆☆☆⚐
*Marrowbone Road, Pokolbin, NSW 2320, ☎ (02) 4991 1770, ⓕ (02) 4991 2482; est 1989; ⚘ 20,000 cases; ♟; A$; 7 days 9-5; ⚹*

Continues to produce consistently full-flavoured, rich Chardonnay, Shiraz and Cabernet Sauvignon under various labels. Exports to the UK and elsewhere.

### Scarborough ☆☆☆☆⚐
*Gillards Road, Pokolbin, NSW 2321, ☎ (02) 4998 7563, ⓕ (02) 4998 7786; est 1985; ⚘ 14,000 cases; ♟; A$; 7 days 9-5*

The vastly experienced Ian Scarborough crafts two styles of Chardonnay: richer (for the local market) and finer (for export). Both are sold with several years' bottle age. Also Semillon and Semillon/Sauvignon Blanc. Exports to the UK and elsewhere.

### Serenella ☆☆☆☆⚐
*Lot 300, Hermitage Road, Pokolbin, NSW 2325, ☎ (02) 4998 7992, ⓕ (02) 4998 7993; est 1971; ⚘ 5,000 cases; ♟; A$; 7 days 9.30-5; S; ⚹*

Reincarnated after the sale of the original Serenella in 1997, with the Cecchini family owning the business and Latitia (Tish) Cecchini in charge of winemaking. Semillon, Botrytis Semillon, and Shiraz are the pick.

### Smithleigh Vineyard ☆☆☆
*53 Osborne Road, Lane Cove, NSW 2066, ☎ 0418 484 565, ⓕ (02) 9420 2014; est 1997; ⚘ 3,000 cases; no visitors*

A partnership between the Smith and Leigh families, which purchased the long-established vineyard from Southcorp in 1996. A lot of work in the vineyard and contract winemaking by Andrew Margan have resulted in consistently excellent Old Vine Reserve Semillon.

### Tamburlaine ☆☆☆
*McDonalds Road, Pokolbin, NSW 2321, ☎ (02) 4998 7570, ⓕ (02) 4998 7763; est 1966; ⚘ 70,000 cases; ♟; A$; 7 days 9.30-5*

A thriving business, which, notwithstanding that it continues to increase already substantial production, sells over ninety per cent of its wines through the cellar door and by mailing list (with an active tasting-club members' cellar programme offering wines held and matured at Tamburlaine). Unashamedly and deliberately focused on the tourist trade (and, of course, its club members).

### Tatler Wines ☆☆☆☆
*Lot 15, Lovedale Road, Lovedale, NSW 2321, ☎ (02) 4930 9139, ⓕ (02) 4930 9145; est 1998; ⚘ 2,000 cases; ♟; A$; 7 days 9.30-5.30; ♚; ⇔; olive oil*

An impressive newcomer, with twenty-one hectares of Chardonnay, Shiraz, Pinot Gris, Cabernet Franc and Sangiovese, and contract making sprinkled across four wineries. Owned by Sydney hoteliers Theo and Spiro Isakidis.

**Tempus Two Wines** ☆☆☆✔ **V**
*Broke Road, Pokolbin, NSW 2321,* ☎ *(02) 4993 3999,* Ⓕ *(02) 4993 3988; est 1997;* ⚱ *50,000 cases;* ⚱ *A$; 7 days 9-5,* ℠; ⚘

Now occupies a striking new winery on Broke Road. Forms part of the McGuigan Wines empire, and draws grapes from many regions. Exports to the UK and elsewhere.

**Thomas Wines** ☆☆☆☆
*C/o The Small Winemakers Centre, McDonalds Road, Pokolbin, NSW 2321,* ☎ *&* Ⓕ *(02) 4991 6801; est 1997;* ⚱ *1,500 cases;* ⚱ *A$; 7 days 10-5*

Andrew Thomas spent thirteen years at Tyrrell's before venturing out on his own, partly as contract winemaker, and partly to develop Thomas Wines. High-quality, single-vineyard Semillon and a Hunter/McLaren Vale Shiraz are both good.

**Tinonee Vineyard NR**
*Milbrodale Road, Broke, NSW 2330,* ☎ *(02) 6579 1308,* Ⓕ *(02) 9719 1833; est 1997;* ⚱ *384 cases;* ⚱ *A$; wkds & public hols 11-4;* ⛺

Ian Craig has established fourteen hectares of vineyards on a mix of red volcanic and river flat soils at Broke. Once all the vines come into bearing, annual production will reach 5,000 cases.

**Tintilla Wines NR**
*725 Hermitage Road, Pokolbin, NSW 2320,* ☎ *(02) 6574 7093,* Ⓕ *(02) 9767 6894; est 1993;* ⚱ *4,000 cases;* ⚱ *A$; wkds 10.30-6, Mon-Fri afternoons by appt*

The Lusby family has established 7.5 hectares of Semillon, Sangiovese, Shiraz, and Merlot, making a promising start with a cherry and chocolate 1998 Shiraz. Estate-grown olives and olive oil add interest.

**Tower Estate** ☆☆☆☆✔
*Corner Broke Road and Hall Road, Pokolbin, NSW 2320,* ☎ *(02) 4998 7989,* Ⓕ *(02) 4998 7919; est 1999;* ⚱ *1,000 cases;* ⚱ *A$; 7 days 10-5;* ⛺, ℠

A prestigious joint venture headed by Len Evans, run in concert with Tower Lodge, a luxury accommodation and conference centre. It draws upon varieties in regions across Australia which have a particular synergy, coupled with the enormous knowledge of Len Evans and the winemaking skills of Dan Dineen. Exports to the UK and elsewhere.

**Tranquil Vale** ☆☆☆
*325 Pywells Road, Luskintyre, NSW 2321,* ☎ *(02) 4930 6100,* Ⓕ *(02) 4930 6105; est 1996;* ⚱ *2,800 cases;* ⚱ *A$; Thurs-Mon 10-4, or by appt;* ⛺

Phil and Lucy Griffiths purchased the property on the banks of the Hunter River sight-unseen from a description in an old copy of *The Weekend Australian* found in the High Commission Office in London. Competent contract winemaking has resulted in quite powerful Semillon and Shiraz.

**Tulloch** ☆☆☆✔
*"Glen Elgin", De Beyers Road, Pokolbin, NSW 2321,* ☎ *(02) 4998 7850,* Ⓕ *(02) 4998 7682; est 1895;* ⚱ *30,000 cases;* ⚱ *A$; 7 days 10-5*

Another near-death experience for a famous brand abandoned by Southcorp, revived in a three-way partnership between Angove's, Inglewood Vineyards (aka Two Rivers) and Jay Tulloch. A new, lavish cellar door opened in late 2003.

**Tyrrell's** ☆☆☆☆☆ **V**
*Broke Road, Pokolbin, NSW 2321,* ☎ *(02) 4993 7000,* Ⓕ *(02) 4998 7723; est 1858;* ⚱ *520,000 cases;* ⚱ *A$; Mon-Sat 8-5;* ⚘

1971 Vat 47 Chardonnay launched a thousand ships. The individual vineyard

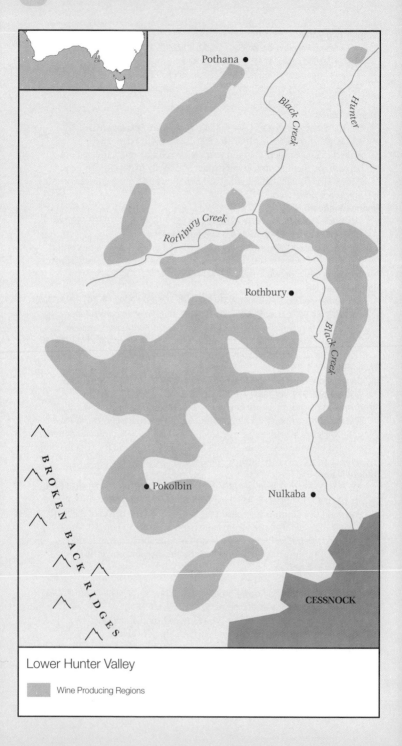

Lower Hunter Valley

Wine Producing Regions

Semillons, released when five years old, are a superb mix of lemon, honey and toast. Vat 9 Shiraz also good. Slimmed down since the sale of the Long Flat brand for an eight-figure sum. Worldwide distribution.

### Vinden Estate ☆☆☆☆
*17 Gillards Road, Pokolbin, NSW 2320, ☎ (02) 4998 7410, Ⓕ (02) 4998 7421; est 1998; ⚑ 2,500 cases; ⚑; A$; 7 days 10-5; ⚑*

Sandra and Guy Vinden have bought their dream home with landscaped gardens in the foreground and nine hectares of vineyard with the Brokenback mountain range in the distance. Much of the winemaking is now done on site, and increasingly drawn from the estate vineyards.

### Wandin Valley Estate ☆☆☆⚐
*Wilderness Road, Lovedale, NSW 2320, ☎ (02) 4930 7317, Ⓕ (02) 4930 7814; est 1973; ⚑ 10,000 cases; ⚑; A$; 7 days 10-5; ⚑; café, cricket ground*

Australian television producer James Davern and family run a quality winery, village green cricket oval, and extensive cottage accommodation. Reserve Chardonnay (toasty, spicy) and Bridie's Shiraz (rich cherry) lead the way. Exports to the UK and elsewhere.

### Warraroong Estate ☆☆☆⚐
*Wilderness Road, Lovedale, NSW 2321, ☎ (02) 4930 7594, Ⓕ (02) 4930 7199; est 1978; ⚑ 2,500 cases; ⚑; A$; Thurs-Mon 10-5, ⚑; ⚑*

Warraroong Estate was formerly Fraser Vineyard, and adopted its new name after it changed hands in 1997. The name "Warraroong" is an Aboriginal word for hillside, reflecting the southwesterly aspect of the property that looks back towards the Brokenback Range and Watagan Mountains. The label design is from a painting by local Aboriginal artist Kia Kiro.

### Wattlebrook Vineyard ☆☆☆⚐ V
*Fordwich Road, Broke, NSW 2330, ☎ & Ⓕ (02) 9929 5668; est 1994; ⚑ 1,000 cases; ⚑; A$; first Sat of each month, or by appt*

NSW Supreme Court Justice Peter McLellan and family began their Hunter Valley vineyard in 1994, adding a Mudgee vineyard in 1988. The well-priced wines are contract-made by Andrew Margan.

### Waverley Estate ☆☆☆
*Waverley-Honour, Palmers Lane, Pokolbin, NSW 2320, ☎ (02) 4998 7953, Ⓕ (02) 4998 7952; est 1989; ⚑ 4,500 cases; ⚑; A$; 7 days 10-5; wine lunches*

Waverley Estate Aged Wines (to give it its full name) is the new name for the Maling Family Estate; as its name suggests, it specializes in offering a range of fully mature wines, going back to 1991.

### Windsors Edge NR
*McDonalds Road, Pokolbin, NSW 2320, ☎ (02) 4998 7737, Ⓕ (02) 4998 7737; est 1996; ⚑ 1,500 cases; ⚑; A$; Fri-Mon 10-5, or by appt; ⚑, ⚑, tennis*

In 1995 Tim Windsor (an oenology graduate) and wife Jessie (an industrial chemist) purchased the old Black Creek Picnic Race Track in Pokolbin. To date seventeen hectares of Shiraz, Semillon, Chardonnay, Tempranillo, Tinta Cão, and Touriga have been planted, then three luxury cottages, followed by a restaurant and cellar door, and a small winery underneath. A quick gallop indeed.

### Wyndham Estate ☆☆☆☆ V
*Dalwood Road, Dalwood, NSW 2335, ☎ (02) 4938 3444, Ⓕ (02) 4938 3422; est 1828; ⚑ one million cases; ⚑; A$; Mon-Fri 9.30-5, wkds 10-4; ⚑*

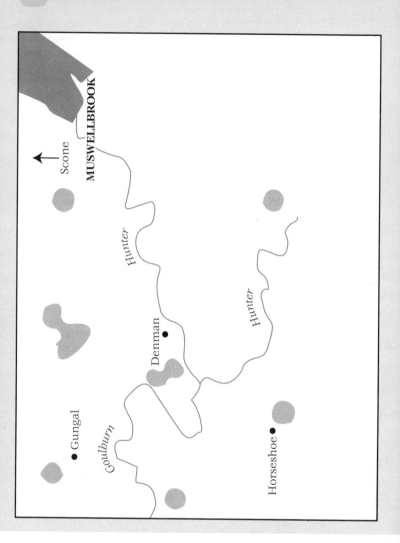

The Hunter Valley fiefdom of the vast Orlando-Wyndham octopus, producing wines of utterly consistent quality and style that will never frighten the horses. Worldwide distribution.

## Upper Hunter Valley

Perversely, the distinction between the Lower and Upper Hunter is not one made under the GI framework. Technically they are one region, which fragments into small sub-regions such as Pokolbin, Rothbury, and Broke-Fordwich. It is an idiosyncratic approach that undoubtedly pleases the vignerons of the Upper Hunter, for which you might as well read Rosemount, the utterly dominant force in the region. Rosemount has come to this position by an unusual path. Viticulture had come and gone between 1870 and 1910. Fifty years later, in 1960, Penfolds made the brave – though not necessarily correct – decision to uproot itself from the Lower Hunter Valley and move lock, stock, and barrel to the Upper Hunter Valley. In 1969, Rosemount Estate arrived and opened its doors for business. By 1978, Penfolds decided it had made a mistake and sold its winery to Rosemount, an act that marked its exit from NSW.

While Rosemount now dominates the Upper Hunter Valley scene, its viticultural and winemaking empire extends to Mudgee and Orange (NSW); McLaren Vale, Coonawarra, and the Adelaide Hills (SA). The reasons for this spread – and Rosemount is not the only winery to draw on fruit from outside the region – are the inherent limitations on viticulture in the Upper Hunter Valley.

It is simply not suited to red wine production; the wines are lacking in concentration and structure. Of the white varieties, the only two worth considering are Semillon (softer and less long-lived than that of the Lower Hunter) and Chardonnay. It is the latter variety that has impressed most, with Rosemount Roxburgh Chardonnay a quirky but acknowledged Australian classic. There are nineteen wine producers in the region.

### Arrowfield ☆☆⭒
*Denman Road, Jerry's Plains, NSW 2330, ☎ (02) 6576 4041, Ⓕ (02) 6576 4144; est 1968; ⬥ 70,000 cases; ⚑; A$; 7 days 10-5*
A chronic under-performer, the wines technically sound but rather dull and prosaic. Exports to the UK and elsewhere.

### Birnham Wood Wines ☆☆☆
*Turanville Road, Scone, NSW 2337, ☎ (02) 6545 3286, Ⓕ (02) 6545 3431; est 1994; ⬥ 8,000 cases; ⚑; A$; wkds & public hols 11-4*
Former Sydney car dealer Mike Eagan and wife Min moved to Scone to establish a horse stud. The vineyard came later but is now a major part of the business, with over thirty hectares of vines. Part of the production is sold, part vinified for Birnham Wood. Exports to the UK and elsewhere.

### Camyr Allyn Wines ☆☆☆⭒
*Camyr Allyn North, Allyn River Road, East Gresford, NSW 2311, ☎ & Ⓕ (02) 4938 9576; est 1999; ⬥ 3,000 cases; ⚑; A$; 7 days 10-5*
The Evers family has quickly established an estate-based operation, with son James Evers and veteran Geoff Broadfield doing the winemaking; a pleasantly savoury and varietal Merlot, regional Shiraz and sparkling Shiraz (pleasingly dry) are the pick.

### Cruickshank-Callatoota Estate ☆☆☆⭒
*2656 Wybong Road, Wybong, NSW 2333, ☎ (02) 6547 8149, Ⓕ (02) 6547 8144; est 1973; ⬥ 5,000 cases; ⚑; A$; 7 days 9-5; 𝒓; camping*
Owned by the Cruickshank family since the word go, with wine quality improving markedly year-on-year; Shiraz and Cabernet Sauvignon now have plenty of stuffing.

### Glendonbrook ☆☆☆
*Lot 2, Park Street, East Gresford, NSW 2311, ☎ (02) 4938 9666, Ⓕ (02) 4938 9766; est 2000; ⬥ 12,000 cases; ⚑; A$; Mon-Fri 9-5, wkds & public hols 10.30-4.30*
Sydney businessman Tom Smith and wife Terese not only purchased a

600-hectare beef cattle property, but diversified into grape-growing and winemaking with an investment of A$3 million in a state-of-the-art winery which also offers contract winemaking services under the direction of Geoff Broadfield.

### Horseshoe Vineyard NR

*Horseshoe Road, Horseshoe Valley via Denman, NSW 2328, ☎ (02) 6547 3528; est 1986; ◈ NFP; ♈; A$; wkds 9-5*

Owner John Hordern showed his winemaking skills early on, but he has largely sidelined his own label as he has become a contract winemaker for others.

### James Estate ☆☆☆☆✓

*951 Bylong Valley Way, Baerami via Denman, NSW 2333, ☎ (02) 6547 5168, ⓕ (02) 6547 5164; est 1971; ◈ 75,000 cases; ♈; A$; 7 days 10-4.30*

The former Serenella Estate, now owned by a substantial corporation with David James Chief Executive and principal shareholder, has made every post a winner, making excellent Reserve Chardonnay and Shiraz from the 100 hectares of estate vineyards. Exports to the UK and elsewhere.

### Polin & Polin Wines ☆☆☆✓

*Wyameta, Bell's Lane, Denman, NSW 2328, ☎ (02) 6547 2955, ⓕ (02) 9969 9665; est 1997; ◈ 1,200 cases; no visitors*

A stylish newcomer with carefully crafted Limb of Addy Shiraz from six hectares of estate plantings.

### Pyramid Hill Wines ☆☆☆

*194 Martindale Road, Denman, NSW 2328, ☎ (02) 6547 2755, ⓕ (02) 6547 2735; est 2002; ◈ 3,000 cases; ♈; A$; by appt; ⇔*

A partnership between the veteran grape-growing Hilder family and international film-makers Nicholas Adler and Caroline Sherwood. Most of the grapes from the seventy-two hectares of high-tech vineyard are sold; Semillon and Merlot are the pick of the five varietals made.

### Rosemount Estate ☆☆☆☆ V

*Rosemount Road, Denman, NSW 2328, ☎ (02) 6549 6450, ⓕ (02) 6549 6499; est 1969; ◈ NFP; ♈; A$; 7 days 10-4; ⦿*

How the mighty are fallen, the debacle of the Southcorp-Rosemount merger being well chronicled. The wines continue as before, with Mudgee and Orange providing the quality end, the whole of southeastern Australia Diamond Label, etc. Worldwide distribution.

### Two Rivers ☆☆☆✓

*Yarrawa Road, Denman, NSW 2328, ☎ (02) 6547 2556, ⓕ (02) 6547 2546; est 1988; ◈ 25,000 cases; no visitors*

Two Rivers is the brand name for the 170-hectare Inglewood Vineyard; the quality of the wine made from a small proportion of the grape intake has steadied in recent years. The business also has a share in the Tulloch brand.

### Winbourne Wines ☆☆☆✓

*Bunnan Road, Scone, NSW 2337, ☎ 0417 650 834, ⓕ (02) 6545 1636; est 1996; 3,000 cases; ♈; A$; by appt*

A local business syndicate headed by a well-known lawyer has established a little under fifty hectares of vineyard, selling most of the grapes, but following the pattern of having a few thousand cases very competently contract-made. Chardonnay, Semillon, and Shiraz lead a surprisingly large portfolio.

### Yarraman Estate ☆☆☆✓

*Yarraman Road, Wybong, NSW 2333, ☎ (02) 6547 8118, ⓕ (02) 6547 8039; est 1958; ◈ 25,000 cases; ♈; A$; 7 days 10-5; ⇔; ⦿*

This is the reincarnation of Penfolds' Wybong Estate, owned by Rosemount for many years, but subsequently going through rapid ownership changes. It buys fruit from many regions to make delicious Semillon, Merlot, and Cabernet Shiraz. Exports to the UK and elsewhere.

# Mudgee

It is not hard to see why the Aborigines bestowed the name Mudgee, meaning "nest in the hills", on this region. The hills in question are a gentler part of the Great Dividing Range. It is also easy to see why the three German families – Roth, Kurtz, and Bucholz – were drawn to this area, establishing vineyards in 1858, and why the Roth and Kurtz families were still actively involved in grape-growing and winemaking 100 years later.

The other key figure in the early days was the remarkable Italian, Dr Thomas Fiaschi, who first arrived in far north Queensland in 1874. In 1879 he established a twenty-hectare vineyard on the banks of the Hawkesbury River and went on to combine an extraordinary army career with his winemaking interests, founding the Tizzana (on the Hawkesbury) and establishing the Augustine Vineyards and Winery in Mudgee. From this point on, the fifty-five vineyards that existed in Mudgee in 1893 slowly dwindled away until, by 1963, only the Roth family's Craigmoor Vineyard was in production. The following year Alf Kurtz established Mudgee Wines, and the recovery of Mudgee was underway. By 1993 there were once again fifty-five growers in the district, tending 430 hectares; by 1999, the area under vine exceeded 1,200 hectares, and it has grown significantly since then.

Mudgee has the distinction of providing a virus-free, pre-phylloxera clone of Chardonnay identified by the famous French ampelographer, Professor Paul Truel. But it is as a red-wine region that Mudgee has made its mark, primarily with deeply coloured Shiraz and Cabernet Sauvignon. The berry-and-chocolate Shiraz develops earthy overtones with ten years' bottle age, while the Cabernet offers lush fruit laced through with balanced tannins. There are thirty-six wine producers in the region.

**Abercorn** ☆☆☆☆↓
*Cassilis Road, Mudgee, NSW 2850, ☎ 1800 000 959, ⑤ (02) 6373 3108; est 1996; ♦ 8,000 cases; ♀; A$; Thurs-Mon 10.30-4.30*
Former journalist Tim Stevens and wife Connie acquired the run-down Abercorn vineyard in 1996. They are making highly attractive wines: sophisticated Chardonnay, rich and powerful Reserve Shiraz, Reserve Cabernet Sauvignon and Reserve Shiraz/Cabernet. Exports to the UK.

**Andrew Harris Vineyards** ☆☆☆↓
*Sydney Road, Mudgee, NSW 2850, ☎ (02) 6373 1213, ⑤ (02) 6373 1296; est 1991; ♦ 65,000 cases; ♀; A$; 7 days 9-5*
Andrew and Debbie Harris lost no time and spared no expense in establishing 106 hectares of vineyards. Careful fruit selection and skilled contract winemaking have resulted in high-quality wines in three ranges: Premium, Reserve, and The Vision (a super-premium Cabernet/Shiraz).

**Blue Wren** ☆☆☆☆
*1 Cassilis Road, Mudgee, NSW 2850, ☎ (02) 6372 6205, ⑤ (02) 6372 6206; est 1985; ♦ 2,000 cases; ♀; A$; 7 days 10.30-4.30; ❖*
James and Diana Anderson have two estate vineyards, with high-quality

Semillon, Shiraz, and Merlot leading the way. All the wines are available at the large on-site restaurant.

**Botobolar** ☆☆☆✓ **V**

*89 Botobolar Road, Mudgee, NSW 2850, ☎ (02) 6373 3840, Ⓕ (02) 6373 3789; est 1971; ♦ 4,000 cases; ⍾; A$; Mon-Sat 10-5, Sun 10-3*

Kevin Karstrom has taken over the mantle of Gil Wahlquist in running this pioneering organic vineyard. His portfolio includes a preservative-free dry red and dry white; but the conventional Shiraz and Cabernet Sauvignon are the best of the bunch. Exports to the UK and elsewhere.

**Burnbrae** ☆☆☆✓

*Hill End Road, Erudgere via Mudgee, NSW 2850, ☎ (02) 6373 3504, Ⓕ (02) 6373 3601; est 1976; ♦ NFP; ⍾; A$; Wed-Mon 9-5*

An estate-based operation with twenty-three hectares of vineyards; owner-winemaker Alan Cox produces good Chardonnay and very good Shiraz and Cabernet. Exports to the UK and elsewhere.

**Clearview Estate Mudgee** ☆☆✓

*Corner Sydney and Rocky Water Hole Road, Mudgee, NSW 2850, ☎ (02) 6372 4546, Ⓕ (02) 6372 7577; est 1995; ♦ 2,200 cases; ⍾; A$; Fri-Mon 10-4, or by appt*

Twelve hectares of vineyard and twelve varieties, including the strange bedfellows of Pinot Grigio, Barbera, and Sangiovese, provide a Joseph's Coat. The "Aussie Farm" cellar door opened in September 2000.

**di Lusso Wines NR**

*Eurunderee Lane, Mudgee, NSW 2850, ☎ (02) 6373 3125, Ⓕ (02) 6373 3128; est 1998; ♦ 3,000 cases; ⍾; A$; Fri-Mon 10-5*

Rob Fairall and Luanne Hill are the unlikely founders of an all-Italian business, with two hectares each of Barbera and Sangiovese, one hectare of Nebbiolo, and half a hectare of Picolit, purchasing Aleatico, Pinot Grigio (from Orange), and more Sangiovese. Deliciously fragrant wines; olives and olive oil, too.

**Elliot Rocke Estate** ☆☆☆☆

*Craigmoor Road, Mudgee, NSW 2850, ☎ (02) 6372 7722, Ⓕ (02) 6372 0680; est 1999; ♦ 5,000 cases; ⍾; A$; 7 days 9-4*

A new label for Mudgee, but planting of its twenty-four hectares of vineyards dates back to 1987, when the property was known as Seldom Seen. Now uses skilled Hunter Valley contract makers; excellent Semillon and Chardonnay.

**Frog Rock** ☆☆☆✓

*Cassilis Road, Mudgee, NSW 2850, ☎ (02) 6372 2408, Ⓕ (02) 6372 6924; est 1973; ♦ 20,000 cases; ⍾; A$; 7 days 10-5*

The former Tallara Vineyard, established almost thirty years ago by leading chartered accountant Rick Turner, with sixty hectares of mature vineyards. Much of the grape production is sold with competent contract winemaking for the remainder: increasing amounts of impressive Semillon, Chardonnay, and Cabernet Sauvignon. Exports to the UK and elsewhere.

**High Valley Wines** ☆☆☆

*137 Cassilis Road, Mudgee, NSW 2850, ☎ (02) 6375 0292, Ⓕ (02) 6375 0228; est 1995; ♦ 2,000 cases; ⍾; A$; 7 days 10-5; pottery studio; light lunches; cheese factory*

Farmers for several generations, the Francis family has ventured into contract grape-growing (twenty-three hectares) and limited winemaking. The Chardonnay and Shiraz have been consistent medal-winners at the Mudgee Wine Show.

**Huntington Estate** ☆☆☆☆☆ **V**
*Cassilis Road, Mudgee, NSW 2850, ☎ (02) 6373 3825, Ⓕ (02) 6373 3730; est*
*1969; ◊ 20,000 cases; Mon-Fri 9-5, Sat 10-5, Sun 10-3; ⚹*
The remarkable Roberts family members have a passion for wine that is
equalled only by their passion for music. The Huntington Music Festival is a
major bi-annual event. The velvety, but long-lived, red wines are outstanding,
and sell for very low prices. The Semillon is classy, too. Eschews exports.

**Lowe Family Wines** ☆☆☆⊰
*Tinja Lane, Mudgee, NSW 2850, ☎ (02) 6372 0800, Ⓕ (02) 6372 0811; est 1987;*
*◊ 6,000 cases; ⚑; A$; Fri-Mon 10-5, or by appt*
Former Rothbury winemaker David Lowe and Jane Wilson make their
elegant Chardonnay, crisp Semillon, and earthy Shiraz from Mudgee,
Orange, and Hunter Valley grapes. Exports to the UK and elsewhere.

**Mansfield Wines** ☆☆☆
*204 Eurunderee Road, Mudgee, NSW 2850, ☎ (02) 6373 3871, Ⓕ (02) 6373*
*3708; est 1975; ◊ 2,000 cases; ⚑; A$; Thurs-Tues & public hols 10-5, or by appt;*
*animal farmyard*
Mansfield Wines has moved with the times, taking the emphasis off
fortified wines and on to table wines, and expanding the product range to
take in cutting-edge varietal reds such as Touriga and Zinfandel.

**Miramar** ☆☆☆ **V**
*Henry Lawson Drive, Mudgee, NSW 2850, ☎ (02) 6373 3874, Ⓕ (02) 6373 3854;*
*est 1977; ◊ 8,000 cases; ⚑; A$; 7 days 9-5*
The silver-bearded, elfin-eyed Ian MacRae runs thirty-three hectares of
vineyard, selling part of the crop to others, and vinifying the remainder. Early
benchmark success with Rosé and Chardonnay has since been supplemented,
indeed supplanted, by dense, long-lived Shiraz and Cabernet Sauvignon.

**Pieter van Gent** ☆☆⊰
*Black Springs Road, Mudgee, NSW 2850, ☎ (02) 6373 3807, Ⓕ (02) 6373 3910;*
*est 1978; ◊ 10,000 cases; ⚑; A$; Mon-Sat 9-5, Sun 11-4; ⛵*
A former fortified-wine business now moving into table winemaking with
success, especially Chardonnay, Verdelho, and Shiraz.

**Poet's Corner Wines** ☆☆☆☆⊰ **V**
*Craigmoor Road, Mudgee, NSW 2850, ☎ (02) 6372 2208, Ⓕ (02) 6372 4464; est*
*1858; ◊ 150,000 cases; ⚑; A$; Mon-Sat 10-4.30, Sun & public hols 10-4; ⏏;*
*museum; cricket grounds*
One of the oldest wineries in Australia to remain in continuous production.
It is now the public face of Orlando-Wyndham's winemaking operations in
Mudgee, with an atmospheric cellar door offering the Craigmoor, Poet's
Corner, Montrose, and Henry Lawson brands. Excels with Semillon,
Chardonnay, Sangiovese, and Shiraz at low prices.

**Robert Stein Vineyard** ☆☆☆⊰
*Pipeclay Lane, Mudgee, NSW 2850, ☎ (02) 6373 3991, Ⓕ (02) 6373 3709; est*
*1976; ◊ 6,500 cases; ⚑; A$; 7 days 10-4.30; ⚹; motorbike museum*
The sweeping panorama from the winery is its own reward for cellar-door
visitors to Robert Stein's set-up. Quality jumps around somewhat, but truly
excellent Reserve Shiraz and Reserve Cabernet are usually at the head.
Exports to the UK and elsewhere.

**Simon Gilbert Wines** ☆☆☆⊰
*1220 Sydney Road, Mudgee, NSW 2850, ☎ (02) 9958 1322, Ⓕ (02) 8920 1333;*
*est 1993; ◊ 35,000 cases; no visitors*

A large, modern contract winemaking business, with public funding, which has hit turbulent financial waters, but will undoubtedly continue in one way or another. Exports to the UK and elsewhere.

**Thistle Hill** ☆☆☆ **V**

*McDonalds Road, Mudgee, NSW 2850, ☎ (02) 6373 3546, ⓕ (02) 6373 3540; est 1976; ✦ 4,000 cases; ⚑; A$; Mon-Sat 9.30-5, Sun & public hols 9.30-4; ⊨*

Produces supremely honest wines, always full of flavour and appropriately reflecting the climate and terroir. Some may be a little short on finesse, but never on character. Chardonnay, Semillon, and Cabernet Sauvignon lead the way, and age well. Exports to the UK and elsewhere.

**Vinifera Wines** ☆☆☆✦

*194 Henry Lawson Drive, Mudgee, NSW 2850, ☎ (02) 6372 2461, ⓕ (02) 6372 6731; est 1997; ✦ 1,500 cases; ⚑; A$; 7 days 10-5.30; olive oil*

The silver lining of severe car-crash injuries was the compensation money which allowed regional medical superintendent Dr Tony McKendry and wife Debbie to build a small winery on their eleven-hectare vineyard, and to produce (inter alia) Tempranillo.

**Wells Parish Wines** ☆☆☆☆

*Benerin Estate, Sydney Road, Kandos, NSW 2848, ☎ (02) 6379 4168, ⓕ (02) 6379 4996; est 1995; ✦ 1,000 cases; ⚑; A$; by appt; ⊨*

The Trounson family has established eighteen hectares at the eastern extremity of the Mudgee region, and at high altitude, producing distinctive mint and blackcurrant Cabernet Sauvignon.

# Cowra

Until 1973, when the first vines were planted, Cowra's chief claim to fame (apart from grazing) was as the site of Australia's prisoner-of-war camp for captured Japanese soldiers and airmen. The war memorial is well worth a visit. The vineyards are situated on gentle slopes within a broad valley on the western side of the Great Dividing Range. They are planted at a lower altitude than Orange, Mudgee, or Hilltops (around 300 metres) and, although further south, have a significantly warmer climate. Cowra was established on the crest of the white-wine boom, and was an early and highly successful entrant in the Chardonnay game. Just when it seemed Chardonnay would be in serious surplus, demand (in 2002) exceeded supply, which is just as well, as its red wines are by and large mediocre, lacking concentration and flavour. A second problem has been the lack of real identity. Until very recently, no wine was made in Cowra; all the grapes were trucked to far-away destinations. Cowra's vignerons are certainly working hard to create a regional image and identity, and the first few wineries have appeared. Yet, it is unlikely that Cowra will break out of the "fighting varietal" sector. There are eighteen wine producers in the region.

**Cowra Estate** ☆☆☆✦ **V**

*Boorowa Road, Cowra, NSW 2794, ☎ (02) 9907 7735, ⓕ (02) 9907 7734; est 1973; ✦ 6,000 cases; ⚑; A$; Tues-Sun 10-4 at The Quarry Restaurant; ⓘ*

A large vineyard acquired by South African businessman and cricket-lover

John Geber in 1995. The Quarry Restaurant offers both the Cowra Estate wines and those of other producers in the region. Quality is improving.

**Falls Wines** ☆☆☆

*Belubula Way, Canowindra, NSW 2804, ☎ (02) 6344 1293, Ⓕ (02) 6344 1290; est 1997; ⚇ 3,200 cases; ⚐; A$; 7 days 10-4; ⊨; meals; ⚔*

Peter and Zoe Kennedy have established Falls Vineyard and Retreat with luxury B&B accommodation. Skilled contract winemaking produces good Semillon, Chardonnay, Merlot, Cabernet Sauvignon, and Shiraz.

**Hamiltons Bluff** ☆☆☆

*Longs Corner Road, Canowindra, NSW 2804, ☎ (02) 6344 2079, Ⓕ (02) 6344 2165; est 1995; ⚇ 2,000 cases; ⚐; A$; wkds & hols 10-4, Mon-Fri by appt, outdoor movies*

Owned by the Andrews family, who planted forty-five hectares of vines in 1995. The first releases came with the 1998 vintage; various styles of Chardonnay have impressed, also Sangiovese.

**Mulligan Wongara Vineyard** ☆☆☆

*603 Grenfell Road, Cowra, NSW 2794, ☎ (02) 6342 9334, Ⓕ (02) 6342 9334; est 1993; ⚇ 2,000 cases; ⚐; A$; Sat & public hols (Sun if a public hol wkd) 10-4; ⊨*

Chardonnay, Shiraz, and Cabernet Sauvignon are contract-made from part of the sixteen-hectare estate. A striking tower cellar door and cellar is now open.

**Mulyan** ☆☆☆⚘

*North Logan Road, Cowra, NSW 2794, ☎ (02) 6342 1289, Ⓕ (02) 6341 1015; est 1994; ⚇ 2,000 cases; ⚐; A$; Sat-Mon & public hols 10-5, or by appt Mon-Fri*

A 1,350-hectare grazing property purchased by the Fagan family in 1886; Peter and Jenni Fagan are on the way to establishing 100 hectares of vineyards by way of diversification. The flavoursome Chardonnay and Shiraz are contract-made by Simon Gilbert.

**Nassau Estate** ☆☆☆⚘

*Fish Fossil Drive, Canowindra, NSW 2804, ☎ (02) 9267 4785, Ⓕ (02) 9267 3844; est 1996; ⚇ 1,500 cases; no visitors*

The Curran family established its 110-hectare vineyard adjacent to the Belubula River at Canowindra in 1996. A significant proportion of the grapes is sold to one of Australia's largest wineries, a small amount retained and competently contract-made by Andrew Margan.

**Rosnay Organic Wines** ☆☆⚘

*Rivers Road, Canowindra, NSW 2804, ☎ (02) 6344 3215, Ⓕ (02) 6344 3229; est 2002; ⚇ 3,000 cases; ⚐; A$; by appt*

A decidedly complex business, with individually owned eight-to-ten-hectare house and vineyard blocks for sale, but with organic farming (under contract) obligatory. Most of the wine is made by organic winemaker specialists Kevin Karstrom of Botobolar and Rodney Hooper of Macaw Creek.

**Wallington Wines NR**

*Nyrang Creek Vineyard, Canowindra, NSW 2904, ☎ (02) 6344 7153, Ⓕ (02) 6344 7105; est 1992; ⚇ 1,500 cases; ⚐; A$; by appt; ⚔*

Anthony and Margaret Wallington have progressively planted fourteen hectares to the classic varieties. Most of the grapes are sold; some Chardonnay, Shiraz, and Cabernet are contract-made.

**Windowrie Estate** ☆☆☆

*Windowrie, Canowindra, NSW 2804, ☎ (02) 6344 3234, Ⓕ (02) 6344 3227; est 1988; ⚇ 32,000 cases; ⚐; A$; 7 days 10-6 at The Mill, Vaux St, Cowra; ⊶; ⚔*

Windowrie Estate was established in 1988 on a substantial grazing property at Canowindra, thirty kilometres north of Cowra. While much of the fruit from the 240-hectare vineyard is sold to other makers, a substantial quantity is made for the Windowrie Estate and The Mill labels; Chardonnay, Verdelho, Sangiovese, and Petit Verdot are all interesting. Exports to the UK and elsewhere.

# Orange

Initially known as the Central Highlands, the Orange region (centred on the slopes of Mount Canobolas) has long been an important orchard area producing apples, pears, and cherries for both local and domestic markets. An experimental station was established at nearby Molong in the 1940s, but vines were first planted commercially in 1980 (at Bloodwood Estate); there are now over thirty wine producers and a number of contract grape-growers. Both white and red wines have the finesse and elegance one expects from a cool climate such as this.

A major development in the region has dramatically increased its profile and its importance as a wine producer. This has been the progressive establishment of a 900-hectare vineyard development (in three stages) known as Little Boomey, and just prior to the 2000 vintage a large winery was erected at Quandong. Extraneous finance problems have marred the project, but in the longer term its worth will be proved. There are thirty wine producers in the region.

**Belgravia Vineyards** ☆☆☆☆
*Belgravia Road, Orange, NSW 2800, ☎ (02) 6365 0633, ⓕ (02) 6365 0646; est 2003; ♦ 6,000 cases; ♗; A$; by appt; ⋈*
Belgravia is a 1,800-hectare mixed farming property, now with 180 hectares of vines contracted to Southcorp, and ten hectares set aside for the Belgravia label. An impressive team is making glorious cool-climate Shiraz/Viognier, fragrant and spicy, with excellent Chardonnay, Viognier, and Shiraz. Exports to the UK.

**Bloodwood Estate** ☆☆☆☆ⁿ **V**
*4 Griffin Road, Orange, NSW 2800, ☎ (02) 6362 5631, ⓕ (02) 6361 1173; est 1983; ♦ 4,000 cases; ♗; A$; by appt; ⋏*
Rhonda and Stephen Doyle were the principal pioneers of this region. Their wines gain both consistency and quality year on year. The cherry-flavoured, crisp Rosé of Malbec is always good; Chardonnay, Riesling (including an occasional ice-wine version), Shiraz, and Cabernet also. Exports to the UK and elsewhere.

**Brangayne of Orange** ☆☆☆☆ⁿ
*49 Pinnacle Road, Orange, NSW 2880, ☎ (02) 6365 3229, ⓕ (02) 6365 3170; est 1994; ♦ 3,500 cases; ♗; A$; by appt*
Orchardists Don and Pamela Hoskins are exciting newcomers who diversified into viticulture in 1994 and now have twenty-five hectares of high-quality vineyards. Skilled contract winemaking has produced elegant and complex Chardonnay, surprising Pinot Noir, and The Tristan, a Cabernet/Shiraz/Merlot blend bursting with ripe fruit. Exports to the UK and Singapore.

**Burke & Hills** ☆☆☆☆
*Cargo Road, Lidster, NSW 2800, ☎ & ⓕ (02) 6365 3456; est 1999; ♦ 3,500 cases; ♗; A$; Fri-Mon 11-5 at Lakeside Cafe, Lake Canobolas; ⋈*

It's all happening in a hurry here under the direction of Doug Burke; ten hectares of high-altitude vineyards, including impressive French clone Pinot Noir; a skilled winemaking and viticultural team, and a 200-tonne winery with contract-making facilities to supplement cash flow. Sauvignon Blanc, Chardonnay, and Pinot Noir are all good wines.

**Canobolas-Smith** ☆☆☆

*Boree Lane, off Cargo Road, Lidster via Orange, NSW 2800, ☏ (02) 6365 6113, Ⓕ (02) 6365 6113; est 1986; ♦ 2,000 cases; ☖; A$; wkds & public hols 11-5; ⦿*
Murray Smith has six hectares of Chardonnay, Pinot Noir, Cabernet Sauvignon, Merlot, Shiraz, and Cabernet Franc. Don't be fooled by the psychedelic blue, wrap-around label design: a quite delicious and serious Chardonnay leads the range.

**Ibis Wines** ☆☆☆⟊

*239 Kearneys Drive, Orange, NSW 2800, ☏ (02) 6362 3257, Ⓕ (02) 6362 5779; est 1988; ♦ 900 cases; ☖; A$; wkds & public hols 11-5, or by appt; ⋌*
Owner-winemaker Phil Stevenson has three separate vineyard sources at different altitudes, and is gaining confidence with a wide range of varietals; Pinot Gris, Unwooded Chardonnay, Shiraz, and Cabernet Franc lead the way.

**Indigo Ridge** ☆☆☆⟊

*Icely Road, Orange, NSW 2800, ☏ (02) 6362 1851, Ⓕ (02) 6362 1851; est 1995; ♦ 600 cases; ☖; A$; first & second wkd of month 12-5, or by appt*
Indigo Ridge has two hectares each of Sauvignon Blanc and Cabernet Sauvignon, and sells the small wine production by cellar door and mail order.

**Jarretts of Orange** ☆☆☆⟊

*Annangrove Park, Cargo Road, Orange, NSW 2800 (postal), ☏ (02) 6364 3118, Ⓕ (02) 6364 3048; est 1995; ♦ 2,000 cases; no visitors*
Justin and Pip Jarrett have established a very substantial vineyard in short order, with 140 hectares in all; they also contract-manage another 120 hectares in the region. Most of the grapes are sold, but the wines made (Marsanne, Sauvignon Blanc, Chardonnay, Shiraz, and Cabernet/Merlot) are all good.

**Logan Wines** ☆☆☆

*1320 Castlereagh Highway, Mudgee, NSW 2850, ☏ (02) 9958 6844, Ⓕ (02) 9958 1258; est 1997; ♦ 20,000 cases; no visitors*
A substantial family operation, founded by businessman Mal Logan assisted by three of his children: Peter (an oenology graduate), Greg (advertising), and Kylie (office administrator). An eclectic range, made from grapes grown in Orange and elsewhere. Exports to the UK and elsewhere.

**Pinnacle Wines** ☆☆☆☆

*50 Pinnacle Road, Orange, NSW 2800, ☏ (02) 6365 3316; est 1999; ♦ 400 cases; ☖; A$; by appt*
Peter Gibson first planted two hectares of Pinot Gris in 1999 at 1,000 metres on Mount Canobolas. The immediate success led to an additional hectare of Viognier and 1.6 hectares of Pinot Noir. Excellent Pinot Gris promises much for the future.

**Prince of Orange NR**

*"Cimbria", The Escort Way, Borenore, NSW 2800, ☏ & Ⓕ (02) 6365 2396; est 1996; ♦ 1,200 cases; ☖; A$; Sat 11-5, or by appt*
Follows the pattern of part grape-grower and part vigneron, using Monarch Winemaking Services in the Hunter Valley. There is a complicated story of direct links between the Prince of Orange and the NSW Surveyor General, hence the name of both the region and the winery.

**Reynolds** ☆☆☆☆⚐

*"Quondong", Cargo Road, Cudal, NSW 2864, ☎ (02) 6364 2330, Ⓕ (02) 6364 2388; est 1994; ⬗ 250,000; no visitors*

Having flown so high, with a 20,000-tonne winery and nine hectares of vineyards producing some remarkably good wines at mouthwatering prices, it seems inconceivable the business will not emerge from its tax scheme fight with the Commissioner of Taxation. The sheer quality of the wines transcends such fights of Mammon. Exports to the UK and elsewhere.

**Ross Hill Vineyard** ☆☆☆

*62 Griffin Road, via Ammerdown, Orange, NSW 2800, ☎ (02) 6360 0175, Ⓕ (02) 6363 1674; est 1994; ⬗ 2,500 cases; ⚑; A$; by appt*

Peter and Terri Robson began planting twelve hectares of vines in 1994 on north-facing, gentle slopes at an elevation of 800 metres, employing soft organic principles. The commendable wines are exported to the UK.

**Templer's Mill** ☆☆☆⚐

*The University of Sydney, Leeds Parade, Orange, NSW 2800, ☎ (02) 6360 5570, Ⓕ (02) 6362 7625; est 1997; ⬗ 1,300 cases; ⚑; A$; 7 days 11-4; ⑂; ⊨*

The Orange Agricultural Campus of Sydney University has established twenty hectares of vineyards as a key enterprise within the Faculty of Rural Management that is also used for viticultural research. Smooth Chardonnay is the star.

**Word of Mouth Wines** ☆☆☆⚐

*Campbell's Corner, Pinnacle Road, Orange, NSW 2800, ☎ (02) 6362 3509, Ⓕ (02) 6365 3517; est 1991; ⬗ 1,500 cases; ⚑; A$; Fri-Sun & public hols 11-5*

The challenging name has an even more challenging label design, the mouth somewhat vampire-like. However, the contract-made Late Harvest Riesling, Sauvignon Blanc, and Pinot Noir soothe rather than lacerate the throat.

# Riverina

This extensive, unprepossessingly flat vineyard area to the southeast of the state stands as a lasting testament to the skills and vision of a group of dedicated Australians. Riverina is hot and dry; the introduction of irrigation by these pioneers was the key to its creation as "The Murrumbidgee Irrigation Scheme Area" between 1906 and 1912. Its subsequent development owes a debt to successive generations of the remarkable McWilliam family, not to mention the influence (both pre- and post-WWII) of Italian immigrants. Until the late 1950s, the Riverina produced only cheap fortified wines. It prospered in so doing until changes in the pattern of wine consumption forced the region to rethink its whole approach to grape-growing and winemaking.

It was Glen McWilliam who then showed the same vision (and skill) as the region's founders. He proved that Riesling, Semillon, and Cabernet Sauvignon could be successfully grown and made into table wines, which, by the standards of the day, were very good. The 1963 Cabernet Sauvignon was a freakish landmark, still vibrant almost twenty years after it was made.

In the following years, the focus was placed relentlessly on holding down the cost of production, and selling wines on price and price alone.

It was left to De Bortoli, with its superb botrytized Noble One Semillon, and to vintages such as 2002 to show how far the quality envelope can be pushed. Then there is the overnight success story of Casella yellow tail, unequalled in the annals of either Australia or the United States. Where next is anyone's guess. There are twenty wine producers in the region.

### Barramundi Wines ☆☆⌐
*Walla Avenue, Griffith, NSW 2680, ☎ (02) 6966 9600, Ⓕ (02) 6962 2888; est 1976; ⚬ NFP: no visitors*
The reincarnation of Cranswick Estate, the latter acquired by Evans & Tate in March 2003. To all intents and purposes an export-only business, with the Barramundi, Aldridge Estate and Cedar Creek brands all at low prices. Worldwide distribution.

### Beelgara Estate ☆☆☆ V
*Farm 576, Beelbangera, NSW 2686, ☎ (02) 6966 0200, Ⓕ (02) 6966 0298; est 1930; ⚬ 600,000 cases; ♟; A$; Mon-Sat 10-5, Sun 11-3; ⚹*
Is another rebirth after the purchase of the sixty-year-old Rossetto Family winery by a group of growers, distributors, and investors. Vintages such as 2002 can come up with excellent wines under the Winemakers Selection banner.

### Casella ☆☆☆ V
*Wakely Road, Yenda, NSW 2681, ☎ (02) 6968 1346, Ⓕ (02) 6968 1196; est 1969; ⚬ 5 million cases; no visitors*
The fairy story to end all fairy stories, with sales of yellow tail growing from zero to five million cases in under two years, largely in the US market courtesy of Rosemount pulling the Lindemans Bin 65 distribution from WJ Deutsch. There are better wines in the stable, but not at the multi-million-case level. Worldwide distribution.

### De Bortoli ☆☆☆☆ V
*De Bortoli Road, Bilbul, NSW 2680, ☎ (02) 6966 0100, Ⓕ (02) 6966 0199; est 1928; ⚬ 3 million cases; ♟; A$; Mon-Sat 9-5, Sun 9-4*
De Bortoli is famous among the cognoscenti for its superb Botrytis Semillon, which in fact accounts for a minute part of its total production. This winery releases low-priced varietal and generic wines that are invariably competently made, and equally invariably good value for money. Worldwide distribution.

### Lillypilly Estate ☆☆☆☆ V
*Lillypilly Road, Leeton, NSW 2705, ☎ (02) 6953 4069, Ⓕ (02) 6953 4980; est 1982; ⚬ 10,000 cases; ♟; A$; Mon-Sat 10-5.30, Sun by appt; ⚹*
Robert Fiumara was the first winemaker to set up a modern, boutique winery in Griffith. He helped bring a sense of identity and character to the Riverina, notably with his Traminer Semillon blend, Tramillon™, and with his unique botrytized Noble Muscat of Alexandria and other Noble (botrytis) varietals.

### McWilliam's ☆☆☆☆ V
*Jack McWilliam Road, Hanwood, NSW 2680, ☎ (02) 6963 0001, Ⓕ (02) 6963 0002; est 1916; ⚬ NFP; ♟; A$; Mon-Sat 9-5; ⚹*
The senior winery in the region, although with the exception of its Botrytis Semillon and Liqueur Muscat, the best wines are limited-release wines sourced from other (premium) regions. Its much-improved Hanwood range is being marketed worldwide in a joint venture with Gallo.

**Miranda Wines** ☆☆☆☆↓ **V**

*57 Jondaryan Avenue, Griffith, NSW 2680, ☎ (02) 6960 3000, ⓕ (02) 6962 6944; est 1939; ⬧ 2.5 million cases; ⚱; A$; 7 days 9-5*

In 2003 Miranda Wines was purchased by the McGuigan/Simeon group, which will, however, presumably keep the brand portfolio largely intact, perhaps investing more in the most successful brands and markets. It can be safely assumed that the plethora of brands and labels will continue, Gold Botrytis the ace in the hole.

**Piromit Wines NR**

*113 Hanwood Avenue, Hanwood, NSW 2680, ☎ (02) 6963 0200, ⓕ (02) 6963 0277; est 1998; ⬧ 60,000 cases; ⚱; A$; Mon-Fri 9-5; ◉*

The Piromit winery was built in 1999 on a six-hectare site previously used as a movie drive-in, and draws upon forty hectares of estate vineyards to produce an attractively priced range of wines. Exports to the UK and elsewhere.

**Riverina Estate** ☆☆☆☆ **V**

*700 Kidman Way, Griffith, NSW 2680, ☎ (02) 6963 8300, ⓕ (02) 6962 4628; est 1969; ⬧ 750,000 cases; ⚱; A$; Mon-Fri 9-5, Sat 10-4*

You pay your money and you take your choice: Warburn Estate, Ballingal Estate, Three Corners, Lizard Ridge, Kanger's Leap, Bushman's Gully, Kimberly Creek, and Lombard Station are all available from Riverina Estate. Worldwide distribution.

**Toorak Estate NR**

*Toorak Road, Leeton, NSW 2705, ☎ (02) 6953 2333, ⓕ (02) 6953 4454; est 1965; ⬧ 400,000 cases; ⚱; A$; Mon-Fri 10-5, Sat by appt; ⚔*

A traditional, long-established Riverina producer with a strong, Italian-based clientele across Australia. Production has skyrocketed, drawing on eighty hectares and purchased grapes, and there is the usual Riverina plethora of brand names.

**Westend Estate** ☆☆☆☆↓ **V**

*1283 Brayne Road, Griffith, NSW 2680, ☎ (02) 6964 1506, ⓕ (02) 6962 1673; est 1945; ⬧ 140,000 cases; ⚱; A$; Mon-Fri 8.30-5, Sat 9.30-4; ⚔*

Another winery sharply lifting quality, packaging, and, above all else, volume, run by Bill Calabria. Particularly successful 3 Bridges Cabernet Sauvignon and Golden Mist Botrytis Semillon, exuding kumquat and mandarin flavours off-set by precisely balanced acidity. To qualify for the 3 Bridges label, the wine must have won at least one gold medal. Exports to the UK and elsewhere.

# Canberra District

It has always struck me as a wry commentary on the unreality of the political hothouse that is Canberra that only one of the Canberra District vignerons actually owns a vineyard in Canberra and that none of them is a politician. The problem is that freehold does not exist within the Australian Capital Territory.

It took the clout of Australia's second-largest wine company to overcome this problem with an enterprise to dwarf all others. In 1997, Hardys entered into an agreement with the territory government for the erection of the 2,000-tonne Kamberra winery and the establishment of a 250-hectare vineyard within the territory. The region's other, much smaller vignerons remain clustered in two areas just outside the territory's borders: in the Yass Valley around Murrumbateman, and along the shores of Lake George. Spring frosts are the main threat here, so very careful site selection is a must. Altitude, too, is a key factor: the highest vineyards produce very creditable Pinot Noir and elegant Chardonnay, while vineyards at lower altitudes still benefit from the strongly Continental climate (warm days, cold nights) to produce stylish Riesling, marvellous Shiraz/Viognier, and elegant Bordeaux-style Cabernet blends. There are thirty-one wine producers in the region.

### Brindabella Hills ☆☆☆☆☆

*Woodgrove Close, via Hall, ACT 2618, ☎ (02) 6230 2583, Ⓕ (02) 6230 2023; est 1989; ⚕ 2,500 cases; ⚐; A$; wkds & public hols 10-5*

Distinguished research scientist Dr Roger Harris developed the method for measuring (in unbelievably tiny amounts) the biochemical flavour agent in Cabernet Sauvignon. He also makes elegant and distinctive hand-crafted Riesling, Sauvignon Blanc/Semillon, Chardonnay, Shiraz, and Cabernet Sauvignon.

### Clonakilla ☆☆☆☆☆

*Crisps Lane, Murrumbateman, NSW 2582, ☎ (02) 6227 5877, Ⓕ (02) 6227 5871; est 1971; ⚕ 3,500 cases; ⚐; A$; 7 days 11-5*

Tim Kirk, son of scientist founder Dr John Kirk, has swept all before him with his brilliant, perfumed, spicy Shiraz/Viognier; Riesling, Viognier, and Shiraz are close behind. Exports to the UK and elsewhere.

### Doonkuna Estate ☆☆☆☆

*Barton Highway, Murrumbateman, NSW 2582, ☎ (02) 6227 5811, Ⓕ (02) 6227 5085; est 1973; ⚕ 3,000 cases; ⚐; A$; 7 days 11-4*

Following the acquisition of Doonkuna by Barry and Maureen Moran in late 1996, the plantings have been increased from a little under four hectares to twenty hectares. The cellar-door prices remain modest, and increased production will follow in the wake of the new plantings.

### Gallagher Estate ☆☆☆☆

*Dog Trap Road, Murrumbateman, NSW 2582, ☎ (02) 6254 9957, Ⓕ (02) 6254 9957; est 1995; ⚕ 2,500 cases; no visitors*

Greg Gallagher was the senior winemaker at Taltarni for twenty years, but he left to establish a small vineyard in Murrumbateman in 1995. He now provides contract winemaking services for a number of wineries in the region. Melon, nectarine, and cashew Chardonnay stands out.

### Helm ☆☆☆☆

*Butt's Road, Murrumbateman, NSW 2582, ☎ (02) 6227 5536, Ⓕ (02) 6227 5953; est 1973; ⚕ 4,000 cases; ⚐; A$; Thurs-Mon 10-5*

Ken Helm is yet another viticultural scientist based in Canberra, and one of the wine industry's more stormy petrels. He is an indefatigable promoter of his wines, and frequently has cause to issue press releases recording the show successes (including bronze medals) of his tightly structured Rieslings and blackberry and cassis Cabernet/Merlots.

### Hillbrook ☆☆☆☆

*639 Doust Road, Geary's Gap via Bungendore, NSW 2621, ☎ & Ⓕ (02) 6236 9455; est 1994; ⚕ 2,000 cases; ⚐; A$; wkds & public hols 10-5*

Adolf and Levina Zanzert began the establishment of 8.5 hectares of vines at Geary's Gap in 1994. The wines, including a fresh, fragrant, and elegant Merlot, have good local distribution; also available through cellar door and mailing list.

**Jeir Creek** ☆☆☆

*Gooda Creek Road, Murrumbateman, NSW 2582, ☎ (02) 6227 5999, ⓕ (02) 6227 0207; est 1984; ◊ 4,500 cases; ⓣ; A$; Fri-Sun & hols 10-5, music & gourmet food first Sun of each month*

Rob Howell came to part-time winemaking through a love of drinking fine wine. Jeir Creek is now a substantial (and still growing) business, the vineyard plantings increased to eleven hectares by the establishment of more Cabernet Sauvignon, Shiraz, and Merlot.

**Kamberra** ☆☆☆☆

*Corner Northbourne Avenue and Fleminton Road, Lyneham, ACT 26002, ☎ (02) 6262 2333, ⓕ (02) 6262 2300; est 2000; ◊ 50,000 cases; ⓣ; A$; 7 days 10-5*

The only winery within the Australian Capital Territory proper, the result of a quasi-joint venture between Hardys and the ACT government. The modern winery processes both estate-grown and locally purchased grapes.

**Kyeema Estate** ☆☆☆⁄

*43 Shumack Street, Weetangera, ACT 2614, ☎ (02) 6254 7536, ⓕ (02) 6254 7557; est 1986; ◊ 750 cases; no visitors*

The Canberra vignerons tend to be a prickly lot and Kyeema's winemaker/owner Andrew McEwin is no exception. But, take note that every wine ever released under this label has won a show award of some distinction!

**Lark Hill** ☆☆☆☆☆

*521 Bungendore Road, Bungendore, NSW 2621, ☎ & ⓕ (02) 6238 1393; est 1978; ◊ 4,000 cases; ⓣ; A$; Wed-Mon 10-5*

Dr (yes, yet another) David and Sue Carpenter are among the region's foremost winemakers. They make elegant but complex Chardonnay, utterly disconcertingly powerful Pinot Noir that consistently shows more varietal character than it ought, and polished, flavourful Cabernet/Merlot. Exports to the UK and elsewhere.

**Lerida Estate** ☆☆☆

*The Wineries, Old Federal Highway, Collector, NSW 2581, ☎ (02) 4848 0231, ⓕ (02) 4848 0232; est 1999; ◊ 1,500 cases; ⓣ; A$; 7 days 11-4.30, or by appt*

Jim Lumbers has established over eight hectares of vineyard (chiefly Pinot Noir) to the immediate south of Lake George Winery. A tasting, barrel, and function room was built in 2001, designed by famous architect Glen Murcott, alongside the open-air winery. Nice Pinot Noir.

**Little Bridge** ☆☆☆⁄ **V**

*PO Box 499, Bungendore, NSW 2621, ☎ (02) 6251 5242, ⓕ (02) 6251 4379; est 1996; ◊ 1,000 cases; no visitors*

A partnership between the Leyshon and Clark families, this is off to a flying start with excellent cassis/blackcurrant Cabernet Sauvignon, aromatic lime, herb, and spice Riesling, and spicy/savoury Pinot Noir.

**Madew Wines** ☆☆☆⁄

*Westering, Federal Highway, Lake George, NSW 2581, ☎ & ⓕ (02) 4848 0026; est 1984; ◊ 2,500 cases; ⓣ; A$; wkds & public hols 11-5; cricket pitch & pavilion*

Originally established within the city limits of Queanbeyan but forced out by urban pressure. The owners then acquired the Westering Vineyard, established by Captain GP Hood. It now boasts scenic views of Lake George, a cricket pitch, and a warning sign reading "Look out for the Great Dane."

**Mount Majura Vineyard** ☆☆☆✦ **V**

*RMB 314 Majura Road, Majura, ACT 2609, ☎ 0403 355 682, Ⓕ (02) 6262 4288; est 1988; ⚘ 2,000 cases; no visitors*

A syndicate including Dr Frank van der Loo, who now makes the wines at Brindabella, has seen a significant rise in quality, with Chardonnay, Pinot Noir, Riesling, Pinot Gris, and Shiraz all firing.

**Pankhurst NR** ☆☆☆☆

*Old Woodgrove, Woodgrove Road, Hall, NSW 2618, ☎ & Ⓕ (02) 6230 2592; est 1986; ⚘ 4,000 cases; ⚲; A$; wkds & public hols, or by appt*

Agricultural scientist Allan Pankhurst and wife Christine established a three-hectare split-canopy vineyard and turned to Sue Carpenter as contract winemaker. Results are convincing, particularly the stylish Pinot Noir and subtly complex Chardonnay.

**Wily Trout** ☆☆☆☆

*Marakei-Nanima Road, via Hall, NSW 2618, ☎ (02) 6230 2487, Ⓕ (02) 6230 2211; est 1998; ⚘ 750 cases; ⚲; A$; 7 days 10-5; ⦿*

The twenty-hectare Wily Trout vineyard shares its home with the Poachers Pantry, a renowned gourmet smokehouse; thus the Smokehouse Café doubles up as a tasting room and cellar door. Skilled contract winemaking produces excellent, fruit-driven Shiraz, powerful, punchy Sauvignon Blanc, and elegant Chardonnay.

**Wimbaliri Wines** ☆☆☆✦

*Barton Highway, Murrumbateman, NSW 2582, ☎ (02) 6227 5921, Ⓕ (02) 6227 5921; est 1988; ⚘ 700 cases; ⚲; A$; wkds 11-5 & by appt*

John and Margaret Andersen chose a smart location to plant a 2.2-hectare mix of Bordeaux blends, Chardonnay, and Shiraz, using sophisticated trellising and close planting.

# Hilltops

A brief flirtation with winemaking occurred here at the end of the nineteenth century, but it was not until the 1970s that the modern romance began. It was left to a local, the late Peter Robertson, to re-introduce vines in 1975. When McWilliam's purchased his 400-hectare Barwang property in 1989, there were still only thirteen hectares under vine. There are now in excess of 150 hectares.

Briefly known as Young, confusingly also the name of the major town around which the region centres, the Hilltops region runs south and east of Young and is defined by the 450-metre contour line as its low point. The climate is cool, with snow in winter, followed by spring frosts that mean careful site selection is needed. Cabernet Sauvignon, Semillon, Chardonnay, and Shiraz are the four most widely planted varieties, and are likely to remain so. Most of the fruit is sold, or, in the case of Barwang, taken to McWilliam's Hanwood winery at Griffith. Both Hungerford Hill and Allandale (in the Hunter Valley) release wines made from Hilltops grapes. There are six wine producers in the region.

**Barwang Vineyard** ☆☆☆☆☆

*Barwang Road, Young, NSW 2594, ☎ (02) 6382 3594, Ⓕ (02) 6382 2594; est 1969; ⚘ NA; no visitors*

These wines (made at McWilliam's) have been of consistent style and quality right from the outset. The range now extends to Chardonnay, Semillon, Shiraz, Merlot, and Cabernet Sauvignon. In each case, oak influence is deliberately down-played, the powerful fruit character providing ample structure and flavour.

**Chalkers Crossing** ☆☆☆☆☆ V

*387 Grenfell Road, Young, NSW 2594, ☎ (02) 6382 6900, Ⓕ (02) 6382 5068; est 2000; ◊ 10,000 cases; ♟; A$; Mon-Fri 9-5, wkds 10-4*

Owned by Ted and Wendy Ambler, this is one of the most exciting newcomers in Australia, with skilled winemaking by the (relatively) young French-trained Celine Rousseau (now an Australian citizen) producing fine, elegant Semillon, Riesling, Sauvignon Blanc, Chardonnay, Pinot Noir, and Cabernet Sauvignon, all from cool regions. Exports to the UK and elsewhere.

**Grove Estate** ☆☆☆☆ V

*Murringo Road, Young, NSW 2594, ☎ (02) 6382 6999, Ⓕ (02) 6382 4527; est 1989; ◊ 2,000 cases; ♟ ; A$; wkds 10-5, or by appt*

Brian Mullany and partners have established a thirty-hectare vineyard planted to mainstream varieties plus Zinfandel, Barbera, and Sangiovese. Wine quality has leapt with skilled contract winemaking; Reserve Cabernet Sauvignon outstanding, Basazi (Zinfandel/Sangiovese/Barbera blend) exotic and plush. Exports to the UK.

**Hansen Hilltops NR**

*Barwang Ridge, 1 Barwang Road, Young, NSW 2594, ☎ (02) 6382 6363, Ⓕ (02) 6382 6363; est 1979; ◊ 2,100 cases; ♟; A$; 7 days 11-6*

Peter Hansen acquired the former Nioka Ridge vineyard, the second oldest in the region. Wines made under his Hansen Hilltops label draw upon five hectares of mature vineyards planted to classic varieties.

# Tumbarumba

This marks the southernmost extension of the state's wine regions, a line that begins just below the Queensland border and runs along the western side of the Great Dividing Range. This is true alpine country, frequented by skiers in winter and by bushwalkers and trout fishermen in summer.

The vineyards lie between 300 and 800 metres, with snow-clad peaks towering above. Spring frosts are a major threat, demanding ultra-careful site selection and (wherever possible) frost protection. The inversion of night-time temperatures – cold air falling, warmer rising – can play tricks, but elevation remains the key factor in the choice of varietal. Chardonnay and Pinot Noir dominate the plantings. In many years, the grapes are destined for sparkling wine, but high-quality table wine can be made in the best warmer vintages.

There are five wine producers in the region: Excelsior Peak, Glenburnie Vineyard, Lighthouse Peak, Tumbarumba Wine Estates, and Tumbarumba Wine Growers.

# Hastings River

Viticulture and winemaking in the Hastings River region date back to 1837, when the first vineyard was planted by Henry Fancourt White, a colonial surveyor. By the 1860s there were thirty-three vineyards in the area.

Following federation and the shift to fortified wines, production inevitably declined. It ceased in the region during the early years of this century.

Sixty years later, in 1980, the French-descended Cassegrain family decided to expand into real estate and associated viticultural and winemaking interests in the region. As a result, they significantly – if improbably – expanded the modern viticultural map of Australia. In the course of meeting the unique climatic challenges of the region (high summer rainfall and humidity), they also pioneered new varieties and new ways of managing vineyards. And they have indirectly encouraged the development of other vineyards and wineries along the northern coast of NSW. There are five wine producers in the region.

### Bago Vineyards ☆☆☆
*Milligans Road, off Bago Road, Wauchope, NSW 2446, ☎ & Ⓕ (02) 6585 7099; est 1985; ♦ 6,000 cases; ♀; A$; 7 days 11-5, jazz wkds; ⚔*
Jim and Kay Mobs began planting the Broken Bago Vineyards in 1985 with one hectare of Chardonnay. There are now twelve hectares of vines, with contract winemaking by Cassegrain.

### Cassegrain ☆☆☆☆
*Hastings River Winery, Fernbank Creek Road, Port Macquarie, NSW 2444, ☎ (02) 6583 7777, Ⓕ (02) 6584 0354; est 1980; ♦ 45,000 cases; ♀; A$; 7 days 9-5; ⅏*
This is a substantial operation. In earlier years, fruit was drawn from many parts of Australia, but the estate now has a 154-hectare vineyard planted with fourteen varieties, including the rare Chambourcin, a French-bred cross resistant to the mildew that bedevils this region. Also now owns Hungerford Hill. Worldwide distribution.

### Inneslake ☆☆☆◁
*The Ruins Way, Inneslake, Port Macquarie, NSW 2444, ☎ (02) 6581 1332, Ⓕ (02) 6581 0391; est 1988; ♦ 1,000 cases; ♀; A$; Mon-Fri 11-5, wkds 10-5; ⅏; ⚔*
A change of name from Charley Brothers, but not ownership. The property on which the vineyards sit has been in the family's ownership since the turn of the century. Since 1988, 7.5 hectares of vines have been established. Cassegrain purchases most of the grapes, vinifying part for the Inneslake label.

### Long Point Vineyard ☆☆☆
*6 Cooinda Place, Lake Cathie, NSW 2445, ☎ (02) 6585 4598, Ⓕ (02) 8584 8915; est 1995; ♦ 600 cases; ♀; A$; Thurs-Sun & public hols 10-6, or by appt*
Graeme (educational psychologist) and Helen (chartered accountant) Davies turned their lives upside down to move from Brisbane to the Barossa Valley (and the Roseworthy Campus of Adelaide University) before returning to the Hastings Valley, establishing their vineyard and self-building their house and winery.

## Shoalhaven Coast

All the wineries hugging the NSW coast from north to south are heavily reliant on general (rather than wine) tourism. They also share humid and often wet summer and autumn seasons, which create difficult viticultural challenges. One solution has been the propagation of Chambourcin, a French-bred hybrid, which is strongly resistant to mildew and has extraordinarily good colour. The other solution, adopted by the two best producers in the Shoalhaven Coast, has been to have their wines contract-made in the Hunter Valley. It has paid big dividends for both; their wines are immeasurably better than most of the other small wineries dotted along the coast of NSW. There are seven wine producers in the region.

**Cambewarra Estate** ☆☆☆⚐

*520 Illaroo Road, Cambewarra, NSW 2540, ☎ & Ⓕ (02) 4446 0170; est 1991; ✦ 3,500 cases; ⚑; A$; Thurs-Sun & hols 10-5; ⋈; ⚔*

Founded by Geoffrey and Louise Cole in 1991, Cambewarra became a pace-setter virtually overnight. Fresh stone-fruit, melon, and citrus Chardonnay, juicy, blackberry Chambourcin, and minty, cassis Cabernet Sauvignon are reliably good.

**Coolangatta Estate** ☆☆☆⚐

*1335 Bolong Road, Shoalhaven Heads, NSW 2535, ☎ (02) 4448 7131, Ⓕ (02) 4448 7997; est 1988; ✦ 5,000 cases; ⚑; A$; 7 days 10-5; ⋈⋅; ⋈; museum, golf course*

Coolangatta Estate is part of a 150-hectare resort. Some of its oldest buildings were constructed by convicts in 1822. One might expect that the wines are tailored purely for the tourist market, but in fact the standard of viticulture is exceptionally high (immaculate Scott-Henry trellising) and the winemaking is wholly professional (contract-made by Tyrrell's). Unsurprisingly, Semillon is best.

**Crooked River Wines** ☆☆⚐

*11 Willow Vale Road, Gerringong, NSW 2534, ☎ (02) 4234 0975, Ⓕ (02) 4234 4477; est 1998; ✦ 6,500 cases; ⚑; A$; 7 days 10.30-4.30*

With 13.5 hectares of vineyards planted to an exotic mix including Arneis, Sangiovese, and Chambourcin, this is the largest vineyard on the south coast. A cellar-door sales, craft shop, and café opened in December 2001.

**The Silos Estate NR**

*Princes Highway, Jaspers Brush, NSW 2535, ☎ (02) 4448 6082, Ⓕ (02) 4448 6246; est 1985; ✦ 1,000 cases; ⚑; A$; 7 days 10-5; ⋈⋅; ⋈*

Since 1995, Gaynor Sims and Kate Khoury, together with viticulturist Jovica Zecevic, have worked hard to improve quality at this estate, both in the five-hectare estate vineyard and in the winery. For the moment, the winery continues to rely on the tourist trade for sales.

# Southern Highlands

Another region to emerge with some impressive results in the first few years of this century. Altitude is the major factor in delivering a cool, Continental-type climate; frost, summer rain, and autumn rain provide challenges, and make site selection particularly important. By and large, the early-ripening varieties perform best. Some look to other parts of New South Wales to supplement their intake and to broaden varietal choice. There are nine wine producers in the region; producers other than those appearing below are Howards Lane Vineyard, Joadja Vineyards, Saint Deryck's Wood Winery, Southern Highland Wines, and Statford Park.

**Centennial Vineyards** ☆☆☆☆⚐

*"Woodside", Centennial Road, Bowral, NSW 2576, ☎ (02) 4861 8700, Ⓕ (02) 4681 8777; est 2002; ✦ 9,000 cases; ⚑; A$; 7 days 10-5; ⋈⋅*

Clearly the pace-setter, with wine industry veteran John Large and investor Mark Dowling purchasing two classic properties, building a 120-tonne winery and opening a hugely popular restaurant. Skilled winemaking by Tony Cosgriff produces singularly impressive Cabernet Sauvignon, Sauvignon Blanc, Cabernet/Merlot, and Chardonnay.

### Cuttaway Hill Estate ☆☆☆↓

*PO Box 2034, Bowral, NSW 2576, ☎ (02) 4862 4551, Ⓕ (02) 4862 2326; est 1998; ⚐ 5,000 cases; no visitors*

Another newcomer, owned by the wealthy O'Neil family, which has established three completely separate vineyard sites with different site climates under the direction of a skilled viticulturist and contract winemaking team. Semillon, Sauvignon Blanc, Chardonnay, and Pinot Gris are the pick.

### McVitty Grove ☆☆☆

*Joadja Road, Berrima, NSW 2577, ☎ (02) 4878 5044, Ⓕ (02) 4878 5524; est 1998; ⚐ 1,000 cases; ⚑; A$; by appt*

Mark and Jane Phillips have established 5.5 hectares of Pinot Noir and Pinot Gris on deep, fertile soils, complemented by a 1.5-hectare olive grove. The Pinot Gris is delivering the goods.

### Mundrakoona Estate NR

*Sir Charles Moses Lane, Old Hume Highway, Woodlands via Mittagong, NSW 2575, ☎ (02) 4872 1311, Ⓕ (02) 4872 1322; est 1997; ⚐ 1,800 cases; ⚑; A$; wkds & public hols 9-6; blacksmithing*

During 1998 and 1999, Anton Balog progressively planted 3.2 hectares of Pinot Noir, Sauvignon Blanc, and Tempranillo at an altitude of 680 metres. He is using wild-yeast ferments, hand-plunging, and other "natural" winemaking techniques.

# Gundagai and Southern New South Wales Zone

The Southern New South Wales Zone has within its boundaries the Canberra District, Hilltops, Tumbarumba and Gundagai, but there are wineries within the Zone falling outside the boundaries of the regions. What is more, while there are significant plantings within the Gundagai region, the number of active wineries is very limited. There are eight wine producers in the Zone/region.

### Bidgeebong Wines ☆☆☆☆

*352 Byrnes Road, Bomen, NSW 2650, ☎ (03) 9853 6207, Ⓕ (03) 9853 5499; est 2000; ⚐ 15,000 cases; ⚑; A$; Mon-Fri 9-4*

A partnership including Andrew Birks, a thirty-year career lecturer at Charles Sturt University, and Simon Robertson, a very experienced viticultural consultant. Together with investors, they have erected a large winery with an ultimate capacity of 2,000 tonnes of grapes, catering for contract winemaking and Bidgeebong's own needs. The wines come from what the founders refer to as "the Bidgeebong triangle lying between Young, Wagga Wagga, Tumbarumba and Gundagai", and the Shiraz, Chardonnay, and Merlot are uniformly good. Exports to the UK and elsewhere.

### Borambola Wines ☆☆☆

*Sturt Highway, Wagga Wagga, NSW 2650, ☎ & Ⓕ (02) 6928 4210; est 1995; ⚐ 3,000 cases; ⚑; A$; 7 days 11-4*

Ten hectares of vines on the historic Borambola Homestead (built circa 1880) property, with wines made by Andrew Birks.

**Charles Sturt University Winery** ☆☆☆⟡ V
*McKeown Drive (off Coolamon Road), Wagga Wagga, NSW 2650, ☎ (02) 6933
2435, Ⓕ (02) 6933 4072; est 1977; ⬥ 15,000 cases; ⬥; A$; Mon-Fri 11-5, wkds 11-4*
A new A$ 2.5 million winery was opened in June 2001; this is a fully
fledged commercial operation, as well as teaching university students.
Good wines at very good prices are the order of the day.

**Paterson's Tumblong Vineyard** ☆☆☆⟡
*474 Old Hume Highway Road, Tumblong, NSW 2729, ☎ (02) 6944 9227, Ⓕ (02)
9880 9176; est 1997; ⬥ 700 cases; ⬥; A$; wkds 9-5; ✗*
The multi-talented and qualified Paterson family have twelve hectares of
vines, entrusting the making to Celine Rousseau at Chalkers Crossing. The
Shiraz and Cabernet Sauvignon are both good wines, full of character.

# Sydney Basin

A proposed region more than likely to be formally recognized in the not too
distant future. It was the birthplace of serious viticulture in Australia, and is
home to some historic vineyards, with Camden Estate Vineyards dating back
to the 1820s and Tizzana Winery built in 1887 by Australia's true renaissance
man, Dr Thomas Fiaschi. There are seven wine producers in the region.

**Tizzana Winery** ☆☆⟡
*518 Tizzana Road, Ebenezer, NSW 2756, ☎ (02) 4579 1150, Ⓕ (02) 4579 1216;
est 1887; ⬥ 300 cases; ⬥; A$; wkds, hols 12-6, or by appt; ⋈*
Tizzana has been a weekend and holiday occupation for Peter Auld for many
years now, operating in one of the great historic wineries built (in 1887) by
Dr Thomas Fiaschi. The wines may not be great, but the ambience is.

**Vicarys** NR
*Northern Road, Luddenham, NSW 2745, ☎ (02) 4773 4161, Ⓕ (02) 4773 4411;
est 1923; ⬥ 1,700 cases; ⬥; A$; Mon-Fri 9-5, wkds 10-5; monthly craft market*
Vicarys justifiably claims to be the Sydney region's oldest continuously
operating winery, having been established in a very attractive, large stone
shearing shed built about 1890. Most of the wines come from other parts of
Australia, but the winery has produced some good wines of all styles over
the years.

# Perricoota

Perricoota, a relatively new region, joins with Riverina as one of the two
regions in the Big Rivers Zone. It hugs the northern side of the Murray
River, with a climate nearly identical to that of South Australia's Riverland
and Victoria's Murray Darling and Swan Hill regions. The three wineries
open to visits are Morrisons Riverview Winery, St Anne's Vineyard, and
Stevens Brook Estate.

**St Anne's Vineyard** ☆☆⟡
*Corner of Perricoota Road and 24 Lane, Moama, NSW 2731, ☎ (03) 5480 0099,
Ⓕ (03) 5480 0077; est 1972; ⬥ 20,000 cases; ⬥; A$; 7 days 9-5*
Richard McLean has established eighty hectares of estate vineyards, with
another 120 hectares of grower vineyards to draw upon. Shiraz, Cabernet
Sauvignon, Grenache, and Mourvèdre account for over seventy-five per
cent of the plantings. The wines are all competently made.

**Stevens Brook Estate** ☆☆☆

*620 High Street, Echuca, Vic 3564, ☎ (03) 5480 1916, Ⓕ (03) 5480 2004; est 1995; ◈ 5,000 cases; ♚; A$; 7 days 10-5*

The best producer in the region, making full-blooded Shiraz, Sangiovese, and Petit Verdot alongside more conventional varieties.

# Western Plains Zone

It seems only yesterday that the Zone existed as a matter of convenience to fill in the gap that would otherwise have existed in New South Wales, stretching as it does towards the centre of Australia. However, in addition to Canonbah Bridge and Red Earth Estate Vineyard, there are four additional wineries that are either open regularly or by appointment:

**Boora Estate NR**

*"Boora", Warrie Road, Dubbo, NSW 2830, ☎ & Ⓕ (02) 6884 2600; ♚; Sat-Tues 10-5, or by appt*

**Lazy River Estate NR**

*29 Old Dubbo Road, Dubbo, NSW 2830, ☎ & Ⓕ (02) 6882 2111; ♚; by appt; ⑩*

**Tombstone Estate NR**

*5 Basalt Road, Dubbo, NSW 2830, ☎ & Ⓕ (02) 6882 6624; ♚; by appt; ⑩*

**Wattagan Estate Winery NR**

*"Wattagan", Oxley Highway, Coonabarabran, NSW 2357, ☎ (02) 6842 2456, Ⓕ (02) 6842 2656; ♚; 7 days 10-5*

**Canonbah Bridge** ☆☆☆☆

*Merryanbone Station, Warren, NSW 2824, ☎ (02) 6833 9966, Ⓕ (02) 6833 9980; est 1999; ◈ 3,600 cases; no visitors*

This twenty-nine-hectare vineyard has been established by Shane McLaughlin on the very large Merryanbone Station. The wines are part estate and part sourced elsewhere. Drought Reserve Shiraz, Semillon/Sauvignon Blanc, and Ram's Leap Semillon/Sauvignon Blanc are all recommended.

**Red Earth Estate Vineyard** ☆☆☆

*18L Camp Road, Dubbo, NSW 2830, ☎ (02) 6885 6676, Ⓕ (02) 6882 8297; est 2000; ◈ 5,000 cases; ♚; A$; 7 days 10-4, or by appt*

If the Macquarie Valley region comes to pass, it will be due to the leadership of Ken and Christine Borchardt at Red Earth Estate Vineyard. They offer contract winemaking facilities to others, and are producing laudable Merlot and Chardonnay under their own brand.

# South Coast Zone

While the Zone extends some distance to the west away from the actual coastline, most of the wineries are in fact on the coast, and heavily reliant on general tourism. There are four wine producers in the Zone; other than the following, there are Cobbity Wines and Remo & Sons.

**Grevillea Estate** ☆☆☆☆

*Buckajo Road, Bega, NSW 2550, ☎ (02) 6492 3006, Ⓕ (02) 6492 5330; est 1980; ◈ 2,000 cases; ♚; A$; Sept-May Mon-Fri 9-5, wkds 10-5; June-Aug 7 days 10-4; ⑩*

While tourist-oriented, has improved its wines greatly over recent years, and also lifted the quality of packaging and labels. Has a patchwork quilt of wines; Reserve Cabernet and Bordeaux blends and a Botrytis Gewurztraminer have been surprisingly good.

**Tilba Valley NR**

*Lake Corunna Estate, 947 Old Highway, Narooma, NSW 2546, ☎ (02) 4473 7308,*
*Ⓕ (02) 4473 7484; est 1978; ⚘ 600 cases; ⛊; A$; Oct-April 7 days 10-5, May-Sept*
*Wed-Sun 11-4 (closed August)*

A strongly tourist-oriented operation, serving a ploughman's lunch daily
from noon to 2pm. Has eight hectares of estate vineyards.

# Central Ranges Zone

A large Zone stretching north to south along the Great Dividing Range,
with Cowra, Mudgee, and Orange all falling well within its boundaries.
These regions, however, do not overlap, leaving a number of wineries
simply entitled to the Central Ranges Zone appellation. Other than those
wineries below, the wineries are Bell River Estate, Chateau Champsaur,
Glenfinlass, Hermes Morrison Wines, Hoppers Hill Vineyards, Sandhills
Vineyard, and Winburndale.

**Bunnamagoo Estate** ☆☆☆⚘

*Bunnamagoo, Rockley, NSW 2795, ☎ 1300 304 707, Ⓕ (02) 6377 5231; est*
*1995; ⚘ 1,000 cases; no visitors*

The property was one of the first land grants in the region in the first half
of the 1800s; a seven-hectare vineyard planted to Chardonnay, Merlot, and
Cabernet Sauvignon has been established by Paspaley Pearls, a famous
name in the pearl industry. Competent contract winemaking produces
good Chardonnay and Cabernet Sauvignon.

**Louee** ☆☆☆⚘

*Cox's Creek Road, Rylstone, NSW 2849, ☎ (02) 8923 5373, Ⓕ (02) 8923 5362;*
*est 1998; ⚘ 1,500 cases; ⛊; A$; 7 days 9-5*

The home vineyard at Rylstone has thirty-two hectares principally planted
to Cabernet Sauvignon, Shiraz, Petit Verdot, and Merlot; the second
vineyard, at an altitude of 1,100 metres, has Riesling, Sauvignon Blanc,
Pinot Noir, Pinot Gris, and Nebbiolo. The elegant style of all of the
contract-made wines reflects the altitude-cooled climate.

**Monument Vineyard** ☆☆☆⚘ **V**

*Corner Escort Way and Manildra Road, Cudal, NSW 2864, ☎ (02) 6364 2294,*
*Ⓕ (02) 6364 2069; est 1998; ⚘ 1,000 cases; ⛊; A$; by appt; ⚘*

In the early 1990s, five mature-age students at Charles Sturt University,
successful in their own professions, decided to form a partnership to
develop a substantial vineyard and winery. After a lengthy search, 110
hectares have been planted, and commendable Shiraz, Reserve
Shiraz/Viognier, and Sangiovese are specially recommended.

# Northern Slopes Zone

A long Zone stretching south from the Queensland border along the Great
Dividing Range. The greatest activity has taken place close to the border at
or near Tenterfield, the grapes headed either to Queensland operations in
the Granite Belt, or south to Hunter Valley makers, including Tyrrell's,
which has its own vineyards in the region. The two largest vineyards are

Richfield Estate (with over twenty-six hectares planted to seven of the classic varieties) and Tangaratta Estate (with twenty-nine hectares planted). In all instances elevation serves to moderate what would otherwise be a distinctly warm climate. Producers are:

**Gilgai Winery NR**
*Tingha Road, Gilgai, NSW 2360, ☎ (02) 6723 1204*

**Kurrajong Downs NR**
*Casino Road, via Tenterfield, NSW 2372, ☎ (02) 6736 4590*

**New England Estate NR**
*Delungra, NSW 2403, ☎ (02) 6724 8508*

**Reedy Creek Vineyard NR**
*Reedy Creek, via Tenterfield, NSW 2372, ☎ (02) 6737 5221*

**Richfield Estate NR**
*Bonshaw Road, Tenterfield, NSW 2372, ☎ (07) 3832 0228*

**Tangaratta Estate NR**
*RMB 637 Old Winton Road, Tamworth, NSW 2340, ☎ (02) 6761 5660*

**Warrina Wines NR**
*Back Road, Kootingal, NSW 2352, ☎ (02) 6760 3985*

**Willowvale Wines NR**
*Black Swamp Road, Tenterfield, NSW 2372, ☎ (02) 6736 3589*

## Northern Rivers Zone

A coastal Zone stretching from Queensland south for roughly the same distance as the Northern Slopes Zone and encompassing one region, the Hastings River, which is covered separately. A strongly maritime climate is warm and humid; the tail end of cyclones working their way south from the northern Queensland coast provide the major challenges, with significant rainfall often occurring in the lead-up to and during vintage. The mildew-resistant Chambourcin is thus a favoured variety. The producers are:

**Divers Luck Wines ☆☆☆**
*Hellenvale, Nelson Bay Road, Bob's Farm, Port Stephens, NSW 2316, ☎ (02) 4982 2471*

**Great Lakes Wines NR**
*115 Herivals Road, Wootton, NSW 2423, ☎ (02) 4997 7255*

**Ilnam Estate ☆☆☆**
*750 Carool Road, Carool, NSW 2486, ☎ (07) 5590 7703*

**Port Stephens Winery NR**
*69 Nelson Bay Road, Bob's Farm, NSW 2316, ☎ (02) 4982 6411*

**Raleigh Winery NR**
*Queen Street, Raleigh, NSW 2454, ☎ (02) 6655 4388*

**Red Tail Wines NR**
*15 Pinnacle Place, Marlee, NSW 2429, ☎ (02) 6550 5084*

**Two Tails Wines NR**
*963 Orara Way, Nana Glen, NSW 2450, ☎ (02) 6654 3633*

**Villa d'Esta Vineyard NR**
*2884 Wallambah Road, Dyers Crossing, NSW 2429, ☎ (02) 6550 2236*

# Victoria

1994     21,047 hectares     31.39 per cent of total plantings
2003     38,284 hectares     24.30 per cent of total plantings
The only state not to keep up with the pace; on the other hand, there has been growth in the plantings in the premium areas in the centre and south. Moreover, Victoria has by far the greatest number of wineries of any state, with 568 compared to South Australia's 419.

## Yarra Valley

When the Swiss settlers came to the Valley in the 1850s, they proved to be highly skilled grape-growers and winemakers. By the late 1880s, the Yarra was one of the most important producers of high-quality wines in Australia. Its demise over the next twenty years was even more rapid than its growth. This was due to a combination of the abolition of state tariffs in 1901, declining soil fertility and, most importantly, the Australia-wide move from fine table wines to cheap fortified wines – a style of wine impossible for the Yarra to achieve. The rebirth came in the late 1960s, with slow, steady growth in the 1980s, and a frenetic pace in the 1990s.

With a climate cooler than Bordeaux and slightly warmer than Burgundy, the Yarra Valley succeeds best with Chardonnay and Pinot Noir, and sparkling wine made from those varieties. Sauvignon Blanc is easy, Riesling curiously reticent, Marsanne and Roussanne excellent. With appropriate site selection and disciplined canopy and yield management, great results can be achieved with Shiraz, Merlot, and Cabernet Sauvignon, especially in the warmer, drier vintages. There are 101 wine producers in the region.

**Ainsworth Estate** ☆☆☆☆
*110 Ducks Lane, Seville, Vic 3139, ☎ (03) 5964 4711, Ⓕ (03) 5964 4311; est 1994; ◊ 3,000 cases; ☗; A$; Thurs-Mon 10.30-5; ⊨; lunches; art & craft*
Part estate-grown and part contract-grown grapes for Denis and Kerri Craig have produced fine, elegant Chardonnay, Pinot Noir, and Cabernet Sauvignon.

**Arthur's Creek Estate** ☆☆☆☆
*Strathewen Road, Arthur's Creek, Vic 3099, ☎ (03) 9714 8202, Ⓕ (03) 9824 0252; est 1975; ◊ 1,500 cases; no visitors*
SEK Hulme planted 1.5 hectares each of Semillon, Chardonnay, and Cabernet in the mid-1970s, with the wines contract-made by various people. It was fifteen years before he took the decision to sell any of it. The deep, ripe but classic Cabernet Sauvignon is outstanding, the elegant Chardonnay an eyelash behind. Exports to the UK and elsewhere.

**Badger's Brook** ☆☆☆
*874 Maroondah Highway, Coldstream, Vic 3770, ☎ (03) 5962 4130, Ⓕ (03) 5962 4238; est 1993; ◊ 5,000 cases; ☗; A$; Thurs-Mon 11-5*
Situated prominently on Maroondah Highway next door to the well-known Rochford Wines. Location is all, although not for all the wines, which come from various sources.

### Bianchet ☆☆☆⌇

*187 Victoria Road, Lilydale, Vic 3140, ☎ (03) 9739 1779, Ⓕ (03) 9739 1277; est 1976; ⅋ 2,500 cases; ⚲ A$; Thurs-Fri 10-4, wkds 10-5; ⱺ*

Recently acquired from the founding family by a small Melbourne-based syndicate. Most of the wines are sold through the cellar door. One of the more unusual offerings is Verduzzo Gold, a late-harvest, sweet white wine made from the Italian grape variety. Chardonnay can also be very good.

### Bulong Estate ☆☆☆⌇

*70 Summerhill Road, Yarra Junction, Vic 3797, ☎ and Ⓕ (03) 5967 2487; est 1994; ⅋ 3,000 cases; no visitors*

Judy and Howard Carter purchased their beautifully situated forty-five-hectare property in 1994, looking down into the valley below and across to the nearby ranges with Mount Donna Buang at their peak. Most of the grapes from the immaculately tended vineyard are sold, with limited quantities made for the Bulong Estate label. Exports to the UK.

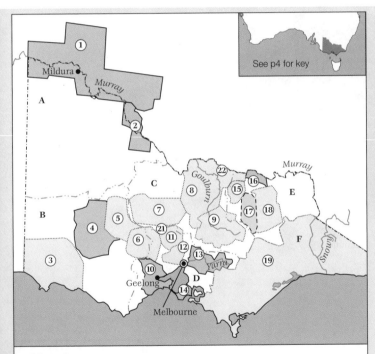

## Victoria

| | | | | | |
|---|---|---|---|---|---|
| | | 4 | Grampians | 13 | Yarra Valley |
| A | Northwest Victoria | 5 | Pyrenees | 14 | Mornington Peninsula |
| B | Western Victoria | 6 | Ballarat | 15 | Glenrowan |
| C | Central Victoria | 7 | Bendigo | 16 | Rutherglen |
| D | Port Phillip | 8 | Goulburn Valley | 17 | King Valley |
| E | Northeast Victoria | 9 | Central Victorian | 18 | Alpine Valleys |
| F | Gippsland | | High Country | 19 | Beechworth |
| 1 | Murray Darling | 10 | Geelong | 20 | Gippsland |
| 2 | Swan Hill | 11 | Macedon | 21 | Heathcote |
| 3 | Henty | 12 | Sunbury | 22 | Upper Goulburn |

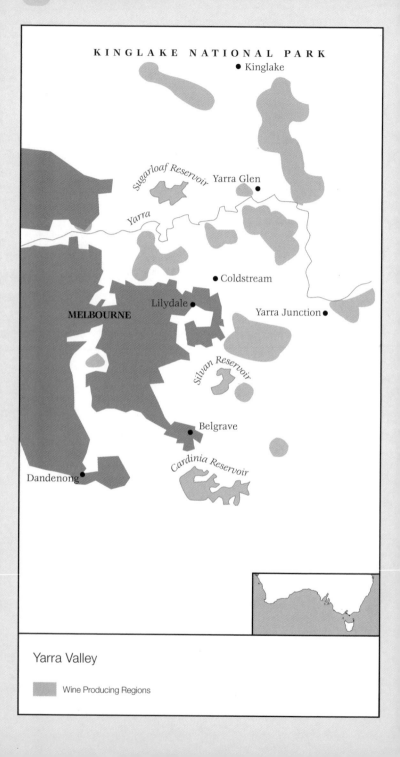

KINGLAKE NATIONAL PARK
● Kinglake

Sugarloaf Reservoir
Yarra Glen ●
Yarra

● Coldstream
Lilydale ●
MELBOURNE
Yarra Junction ●

Silvan Reservoir

Belgrave ●

Cardinia Reservoir

Dandenong ●

Yarra Valley

Wine Producing Regions

**Cahillton** ☆☆☆⁴
*93A Killara Road, Gruyere, Vic 3770;* ☎ *(03) 5964 9000,* Ⓕ *(03) 5964 9313;*
*est 1999;* ⚭ *2,000 cases; no visitors*
The tip of a multi-million dollar investment by the Indonesian Widjaja
family, with twelve varieties planted in the Yarra Valley, and another seven
in a much larger vineyard at Heathcote, amounting to 128 hectares in all.

**Carlei Estate & Green Vineyards** ☆☆☆☆☆
*1 Albert Road, Upper Beaconsfield, Vic 3808,* ☎ *and* Ⓕ *(03) 5944 4599; est 1994;*
⚭ *10,000 cases;* ⚑ *; A$; wkds by appt;* 𝄆
Sergio Carlei is an oenological wizard of Oz, taking small parcels of grapes
from here, there, and everywhere, and producing a range of wonderfully
complex wines with a strong organic bent. Exports to the UK and elsewhere.

**Coldstream Hills NR**
*31 Maddens Lane, Coldstream, Vic 3770,* ☎ *(03) 5964 9410,* Ⓕ *(03) 5964 9389;*
*est 1985;* ⚭ *55,000 cases;* ⚑ *; A$; 7 days 10-5*
Founded by the author, who continues as a consultant following the
acquisition of Coldstream by Southcorp in mid-1996. Well in excess of 100
hectares of owned or managed estate vineyards are the base. Chardonnay
and Pinot Noir are the focus; Sauvignon Blanc, Merlot, and Cabernet
Sauvignon also important. Exports to the UK and elsewhere.

**De Bortoli** ☆☆☆☆☆ **V**
*Pinnacle Lane, Dixon's Creek, Vic 3775,* ☎ *(03) 5965 2271,* Ⓕ *(03) 5965 2442;*
*est 1987;* ⚭ *400,000 cases;* ⚑ *; A$; 7 days 10-5;* 🍴*;* 𝄆*; gardens*
The quality arm of the bustling De Bortoli group, run by Leanne De Bortoli
and husband Stephen Webber, an ex-Lindemans winemaker. The top label
(De Bortoli), the second (Gulf Station), and the third (Windy Peak) offer
wines of consistently good quality and excellent value. Chardonnay
is outstanding.

**Diamond Valley Vineyards** ☆☆☆☆☆
*2130 Kinglake Road, St Andrews, Vic 3761,* ☎ *(03) 9710 1484,* Ⓕ *(03) 9710 1369;*
*est 1976;* ⚭ *7,000 cases; no visitors*
Run by the tightly knit Lance family, one of the Yarra Valley's finest
producers of true Pinot Noirs, fragrant and intense wines of tremendous
style and crystal-clear varietal character. Chardonnay is of equal quality
and similar style. Exports to the UK and elsewhere.

**Domaine Chandon (Green Point)** ☆☆☆☆☆
*Green Point, Maroondah Highway, Coldstream, Vic 3770,* ☎ *(03) 9739 1110,*
Ⓕ *(03) 9739 1095; est 1986;* ⚭ *150,000 cases;* ⚑ *; A$; 7 days 10.30-4.30;* 𝄆
Wholly owned by Champagne Moët & Chandon, in a superb location with
luxurious tasting facilities. A complex blend of French and Australian styles,
thought by many to be the best Moët produces overseas. Exported under
the Green Point label, also used for the increasing production of table
wines, notably Pinot Noir and Chardonnay. Worldwide distribution.

**Dominique Portet** ☆☆☆☆☆
*870-872 Maroondah Highway, Coldstream, Vic 3770,* ☎ *(03) 5962 5760,* Ⓕ *(03)*
*5962 4938; est 2000;* ⚭ *8,000 cases;* ⚑ *; A$; 7 days 10-5*
Dominique Portet spent his early years at Château Lafite (his father was
*régisseur*) and was one of the first flying winemakers, commuting to Clos
Duval in the Napa Valley, then twenty years at Taltarni. Now he has realized
a long-held ambition to establish his own winery in the Yarra Valley, opened
early in 2002, with outstanding Heathcote Shiraz and Cabernet Sauvignon
complementing Yarra Sauvignon Blanc and Cabernet Sauvignon.

**Evelyn County Estate** ☆☆☆☆↓

*55 Eltham-Yarra Glen Road, Kangaroo Ground, Vic 3097, ☏ (03) 9437 2155,*
*Ⓕ (03) 9437 2188; est 1994; ♦ 2,000 cases; ♟; A$; Mon-Wed 11-5, Thurs-Fri*
*11am-10pm, Sat 9-midnight, Sun 9am-10pm; ⊯; art gallery*

The seven-hectare estate is that of former Coopers & Lybrand managing
partner Roger Male and his wife Robyn. A cellar-door sales, gallery, and
restaurant opened in 2001. Merlot, Pinot Noir, and Cabernet Sauvignon
have all succeeded handsomely.

**Fergusson** ☆☆☆↓

*Wills Road, Yarra Glen, Vic 3775, ☏ (03) 5965 2237, Ⓕ (03) 5965 2405; est 1968;*
*♦ 5,000 cases; ♟; A$; 7 days 11-5; ⊯; ⇌; hot air balloon flights*

Best known as a popular tourist destination, particularly for coach parties.
Offers hearty fare in comfortable surroundings, accompanied by estate-
grown wines (more expensive), or the Tartan range from other regions
(less expensive). The Yarra wines are consistently full-flavoured. Exports to
the UK and US.

**Five Oaks Vineyard** ☆☆☆ V

*60 Aitken Road, Seville, Vic 3139, ☏ (03) 5964 3704, Ⓕ (03) 5964 3064; est 1997;*
*♦ 2,000 cases; ♟; A$; wkds & public hols 10-5, or by appt*

Wally Zuk, together with wife Judy, runs all aspects of Five Oaks, far
removed from Wally's background in nuclear physics. He has, however,
completed his wine-science degree at Charles Sturt University, and is thus
more than qualified to make the Five Oaks wines.

**Gembrook Hill** ☆☆☆☆↓

*Launching Place Road, Gembrook, Vic 3783, ☏ (03) 5968 1622, Ⓕ (03) 5968*
*1699; est 1983; ♦ 2,000 cases; ♟; A$; by appt*

Ian Marks, Melbourne dentist by day and fastidious viticulturist otherwise,
tends the six-hectare vineyard planted on red volcanic soil and has committed
the ultimate folly by building an on-site winery. All wines are fine and elegant,
with Sauvignon Blanc, Chardonnay, and Pinot Noir the stars.

**Giant Steps** ☆☆☆↓

*10-12 Briarty Road, Gruyere, Vic 3770; ☏ (03) 5964 9555, Ⓕ (03) 5964 9551;*
*est 1998; ♦ 10,000 cases; ♟; A$; by appt*

The newest wine venture of the mercurial Phil Sexton (and wife Allison),
founder of Devil's Lair, and now of designer beer Little Creatures. North-
facing hillside vineyards promise much.

**Hanson-Tarrahill Vineyard** ☆☆☆

*49 Cleveland Avenue, Lower Plenty, Vic 3093, ☏ (03) 9439 7425, Ⓕ (03) 9439*
*4217; est 1983; ♦ 900 cases; no visitors*

Dental surgeon Ian Hanson is a red-wine specialist, producing Pinot Noir
and various Cabernet-based wines from two vineyard resources, the
oldest dating back to the late 1960s. What the wines lack in finesse, they
make up for in flavour. Exports to the UK.

**Hillcrest Vineyards** ☆☆☆☆↓

*31 Phillip Road, Woori Yallock, Vic 3139, ☏ (03) 5964 6689, Ⓕ (03) 5961 5547;*
*est 1971; ♦ 250 cases; ♟; A$; by appt*

David and Tanya Bryant have acquired a dry-grown thirty-three-year-
old vineyard, and produce tiny quantities of outstanding Pinot Noir
and Chardonnay.

**Kellybrook** ☆☆☆↓

*Fulford Road, Wonga Park, Vic 3115, ☏ (03) 9722 1304, Ⓕ (03) 9722 2092; est*
*1960; ♦ 3,000 cases; ♟; A$; Mon 11-5, Tues-Sat 9-6, Sun 11-6; ⊯; ⚲; pétanque*

The eight-hectare vineyard at Wonga Park lies at the entrance to the principal wine-growing areas of the Yarra Valley, replete with picnic area and a full-scale restaurant. Also a very competent producer of both cider and apple brandy (in Calvados style). Exports to the UK.

**Killara Park Estate** ☆☆☆✐

*Suite 1230, 1 Queens Road, Melbourne, Vic 3004 (postal), ☎ (03) 9863 7505, Ⓕ (03) 9863 7510; est 1997; ❖ 3,500 cases; no visitors*

With sixty hectares of vineyards established since 1997, primarily on steep slopes, an important contract grape supplier in the Yarra Valley. A small amount is kept back to make Chardonnay, Pinot Noir, Shiraz, and Merlot.

**Lillydale Estate** ☆☆☆☆☆ V

*Lot 10, Davross Court, Seville, Vic 3139, ☎ (03) 5964 2016, Ⓕ (03) 5964 3009; est 1975; ❖ NFP; ☗; A$; 7 days 11-5; ▐●▌*

Acquired by McWilliam's Wines in 1994 from the founding partnership. The elegant wines are now made at McWilliam's in the Riverina: snappy Sauvignon Blanc, lingering Chardonnay, and spicy, savoury Pinot Noir. A winery restaurant opened in 1997.

**Lirralirra Estate** ☆☆☆✐

*Paynes Road, Lilydale, Vic 3140, ☎ & Ⓕ (03) 9735 0224; est 1981; ❖; ☗; A$; wkds & hols 10-6 (7 days in Jan)*

Off the beaten track. Owner Alan Smith originally intended to make a Sauternes-style wine from Semillon, Sauvignon Blanc, and Muscadelle, but found the conditions unfavourable for the development of botrytis. He now makes dry red and white wines: the Pinot Noir is best.

**Long Gully Estate** ☆☆☆✐

*Long Gully Road, Healesville, Vic 3777, ☎ (03) 9510 5798, Ⓕ (03) 9510 9859; est 1982; ❖ 150,000 cases; ☗; A$; 7 days 11-5*

One of Yarra's larger producers to have successfully established a number of export markets. Offers a range of wines, and the quality is consistent. Recent vineyard extensions underline its commercial success. Exports to the UK and elsewhere.

**Lovegrove Vineyard and Winery** ☆☆☆✐

*1420 Heidelberg-Kinglake Road, Cottles Bridge, Vic 3099, ☎ (03) 9718 1569, Ⓕ (03) 9718 1028; est 1983; ❖ 1,500 cases; ☗; A$; wkds & public hols 11-6, Mon-Fri by appt; light food platters; ✗*

While production is limited, visitors are offered much to enjoy, with picturesque gardens overlooking the Kinglake Ranges; light food; barbecue and picnic tables; occasional art exhibitions; and live music on the second Sunday of each month. Exports to the UK.

**Metier Wines** ☆☆☆☆☆

*Tarraford Vineyard, 440 Healesville Road, Yarra Glen, Vic 3775, ☎ 0419 678 918, Ⓕ (03) 5962 2194; est 1995; ❖ 2,000 cases; no visitors*

*Métier* is the French word for craft, trade, or profession; the business is that of Martin Williams MW, who operates chiefly as a contract winemaker. Individual vineyard wines under the Metier label have been exceptionally good, with Pinot Noir, Chardonnay, and Viognier leading the way – all fine but complex. Exports to the UK and elsewhere.

**Morgan Vineyards** ☆☆☆☆

*30 Davross Court, Seville, Vic 3139, ☎ (03) 5964 4807; est 1987; ❖ 1,000 cases; ☗; A$; Mon-Fri 11-4, wkds & public hols 11-5; ✗*

Roger and Ally Morgan have adopted a softly, softly approach, slowly increasing the small patch of vines planted in 1971 to the present total of

5.66 hectares. While this was happening, Roger completed the academic requirements of the wine science degree course at Charles Sturt University, and very competently makes Chardonnay, Pinot Noir, Merlot, and Cabernet Sauvignon.

### Mount Mary ☆☆☆☆☆

*Coldstream West Road, Lilydale, Vic 3140, ☎ (03) 9739 1761, Ⓕ (03) 9739 0137; est 1971; ♦ 3,000 cases; no visitors*

The grand old lady of the Yarra Valley, producing superbly refined, elegant, and intense Cabernets, and usually outstanding, long-lived Pinot Noirs that justify its exalted reputation. Owner and founding winemaker Dr John Middleton does not suffer fools (for which read wine writers) gladly. Exports to the UK and elsewhere.

### Naked Range Wines ☆☆☆

*125 Rifle Range Road, Smith's Gully, Vic, 3760, ☎ (03) 9710 1575, Ⓕ (03) 9710 1655; est 1996; ♦ 2,500 cases; ♈; A$; by appt*

Mike Jansz has established seven hectares of vineyard, planted to Sauvignon Blanc, Pinot Noir, Cabernet Sauvignon, Merlot, and Cabernet Franc. The wines are marketed under a striking Naked Range label, calculated to give the United States BATF cardiac arrest if ever the wines were to be exported there.

### Oakridge Estate ☆☆☆☆

*864 Maroondah Highway, Coldstream, Vic 3770, ☎ (03) 9739 1920, Ⓕ (03) 9739 1923; est 1978; ♦ NFP; ♈; A$; 7 days 10-5; ▮◗; ⚹*

Acquired by Evans & Tate in 2001, Oakridge Estate now has the former De Bortoli winemaker David Bicknell in charge, raising both the quality and consistency of the wines. Rumours persist that there may be a sale. Exports to the UK and elsewhere.

### Punt Road ☆☆☆☆

*10 St Huberts Road, Coldstream, Vic 3770, ☎ (03) 9739 0666, Ⓕ (03) 9739 0633; est 2000; ♦ 6,000 cases; ♈; A$; 7 days 10-5; ⚹*

Brings together a syndicate headed by Rob Dolan (as winemaker) and Joe Napoleone and Malcolm Fell (as viticulturists). The venture controls three vineyards totalling 100 hectares. A consistent producer of elegant Chardonnay and Pinot Noir (among other varietals). Exports to the UK and US.

### Ridgeback Wines ☆☆☆☆

*New Chum Gully Estate, Howards Road, Panton Hill, Vic 3759, ☎ (03) 9719 7687, Ⓕ (03) 9719 7667; est 2000; ♦ 1,200 cases; ♈; A$; by appt*

Ron and Lynne Collings have established four hectares of hillside vineyards and Ron has completed the wine degree at Charles Sturt University with honours. The wines are made at contract facilities under Ron's direction, recent vintages being particularly impressive. Exports to the UK.

### Rochford Wines ☆☆☆☆☆

*Corner Maroondah Highway and Hill Road, Coldstream, Vic 3770, ☎ (03) 5962 2119, Ⓕ (03) 5962 5319; est 1993; ♦ 14,000 cases; ♈; A$; 7 days 10-5; ▮◗; ⚹; concerts; art gallery*

The former Eyton-on-Yarra is now owned by the founder owners of Rochford in the Macedon Ranges, who have consolidated the two businesses in the Yarra Valley, but with a diverse range of regional/varietal wines of impressive quality.

**Roundstone Winery & Vineyard** ☆☆☆⬪

*54 Willow Bend Drive, Yarra Glen, Vic 3775, ☎ (03) 9730 1181, Ⓕ (03) 9730 1151;*
*est 1998; ⬪ 2,000 cases; ♟; A$; Thurs-Sun & public hols 10-5, or by appt;*
*🍴; pétanque*

John and Lynne Derwin have established their eight-hectare vineyard, cellar
door, and restaurant in a pretty part of the Yarra Valley, looking out over a large
dam. The wines are good, and so is the food, with Lynne as the inspiration.

**Samson Hill Estate** ☆☆☆⬪

*360 Eltham-Yarra Glen Road, Kangaroo Ground, Vic 3097, ☎ (03) 9712 0715,*
*Ⓕ (03) 9712 0815; est 1997; ⬪ 3,000 cases, ♟; A$; Thurs-Sun 11-8, or by appt;*
*light meals, gifts*

In a region noted for its spectacular scenery, Samson Hill Estate has been
established by Steven and Pago Sampson on one of the most spectacular
sites of all. At the very top of Kangaroo Ground, it looks to the city of
Melbourne, thence to Kinglake, then the Dandenongs, then Mount Macedon.
The cellar door offers casual dining and catering for all functions.

**Seville Estate** ☆☆☆☆☆

*65 Linwood Road, Seville, Vic 3139, ☎ (03) 5964 2622, Ⓕ (03) 5964 2633; est*
*1970; ⬪ 5,000 cases; ♟; A$; by appt; ⚹*

The ownership of Seville Estate has been restructured, now making it a
sister company to Brokenwood, rather than a subsidiary. The quality of the
wines continues at the highest level: Chardonnay and Pinot Noir in the
usual precise Yarra Valley style and spicy, peppery, cherryish Shiraz from
old vines. Exports to the UK and elsewhere.

**Shantell** ☆☆☆☆ **V**

*1974 Melba Highway, Dixon's Creek, Vic 3775, ☎ (03) 5965 2264, Ⓕ (03) 5965*
*2331; est 1980; ⬪ 2,500 cases; ♟; A$; 7 days 10.30-5; 🍴*

Dr Shan Shanmugam and biochemist Turid have slowly but surely developed
Shantell. They still sell some of the grapes from the ten-hectare estate, but
also make some extraordinarily intense and richly tangy Chardonnay, and
pure Cabernet Sauvignon. Exports to the UK and elsewhere.

**Shelmerdine Vineyards** ☆☆☆☆⬪

*PO Box 18152, Collins Street East, Melbourne, Vic 8001 (postal), ☎ (03) 9207 3090,*
*Ⓕ (03) 9207 3061; est 1989; ⬪ NFP; no visitors*

Stephen Shelmerdine has been a major figure in the wine industry for well
over twenty years, like his family before him (who founded Mitchelton
Winery), and has been honoured for his many services to the industry. The
venture has 130 hectares of vines in the Yarra Valley and Heathcote
regions; most of the grapes are sold, a small portion of the usual suspects
contract-made at Punt Road.

**SpringLane** ☆☆☆⬪

*PO Box 390, Yarra Glen, Vic 3775, ☎ (03) 9730 1107, Ⓕ (03) 9739 0135; est 1998;*
*⬪ 1,800 cases; no visitors*

SpringLane is the separately owned wine business of Graeme Rathbone,
brother of Doug Rathbone, who is the (corporate) owner of Yering
Station. The wines are made at Yering Station from grapes grown on the
fourteen-hectare SpringLane Vineyard; Viognier, Rosé, and Merlot are
points of difference.

**St Hubert's** ☆☆☆⬪

*Maroondah Highway, Coldstream, Vic 3770, ☎ (03) 9739 1118, Ⓕ (03) 9739*
*1096; est 1966; ⬪ 15,000 cases; ♟; A$; Mon-Fri 9-5, wkds 10.30-5.30; jazz*

A once famous wine (in the context of the Yarra Valley) which seems to have lost its focus since the merger of Mildara with Blass, and now part of Beringer Blass. However, the wines are reliable, and the cellar door – if somewhat humble – is well situated. Orange blossom Roussanne is a winery specialty.

### Sticks ☆☆☆☆ V

*St Huberts Road, Coldstream, Vic 3770, ☏ (03) 9739 0666, Ⓕ (03) 9739 0633; est 2000; ⚭ 20,000 cases; ⚲; A$; 7 days 10-5*

Rob Dolan, the affable, towering, (former) long-serving winemaker at Yarra Ridge, has long had the nickname "Sticks". Now at Punt Road, he has developed the well-priced Sticks range of Sauvignon Blanc/Semillon, Chardonnay, Pinot Noir, and Cabernet Sauvignon. Exports to the UK and US.

### Strathewen Hills ☆☆☆☆

*1090 Strathewen Road, Strathewen, Vic 3099, ☏ & Ⓕ (03) 9714 8464; est 1991; ⚭ NFP; ⚲; A$ by appt; ⊨*

Former amateur winemaker and Coldstream Hills viticulturist Bill Christophersen now makes small quantities of tightly focused, strongly structured wines led by Tribal Elder Shiraz. Exports to the US.

### Sutherland Estate ☆☆☆☆

*2010 Melba Highway, Dixons Creek, Vic 3775, ☏ 0402 052 287, Ⓕ (03) 9762 1122; est 2000; ⚭ 2,000 cases; ⚲; A$; Thurs-Mon 10-5*

The Phelan family (father Ron, mother Sheila, daughter Catherine, and partner Angus Ridley) acquired an existing two-hectare vineyard and planted an additional three-plus hectares in 2000. Catherine and Angus are nearing the end of the five-year Charles Sturt University viticulture and oenology course, and will take over winemaking when an on-site winery is completed, with Tempranillo down the track.

### Tarrawarra Estate ☆☆☆☆⚘

*Healesville Road, Yarra Glen, Vic 3775, ☏ (03) 5962 3311, Ⓕ (03) 5962 3887; est 1983; ⚭ 25,000 cases; ⚲; A$; 7 days 11-5; art gallery; light meals*

Established by the clothing magnate Marc Besen and family. The winery specialty is a slowly evolving Chardonnay of great structure and complexity; robust, age-worthy Pinot Noir. The second-label wines, the curiously named Tin Cows, are more accessible when young. A multi-million-dollar art gallery opened in 2004. Exports to the UK and elsewhere.

### Tokar Estate ☆☆☆⚘

*6 Maddens Lane, Coldstream, Vic 3770, ☏ (03) 5964 9585, Ⓕ (03) 9706 4033; est 1996; ⚭ 1,500 cases; ⚲; A$; Fri-Sun & long weekends 10-5; ▥*

One of the new arrivals in Maddens Lane, with five hectares of vines including Tempranillo. A cellar door, barrel room, and restaurant opened late 2002. Exports to the UK and elsewhere.

### Toolangi Vineyards ☆☆☆☆⚘

*2 Merriwee Crescent, Toorak, Vic 3142 (postal), ☏ (03) 9822 9488, Ⓕ (03) 9804 3365; est 1995; ⚭ 4,000 cases; no visitors*

Garry and Julie Hounsell have established thirteen hectares of vines at the edge of the Toolangi State Forest, sharing the contract winemaking with a trio of winemakers with impressive credentials, and predictable outcomes for the excellent wines, Chardonnay (made by Rick Kinzbrunner) in the vanguard. Exports to the UK.

### Wantirna Estate NR

*Bushy Park Lane, Wantirna South, Vic 3152, ☏ (03) 9801 2367, Ⓕ (03) 9887 0225; est 1963; ⚭ 800 cases; no visitors*

Solicitor Reg Egan became a pioneer of the area when he purchased Wantirna Estate, part of a nature reserve. Not rated, in deference to Reg Egan's firmly held views, but produces very good wines, particularly Isabella Chardonnay and Lily Pinot Noir.

### Warramate ☆☆☆☆

*27 Maddens Lane, Gruyere, Vic 3770, ☎ (03) 5964 9219, Ⓕ (03) 5964 9219; est 1970; ❧ 900 cases; ♟; A$; 7 days 10-6*

Two generations of the Church family are involved, with son David taking over winemaking responsibilities and doubling the size of the vineyard in 2000–1. For the time being, Shiraz and Riesling are the pick.

### Wedgetail Estate ☆☆☆☆☆

*40 Hildebrand Road, Cottles Bridge, Vic 3099, ☎ (03) 9714 8661, Ⓕ (03) 9714 8676; est 1994; ❧ 1,500 cases; ♟; A$; wkds & public hols 12-5, or by appt, closed 25 Dec-24 Jan*

Canadian-born photographer Guy Lamothe and partner Dena Ashbolt have graduated from home winemaking to producing Pinot Noir of the highest quality, Guy having worked vintages around the world. Highly recommended. Exports to the UK and elsewhere.

### Yarra Burn ☆☆☆☆⚘

*Settlement Road, Yarra Junction, Vic 3797, ☎ (03) 5967 1428, Ⓕ (03) 5967 1146; est 1975; ❧ 15,000 cases; ♟; A$; 7 days 10-5; ⑩*

Acquired by Hardys in 1995 and the lead brand for its substantial Yarra Valley operations. Bastard Hill Chardonnay and Pinot Noir are outstanding Reserve wines, affectionately named by the vineyard workers who have to negotiate twenty-five extremely steep slopes. Exports to the UK and elsewhere.

### Yarra Edge ☆☆☆⚘

*PO Box 390, Yarra Glen, Vic 3775, ☎ (03) 9730 0100, Ⓕ (03) 9739 0135; est 1984; ❧ 2,000 cases; ♟; A$; at Yering Station 7 days 10-5*

Now leased to Yering Station, which makes the wines and continues to use the Yarra Edge brand for grapes from this estate. Tom Carson, Yering Station winemaker, was briefly winemaker/manager at Yarra Edge and knows the property intimately, so the rich style can be expected to continue.

### Yarra Ridge ☆☆☆☆

*Glenview Road, Yarra Glen, Vic 3775, ☎ (03) 9730 1022, Ⓕ (03) 9730 1131; est 1983; ❧ 45,000 cases; ♟; A$; 7 days 10-5*

Has had various changes in winemaking and brand-positioning since being wholly owned by Beringer Blass, some subtle, some not, but now seems to be reverting to its Yarra Valley roots. Pinot Grigio is a point of difference. Exports to the UK and elsewhere.

### Yarra Track Wines ☆☆☆☆

*518 Old Healesville Road, Yarra Glen, Vic 3775, ☎ (03) 9730 1349, Ⓕ (03) 9730 1910; est 1989; ❧ 800 cases; ♟; A$; 7 days 10.30-5.30; gourmet platters*

Jim and Diana Viggers began the establishment of their vineyard back in 1989; it now has 3.1 hectares of Chardonnay and 3.4 hectares of Pinot Noir. Both varieties have produced some excellent wines.

### Yarra Yarra ☆☆☆☆☆

*239 Hunts Lane, Steels Creek, Vic 3775, ☎ (03) 5965 2380, Ⓕ (03) 5965 2086; est 1979; ❧ NFP; ♟; A$; by appt*

Notwithstanding its tiny production, the wines of Yarra Yarra have found their way into Melbourne's best restaurants. Ian Maclean has increased the estate plantings from two hectares to over seven. The Semillon/Sauvignon

Blanc and Cabernets (Bordeaux blend) have exceptional finesse, balance, and longevity. Exports to the UK and elsewhere.

**Yarra Yering** ☆☆☆☆☆

*Briarty Road, Coldstream, Vic 3770, ☎ (03) 5964 9267, Ⓕ (03) 5964 9239; est 1969; ⚬ NA; ⚐; A$; first Sat in May*

Dr Bailey Carrodus makes extremely powerful, occasionally idiosyncratic wines from his twenty-five-year-old, low-yielding, unirrigated vineyards. Both red and white wines have an exceptional depth of flavour and richness; I believe his reds to be greatest. Exports to the UK and elsewhere.

**Yarrabank** ☆☆☆☆☆

*38 Melba Highway, Yarra Glen, Vic 3775, ☎ (03) 9730 0100, Ⓕ (03) 9739 0135; est 1993; ⚬ 5,000 cases; ⚐; A$; at Yering Station 7 days 10-5*

Shares the same spectacular winery facility built in 1997 by joint venture partners Yering Station and Champagne Devaux (the owner). The sparkling wine is one of the finest and best traditional-method fizzes in Australia, made from fruit sourced from the Yarra Valley and elsewhere in southern Victoria.

**Yering Farm** ☆☆☆↑

*St Huberts Road, Yering, Vic 3770, ☎ (03) 9739 0461, Ⓕ (03) 9739 0467; est 1988; ⚬ 7,000 cases; ⚐; A$; 7 days 10-5; pruners' lunch*

Alan and Louise Johns established their twelve-hectare vineyard in 1989 on the site of the original Yeringa winery built by the Deschamps family in the last century. Yarra Ridge buys part of the fruit and makes very competent wines for this label.

**Yering Station** ☆☆☆☆☆

*38 Melba Highway, Yering, Vic 3770, ☎ (03) 9730 0100, Ⓕ (03) 9739 0135; est 1988; ⚬ 50,000 cases; ⚐; A$; 7 days 10-5; ⏹; ⚑*

The historic Yering Station was purchased by the Rathbone family in 1996; a joint venture with Champagne Devaux has resulted in a spectacular winery, handling the Yarrabank sparkling wines, Yering Station, and Yarra Edge wines. A focal point of the Yarra Valley, particularly with the historic Chateau Yering next door, and superb Shiraz/Viognier a point of difference. Exports to the UK and elsewhere.

**Yeringberg** ☆☆☆☆↑

*Maroondah Highway, Coldstream, Vic 3770, ☎ (03) 9739 1453, Ⓕ (03) 9739 0048; est 1863; ⚬ 1,000 cases; ⚐; A$; by appt*

Established by Guill de Pury's great-grandfather, Yeringberg has the only working winery from the nineteenth century (built in the 1880s). Superbly sited hillside vineyards produce a Marsanne/Roussanne blend that harks back to the last century, powerful Pinot Noir, and a Cabernet blend that soars in warmer vintages. Extensive new plantings herald an increased output by 2005. Exports to the UK and elsewhere.

# Mornington Peninsula

Traditionally the major lure for summer visitors, the ocean also plays a very important role in shaping the viticultural climate, as there are places on the Peninsula that are simply too cool for commercially viable grape-growing. Site and varietal selection are matters of financial life or death for would-be vignerons. Of these, there is no shortage: the growth in their numbers has been every bit as great as in the Yarra Valley. Yet in stark contrast to the Yarra, most properties are relatively small, due to a deliberate life-style choice by the doctor/lawyer/banker owner, the lack of and high costs of land, and the shortage of large holdings (over 100 hectares). The largest of the local wineries is Stonier, in which Petaluma has a seventy per cent interest.

Overall, grapes ripen on the Peninsula several weeks after the Yarra. Its most successful varieties are Chardonnay, Pinot Gris, and Pinot Noir, its least successful Cabernet and Merlot. Shiraz is the odd man out; a couple of producers (Merricks, Paringa Estate, and Port Phillip Estate) have made striking wines in good years. There are seventy-five wine producers in the region.

### Barrymore Estate ☆☆☆⯪
*76 Tuerong Road, Tuerong, Vic 3933, ☎ (03) 5974 8999, ⓕ (03) 9789 0821; est 1998; ⚐ 1,500 cases; ⚑; A$; wkds 11-5, or by appt; bush and wetland walks*
The eleven-hectare vineyard is part of a much larger, historic property first settled in the 1840s. Peter Cotter sells most of the grapes, keeping enough to make spicy, savoury Pinot Noir, off-dry Pinot Gris, and Retro Rosé. Exports to the UK and elsewhere.

### Bayview Estate NR
*365 Purves Road, Main Ridge, Vic 3928, ☎ (03) 5989 6130, ⓕ (03) 5989 6373; est 1984; ⚐ 10,000 cases; ⚑; A$; 7 days 11-7; ⦿; tavern; beer garden*
A tourist mecca. It has a hotel with 70 beers from around the world, an 80-seat beer garden; offers fly fishing on the vineyard dam, and rose and lavender gardens. Almost incidental are the ten hectares of Pinot Gris and Pinot Noir, which produce 10,000 cases of wine a year.

### Box Stallion ☆☆☆☆
*64 Turrarubba Road, Merricks North, Vic 3926, ☎ (03) 5989 7444, ⓕ (03) 5989 7688; est 2001; ⚐ 9,000 cases; ⚑; A$; 7 days 11-5; ⦿*
A joint venture between the Wharton, Gillies, and Zerbe families, linking twenty hectares of vines on a former thoroughbred estate property. Veteran Alex White is the contract winemaker; powerful Pinot Noir and spicy Shiraz lead the way.

### Charlotte's Vineyard ☆☆☆☆
*Kentucky Road, Merricks North, Vic 3926, ☎ (03) 5989 7266, ⓕ (03) 5989 7500; est 1987; ⚐ NFP; ⚑; A$; 7 days 11-5; ⦿*
Michael and Susan Wyles have purchased the three-hectare former Hanns Creek Vineyard and renamed it. Their first release of Pinot Noir (2002) is outstanding, the Chardonnay not far behind.

### Crittenden at Dromana ☆☆☆⯪
*25 Harrisons Road, Dromana, Vic 3936, ☎ (03) 5981 8322, ⓕ (03) 5981 8366; est 2003; ⚐ NFP; ⚑; A$; 7 days 11-5; ⦿; wine bar*
Like a phoenix from the ashes, Garry Crittenden has risen again, soon after his formal ties with Dromana Estate Limited were severed. He now has the Schinus range of five mainstream varietals; Sangiovese and Arneis due for release under the Pinocchio label; and super-premium Chardonnay and Pinot Noir under the Crittenden banner. Exports to the UK and Singapore.

### Darling Park ☆☆☆☆
*232 Red Hill Road, Red Hill, Vic 3937, ☎ (03) 5989 2324, ⓕ (03) 5989 2324; est 1986; ⚐ 3,000 cases; ⚑; A$; wkds & public hols 11-5, 7 days in January; ⦿; ⚶*
Josh Liberman (and wife Karen) and David Coe purchased Darling Park prior to the 2002 vintage. The Winenet consultancy group is providing

advice on both the viticultural and winemaking side, and the quirky product range has been revamped, including Merlot from the Adelaide Hills.

## Dromana Estate ☆☆☆◝

*RMB 555 Old Moorooduc Road, Tuerong, Vic 3933, ☎ (03) 5974 4400, Ⓕ (03) 5974 1155; est 1982; ✵ 30,000 cases; ⚱; A$; 7 days 11-4; café; gallery*

In the wake of father Garry's departure, son Rollo Crittenden has taken over winemaking responsibility at Dromana Estate, which is now owned by an investment group. Exports to the UK and elsewhere.

## Eldridge Estate ☆☆☆☆☆

*120 Arthurs Seat Road, Red Hill, Vic 3937, ☎ (03) 5989 2644, Ⓕ (03) 5989 2644; est 1985; ✵ 800 cases; ⚱; A$; wkds & public hols, Jan 1-26 11-5*

David Lloyd had made wine nearly everywhere before he and wife Wendy purchased this 3.5-hectare estate, planted with seven varieties, in 1995. He is producing potent Pinot Noir, delicious Gamay, and grapefruit/melon/cashew Chardonnay of immaculate quality.

## Foxeys Hangout ☆☆☆◝

*795 White Hill Road, Red Hill, Vic 3937, ☎ (03) 0402 117 104, Ⓕ (03) 9809 0495; est 1998; ✵ 3,000 cases; no visitors*

Brothers Michael and Tony Lee, with twenty years in the hospitality industry behind them, have planted five hectares of Pinot Noir, Chardonnay, and Pinot Gris, and made an encouraging start. The name comes from the bygone days of fox hunters hanging their dead prey from the limbs of a large tree.

## Hickinbotham NR

*Nepean Highway (near Wallaces Road), Dromana, Vic 3936, ☎ & Ⓕ (03) 5981 0355; est 1981; ✵ 3,000 cases; ⚱; A$; 7 days 11-5; ⦿*

Grandfather Alan Hickinbotham was a brilliant wine scientist who led world research into the role of pH in winemaking. Father Ian also contributed much, but the spark seems to have gone from this family business, which keeps a far lower profile than in bygone days. Exports to the UK and elsewhere.

## Hurley Vineyard ☆☆☆☆◝

*101 Balnarring Road, Balnarring, Vic 3926, ☎ (03) 5931 3000, Ⓕ (03) 5931 3200; est 1998; ✵ 500 cases; ⚱; A$; first wkd of each month, or by appt*

Kevin Bell is a Melbourne Queen's Counsel, his wife a family law specialist, but they have found time to establish a Pinot-only winery. Kevin has completed the five-year wine science degree at Charles Sturt University, and makes wonderfully spicy, complex, and long Pinot Noir.

## Karina Vineyard ☆☆☆☆ V

*35 Harrisons Road, Dromana, Vic 3936, ☎ (03) 5981 0137, Ⓕ (03) 5981 0137; est 1984; ✵ 2,000 cases; ⚱; A$; wkds 11-5, Jan 7 days*

Just three kilometres from the shores of Port Phillip Bay. Immaculately tended and with picturesque gardens. Fragrant Riesling and cashew-accented Chardonnay are its best wines.

## Kooyong ☆☆☆☆

*PO Box 153, Red Hill South, Vic 3937, ☎ (03) 5989 7355, Ⓕ (03) 5989 7677; est 1996; ✵ 5,000 cases; no visitors*

One of the larger, if not the largest, new entrants on the Peninsula; thirty-four hectares of vines (two-thirds Pinot, one-third Chardonnay) have been planted. The wines are made on-site by oenology graduate Sandro Mosele, and the quality of both is impressive, promising much for the future. Exports to the UK and US.

**Main Ridge Estate** ☆☆☆☆☆

*80 William Road, Red Hill, Vic 3937, ☎ (03) 5989 2686, Ⓕ (03) 5931 0000; est 1975; ☙ 1,000 cases; ☕; A$; Mon-Fri 12-4, wkds 12-5; Sun lunch; gardens*

Nat White pays meticulous attention to every aspect of his viticulture and winemaking, doing annual battle with one of the cooler sites on the Peninsula. The same attention to detail extends to the winery and the winemaking. The Half Acre Pinot Noir is a measure of the size of the business, the Chardonnay is also superb. Exports to the UK and Singapore.

**Mantons Creek Vineyard** ☆☆☆☆

*Tucks Road, Main Ridge, Vic 3928, ☎ (03) 5989 6264, Ⓕ (03) 5989 6348; est 1994; ☙ 4,500 cases; ☕; A$; 7 days 11-5; ⑩; ⊨*

The fourteen-hectare vineyard, planted in 1990, included three hectares of Tempranillo. It has fulfilled owner John Williams' optimism, with spicy, vibrant fruit aromas and a long and piercing palate. The mainstream wines also please.

**Marinda Park Vineyard** ☆☆☆☆

*238 Myers Road, Balnarring, Vic 3926, ☎ & Ⓕ (03) 5989 7613; est 1999; ☙ 2,100 cases; ☕; A$; Thurs-Mon 11-5, Jan 7 days; ⑩*

An Australian-US partnership producing stylish wines from ten hectares of Chardonnay, Sauvignon Blanc, Pinot Noir, and Merlot. Exports to the US and Singapore, coupled with sales through the provincial-style café, quickly run through the stock of the wines.

**Maritime Estate** ☆☆☆☆

*Tucks Road, Red Hill, Vic 3937, ☎ (03) 9848 2926, Ⓕ (03) 9848 2926; est 1988; ☙ 2,000 cases; ☕; A$; wkds & public hols 11-5, Dec 27-Jan 26 7 days*

John and Linda Ruljancich have enjoyed great success since their first vintage in 1994. This is no doubt due in part to skilled contract winemaking, but also to the situation of their vineyard, looking across the hills and valleys of the Red Hill sub-region.

**Massoni Wines** ☆☆☆◌

*PO Box 298, Newport, Vic 3015, ☎ 1300 131 175, Ⓕ 1300 131 185; est 1984; ☙ 10,000 cases; no visitors*

Became part of an ambitious expansion plan with Warrenmang (q.v.) in 2004, but at the time of writing it seemed unlikely the merger would proceed.

**Merricks Estate** ☆☆☆◌

*Thompsons Lane, Merricks, Vic 3916, ☎ (03) 5989 8416, Ⓕ (03) 9613 4242; est 1977; ☙ 2,000 cases; ☕; A$; first wkd each month, every wkd in Jan & public hol wkds 12-5*

Melbourne solicitor George Kefford, with wife Jacquie, runs Merricks Estate as a weekend and holiday enterprise as a relief from professional practice. Produces distinctive, spicy, cool-climate Shiraz and Pinot Noir, also pleasant Chardonnay and Pinot Noir. Exports to the UK and Hong Kong.

**Miceli** ☆☆☆☆

*60 Main Creek Road, Arthurs Seat, Vic 3936, ☎ (03) 5989 2755, Ⓕ (03) 5989 2755; est 1991; ☙ 3,000 cases; ☕; A$; first wkd each month 12-5, also Jan, every wkd, or by appt*

This may be a part-time labour of love for Dr Anthony Miceli, but this hasn't prevented him taking the venture very seriously. While establishing the three-hectare vineyard, he studied wine science at University. Pinot Grigio, Olivia's Chardonnay, and Reserve Pinot Noir are usually excellent.

## Montalto Vineyards ☆☆☆☆☆ V

*33 Shoreham Road, Red Hill South, Vic 3937, ☎ (03) 5989 8412, Ⓕ (03) 5989 8417; est 1998; 3,500 cases; 7 days 12-5; ⦿*

John Mitchell and family have an eleven-hectare estate producing wines under two labels: Montalto and Pennon (the later a second label). This is one of the stars among the new arrivals, offering both quality and value, especially silky Pinot Noir.

## Moorooduc Estate ☆☆☆☆☆

*501 Derril Road, Moorooduc, Vic 3936, ☎ (03) 5971 8506, Ⓕ (03) 5971 8550; est 1983; ❀ 2,500 cases; ⚱; A$; wkds 11-5, Jan 7 days; ⦿; ⇴*

Dr Richard McIntyre regularly produces one of the richest and most complex Chardonnays in the region. Sauvignon Blanc and Pinot Noir are more elegant; McIntyre continues to push the envelope with wild yeast and nil filtration. Exports to the UK and elsewhere.

## Morning Star Estate ☆☆☆☆

*1 Sunnyside Road, Mount Eliza, Vic 3930, ☎ (03) 9787 7760, Ⓕ (03) 9787 7160; est 1992; ❀ 4,000 cases; ⚱; A$; 7 days 10-5; ⦿; ⇴*

A historic property, the house built in 1867, owned by Judy Barrett and family, with ten hectares each of Pinot Gris, Chardonnay, and Pinot Noir now in production. Most of the grapes are sold, a percentage held for the estate label, skilfully contract-made by Sandro Mosele, the Pinot Noir exceptional.

## Mount Eliza Estate ☆☆☆⟆

*Corner Sunnyside Road and Nepean Highway, Mt Eliza, Vic 3930, ☎ (03) 9787 0663, Ⓕ (03) 9708 8355; est 1997; ❀ 8,500 cases; ⚱; A$; 7 days 11-5; ⦿*

The Thurleys have planted fifteen hectares of Chardonnay, Sauvignon Blanc, Shiraz, Pinot Noir, and Cabernet Sauvignon, the wines contract-made in Geelong by Scott Ireland. The cellar door has great views across Port Phillip Bay to the Melbourne city skyline.

## Osborns ☆☆☆☆

*166 Foxeys Road, Merricks North, Vic 3926, ☎ (03) 5989 7417, Ⓕ (03) 5989 7510; est 1988; ❀ 1,500 cases; ⚱; A$; wkds Oct-June, or by appt; antipasti platters*

Frank and Pamela Osborn have taken the slow boat to commercial winemaking. They began planting in 1988 and opened for business in 1997 with six vintages each of complex, nutty Chardonnay and sappy, spicy Pinot Noir, in tiny quantities. Stocks (and vintages) have shrunk since then, the quality not. Exports to the UK and Singapore.

## Paringa Estate ☆☆☆☆☆

*44 Paringa Road, Red Hill South, Vic 3937, ☎ (03) 5989 2669, Ⓕ (03) 5931 0135; est 1985; ❀ 5,000 cases; ⚱; A$; 7 days 11-5; ⦿; ⚵*

Former schoolteacher Lindsay McCall makes wines with an unequalled depth, complexity, and power. The Pinot Noir, in particular, is usually awesome, but then so are the Chardonnay and Shiraz. Only the wet, cold vintages show he is human.

## Port Phillip Estate ☆☆☆☆☆

*261 Red Hill Road, Red Hill, Vic 3937, ☎ (03) 5989 2708, Ⓕ (03) 5989 3017; est 1987; ❀ 4,000 cases; ⚱; A$; wkds & public hols 11-5*

Purchased by the Gjergja family in February 2000, with Lindsay McCall of Paringa Estate continuing as contract winemaker working similar magic here. It is hard to choose between the Reserve Pinot Noir and the Reserve Shiraz; both have extra dimensions of flavour.

**Red Hill Estate** ☆☆☆☆☆
*53 Redhill-Shoreham Road, Red Hill South, Vic 3937, ☎ (03) 5989 2838, Ⓕ (03)*
*5989 2855; est 1989; ⚘ 30,000 cases; ⚲; A$; 7 days 11-5; ⚬; ⚔*
With three vineyard sites totalling thirty-one hectares, Red Hill Estate is a
major player. Michael Kyberd has managed to lift the quality as well as the
quantity of the Chardonnay, Pinot Noir, Shiraz, Pinot Grigio, and sparkling
wines. Exports to the UK and elsewhere.

**Scorpo Wines** ☆☆☆☆☆
*23 Old Bittern-Dromana Road, Merricks North, Vic 3926, ☎ (03) 5989 7697,*
*Ⓕ (03) 9813 3371; est 1997; ⚘ 2,000 cases; ⚲; A$; by appt*
The Scorpo family, with help from contract winemaker Sandro Mosele, has
burst onto the scene with dense, powerful Pinot Noir, rich and complex
Chardonnay, and beguiling lychee and musk Pinot Gris.

**Stonier Wines** ☆☆☆☆⚘ V
*362 Frankston-Flinders Road, Merricks, Vic 3916, ☎ (03) 5989 8300, Ⓕ (03) 5989*
*8709; est 1978; ⚘ 25,000 cases; ⚲; A$; 7 days 11-5; cheese platters*
One of the most senior wineries on the Mornington Peninsula, now part of
the Petaluma group, which is in turn owned by Lion Nathan of New Zealand.
Wine quality is assured, as is the elegant, restrained style of the majority of
the wines. Exports to the UK and elsewhere.

**Stumpy Gully** ☆☆☆⚘
*1247 Stumpy Gully Road, Moorooduc, Vic 3933, ☎ (03) 5978 8429, Ⓕ (03) 5978*
*8419; est 1988; ⚘ 4,000 cases; ⚲; A$; wkds 11-5*
Two generations of the Zantvoort family are now involved, producing
everything from Marsanne and Riesling to Cabernet Sauvignon and
fortified Sauvignon Blanc. Exports to the UK and Netherlands.

**T'Gallant** ☆☆☆☆
*1385 Mornington-Flinders Road, Main Ridge, Vic 3928, ☎ (03) 5989 6565, Ⓕ (03)*
*5989 6577; est 1990; ⚘ 30,000 cases; ⚲; A$; 7 days 10-5; ⚬; ⚔*
Acquired (quixotically, in the view of some) by Beringer Blass in April 2003.
Founders Kathleen Quealy and Kevin McCarthy continue to be involved,
and the focus on Pinot Gris remains. Exports to the UK and US.

**Tuck's Ridge** ☆☆☆☆
*37 Shoreham Road, Red Hill South, Vic 3937, ☎ (03) 5989 8660, Ⓕ (03) 5989*
*8579; est 1993; ⚘ 14,000 cases; ⚲; A$; 7 days 12-5; cheese platters*
After an initial burst of frenetic activity following its launch in July 1993,
Tuck's Ridge has slowed down a little. But plantings have increased to
over twenty-five hectares, making it one of the largest vineyards in this
region. Fragrant Riesling is good value, Pinot Noir fragrant and silky.
Exports to the UK and elsewhere.

**Turramurra Estate** ☆☆☆⚘
*RMB 4327 Wallaces Road, Dromana, Vic 3926, ☎ (03) 5987 1146, Ⓕ (03) 5987*
*1286; est 1989; ⚘ 6,000 cases; ⚲; A$; Wed-Sun 12-5, or by appt; cooking school*
Dr David Leslie gave up his job as a medical practitioner to concentrate on
developing the family's ten-hectare estate at Dromana. Wife Paula is the
viticulturist, tending Sauvignon Blanc, Chardonnay, Pinot Noir, Shiraz, and
Cabernet Sauvignon. Exports to the UK and elsewhere.

**Vale Vineyard** ☆☆☆☆⚘
*2914 Frankston-Flinders Road, Balnarring, Vic 3926, ☎ (03) 5983 1521, Ⓕ (03)*
*5983 1942; est 1991; ⚘ 1,000 cases; no visitors*
After a lifetime in the retail liquor industry, John and Susan Vale took a

busman's retirement by purchasing a grazing property at Balnarring in 1991. John added what he says was "formal winemaking training" before building a twenty-tonne on-site winery. Quite lovely Chardonnay, Riesling, and Tempranillo, with Verduzzo and Arneis in the pipeline.

**Willow Creek** ☆☆☆☆✓

*166 Balnarring Road, Merricks North, Vic 3926, ☎ (03) 5989 7448, ℉ (03) 5989 7584; est 1989; ♦ 10,000 cases; ☨; A$; 7 days 10-5; ¶*

Immaculately crafted Chardonnay and fine Pinot Noir lead the way. Exports to the UK and elsewhere. The restaurant is open for lunch seven days and Friday and Saturday nights for dinner.

# Geelong

Geelong sits to the southwest of Melbourne. Like the Yarra Valley, the initial impetus for viticulture in Geelong was created by Swiss settlers, and until 1874 it seemed the two regions would vie with each other for supremacy. Then their paths diverged dramatically: phylloxera was discovered in Geelong, and the Victorian parliament swiftly passed controversial legislation requiring the uprooting of all the vineyards. Compensation was inadequate. Viticulture did not return to Geelong until 1966 and the arrival of the Seftons at Idyll Vineyard. They planted Gewurztraminer, Shiraz, and Cabernet Sauvignon. Chardonnay and Pinot Noir followed in due course, but not to the exclusion of later-ripening varieties such as Riesling, Shiraz, and Cabernet Sauvignon.

Geelong is a windswept place, yet vineyards established in hollows or on river banks sheltered from the wind have found frost the greater of the two evils. The soils and climate are very different to those of the Yarra Valley; Chardonnay and Pinot Noir are more robust here. Then there is Shiraz. A fascinating contemporary battle is being waged over a variety that may be statistically unimportant, but is capable of great things. There are thirty wine producers in the region.

**Austin's Barrabool** ☆☆☆☆ V

*870 Steiglitz Road, Sutherlands Creek, Vic 3331, ☎ (03) 5281 1799, ℉ (03) 5281 1673; est 1982; ♦ 8,000 cases; ☨; A$; by appt*

After a slow start, Austin's has laid the foundation for major growth. Richard and Pamela Austin have four different properties in the Geelong region, totalling more than 580 hectares with sixty-four hectares of vines, led by Pinot Noir and Shiraz. A large on-site winery has been built and production is set to increase rapidly in the years ahead.

**Bannockburn Vineyards** ☆☆☆☆☆

*Midland Highway, Bannockburn, Vic 3331, ☎ (03) 5281 1363, ℉ (03) 5281 1349; est 1974; ♦ 10,000 cases; no visitors*

One of Australia's foremost producers of Pinot Noir and Chardonnay (and excellent Shiraz), the driving force has been low-yielding estate vineyards and the French-influenced winemaking of Gary Farr. Exports to the UK and elsewhere.

**Bellarine Estate** ☆☆☆☆

*2270 Port Arlington Road, Bellarine, Vic 3222, ☎ (03) 5259 3310, ℉ (03) 5259 3393; est 1995; ♦ 7,000 cases; ☨; A$; 7 days 10-4; ¶; ⊨; ✗*

A substantial enterprise, with thirteen hectares of Chardonnay, Pinot Noir,

Shiraz, Merlot, Pinot Gris, and Viognier. The wines are made by Robin Brokett at Scotchmans Hill (*q.v.*). James Paddock Chardonnay (complex and intense) and Phil's Fetish Pinot Noir (concentrated, ultra-ripe plum, spice and prune) stand out.

**By Farr** ☆☆☆☆☆

*PO Box 72, Bannockburn, Vic 3331, ☎ (03) 5281 1979, Ⓕ (03) 5281 1979; est 1999; ♦ 2,000 cases; no visitors*

In 1994 Gary Farr and family planted just under five hectares of clonally selected Viognier, Chardonnay, Pinot Noir, and Shiraz on a north-facing hill directly opposite the Bannockburn winery. The quality of the wines is exemplary, their character subtly different to those of Bannockburn, due, in Farr's view, to the interaction of the terroir and the clonal selection. Exports to the UK and elsewhere.

**Clyde Park** ☆☆☆☆☆

*2490 Midland Highway, Bannockburn, Vic 3331, ☎ & Ⓕ (03) 5281 7274; est 1979; ♦ 2,800 cases, ♚; A$; wkds & public hols 11-4*

Terry Jongebloed and Sue Jongebloed-Dixon acquired this ten-hectare vineyard from Gary Farr; after a period of obscurity, superb Shiraz, Chardonnay, and Pinot Noir have appeared, displaying strong terroir characteristics.

**Curlewis Winery** ☆☆☆☆☆

*55 Navarre Road, Curlewis, Vic 3222, ☎ (03) 5250 4567, Ⓕ (03) 5250 4567; est 1998; ♦ 1,000 cases; ♚; A$; by appt*

Self-confessed "Pinotphiles" Rainer Breit and partner Wendy Oliver have achieved a great deal in a short period of time. In 1996 they purchased their property at Curlewis with 1.6 hectares of what were then eleven-year-old Pinot Noir vines; until 1998 the grapes were sold. They then set to and established an on-site winery and have succeeded in making highly complex Pinot Noir and Chardonnay.

**del Rios** ☆☆☆☆☆

*2320 Ballan Road, Anakie, Vic 3221, ☎ (03) 5284 1221, Ⓕ (03) 9497 4644; est 1996; ♦ 5,000 cases; ♚; A$; wkds 10-4, bus tours by appt*

German del Rio was born in northern Spain in 1920; after three generations in Australia, his family has established fifteen hectares of vines on the slopes of Mount Anakie, winemaking moving on-site in 2004. Outstanding Pinot Noir.

**Farr Rising** ☆☆☆☆☆

*27 Maddens Road, Bannockburn, Vic 3331, ☎ & Ⓕ (03) 5281 1979; est 2001; ♦ 1,500 cases; no visitors*

Nicholas Farr, son of Gary Farr, has selectively sourced Mornington Pinot Noir and Geelong Chardonnay, Merlot and (again) Pinot Noir to produce a series of outstanding wines.

**Innisfail Vineyards** ☆☆☆☆

*Cross Street, Batesford, Vic 3221, ☎ (03) 5276 1258, Ⓕ (03) 5276 1258; est 1980; ♦ 2,000 cases; ♚; A$; by appt*

This six-hectare vineyard released its first wines in 1988, made in a small on-site modern winery. Chewy, complex Chardonnay, potent Pinot Noir, and Cabernet Sauvignon/Merlot are contract-made by Nicholas Farr.

**Jindalee Wines** ☆☆☆☆ V

*265 Ballan Road, Moorabool, North Geelong, Vic 3221, ☎ (03) 5276 1280, Ⓕ (03) 5276 1537; est 1997; ♦ 500,000 cases; ♚; A$; 7 days 10-5*

Jindalee is part of the Littore group, and has absorbed the former Idyll Estate as its head office and flagship vineyard producing the Fettlers Rest range. The real business is based on 500 hectares of vines in the Riverland which provide the Jindalee label; the Chardonnay is a super bargain. Exports to the UK and elsewhere.

### Lethbridge Wines ☆☆☆☆

*74 Burrows Road, Lethbridge, Vic 3222, ☎ (03) 5281 7221, Ⓕ (03) 5281 7221; est 1996; ♦ 1,500 cases; ⚑; A$; Fri-Sun & public hols 10.30-5, or by appt; Ⲕ*

Established by three scientists, including Ray Nadeson, who says, "Our belief is that the best wines express the unique character of special places. With this in mind our philosophy is to practise organic principles in the vineyard complemented by traditional winemaking techniques to allow the unique character of the site to be expressed in our fruit and captured in our wine." The Pinot Noir is especially good.

### Leura Park Estate ☆☆☆☆⁄

*1400 Portarlington Road, Curlewis, Vic 3222, ☎ (03) 5253 3180, Ⓕ (03) 5251 1262; est 1995; ♦ 600 cases; ⚑; A$; wkds 11-5; coffee & snacks*

Famed restaurateurs Stephen and Lisa Cross have established twenty hectares of vines, selling most of the grapes to De Bortoli but having tiny quantities of Chardonnay, Sauvignon Blanc, Pinot Gris, and Pinot Noir – all with elegance, line, and length – contract-made by De Bortoli.

### Pettavel ☆☆☆☆

*65 Pettavel Road, Waurn Ponds, Vic 3216, ☎ (03) 5266 1120, Ⓕ (03) 5266 1140; est 2000; ♦ 20,000 cases; ⚑; A$; 7 days 10-5.30*

A major new landmark in the Geelong region, with a striking and substantial winery built for the 2002 vintage, plus a large tasting area and restaurant capable of seating 180 people. The excellent wines are full of interest, none more so than the Platina Merlot/Petit Verdot. Exports to the UK and elsewhere.

### Prince Albert ☆☆☆☆

*100 Lemins Road, Waurn Ponds, Vic 3216, ☎ & Ⓕ (03) 5241 8091; est 1975; ♦ 100 cases; ⚑; A$; by appt*

Bruce Hyett re-established Prince Albert on the north-facing slope of a nineteenth-century vineyard, which then, as today, produced only Pinot Noir. The wine always has pure varietal character, and is on the lighter side. Exports to the UK.

### Provenance Wines ☆☆☆☆☆

*870 Steiglitz Road, Sutherlands Creek, Vic 3331, ☎ (03) 5272 2362, Ⓕ (03) 5272 1551; est 1995; ♦ 2,000 cases; ⚑; A$; by appt*

Owner-winemaker Scott Ireland now makes the Provenance wines (and the Austin's Barrabool wines) at the new winery owned by the Austins at Sutherlands Creek. His Geelong Shiraz is in full-blown Côte-Rôtie style. Pinot Noir, Pinot Gris, and Chardonnay are all excellent.

### Scotchmans Hill ☆☆☆☆⁄

*190 Scotchmans Road, Drysdale, Vic 3222, ☎ (03) 5251 3176, Ⓕ (03) 5253 1743; est 1982; ♦ 50,000 cases; ⚑; A$; 7 days 10.30-5.30, ⧉; Ⲕ*

The Browne family owns and runs two adjacent vineyards, and specializes in aromatic, fresh Chardonnay and Pinot Noir. Scotchmans has more weight than second label Swan Bay, but both are relatively understated and certainly not over-oaked. Spicy, liquorice-accented Shiraz is a notable addition to the range. Exports to the UK and elsewhere.

**Shadowfax Vineyard and Winery** ☆☆☆☆☆
*K Road, Werribee, Vic 3030, ☎ (03) 9731 4420, Ⓕ (02) 9731 4421; est 2000;*
*♦ 15,000 cases; ♥; A$; 7 days 11-5; ⦿; 🚗; ⚹*

Shadowfax is part of an awesome development at Werribee Park, situated twenty minutes from Melbourne towards Geelong. The truly striking winery was erected in time for the 2000 vintage. The Mansion Hotel and restaurant (circa 1880), with ninety-two rooms and suites, emphasizes conference bookings during the week, and tourism on the weekend. Winemaker Matt Harrop is producing quite wonderful Shiraz, Chardonnay, Pinot Noir, and Viognier from diverse cool-climate sources. Exports to the UK and elsewhere.

# Macedon Ranges

The hills of the Macedon Ranges, though not the vineyards, ascend to over 700 metres above sea level. Site selection, aspect, slope, and varietal selection are therefore all-important in this decidedly mountainous area, for many parts of this region tremble on the brink of commercial viability. Wind (often biting and bleak, even in summer) and frost are obvious dangers, but in the cooler, wetter vintages there may simply be insufficient sunshine hours and warmth to properly ripen the grapes.

All that said, there are some excellent producers of sparkling wines (Cope-Williams and Hanging Rock) and a growing band of Chardonnay and Pinot Noir producers, of which Bindi is the brightest and most recent star. Then there are the long-established Virgin Hills and Granite Hills, both of whom bypassed Pinot Noir and Chardonnay in favour of Riesling (Granite Hills), Cabernet Sauvignon, and Shiraz (both). There are thirty-eight wine producers in the region.

**Big Shed Wines** ☆☆☆☆
*1289 Malmsbury Road, Glenlyon, Vic 3461, ☎ & Ⓕ (03) 5348 7825; est 1999;*
*♦ 1,200 cases; ♥; A$; 7 days, winter 10-6, summer 10-7*

Founder and winemaker Ken Jones is a former geneticist and molecular biologist (at Edinburgh University), which made the chemistry of winemaking easy. Black cherry, plum, spice, and liquorice Reserve Shiraz, complex, spicy Pinot Noir, and smooth Chardonnay are all very good.

**Bindi Wine Growers** ☆☆☆☆☆
*343 Melton Road, Gisborne, Vic 3437, ☎ (03) 5428 2564, Ⓕ (03) 5428 2564;*
*est 1988; ♦ 1,200 cases; no visitors*

This house has gone from strength to strength. The Chardonnay is top-shelf, the ultra-concentrated Pinot Noir as remarkable (in its own idiom) as Bass Phillip, Giaconda, or any of the other tiny-production icon wines. Exports (in tiny quantities) to the UK and elsewhere.

**Candlebark Hill** ☆☆☆☆
*Fordes Lane, Kyneton, Vic 3444, ☎ (03) 9836 2712, Ⓕ (03) 9836 2712; est 1987;*
*♦ 600 cases; ♥; A$; by appt*

David Forster has established a marvellously scenic 3.5-hectare vineyard, planted predominantly with Pinot Noir but also with Chardonnay, the three Bordeaux varieties, Shiraz, and Malbec. Pinot Noir is by far the best, the Reserve version outstanding.

**Cobaw Ridge** ☆☆☆☆⚘

*31 Perc Boyer's Lane, East Pastoria via Kyneton, Vic 3444, ☎ (03) 5423 5227,*
*Ⓕ (03) 5423 5227; est 1985; ⚘ 1,200 cases; ⚑; A$; 7 days 10-5*

Nelly and Alan Cooper have established a six-hectare vineyard at an altitude of 610 metres above Kyneton, complete with pole-framed mud-brick house and winery. Chardonnay and Shiraz/Viognier do very well in warm vintages, and have been joined by the rare northern Italian grape, Lagrein. Exports to the UK and US.

**Cope-Williams** ☆☆☆☆

*Glenfern Road, Romsey, Vic 3434, ☎ (03) 5429 5428, Ⓕ (03) 5429 5655;*
*est 1977; ⚘ 7,000 cases; ⚑; A$; 7 days 11-5; ⑩; cricket, royal tennis*

Anyone with a penchant for cricket must visit this gloriously situated property (it has its own village-green cricket ground for hire). Architect Gordon Cope-Williams and wife Judy are the driving forces of the tourism aspect, but there are also excellent sparkling wines, plus a diverse range of table wines using fruit drawn from elsewhere.

**Curly Flat** ☆☆☆☆☆

*Collivers Road, Lancefield, Vic 3435, ☎ (03) 5429 1956, Ⓕ (03) 5429 2256;*
*est 1991; ⚘ 2,500 cases; ⚑; A$; first Sun of month, or by appt*

Banker Phillip and wife Jeni Moraghan have painstakingly established fourteen hectares of Pinot Noir (chiefly), Chardonnay, and Pinot Gris. They have adopted a sophisticated marketing model, with the moderately high prices reflecting both the capital investment and attention to detail.The complex and textured Pinot Noir and Chardonnay are both outstanding. Exports to the UK and US.

**Epis/Epis & Williams** ☆☆☆☆

*Lot 16, Calder Highway, Woodend, Vic 3442, ☎ (03) 5427 1204, Ⓕ (03) 5427*
*1204; est 1990; ⚘ 850 cases; by appt*

Three legends are involved in the Epis and Epis & Williams wines, two of them in their own lifetime. They are long-term Essendon guru and former player Alec Epis, who owns the two quite separate vineyards and brands; Stuart Anderson, who makes the wines, with Alec Epis doing all the hard work; and the late Laurie Williams, the father of viticulture in the Macedon region.

**Granite Hills** ☆☆☆☆☆ **V**

*1481 Burke and Wills Track, Baynton, Kyneton, Vic 3444, ☎ (03) 5423 7264,*
*Ⓕ (03) 5423 7288; est 1970; ⚘ 7,000 cases, ⚑; A$; Mon-Sat 10-6, Sun 12-6*

This was Macedon's pace-setter for cool-climate, spicy Shiraz and intense, long-lived, limey, citrus Riesling. A consistently top-flight performer in wine shows. Exports to the UK and elsewhere.

**Hanging Rock Winery** ☆☆☆☆⚘

*88 Jim Road, Newham, Vic 3442, ☎ (03) 5427 0542, Ⓕ (03) 5427 0310; est*
*1982; ⚘ 40,000 cases; ⚑; A$; 7 days 10-5; ✉*

Takes its name from a celebrated rock formation which can be seen from the vineyard. John Ellis, veteran winemaker of twenty-five years' standing, makes Australia's most complex sparkling wine, Macedon Cuvée, in the style of Bollinger. Local zesty Jim Jim Sauvignon Blanc and opulent Heathcote Shiraz are quality leaders. Exports to the UK and elsewhere.

**Kyneton Ridge Estate** ☆☆☆☆⚘

*90 Blackhill School Road, Kyneton, Vic 3444, ☎ (03) 5422 7377, Ⓕ (03) 5422*
*3747; est 1997; ⚘ 300 cases, ⚑; A$; by appt; ✉*

John and Ann Boucher have winemaking roots going back four generations, and, with Pauline Russell, have found an ideal site for Pinot Noir near Kyneton. The wine has extraordinary colour, concentration, and richness.

**Mount Gisborne Wines** ☆☆☆⵿

*83 Waterson Road, Gisborne, Vic 3437, ☎ (03) 5428 2834, Ⓕ (03) 5428 2834; est 1986; ✸ 1,500 cases; ☗; A$; wkds 10-5*

This is a weekend and holiday occupation for proprietor David Ell. He makes the Chardonnay and Pinot Noir from his six-hectare vineyard under the watchful and skilled eye of industry veteran Stuart Anderson (the Balgownie founder), who now lives in semi-retirement high in the Macedon Hills.

**Mount William Winery** ☆☆☆⵿

*Mount William Road, Tantaraboo, Vic 3764, ☎ (03) 5429 1595, Ⓕ (03) 5429 1998; est 1987; ✸ 1,500 cases; ☗; A$; by appt*

Adrienne and Murray Cousins established seven hectares of vineyards between 1987 and 1999, planted with Pinot Noir, Cabernet Franc, Semillon, and Chardonnay. They also buy Riesling. The wines are contract-made (Hanging Rock) and sold through a stone-built tasting and cellar-door facility.

**O'Shea & Murphy Rosebery Hill Vineyard** ☆☆☆⵿

*Rosebery Hill, Pastoria Road, Pipers Creek, Vic 3444, ☎ (03) 5423 5253, Ⓕ (03) 5424 5253; est 1984; ✸ 1,500 cases; ☗; A$; by appt*

Planting of the eight-hectare vineyard began in 1984 on a north-facing slope of red basalt soil, without the aid of irrigation or sprays. Part of the production is made for the Rosebery Hill label, and part sold to others, all of whom attest to the quality of the fruit.

**Patrick's Vineyard** ☆☆☆☆☆

*Croziers Road, Cobaw via Mount Macedon, Vic 3441, ☎ 0419 598 401, Ⓕ (03) 9521 6266; est 1996; ✸ 350 cases; no visitors*

A Pinot Noir specialist, with two hectares planted over the 1996 and 1997 seasons high on the southern slopes of the Cobaw Range. In warmer vintages an intense, stylish Pinot Noir is the result.

**Portree** ☆☆☆☆

*72 Powells Track via Mount William Road, Lancefield, Vic 3455, ☎ (03) 5429 1422, Ⓕ (03) 5429 2205; est 1983; ✸ 1,000 cases; ☗; A$; wkds & public hols 11-5*

All the wines show distinct cool-climate characteristics, the Quarry Red having similarities to the wines of Chinon in the Loire Valley. But it is with its principal wine, the multi-layered and multi-faceted Chardonnay, that Portree has done best, the Pinot in close company.

**Straws Lane** ☆☆☆☆

*1282 Mount Macedon Road, Hesket, Vic 3442, ☎ (03) 9654 9380, Ⓕ (03) 9663 6300; est 1987; ✸ 1,800 cases; wkds & public hols 10-4, or by appt*

Stuart Anderson guides the making of the Pinot Noir, Hanging Rock Winery handles the Gewurztraminer and the sparkling-wine base, and Cope-Williams looks after the second fermentation and maturation of the sparkling wine. It's good to have cooperative neighbours.

**Virgin Hills** ☆☆☆☆☆

*Salisbury Road, Lauriston West via Kyneton, Vic 3444, ☎ (03) 5422 7444, Ⓕ (03) 5422 7400; est 1968; ✸ 2,500 cases; ☗; A$; by appt*

Virgin Hills has passed through several ownership changes in a short period of time, now resting with Michael Hope of the Hunter Valley's Hope Estate. No longer made without the use of $SO_2$, and queries about direction have subsided. Exports to the UK and US.

# Sunbury

Sunbury has gentle hills that rise from dead flat country to the south and west. The nearest region to Melbourne, it has a great history, much of it miraculously preserved. In 1858, one-time Victorian premier James Francis Goodall planted the first vines at Goona Warra. James S Johnstone followed on quickly, establishing Craiglee in 1864. In 1872, he made a Shiraz that I have been lucky enough to taste (found in the 1950s) – a powerful testament to the suitability of Sunbury for the production of long-lived Shiraz. However, Shiraz by no means dominates the plantings in this unambiguously cool region; Chardonnay, Semillon, Pinot Noir, and the Bordeaux varieties are all grown here. There are thirteen wine producers in the region.

**Andraos Bros** ☆☆☆☆
*Winilba Vineyard, 150 Vineyard Road, Sunbury, Vic 3429, ☎ (03) 9740 9703, Ⓕ (03) 9740 9795; est 1989; ⚭ 2,500 cases; ⚲; A$; Fri-Sun & public hols 11-5, or by appt; ⦿*
The Winilba Vineyard was first planted in 1863, and remained in production until 1889. Exactly one hundred years later, the Andraos brothers commenced replanting; over the following years they built a winery from the ruins of the original bluestone cellar, producing excellent Chardonnay, Shiraz, and Cabernet Sauvignon.

**Arundel** ☆☆☆☆☆
*Arundel Farm Estate, PO Box 136, Keilor, Vic 3036, ☎ (03) 9335 3422, Ⓕ (03) 9335 4912; est 1995; ⚭ 200 cases; no visitors*
While production of the rich, layered, and powerful Shiraz is as yet in tiny quantities, the vineyard has been increased from 1.6 to 8.8 hectares, and production will then rise significantly.

**Craiglee** ☆☆☆☆☆ V
*Sunbury Road, Sunbury, Vic 3429, ☎ (03) 9744 4489, Ⓕ (03) 9744 4489; est 1976; ⚭ 3,000 cases; ⚲; A$; Sun & public hols 10-5, or by appt*
A historic winery with a proud nineteenth-century record, which re-opened for winemaking in 1976 after a prolonged hiatus. Pat Carmody produces one of the finest cool-climate Shirazes in Australia, redolent of cherry, liquorice, and spice in the better (*i.e.* warmer) vintages, lighter-bodied in the cooler ones. Maturing vines and improved viticulture have yielded more consistent (and even better) wines over the past ten years or so. Exports to the UK and elsewhere.

**Fenton Views Winery** ☆☆☆✦
*182 Fenton Hill Road, Clarkefield, Vic 3430, ☎ (03) 5428 5429, Ⓕ (03) 5428 5304; est 1994; ⚭ 800 cases; ⚲; A$; wkds 11-5, or by appt*
Situated on the north-facing slopes of Fenton Hill, overlooking the Hume and Macedon Ranges, providing a spectacular and tranquil setting, with plantings of Shiraz, Chardonnay, Pinot Noir, and Cabernet Sauvignon. Co-owner David Spiteri studied winemaking at Charles Sturt University, with vintage experience in both Australia and California.

**Galli Estate** ☆☆☆☆✦
*1507 Melton Highway, Rockbank, Vic 3335, ☎ (03) 9747 1444, Ⓕ (03) 9747 1481; est 1997; ⚭ 12,000 cases; ⚲; A$; 7 days 11-5; ⦿*
The Galli family has moved quickly, with thirty-two hectares of vineyard and a large underground cellar and winery. Succulent Shiraz, Chardonnay, and

Pinot Noir are the best of a large portfolio under the direction of winemaker Stephen Phillips (ex-Coldstream Hills).

**Goona Warra Vineyard** ☆☆☆☆⊰

*Sunbury Road, Sunbury, Vic 3429, ☎ (03) 9740 7766, Ⓕ (03) 9744 7648; est 1863; ⬩ 3,000 cases; ⚱; A$; 7 days 10-5; Sun lunch only*

Historic stone winery, with excellent tasting facilities. Outstanding venue for celebrations. Chardonnay, Pinot Noir, and Cabernet Franc can excel. Exports to the UK and Hong Kong.

**Wildwood Vineyards** ☆☆☆☆

*St John's Lane, Wildwood, Bulla, Vic 3428, ☎ (03) 9307 1118, Ⓕ (03) 9331 1590; est 1983; ⬩ 2,000 cases; ⚱; A$; 7 days 10-6; ⑩*

Situated four kilometres past Melbourne Airport in the Oaklands Valley. Plastic surgeon Wayne Stott has taken what is very much a part-time activity rather more seriously than most by completing the wine-science degree at Charles Sturt University. Pinot Noir, Shiraz, and Cabernets are the pick.

**Witchmount Estate** ☆☆☆☆

*557 Leakes Road, Rockbank, Vic 3335, ☎ (03) 9747 1088, Ⓕ (03) 9747 1066; est 1991; ⬩ 8,000 cases; ⚱; A$; Wed-Sun 10-5; ⑩*

An Italo-Australian flavour, with an on-site Italian restaurant and function rooms; the twenty-one hectares of vineyards include Nebbiolo, Picolit (both Italian), and Tempranillo. The arrival of former Seppelt senior winemaker Steve Goodwin bodes well.

# Grampians

For old-timers, this region remains known as Great Western. The reasons for the change need not detain us, but some are due to the imperatives of the GI legislation. The history of the Grampians is inextricably woven with the discovery of gold in 1851. When the gold started to run out, Joseph Best employed the out-of-work miners to dig underground tunnels for his winery. His brother Henry also established a vineyard near Concongella Creek in 1866; it is now the jewel in the crown of Best's Wines. There has never been any doubt that the region is ideally suited to Shiraz. The three leading exponents are Seppelt, Best's, and Mount Langi Ghiran. While Shiraz is the outstanding variety, Riesling, too, does particularly well, while Chardonnay and Cabernet Sauvignon are good. There are fifteen wine producers in the region.

**Armstrong Vineyards** ☆☆☆☆⊰

*Lot 1, Military Road, Armstrong, Vic 3381, ☎ (08) 8277 6073, Ⓕ (08) 8277 6035; est 1989; ⬩ 800 cases; no visitors*

The brainchild of Tony Royal, former Seppelt Great Western winemaker who now runs the Australian arm of Seguin Moreau (French coopers). His five hectares of Shiraz make lush wine of consistently high quality.

**Best's Wines** ☆☆☆☆☆

*111 Best's Road, Great Western, Vic 3377, ☎ (03) 5356 2250, Ⓕ (03) 5356 2430; est 1866; ⬩ 30,000 cases; ⚱; A$; Mon-Sat 10-5, Sun 11-4; �*

Historic winery, owning some priceless vineyards planted as long ago as 1867. Consistently produces elegant, supple wines that deserve far greater recognition than they receive. The Shiraz is a classic; the deluxe Thomson Family Shiraz is magnificent. Exports to the UK and elsewhere.

### The Gap Vineyard ☆☆☆☆

*Pomonal Road, Halls Gap, Vic 3381, ☎ (03) 5356 4252, Ⓕ (03) 5356 4645; est 1969; ⬥ 1,500 cases; ♟; A$; Wed-Sun 10-5, 7 days during school & public hols*

The former Boroka winery purchased by Mount Langi Ghiran in 1998 boasts a spectacular vineyard site near the famous Halls Gap. Former indifferent wine quality is improving exponentially, led by Riesling, Cabernet Sauvignon, and Shiraz.

### Garden Gully Vineyards ☆☆☆☆ V

*Western Highway, Great Western, Vic 3377, ☎ (03) 5356 2400, Ⓕ (03) 5356 2400; est 1987; ⬥ 2,000 cases; ♟; A$; by appt*

Brian Fletcher and Warren Randall, former Seppelt winemakers, use their intimate knowledge of the Grampians to guide the fortunes of Garden Gully from afar. Both limey Riesling and dark, cherry/plum Shiraz are excellent, as is sparkling Shiraz.

### Kimbarra Wines ☆☆☆☆

*422 Barkly Street, Ararat, Vic 3377, ☎ (03) 5352 2238, Ⓕ (03) 5342 1950; est 1990; ⬥ 1,000 cases; ♟; A$; Mon-Fri 9-5*

Peter and David Leeke have established twelve hectares of Riesling, Shiraz, and Cabernet Sauvignon, the three varieties best suited to the Grampians.

### Michael Unwin Wines ☆☆☆☆✓

*2 Racecourse Road, Beaufort, Vic 3373, ☎ (03) 5349 2021, Ⓕ (03) 5349 2032; est 2000; ⬥ 1,000 cases; ♟; A$; 7 days 10-6*

Michael Unwin was a long-term flying winemaker, and has still been hopping around central Victoria deciding where to make his impressive wines. The Acrobat range tops the tree.

### Montara ☆☆☆✓ V

*Chalambar Road, Ararat, Vic 3377, ☎ (03) 5352 3868, Ⓕ (03) 5352 4968; est 1970; ⬥ NFP; ♟; A$; Mon-Sat 10-5, Sun 12-4*

Achieved considerable attention for its Pinot Noirs during the 1980s. Nowadays the wines have a fragrance and elegance, yet sometimes lack richness and concentration. Prices and labels are attractive. Exports to the UK and elsewhere.

### Mount Langi Ghiran Vineyards ☆☆☆☆✓

*Warrak Road, Buangor, Vic 3375, ☎ (03) 5354 3207, Ⓕ (03) 5354 3277; est 1969; ⬥ 45,000 cases; ♟; A$; Mon-Fri 9-5, wkds 12-5*

The Shiraz leads the way for cool-climate examples of this variety: weight, texture, and spicy, fruity richness. The business was acquired by Yering Station in 2003, which should lead to greater focus and restore the wines to a five-star rating. Exports to the UK and elsewhere.

### Seppelt Great Western ☆☆☆☆☆ V

*Moyston Road, Great Western via Ararat, Vic 3377, ☎ (03) 5361 2222, Ⓕ (03) 5361 2200; est 1865; ⬥ NFP; ♟; A$; 7 days 10-5; ⚲*

Constant name and label changes have bedevilled Seppelt for many years. This, coupled with the big company syndrome, tends to obscure the real quality and value of the wines. Drumborg Riesling, St Peters Shiraz, and Show Reserve Sparkling Shiraz are absolutely outstanding; all of the other wines are under-priced and reliably good. Exports to the UK and elsewhere.

# Pyrenees

The Australian Pyrenees is a quiet region, like many wine areas on the road to nowhere in particular. While viticulture played a role between 1848 and 1945, it was a minor one. Then, in 1963, the French brandy producer Rémy Martin arrived. It believed the region was particularly suited for the production of good-quality Australian brandy. The large Chateau Remy vineyard was accordingly planted with Trebbiano. When the brandy market was destroyed by federal excise taxation, Chateau Remy moved from spirits to sparkling wine production. Over the years, Chardonnay and Pinot Noir have replaced the Trebbiano.

Meanwhile, other wineries in the region, like Dalwhinnie, Redbank, and Taltarni, set out to prove that the Pyrenees is an excellent region for the production of full-bodied reds, based primarily on Shiraz, Cabernet Sauvignon, and Merlot.

Initially unaffected by the rush to establish new vineyards, in the latter part of the 1990s and early 2000s Pyrenees joined the viticultural rat-race. There are twenty wine producers in the region.

**Berrys Bridge** ☆☆☆☆
*Forsters Road, Carapooee, St Arnaud, Vic 3478, ☎ (03) 5496 3220, ⓕ (03) 5496 3322; est 1990; ☖ 1,500 cases; ☗; A$; wkds by appt*
Geologist-cum-winemaker Roger Milner, now joined by partner Jane Holt with dual degrees in viticulture and wine science, have succeeded in producing powerful, concentrated, complex Shiraz and Cabernet Sauvignon since the inaugural 1997 vintage. The annual offering sells out rapidly.

**Blue Pyrenees Estate** ☆☆☆☆✓
*Vinoca Road, Avoca, Vic 3467, ☎ (03) 5465 3202, ⓕ (03) 5465 3529; est 1963; ☖ 100,000 cases; ☗; A$; Mon-Fri 10-4.30, wkds & public hols 10-5; meals at wkds; ✗*
Founded by Rémy Martin as Chateau Remy, this estate is increasing its focus on table wines, with the Estate Reserve wines at the top, next the Blue Pyrenees varietals, and at the bottom budget-priced Fiddlers Creek. Sparkling wines remain a significant part of the business. Exports to the UK and elsewhere.

**Dalwhinnie** ☆☆☆☆☆
*448 Taltarni Road, Moonambel, Vic 3478, ☎ (03) 5467 2388, ⓕ (03) 5467 2237; est 1976; ☖ 5,500 cases; ☗; A$; 7 days 10-5*
The wines all show tremendous depth of fruit flavour, reflecting the relatively low-yielding, well-maintained thirty-three hectares of estate vineyards. It is hard to say whether the Chardonnay, Shiraz, or the Cabernet Sauvignon is the more distinguished; the Pinot Noir borders on the astonishing, given the climate. It, along with the Eagle Series Shiraz, is made at a fifty-tonne winery established on-site in 2002. Exports to the UK and elsewhere.

**Landsborough Valley Estate** ☆☆☆☆
*850 Landsborough-Elmhurst Road, Landsborough, Vic 3385, (03) 5356 9390, ⓕ (03) 5356 9130; est 1996; ☖ 3,000 cases; ☗; A$; by appt*
District veterans Wal Henning and Geoff Oliver first saw the potential vineyard site in 1963, and coveted it until its acquisition in 1996. They have established twenty hectares of vines, the lion's share to Shiraz, with lesser amounts of Cabernet, Pinot Noir, Chardonnay, and Riesling. The red wines carry the day.

**Mount Avoca Winery** ☆☆☆☆⁴ **V**

*Moates Lane, Avoca, Vic 3467, ☏ (03) 5465 3282, ⓕ (03) 5465 3544; est 1970;*
*☀ 15,000 cases; ☗; A$; Mon-Fri 9-5, wkds 10-5; cheese platters, pétanque*

After being briefly embroiled in the Barrington Estates financial collapse,
Mount Avoca has reverted to family ownership under the direction of
Matthew Barry, who has shown equal skills with Sauvignon Blanc and
Semillon, as well as Shiraz and Cabernet Sauvignon. Exports to the UK
and elsewhere.

**Peerick Vineyard** ☆☆☆☆

*Wild Dog Track, Moonambel, Vic 3478, ☏ (03) 5467 2207, ⓕ (03) 5467 2207;*
*est 1990; ☀ 2,500 cases; ☗; A$; wkds & public hols 11-4*

The venture of Melbourne lawyer Chris Jessup and wife Meryl. Despite
rationalization of the plantings, they still manage to grow Cabernet
Sauvignon, Shiraz, Cabernet Franc, Merlot, Sauvignon Blanc, and Viognier
in the six hectares under vine. Quality has improved significantly, the
perfumed, musk, and spice Viognier particularly meritorious.

**Pyrenees Ridge Vineyard** ☆☆☆☆⁴

*532 Caralulup Road, Lamplough via Avoca, Vic 3467, ☏ (03) 5465 3710,*
*ⓕ (03) 5465 3320; est 1998; ☀ 1,500 cases; Thurs-Mon & public hols 10-5; ↸*

Highly qualified oenologist Graeme Jukes (with wife Sally-Ann) is taking a
*garagiste* approach, with the quality of the powerful blackberry and plum
Cabernet/Shiraz more than compensating for the small production. Ditto
Reserve Shiraz.

**Redbank Winery** ☆☆☆☆

*1 Sally's Lane, Redbank, Vic 3467, ☏ (03) 5467 7255, ⓕ (03) 5467 7248; est 1973;*
*☀ 58,000 cases; ☗; A$; Mon-Sat 9-5, Sun 10-5; deli*

Neill and Sally Robb might seem laid-back in the best Aussie style, but
they have built a thriving business, ranging from the estate-grown flagship
Sally's Paddock (a Cabernet/Shiraz/Malbec) and, at the other end, the
export-oriented, budget-priced Long Paddock wines, made for them
elsewhere. The Hundred Tree Hill brand (and twenty hectares of vineyard)
are owned by their three children. Worldwide distribution.

**Summerfield** ☆☆☆☆☆ **V**

*Main Road, Moonambel, Vic 3478, ☏ (03) 5467 2264, ⓕ (03) 5467 2380; est*
*1979; ☀ 3,500 cases; ☗; A$; 7 days 9-5.30; ⇔; airstrip*

Ian and Mark Summerfield are specialist red-wine producers, their particular
forté Shiraz. Since 1988, the wines have been consistently excellent, luscious,
full-bodied, and fruit-driven, yet with a slice of vanilla oak to top them off.
Ranks second only to Dalwhinnie in the region. Exports to the UK and US.

**Taltarni** ☆☆☆☆⁴ **V**

*339 Taltarni Road, Moonambel, Vic 3478, ☏ (03) 5459 7900, ⓕ (03) 5467 2306;*
*est 1972; ☀ 80,000 cases; ☗; A$; 7 days 10-5; ↸; gardens; pétanque*

A new order headed by multi-talented Peter Steer has brought about the
style change (and quality improvement) which Taltarni needed so badly.
Tasmanian Lalla Gully Vineyard brings brightness and focus to the
Riesling, Sauvignon Blanc, and Chardonnay, while Cephas heads the red
varietal range with an exuberant display of black fruits, cedar, and spice.
Exports to the UK and elsewhere.

**Warrenmang Vineyard** ☆☆☆☆

*Mountain Creek Road, Moonambel, Vic 3478, ☏ (03) 5467 2233, ⓕ (03) 5467*
*2309; est 1974; ☀ 8,500 cases; ☗; A$; 7 days 10-5; ⇔; ↸; resort*

At the time of going to print, the future direction for Warrenmang was uncertain. An ambitious plan to raise funds through a proposed public listing on the Stock Exchange, taking in Massoni as part of the expanded business, had stalled. It's a case of "watch this space".

# Henty

Henty, previously known as the Far Southwest, is a remote corner of Victoria that might be far better known were it not for the arbitrary placement of the state border with South Australia. It lies a relatively few kilometres east of some of Australia's well-known wine regions, including Coonawarra and Padthaway. As it is, Drumborg is the only significant wine district in Henty, and Seppelt the only substantial vine-grower. The soil and the plentiful supply of underground water are links in common with those regions over the border to the west. That said, the climate of Drumborg is significantly cooler. Pinot Noir and Chardonnay are tailor-made for fine sparkling wine in the cooler vintages, and for table wine in most years. Riesling usually produces a fragrant yet steely wine, and in the warmer vintages intense Pinot Noir, Cabernet Sauvignon, and Shiraz come to the fore. Overall, Henty remains one of the last frontiers. When the next wave of viticulture comes in ten or twenty years' time, it must surely sweep over this region. There are eight wine producers here.

**Barretts Wines** ☆☆☆⚐
*Portland-Nelson Highway, Portland, Vic 3305, ☎ (03) 5526 5251; est 1983;*
*⚱ 1,000 cases; ⚲; A$; 7 days 11-5*
Rod Barrett makes the wines on-site, and has learned steadily as the years have gone by since he took responsibility in 1992. In the warmer vintages Riesling and Pinot Noir can excel.

**Bochara Wines** ☆☆☆☆⚐ **V**
*Glenelg Highway, Bochara, Vic 3300, ☎ (03) 5571 9309, Ⓕ (03) 5570 8334; est 1998; ⚱ 1,000 cases; ⚲; A$; Thurs-Mon 11-5, or by appt*
This is the small husband and wife business of experienced winemaker Martin Slocombe and former Yalumba viticulturist Kylie McIntyre. Their 2.5-hectare vineyard is supplemented by grape purchases from within the region. The wine style is subtle but intense, and the wines are well worth seeking out.

**Crawford River Wines** ☆☆☆☆☆
*Hotspur Upper Road, Condah, Vic 3303, ☎ (03) 5578 2267, Ⓕ (03) 5578 2240;*
*est 1975; ⚱ 4,000 cases; ⚲; A$; by appt*
Part-time grazier, part-time winemaker, John Thomson has the winemaker's equivalent of a gardener's "green fingers". He makes exemplary wines right across the range. The Riesling and Semillon/Sauvignon Blanc are consistently outstanding, the Cabernet-based wines excellent in warmer vintages. Exports to the UK and elsewhere.

**Tarrington Vineyards** ☆☆☆☆☆
*Hamilton Highway, Tarrington, Vic 3301, ☎ (03) 5572 4509, Ⓕ (03) 5572 4509;*
*est 1993; ⚱ 300 cases; ⚲; A$; by appt*
Right from the word go, the grape-growing and winemaking practices of Burgundy have been adopted by winemaker-owner Tamara Irish.

The quantities may be minuscule (get on the mailing list), but the quality is celestial. The Chardonnay is modelled on Chablis, and the Pinot Noir is beyond comparison.

# Bendigo

By 1864, there were more than forty vineyards in the Bendigo region. By 1880, 216 hectares supported over 100 wineries (one must suppose this number included lean-tos at the back of the house). Phylloxera heralded a brutal end to winemaking when it arrived in 1893, but no doubt the bank crash of the same year and the move to fortified wines also played their roles in the cessation of winemaking in the region. A gap of over sixty years followed, until Bendigo pharmacist Stuart Anderson planted vines at Balgownie in 1969, making startling red wines. Bendigo continues to make great red wines, but the excision of the Heathcote region in 2003, and the explosive expansion of that area, have, perhaps, robbed Bendigo of some of the lustre it had in the 1980s and 1990s. There are thirty-two wine producers in the region.

**Balgownie Estate** ☆☆☆☆✓
*Hermitage Road, Maiden Gully, Vic 3551, ☎ (03) 5449 6222, Ⓕ (03) 5449 6506; est 1969; ⚱ 5,000 cases; ⚱; A$; 7 days 11-5,* ⊨
In mid-1999, Mildara Blass sold Balgownie Estate to the Forrester family of Queensland. Major changes have seen the doubling of vineyards to thirty-six hectares, a A$3 million winery upgrade, and a new winemaker installed. All of these investments have paid off handsomely, with wine quality headed back to the halcyon days of founder Stuart Anderson. Exports to the UK and elsewhere.

**BlackJack Vineyards** ☆☆☆☆✓
*Corner Blackjack Road and Calder Highway, Harcourt, Vic 3453, ☎ (03) 5474 2355, Ⓕ (03) 5474 2355; est 1987; ⚱ 2,500 cases; ⚱; A$; wkds & public hols 11-5*
Ian McKenzie (no relation to Seppelt's eponymous former chief winemaker) and Ken Pollock make full-blooded, sometimes rustic, sometimes compelling red wines from a vineyard established on an old apple and pear orchard in the Harcourt Valley.

**Chateau Leamon** ☆☆☆☆
*5528 Calder Highway, Bendigo, Vic 3550, ☎ (03) 5447 7995, Ⓕ (03) 5447 0855; est 1973; ⚱ 2,500 cases; ⚱; A$; Wed-Mon 10-5*
Ian Leamon uses locally grown grapes, but also looks to the Strathbogie Ranges for fruit for other wines. In the better vintages Reserve Shiraz and Reserve Cabernet Sauvignon are truly excellent. Exports to the UK and elsewhere.

**Harcourt Valley Vineyards** ☆☆☆☆
*3339 Calder Highway, Harcourt, Vic 3453, ☎ (03) 5474 2223, Ⓕ (03) 5474 2293; est 1976; ⚱ 1,000 cases; ⚱; A$; 7 days 11-5, 11-6 during daylight savings; special events*
A picturesque setting where the granite cellars, hewn from local rock, are set among river gums. Owner John Livingstone continues to make Barbara's Shiraz and Barbara's Shiraz Pressings; also Chardonnay, Riesling, and Cabernet, the reds in a rich, full-bodied style typical of the region.

**Nuggetty Vineyard** ☆☆☆☆

*280 Maldon-Shelbourne Road, Nuggetty, Vic 3463, ☎ (03) 5475 1347, Ⓕ (03) 5475 1647; est 1993; ♦ 1,000 cases; ⚐; A$; wkds 10-4 & public hols 10-4, or by appt*

A highly qualified husband and wife team of Greg and Jackie Dedman are quietly building the Nuggetty Vineyard brand, with appropriately powerful Shiraz and Cabernet Sauvignon leading the way, supported by Barrel Fermented Semillon. Exports to the UK and US.

**Passing Clouds** ☆☆☆☆☆

*RMB 440 Kurting Road, Kingower, Vic 3517, ☎ (03) 5438 8257, Ⓕ (03) 5438 8246; est 1974; ♦ 4,000 cases; ⚐; A$; wkds 12-5, Mon-Fri by appt*

Graeme Leith is one of the great personalities of the industry, with a superb sense of humour. He makes lovely regional reds, packed with cassis, berry, and minty fruit. Angel Blend and Graeme's Blend usually lead the way; Yarra-Valley-sourced Pinot Noir an impressive newcomer. Exports to the UK.

**Pondalowie Vineyards** ☆☆☆☆☆

*6 Main Street, Bridgewater-on-Loddon, Vic 3516, ☎ & Ⓕ (03) 5437 3332; est 1997; ♦ 1,500 cases; ⚐; A$; wkds & public hols 12-5, or by appt*

Dominic and Krystina Morris both have a strong winemaking background, gained from working alternate vintages in Australia, Portugal, and France. They have established eleven hectares of vineyard, planted to Shiraz, Tempranillo, and Cabernet Sauvignon, plus a little Viognier, Malbec, and Touriga. The Shiraz/Viognier has the exuberant synergy one expects of the marriage; the Unoaked Tempranillo is wonderfully perfumed and authentic. Exports to the UK.

**Sandhurst Ridge** ☆☆☆☆☆

*156 Forest Drive, Marong, Vic 3515, ☎ (03) 5435 2534, Ⓕ (03) 5435 2548; est 1990; ♦ 2,500 cases; ⚐; A$; Wed-Mon 12-5, or by appt*

With their complementary background skills, the four Greblo brothers have established a 6.6-hectare vineyard (principally Cabernet Sauvignon and Shiraz) and built a full-scale winery in 1996. The red wines have gone from strength to strength, opulently ripe and complex in vintages such as 2002.

**Water Wheel** ☆☆☆☆ V

*Bridgewater-on-Loddon, Bridgewater, Vic 3516, ☎ (03) 5437 3060, Ⓕ (03) 5437 3082; est 1972; ♦ 35,000 cases; ⚐; A$; Oct-Apr 7 days 11-5, May-Sept Mon-Fri 11-5, wkds & public hols 1-4*

Peter Cumming quietly goes about the business of making significant quantities of competitively priced, unfailingly honest, smooth, and varietally distinctive wines, of which the Chardonnay, Shiraz, and Cabernet Sauvignon are the best. Watch for the 2002 vintage. Exports to the UK and elsewhere.

# Heathcote

If you are thinking of setting up shop as a maker of Australian Shiraz, it is likely you will put Heathcote at the top of your shopping list. The number and size of new plantings in the region is extraordinary, particularly given the scarcity of water resources for irrigation, without which vine establishment is problematic if there is normal rainfall, nigh-on impossible if there is a continuation of the drought cycle of the first years of this century. The attraction is the 500-million-year-old decomposed Cambrian igneous rock, ironically called Greenstone: ironically, because it is now a vivid red. It runs from just south of the town of Heathcote north to Colbinabbin along the dominant geographic structure of the Mount Camel range, which provides ideal slopes. If the vines are established, such as those of Jasper Hill, the depth of the soil makes irrigation largely redundant, but there is a chicken-and-egg issue here, as some aspirants have found out to their cost. At its best, Heathcote Shiraz has a majestically velvety texture to its deeply resonant red and black fruit flavours, and soaks up new oak without blinking. There are twenty-five wine producers in the region.

### Barnadown Run ☆☆☆☆

*390 Cornella Road, Toolleen, Vic 3551, ☎ (03) 5433 6376, ⓕ (03) 5433 6386; est 1995; ◈ 1,500 cases; ♟; A$; 7 days 10-5*

Named after the original pastoral lease of which the vineyard forms part and established on rich terra rossa soil for which the best Heathcote vineyards are famous. Owner Andrew Millis carries out both the viticulture and winemaking at the five-hectare vineyard planted to Shiraz, Merlot, and Cabernet Sauvignon. Exports to the US and UK.

### Burke and Wills Winery ☆☆☆☆

*3155 Burke and Wills Track, Mia Mia, Vic 3444, ☎ (03) 5425 5400, ⓕ (03) 5425 5401; est 2003; ◈ 1,000 cases; ♟; A$; by appt; open air concerts in summer*

Owner/winemaker Andrew Pattison has moved from Macedon to Heathcote, the grapes and wine sources in transition as he does so, but with an exceptional French Oak Shiraz and good Pattison Bordeaux Blend from the 2001 vintage. Not to be confused with Burke & Hills of Orange.

### Domaines Tatiarra ☆☆☆☆☆

*2/102 Barkers Road, Hawthorn, Vic 3124 (postal), ☎ 0411 240 815, ⓕ (03) 9890 5322; est 1991; ◈ 1,800 cases; no visitors*

A virtual winery under the winemaking control of Ben Riggs (McLaren Vale) but with a sixty-hectare property of Cambrian earth already producing glorious Shiraz under the Cambrian, Caravan of Dreams, and Trademark labels. The wines are made at Pettavel in Geelong (*q.v.*).

### Heathcote Winery ☆☆☆☆

*183-185 High Street, Heathcote, Vic 3523, ☎ (03) 5433 2595, ⓕ (03) 5433 3081; est 1978; ◈ 5,000 cases; ♟; A$; 7 days 11-5; ⚐; art gallery*

The Heathcote Winery is back in business with a vengeance. The wines are being produced predominantly from the twenty-six hectares of estate vineyard, and some from local and other growers under long-term contracts, and the tasting room facilities restored and upgraded. The various Shiraz and Shiraz/Viogniers are the pick.

### Jasper Hill ☆☆☆☆☆

*Drummonds Lane, Heathcote, Vic 3523, ☎ (03) 5433 2528, ⓕ (03) 5433 3143; est 1975; ◈ 3,500 cases; ♟; A$; by appt*

Ron and Elva Laughton, together with their daughters Georgia and Emily, make some of Australia's greatest Shiraz. Georgia's Paddock (9.5 hectares) is 100 per cent Shiraz; Emily's Paddock (3.2 hectares) has a dash of Cabernet Franc to accompany the Shiraz. Ron is unapologetic about the high alcohol of his rich, velvety, tapestried wines. Exports to the UK and elsewhere.

### McIvor Estate ☆☆☆☆

*80 Tooborac-Baynton Road, Tooborac, Vic 3522, ☎ (03) 5433 5266, ⓕ (03) 5433 5358; est 1997; ◈ 1,200 cases; ♟; A$; wkds & public hols 10-5, or by appt; olive oil*

Adrian Munari is the contract winemaker for this interesting 5.5-hectare vineyard, with its exotic array of Marsanne (excellent wine already), Roussanne, Shiraz, Cabernet Sauvignon, Merlot, Nebbiolo, and Sangiovese (the last high-toned, exuberant, red cherry, spice, tobacco, and leaf). Not to be confused with longer-established McIvor Creek of the same region.

### Mount Burrumboot Estate ☆☆☆☆✓

*3332 Heathcote-Rochester Road, Colbinabbin, Vic 3559, ☎ & Ⓕ (03) 5432 9238; est 1999; ❧ 500 cases; ☗; A$; wkds & public hols 11-5, or by appt; ▯◀*

Andrew and Cathy Branson have a mixed farm on the slopes of the Mount Camel Range above Colbinabbin, and in 1999 planted Verdelho, Shiraz, and Merlot. Cathy Branson took ownership of the 2002 vintage made in a tractor shed (*tractoriste*?). The result was so good a fifty-tonne winery was built later the same year. Shiraz and Merlot are excellent and production will increase.

### Mount Ida ☆☆☆☆

*Northern Highway, Heathcote, Vic 3253, ☎ (03) 8626 3340; est 1978; ❧ 2,000 cases; no visitors*

Planted by the famous Australian artist Leonard French and Dr James Munro, Mount Ida was acquired by Tisdall, itself swallowed up in turn by Beringer Blass. Consistently sumptuous Shiraz, in typical Heathcote style, sells out rapidly each year.

### Paul Osicka ☆☆☆☆

*Majors Creek Vineyard at Graytown, Vic 3608, ☎ (03) 5794 9235, Ⓕ (03) 5794 9288; est 1955; ❧ NFP; ☗; A$; Mon-Sat 10-5, Sun 12-5*

A low-profile producer but reliable, particularly when it comes to smooth but rich Shiraz. Has the distinction of being the only winery open for business in Victoria between 1930 and 1963. Exports to the UK and elsewhere.

### Red Edge ☆☆☆☆

*Golden Gully Road, Heathcote, Vic 3523, ☎ (03) 9337 5695, Ⓕ (03) 9337 7550; est 1971; ❧ 1,000 cases; ☗; A$; by appt*

Red Edge is a new name, but the vineyard dates back to 1971 and the renaissance of the Victorian wine industry. In the early 1980s, it yielded the wonderful wines of Flynn & Williams. Peter and Judy Dredge have now revived the estate, producing dense Shiraz and Cabernet Sauvignon. Exports to the UK and US.

### Redesdale Estate Wines ☆☆☆☆✓

*North Redesdale Road, Redesdale, Vic 3444, ☎ (03) 5425 3236, Ⓕ (03) 5425 3122; est 1982; ❧ 1,000 cases; ☗; A$; Nov-April wkds 11-4, or by appt; ▱*

A part lifestyle venture by Peter Williams and wife Suzanne Arnall-Williams, who purchased a derelict vineyard in 1988, rejuvenated it and then established a luxury two-storey cottage surrounded by a superb garden (linked to their villa in Tuscany). Contract winemaking at Balgownie has delivered the goods for the intense and luscious Shiraz and Cabernets.

### Toolleen Vineyard ☆☆☆☆

*2004 Gibb Road, Toolleen, Vic 3551, ☎ & Ⓕ (03) 5433 6397; est 1996; ❧ 1,000 cases; no visitors*

Owned by Mr KC Huang and family, with 14.7 hectares of Shiraz and Cabernet Sauvignon (plus a few others) on the western slope of Mount Camel. The wines are contract-made by Dominique Portet (Yarra Valley) and the densely fruited Shiraz and Cabernet Sauvignon are typical of the region at its best; eighty per cent of the production is exported to Asia.

**Wild Duck Creek Estate NR**
*Spring Flat Road, Heathcote, Vic 3523,* ☎ & Ⓕ *(03) 5433 3133; est 1980;* ❧ *4,000 cases;* ♇; *A$; by appt;* 🖂

David and Diana Anderson slowly built the tiny, part-time vineyard and winery between 1980 and 1993 to become red-wine specialists. The Duck Muck label has gained icon status in the US. Worldwide distribution.

# Goulburn Valley/Nagambie Lakes

The Nagambie Lakes is a sub-region of the Goulburn Valley, situated at its southern end, and was a major viticultural centre as long ago as 1860. It is a logical place to grow grapes, as it is as warm as the Barossa Valley, and has ample underground (and river) water off-setting the dry, low-humidity summers. It is noted for long-lived Shiraz, Cabernet, and Marsanne. The Goulburn Valley proper runs along the southern side of the Murray River, and the overall focus switches from red to white. The climate is warmer again, and drier, but water is even more freely available. Yields are even higher than the already generous crops of the Nagambie Lakes, where the key wineries are Tahbilk and Mitchelton. There are few wineries in the world with such charm as Tahbilk's; Mitchelton was built one hundred or so years later, but also in grand style. There are twenty-six wine producers in the region.

**Burramurra** ☆☆☆✬
*Barwood Park, Nagambie, Vic 3608,* ☎ *(03) 5794 2181,* Ⓕ *(03) 5794 2755; est 1988;* ❧ *1,000 cases; Fri-Sun & public hols 10-5, or by appt*

Burramurra is the relatively low-profile vineyard operation of the former deputy premier of Victoria, Pat McNamara. Most of the grapes are sold to Mitchelton; a small amount is contract-made for the Burramurra label, much of it sold to the US.

**Cape Horn Vineyard** ☆☆☆
*Echuca-Picola Road, Kanyapella, Vic 3564,* ☎ *(03) 5480 6013,* Ⓕ *(03) 5480 6013; est 1993;* ❧ *1,500 cases;* ♇; *A$; 7 days 10.30-5; river cruises; light meals*

The unusual name comes from a bend in the Murray River which was considered by the riverboat owners of the nineteenth century to resemble Cape Horn, a resemblance now depicted on the wine label. Fourteen hectares of vines produce pleasantly soft wines contract-made at Hanging Rock (*q.v.*), the best Durif and Marsanne.

**Dalfarras** ☆☆☆✬
*PO Box 123, Nagambie, Vic 3608,* ☎ *(03) 5794 2637,* Ⓕ *(03) 5794 2360; est 1991;* ❧ *18,000 cases; no visitors*

The personal project of Alister Purbrick (of Tahbilk) and artist-wife Rosa (née Dalfarra), whose paintings adorn the labels of the wines. It has its own thirty-seven hectares of vines and, to use Alister's words, "It allows me to expand my winemaking horizons and mould wines in styles different to Tahbilk."

**David Traeger** ☆☆☆✬
*139 High Street, Nagambie, Vic 3608,* ☎ *(03) 5794 2514,* Ⓕ *(03) 5794 1776; est 1986;* ❧ *10,000 cases;* ♇; *A$; 7 days 10-5*

David Traeger learned much during his years as assistant winemaker at Mitchelton, and knows central Victoria well. Shiraz and Verdelho are best.

Now owned by the Dromana Estate group, but David Traeger still owns the super-premium Baptista Shiraz. Exports to the UK and elsewhere.

**Longleat Estate** ☆☆☆☆ **V**

*105 Old Weir Road, Murchison, Vic 3610, ☎ (03) 5826 2294, ⓕ (03) 5826 2510; est 1975; ⬥ 4,000 cases; ⚑; A$; Fri-Mon & public hols 10-5, or by appt*

Sandra and Guido Vazzoler acquired the long-established Longleat Estate vineyard in 2003. The wines are estate-grown, and the 2002 vintage in particular marked a significant lift in quality.

**McPherson Wines** ☆☆☆ **V**

*PO Box 529, Artarmon, NSW 1570, ☎ (02) 9436 1644, ⓕ (02) 9436 3144; est 1993; ⬥ 300,000 cases; no visitors*

Has hitherto focused almost exclusively on exports to the UK and elsewhere, with wines made at various locations from contract-grown grapes or purchased in bulk and blended; a joint venture between Andrew McPherson and Alister Purbrick of Tahbilk (*q.v.*). The Reserve range provided a quality lift at the top end. Worldwide distribution.

**Mitchelton** ☆☆☆☆ **V**

*Mitchellstown via Nagambie, Vic 3608, ☎ (03) 5736 2222, ⓕ (03) 5736 2266; est 1969; ⬥ 200,000 cases; ⚑; A$; 7 days 10-5; ⚶; gallery; river cruises*

Acquired by Petaluma in 1994, Mitchelton boasts an impressive array of wines across a broad spectrum of style and price. Exemplary Blackwood Park Riesling, Goulburn Valley Marsanne, and Print Label Shiraz. Exports to the UK and elsewhere.

**Tahbilk** ☆☆☆☆⚶ **V**

*Goulburn Valley Highway, Tabilk, Vic 3608, ☎ (03) 5794 2555, ⓕ (03) 5794 2360; est 1860; ⬥ 110,000 cases; ⚑; A$; Mon-Sat 9-5, Sun 11-5; ⚶*

A winery steeped in tradition (with high National Trust classification) and which makes wines in keeping with that tradition. Age-worthy Marsanne, Shiraz from 1860s vines, Riesling, Viognier, and Cabernet Sauvignon are all impressive. Worldwide distribution.

# Strathbogie Ranges

This is the northern half of what was previously (unofficially) known as Central Victorian High Country. The climate is cool (due mainly to its elevation) but not as cool as that of its southern neighbour, the Upper Goulburn. Thus it does allow the later-ripening varieties such as Shiraz, Cabernet Sauvignon, and Merlot to ripen satisfactorily in most years; these three and Chardonnay are the most important varieties. There are eight wine producers in the region.

**Antcliff's Chase** ☆☆☆⚶

*RMB 4510 Caveat via Seymour, Vic 3660, ☎ (03) 5790 4333, ⓕ (03) 5790 4333; est 1982; ⬥ 800 cases; ⚑; A$; wkds 10-5*

A scarecrow on the label tells its own story of the problems caused by birds in small, remote vineyards. The grapes from the four hectares are principally sold; a small amount is vinified under the Antcliff's Chase label, and the quality is generally good.

**Dominion Wines** ☆☆⚶

*Upton Road, Strathbogie Ranges via Avenel, Vic 3664, ☎ (03) 5796 2718, ⓕ (03) 5796 2719; est 1999; ⬥ 140,000 cases; ⚑; A$; by appt; ⚶*

A major newcomer; a 7,500-tonne winery was built prior to the 2000 vintage, supported in part by ninety hectares of estate vineyards and in part as a contract winemaker for other major Australian wine companies. Exports to the UK and elsewhere.

**Maygars Hill Winery** ☆☆☆☆☆
*53 Longwood-Mansfield Road, Longwood, Vic 3665, ☎ (03) 5798 5417, Ⓕ (03) 5798 5457; est 1997; ♦ 900 cases; ⚲; A$; by appt; ⛌; ✗*

The name of the Hill comes from Lieutenant Colonel Maygar, who won a VC in the Boer War in South Africa in 1901. Jenny Houghton (no relative) has a combined vineyard and B&B operation, gaining much publicity with the trophy-winning 2002 Cabernet Sauvignon, full of expressive and attractive cassis/blackcurrant fruit (contract-made by Plunkett).

**Nillahcootie Estate** ☆☆☆☆
*RMB 1637 Lima South, Vic 3673, ☎ (03) 5768 2666, Ⓕ (03) 5768 2678; est 1988; ♦ 700 cases; ⚲; A$; by appt*

Karen Davy and Michael White decided to diversify their primary business of beef cattle production on their 280-hectare property in 1988. They planted seven hectares, initially content to sell the production to other local wineries, but have retained the equivalent of 700 cases of wine. In 2001 they purchased a property overlooking Lake Nillahcootie, renovated a homestead (available for rent), and commenced construction of the cellar door, due for completion by autumn 2004.

**Plunkett** ☆☆☆☆☆
*Corner Hume Highway and Lambing Gully Road, Avenel, Vic 3664, ☎ (03) 5796 2150, Ⓕ (03) 5796 2147; est 1980; ♦ 15,000 cases; ⚲; A$; 7 days 11-5 (cellar door), Thurs-Mon 11-5 (restaurant); ⛏; ✗*

Grape-growers since 1980, turning part-winemakers in 1992, the Plunkett family has 100 hectares under vine. Part of the grape production is sold; the remainder is made into the top-level Strathbogie Ranges label, Blackwood Ridge the second. Exports to the UK and elsewhere.

# Upper Goulburn

Variations in elevation (150 meters to 600 meters), and hence climate, see the full range of early- (Pinot Noir, Chardonnay), mid- (Sauvignon Blanc, Cortese), and late- (Riesling, Marsanne, Shiraz, Merlot, Cabernet Sauvignon) ripening varietals being planted. Degree of slope, aspect (north and northeast preferred), and soil all play a role in site selection, but spring frosts are a major limiting factor. The hilly scenery is beautiful, sometimes spectacular, as at Delatite. There are nineteen wine producers in the region.

**Cheviot Bridge/Long Flat** ☆☆☆☆ V
*10/499 St Kilda Road, Melbourne, Vic 3004, ☎ (03) 9820 9080, Ⓕ (03) 9820 9070; est 1998; ♦ 50,000 cases; no visitors*

Cheviot Bridge/Long Flat brings together a highly experienced team of wine industry professionals and investors who provided the A$10 million-plus required to purchase the Long Flat range of wines from Tyrrell's, the purchase taking place in the second half of 2003. The only vineyards owned by Cheviot Bridge are at Yea, which provide the top of the range,

followed by CB range, the Long Flat Wine Co. and Long Flat labels.
Kissing Bridge and Thirsty Lizard are export-only; worldwide distribution.

**Delatite** ☆☆☆☆
*Stoneys Road, Mansfield, Vic 3722, ☎ (03) 5775 2922, Ⓕ (03) 5775 2911; est 1982; ⚭ 12,000 cases; ⚱; A$; 7 days 10-5*
Rosaland Ritchie (and family) run this acclaimed winery. With its sweeping views across to the snow-clad peaks, this is an uncompromisingly cool-climate viticultural enterprise and the wines naturally reflect the climate. Light but intense Riesling and spicy Traminer flower with a year or two in bottle, and in the warmer vintages the red wines achieve flavour and texture, albeit with a distinctive mintiness. The vineyard is being converted to biodynamics, an interesting move. Exports to the UK and elsewhere.

**Lost Valley Winery** ☆☆☆☆
*Strath Creek, Vic 3658, ☎ (03) 9592 3531, Ⓕ (03) 9592 6396; est 1995; ⚭ 2,500 cases; no visitors*
Dr Robert Ippaso owns a three-hectare vineyard at 450 metres above sea level on the slopes of Mount Tallarook. It is planted with Shiraz, Merlot, Verdelho, and Cortese. The latter is the only planting of this variety in Australia and pays homage to Dr Ippaso's birthplace in the Franco-Italian Alps, where the grape flourishes. Exports to the UK and elsewhere.

**Murrindindi** ☆☆☆☆
*Cummins Lane, Murrindindi, Vic 3717, ☎ (03) 5797 8448, Ⓕ (03) 5797 8448; est 1979; ⚭ 1,500 cases; ⚱; A$; Mon-Wed 9-4, Thurs-Sat 9-8.30 at Marmalades Café, Yea*
Owned and run by the Cuthbertson family. Its unequivocally cool climate means that special care has to be taken in the vineyard to produce ripe fruit. Hard work is rewarded with elegant Chardonnay, Shiraz, and Cabernet/Merlot.

**Penbro Vineyard** ☆☆☆☆
*Corner Melba Highway and Murrindindi Road, Glenburn, Vic 3717, ☎ (03) 9215 2229, Ⓕ (03) 9215 2346; est 1997; ⚭ 3,500 cases; ⚱; A$; by appt, cellar door at Glenburn Pub*
Since 1997 the Bertalli family has established forty hectares of Chardonnay, Pinot Noir, Merlot, Cabernet Sauvignon, and Shiraz. The wines have won several silver and bronze medals at the Victorian Wine Show. Part of the grape production is sold, part vinified for the Penbro brand.

**Rees Miller Estate** ☆☆☆☆
*5355 Goulburn Highway, Yea, Vic 3717, ☎ (03) 5797 2101, Ⓕ (03) 5797 3276; est 1996; ⚭ 3,000 cases; ⚱; A$; wkds & public hols 10-5; ⚔*
Sylke Rees and David Miller run 7.5 hectares of vineyard on a low-input, low-yield basis, making Chardonnay, Pinot Noir, Shiraz, Shiraz/Viognier, and a Bordeaux blend on-site.

**Tallarook** ☆☆☆☆
*2 Delaney's Road, Warranwood, Vic 3134, ☎ (03) 9876 7022, Ⓕ (03) 9876 7044; est 1987; ⚭ 11,000 cases; no visitors*
Now has a permanent winery home in the Yarra Valley under the direction of MasterWineMakers with a consequent expansion both in production and varietal range which extends to Marsanne, Shiraz, Chardonnay, Pinot Noir, and Merlot/Cabernet. Exports to the UK and elsewhere.

# Rutherglen

Rutherglen has a character and personality second to none. It is steeped in history and legend. As in so much of Victoria, gold and wine remained intertwined during the boom years from 1860 to 1893. It was an environment in which vast winery and vineyard enterprises flourished. There was Mount Ophir, with 280 hectares and way-out architecture; Fairfield, home to the Morris family and the largest winery in the southern hemisphere, and Graham's, owner of 250 hectares. This region's decline resulted as exports to the UK fell and the domestic market's taste shifted from fortified wines to table wines. Happily, all was not lost. Production of the sublime Muscats and Tokays, virtually without parallel elsewhere in the world, continues, drawing on base wines aged in a *solera*-style system that dates back to the turn of the century. The Winemakers of Rutherglen have banded together to formulate a classification system for their Muscats (and, by extension, their Tokays). They hold periodic tastings to ensure quality and style parameters are being observed. At the bottom is Rutherglen Muscat, the emphasis on fresh raisin aromas and flavours. Next up is Classic, with a greater level of richness and complexity, and the development of rancio. Grand moves to a new level of intensity, depth, and concentration, the rancio characters imparting layers of texture and flavour. Finally comes Rare, bottled in tiny quantities each year, the amount limited by the very old reserves in the *solera*. It is one of the great wines of the world. The Winery Walkabout, held on the long weekend of the Queen's birthday at the start of June, rivals the Barossa Vintage Festival in popularity. This is one of the truly great wine-tourism destinations. There are twenty-one wine producers in the region.

### All Saints ☆☆☆☆☆
*All Saints Road, Wahgunyah, Vic 3687, ☎ (02) 6035 2222, Ⓕ (02) 6035 2200; est 1864; ◈ 35,000 cases; Mon-Sat 9-5.30, Sun 10-5.30; Ⲕ; gardens*
One of the great, if whimsical, landmarks on the Australian scene. This castellated, red-brick Scottish castle, owned by Peter Brown (of Brown Brothers), offers good table wines, great fortified Tokay and Muscat (the Museum Rare releases are sublime), and an excellent restaurant.

### Bullers Calliope ☆☆☆☆☆
*Three Chain Road, Rutherglen, Vic 3685, ☎ (02) 6032 9660, Ⓕ (02) 6032 8005; est 1921; ◈ 4,000 cases; ⲣ; A$; Mon-Sat 9-5, Sun 10-5; bird park*
The winery rating is for the superb releases of Rare Liqueur Muscat and Rare Liqueur Tokay, dazzlingly beautiful examples of their style. Limited releases of Calliope Shiraz and Shiraz Mondeuse can also be good. Exports to the UK and elsewhere.

### Campbells ☆☆☆☆☆
*Murray Valley Highway, Rutherglen, Vic 3685, ☎ (02) 6032 9458, Ⓕ (02) 6032 9870; est 1870; ◈ 60,000 cases; ⲣ; A$; Mon-Sat 9-5, Sun 10-5; Ⲕ*
Offers a wide range of table and fortified wines of ascending quality and price which are always honest. As so often happens in this part of the world, the fortified wines are the best, with the extremely elegant Isabella Rare Tokay and Merchant Prince Rare Muscat at the top of the tree. Exports to the UK and elsewhere.

**Chambers Rosewood** ☆☆☆☆☆
*Barkly Street, Rutherglen, Vic 3685, ☎ (02) 6032 8641, Ⓕ (02) 6032 8101;*
*est 1858; ⚭ 10,000 cases; ♟ A$; Mon-Sat 9-5, Sun 11-5; playground*
The rating is given for the tiny quantities of Rare Rutherglen Muscat and
Rare Rutherglen Tokay, which Bill Chambers grudgingly hands out. He
tends to raise the price every time someone has the temerity to buy these
classics. Exports to the UK and elsewhere.

**Cofield** ☆☆☆☆⚬ V
*Distillery Road, Wahgunyah, Vic 3687, ☎ (02) 6033 3798, Ⓕ (02) 6033 0798;*
*est 1990; ⚭ 11,000 cases; ♟ A$; Mon-Sat 9-5, Sun 10-5; 𝘒; gourmet barbecue*
*packs; Pickled Sisters Café*
District veteran Max Cofield, together with wife Karen and sons Damien,
Ben, and Andrew, is developing a strong cellar-door sales base by staging
winery functions with guest chefs, and also providing a large barbecue
and picnic area. The quality of the red wines, in particular, is good, and
improving all the time.

**drinkmoor wines** ☆☆☆☆⚬
*All Saints Road, Wahgunyah, Vic 3687, ☎ (02) 6033 5544, Ⓕ (02) 6033 5645;*
*est 2002; ⚭ 2,500 cases; ♟ A$; 7 days 10-5; art & craft gallery*
An exemplar of targeted marketing, offering non-vintage varietal wines in
unpretentious packaging and at one price for the whites, one for reds, all
designed to take out the fear factor. The red wines, in particular, are
thoroughly commendable.

**Morris** ☆☆☆☆☆ V
*Mia Mia Road, Rutherglen, Vic 3685, ☎ (02) 6026 7303, Ⓕ (02) 6026 7445;*
*est 1859; ⚭ 100,000 cases; ♟ A$; Mon-Sat 9-5, Sun 10-5; 𝘒*
One of the greatest, some would say the greatest, of the fortified
winemakers. To test that view, try the Old Premium Rare Muscat and Old
Premium Rare Tokay, the reasons for the winery rating. They are absolute
bargains given their age and quality. Table wines are dependable; Durif is
the best by far. Exports to the UK and US.

**Mount Prior Vineyard** ☆☆☆☆⚬ V
*Gooramadda Road, Rutherglen, Vic 3685, ☎ (02) 6026 5591, Ⓕ (02) 6026 5590;*
*est 1860; ⚭ 10,000 cases; ♟ A$; 7 days 9-5; 🍴; 🛏; gift shop*
Yet another great legacy of the 1800s, with a thoroughly modern range of
well-executed wines and a much-awarded restaurant. The Director's
Selection Muscat offers exceptional value for money.

**Pfeiffer** ☆☆☆☆⚬
*167 Distillery Road, Wahgunyah, Vic 3687, ☎ (02) 6033 2805, Ⓕ (02) 6033 3158;*
*est 1984; ⚭ 20,000 cases; ♟ A$; Mon-Sat 9-5, Sun 10-5; playground*
Ex-Lindemans fortified winemaker Chris Pfeiffer occupies one of the
historic wineries (built in 1880) that abound in northeast Victoria. Worth a
visit on this score alone. The fortified wines are good, and the table wines
have improved considerably, drawing upon thirty-two hectares of estate
plantings. Exports to the UK and elsewhere.

**Rutherglen Estates** ☆☆☆☆⚬
*Corner Great Northern Road and Murray Valley Highway, Rutherglen, Vic 3685,*
*☎ (02) 6032 8516, Ⓕ (02) 6032 8517; est 2000; ⚭ 25,000 cases; no visitors*
The Rutherglen Estates brand is an offshoot of a far larger contract crush
and make business, with a winery capacity of 4,000 tonnes (roughly
equivalent to 280,000 cases). The wines released are Chardonnay/Marsanne,

Shiraz, Shiraz/Mourvèdre, Durif, and Sangiovese. Exports to the UK and elsewhere.

**St Leonards** ☆☆☆☆✈ **V**

*Wahgunyah, Vic 3687, ☎ (02) 6033 1004, ⓕ (02) 6033 3636; est 1860; ⚱ NFP;*
*ⓨ; A$; Mon-Fri 9-5, Sat 10-5; ⚹; wkd barbecues 11-3; live music*

An old favourite on the banks of the Murray, also owned by Peter Brown, its wines cleverly marketed at the cellar door and bistro.

**Stanton & Killeen Wines** ☆☆☆☆☆ **V**

*Jacks Road, Murray Valley Highway, Rutherglen, Vic 3685, ☎ (02) 6032 9457,*
*ⓕ (02) 6032 8018; est 1875; ⚱ 15,000 cases; ⓨ; A$; Mon-Sat 9-5, Sun 10-5*

Chris Killeen has skilfully expanded the portfolio here, but without in any way compromising its reputation as a traditional maker of smooth, rich reds and attractive, fruity Muscats and Tokays. His great "Vintage Ports" equal the very best in Australia, made from the correct varieties and not too sweet. Exports to the UK and US.

**Warrabilla** ☆☆☆☆✈ **V**

*Murray Valley Highway, Rutherglen, Vic 3685, ☎ (02) 6035 7242, ⓕ (02) 6035*
*7298; est 1990; ⚱ 9,000 cases; ⓨ; A$; 7 days 10-5*

Former All Saints winemaker Andrew Sutherland-Smith has leased a small winery at Corowa to make the Warrabilla wines from a four-hectare vineyard developed by himself and Carol Smith in the Indigo Valley. The reds and in particular the Durif and the Shiraz, have reached cult status, selling out well before the release of the following vintage.

# Glenrowan

The advent of the GI legislation has seen the division of northeast Victoria into five regions: Rutherglen, Glenrowan, King Valley, Alpine Valleys, and Beechworth. The first two walk together (as do the last two), for Glenrowan is every bit as famous for its Muscats and its Tokays as Rutherglen. It is no less renowned for its red wine. The special features of Glenrowan, which do legitimately differentiate it from Rutherglen, are the deep red, friable soils and the tempering climatic influence of Lake Mokoan. The key Glenrowan producer is Baileys, a somewhat ill-fitting outpost of the Beringer Blass wine empire (in near-identical fashion to Morris's place in the Orlando Wyndham group). In each case their corporate masters have, by and large, left well alone. There are five wine producers in the region.

**Auldstone** ☆☆☆

*Booths Road, Taminick via Glenrowan, Vic 3675, ☎ (03) 5766 2237, ⓕ (03) 5766*
*2131; est 1987; ⚱ 2,000 cases; ⓨ; A$; Thurs-Sat & school hols 9-5, Sun 10-5*

Michael and Nancy Reid have restored the century-old stone winery and replanted the largely abandoned twenty-six-hectare vineyard that surrounds it and produce a wide range of table and fortified wines.

**Baileys of Glenrowan** ☆☆☆☆

*Corner Taminick Gap Road and Upper Taminick Road, Glenrowan, Vic 3675,*
*☎ (03) 5766 2392, ⓕ (03) 5766 2596; est 1870; ⚱ 15,000 cases; ⓨ; A$;*
*Mon-Fri 9-5, wkds 10-5; museum*

Baileys of Glenrowan is part of the Beringer Blass empire, but, thankfully, it is left pretty much to its own devices. Ripe, black-cherry 1920s Block Shiraz impressively heads the list of table wines, the Founder Tokay, Muscat, and Port are reliably good fortifieds. Exports to the UK and New Zealand.

**Goorambath** ☆☆☆☆
*103 Hooper Road, Goorambat, Vic 3725, ☎ (03) 5764 1380, Ⓕ (03) 5764 1320; est 1997; ♦ 600 cases; ♀; A$; by appt*
Professional viticulturists Lyn and Geoff Bath have demonstrated their expertise by selecting and planting this small vineyard. Inky Shiraz and fruit-salad Verdelho both impress.

**Taminick Cellars** ☆☆☆⚘
*Booth Road, Taminick, Vic 3675, ☎ (03) 5766 2282, Ⓕ (03) 5766 2151; est 1904; ♦ 4,000 cases; ♀; A$; Mon-Sat 9-5, Sun 10-5*
Traditional producer of massively flavoured and very long-lived red wines, most sold to long-term customers and through cellar door. Premium Shiraz and Special Release Cabernet Sauvignon are the pick of the table wines.

**Warby Range Estate** ☆☆☆☆⚘ **V**
*Jones Road, Taminick via Glenrowan, Vic 3675, ☎ (03) 5765 2314; est 1989; ♦ 500 cases; ♀; A$; Thurs-Mon 10-5, or by appt*
Starting as contract grape-growers in 1989, in 1996 Ralph and Margaret Judd made their first barrel of wine, and have now moved to opening a small cellar-door sales facility. The Shiraz and Durif are monumental in flavour and depth, in best Glenrowan tradition, and will richly repay extended cellaring.

# King Valley

Vineyard altitudes range from 150 to 630 metres, creating a spread of climate, ranging from very warm (similar to Rutherglen) to very cool (similar to Macedon). It is a beautiful region, blessed by its deep, rich soils. In 1970, two farmers (of Anglo-Saxon descent) decided to diversify into grape production: John Levigny at Meadow Creek and Guy Darling at Koombahla. Thereafter, the number of grape-growers (mainly Italian) grew exponentially until 1989, as did tonnage. Yet there was only one purchaser: Brown Brothers had made the area its fiefdom. The informal exclusivity broke in 1989 and now King Valley grapes are used in wines made as far afield as the Hunter and Barossa valleys. A large winery, Miranda, was built at the end of the 1990s; all the others (other than the long-established Brown Bros) are small.

Chardonnay and Riesling are the most widely planted white grapes, and Cabernet Sauvignon heads a contingent of all the main red varieties. The two areas in which the King Valley can excel are with sparkling wines and the principal Italian varieties: Nebbiolo, Sangiovese, and Barbera. With the qualified exception of sparkling wine, the best results will come from growers who take steps to control the usually prolific yields. They cannot afford to become mountain cousins of the traditional Riverland growers. There are nineteen wine producers in the region.

**Avalon Vineyard** ☆☆☆☆⚘
*RMB 9556 Whitfield Road, Wangaratta, Vic 3678, ☎ (03) 5729 3629, Ⓕ (03) 5729 3635; est 1981; ♦ 1,000 cases; ♀; A$; 7 days 10-5*
Much of the production from the ten-hectare vineyard is sold, with limited quantities made by Doug Groom, a graduate of Roseworthy, and one of Avalon's owners.

**Boggy Creek Vineyards** ☆☆☆✓

*1657 Boggy Creek Road, Myrrhee, Vic 3732, ☎ (03) 5729 7587, Ⓕ (03) 5729 7600; est 1978; ⊛ NA; ⚑; A$; by appt*

Graeme and Maggie Ray started their vineyard as a hobby in 1978; it is a hobby no more, with thirty hectares planted on northeast-facing slopes at an altitude of 350 metres. A Barbera/Sangiovese is the pick of the vinified production (most is sold as grapes).

**Brown Brothers** ☆☆☆☆ V

*Snow Road, Milawa, Vic 3678, ☎ (03) 5720 5500, Ⓕ (03) 5720 5511; est 1885; ⊛ 790,000 cases; ⚑; A$; 7 days 9-5; epicurean centre; playground*

Deservedly one of the most successful family wineries in Australia, drawing on vineyards spread throughout a range of climates, varying according to altitude from very warm to very cool. It is also known for the diversity of grape varieties with which it works. It has the most successful cellar-door operation in Australia today. Worldwide distribution.

**Dal Zotto Wines** ☆☆☆✓

*1944 Edi Road, Cheshunt, Vic 3678, ☎ (03) 5729 8321, Ⓕ (03) 5729 8490; est 1987; ⊛ 10,000 cases; ⚑; A$; 7 days 11-5*

Remains a contract grape-grower, with almost twenty-six hectares of vineyards including plantings of Sangiovese and Barbera, but makes increasing quantities of tidy Riesling, Chardonnay, and Shiraz.

**Pizzini** ☆☆☆☆ V

*King Valley Road, Wangaratta, Vic 3768, ☎ (03) 5729 8278, Ⓕ (03) 5729 8495; est 1980; ⊛ 12,000 cases; ⚑; A$; 7 days 12-5; ⚑; fishing, swimming*

Fred and Katrina Pizzini have been grape-growers in the King Valley for over twenty years, cultivating over sixty hectares of vineyard. Grape-growing still continues to be the major focus of activity, but their move into winemaking has been particularly successful, notably with Sangiovese.

**Symphonia Wines** ☆☆☆☆✓ V

*1699 Boggy Creek Road, Myrrhee, Vic 3732, ☎ (03) 5729 7519, Ⓕ (03) 5729 7519; est 1998; ⊛ 1,500 cases; ⚑; A$; by appt*

Peter Read is a veteran of the King Valley, first planting in 1981 to supply Brown Brothers. After subsequent trips to Western and Eastern Europe, the Symphonia wines offer a galaxy of varietals and blends which include Arneis, Saperavi, Tannat, Petit Manseng, and Tempranillo alongside classic varieties. These unusual varieties all work particularly well in the region, and are strongly recommended.

**Wood Park** ☆☆☆✓

*RMB 1139 Bobinawarrah-Whorouly Road, Milawa, Vic 3678, ☎ (03) 5727 3367, Ⓕ (03) 5727 3682; est 1989; ⊛ 4,000 cases; ⚑; A$; Wed-Mon 10-5 at Milawa Cheese Factory*

Grazier and farmer John Stokes diversified into grape-growing in 1989. He sells most of the grapes but makes a Chardonnay and Shiraz/Cabernet with the assistance of the exceptionally talented Rick Kinzbrunner. Pinot Gris and Kneebone's Gap Shiraz are the pick. Exports to the UK and elsewhere.

# Alpine Valleys

The battle to secure the name Alpine Valleys for the region was protracted and intense, and for a long time it seemed common sense might not prevail. But it did, and the name conveys an accurate sense of the often spectacular and beautiful mountain scenery with which the region has been blessed. The region consists of four river basins or valleys, created by the Ovens, Buffalo, Buckland, and Kiewa rivers, which have given rise to the application of the Kiewa River Valley and the Ovens Valley as sub-regions, leaving the more elevated Beechworth region as a region to the northeast.

The diversity of climate and of growing conditions within the region is wholly driven by altitude, ranging as it does between 150 metres (411 feet) and well over 300 metres (822 feet). So it is that full-bodied red wines are produced at the lowest levels – witness the once famous and now discontinued Wynns Ovens Valley Burgundy – with both style and the grape variety changing as the altitude increases. There are nine wine producers in the region.

### Boynton's ☆☆☆✦

*Great Alpine Road, Porepunkah, Vic 3741, ☎ (03) 5756 2356, Ⓕ (03) 5756 2610; est 1987; ⚱ 11,000 cases; ⚱; A$; 7 days 10-5; playground; garden; 𝒦*

Kel Boynton has a beautiful sixteen-hectare vineyard, framed by Mount Buffalo rising into the skies above it. Overall, the red wines have always outshone the whites. The initial very strong American oak input has been softened in more recent vintages to give a better fruit/oak balance. The Paiko label is for wines grown near Mildura by business partner and famed nurseryman Bruce Chalmers.

### Gapsted Wines ☆☆☆☆

*Great Alpine Road, Gapsted, Vic 3737, ☎ (03) 5751 1383, Ⓕ (03) 5751 1368; est 1997; ⚱ 14,000 cases; ⚱; A$; 7 days 10-5; 𝒦; light meals; amphitheatre*

The premier brand of the Victorian Alps Wine Co, the latter primarily a contract-crush facility for forty-eight growers in the King and Alpine valleys. The labels incorporate the "ballerina canopy" tag, a particular training method which is ideally suited to these regions. The quality is consistently good; look also for Petit Manseng, Saperavi, and Tempranillo varietal releases.

### Michelini Wines ☆☆☆

*Great Alpine Road, Myrtleford, Vic 3737, ☎ (03) 5751 1990, Ⓕ (03) 5751 1410; est 1982; ⚱ 5,000 cases; ⚱; A$; 7 days 10-5; 𝒦*

Italian-born tobacco farmers-turned-grape-growers, the Michelinis have forty-two hectares of vineyard established on terra rossa soil. Most of the production is sold, but since 1996 a large (1,000-tonne) on-site winery has seen the first wines made under the Michelini label. Here look for exotics such as Marzemino and Fragolino.

## Beechworth

Gold brought Beechworth into existence after its discovery in March 1852. The town was proclaimed the following year, and was built with gold. Perched precariously on a steep hillside, with streets plunging at precipitous and unexpected angles, its stone buildings and array of exotic (English) trees are a sight to behold in autumn. The first land sales took place in 1855, and the first vines were planted in 1856 by a Mr Rochlitz (who had obtained ninety-five varieties from Adelaide). Plantings reached their peak in 1891, but quickly dwindled thereafter to almost disappear by 1916. It was not until the early 1970s that commercial plantings recommenced and not until the last moment that Beechworth successfully sought registration as a Geographic Indication. Giaconda is the stellar wine producer, but the town of Beechworth, clinging precariously to the steep mountainside, is a tourist magnet, reaching its full glory when its exotic trees burst into a symphony of yellow, gold, orange, and red. There are twelve wine producers in the region.

### Amulet Vineyard ☆☆☆⚘

*Wangaratta Road, Beechworth, Vic 3747, ☎ (03) 5727 0420, Ⓕ (03) 5727 0421; est 1998; ⚘ 1,300 cases; ⚏; A$; Fri-Mon, public & school hols 10-5, or by appt*
Sue and Eric Thornton have planted a patchwork quilt four-hectare vineyard, with Sangiovese taking one hectare, the other varieties half a hectare or less; in descending order of magnitude are Barbera, Shiraz, Cabernet Sauvignon, Merlot, Nebbiolo, Orange Muscat, Pinot Gris, and Pinot Blanc.

### Castagna Vineyard ☆☆☆☆⚘

*Ressom Lane, Beechworth, Vic 3747, ☎ (03) 5728 2888, Ⓕ (03) 5728 2898; est 1997; ⚘ 2,000 cases; ⚏; A$; by appt*
The elegantly labelled and highly regarded wines of Castagna come from four hectares of estate Shiraz and Viognier. Winemaker Julian Castagna is intent on making wines which reflect the terroir as closely as possible, declining to use cultured yeast or filtration. Genesis Syrah deserves its cult status. Exports to the UK and elsewhere.

### Giaconda ☆☆☆☆☆

*McClay Road, Beechworth, Vic 3747, ☎ (03) 5727 0246, Ⓕ (03) 5727 0246; est 1985; ⚘ 2,000 cases; by appt*
Rick Kinzbrunner makes wines that command a super-cult status. Given the tiny production, this makes them extremely difficult to find; they are sold chiefly through restaurants and mail order. All have a cosmopolitan edge, as befits Kinzbrunner's international winemaking experience. The Chardonnay, often with slightly feral Burgundian overtones, is regarded by many as Australia's best, the 1996 a masterpiece. Exports to the UK and elsewhere.

### Pennyweight Winery ☆☆☆

*Pennyweight Lane, Beechworth, Vic 3747, ☎ (03) 5728 1747, Ⓕ (03) 5728 1704; est 1982; ⚘ 1,000 cases; ⚏; A$; 7 days 10-5; ✗*
Established by Stephen Morris (and wife Elizabeth), great-grandson of GF Morris, founder of Morris Wines. The three hectares of vines are not irrigated, and are organically grown.

### Sorrenberg ☆☆☆⚘

*Alma Road, Beechworth, Vic 3747, ☎ (03) 5728 2278, Ⓕ (03) 5728 2278; est 1986; ⚘ 1,200 cases; ⚏; A$; Mon-Fri by appt, most wkds 1-5 by appt*
Barry and Jan Morey made their first wines in 1989 from the 2.5-hectare vineyard on the outskirts of Beechworth. Wine quality has improved steadily since the early days, with a particular following for the Chardonnay and Gamay. Some, indeed, would accord it a higher rating.

# Gippsland

This is one of the most far-flung and climatically diverse of all Victoria's regions. Indeed, it is both a Zone and region, and it seems only a matter of time before it divides itself into sub-regions. Phillip Jones of Bass Phillip believes there are six climatically distinct sub-regions, but most content themselves with three: east, west, and south. South Gippsland is the coolest and wettest, similar to Burgundy and the Loire Valley. It has proved itself absolutely ideal for Pinot Noir and excellent for Chardonnay. West Gippsland is drier and a little warmer than either the south or east, and periodic droughts make irrigation essential. East Gippsland has a more Mediterranean climate, with lower rainfall again making irrigation highly desirable. Its weather patterns are complex, some coming from the north, others moving in from the west. It is capable of producing spectacularly rich Chardonnay from its generally low-yielding vineyards, provided botrytis is kept at bay. Although centred on Pinot Noir and Chardonnay, the Gippsland wines extend across the full range of styles from Sauvignon Blanc to Bordeaux blends. The regional style is one of richness and robustness, with the exception of some elegant and fine Pinot Noirs. There are thirty-seven wine producers in the region.

### Ada River ☆☆☆☆

*2330 Main Road, Neerim South, Vic 3831, ☎ (03) 5628 1661, Ⓕ (03) 5628 1661; est 1983; ⚗ 2,000 cases; ⚐; A$; wkds & public hols 10-6*

The Kelliher family has effectively reinvented Ada River, with two Gippsland vineyards (the Chardonnay is excellent) and one in Heathcote replacing the Yarra Valley. The Heathcote-sourced Shiraz and Cabernet Sauvignon are intensely rich, typical of the region.

### Bass Phillip ☆☆☆☆☆

*Tosch's Road, Leongatha South, Vic 3953, ☎ (03) 5664 3341, Ⓕ (03) 5664 3209; est 1979; ⚗ 1,500 cases; ⚐; A$; by appt*

Phillip Jones has retired from the Melbourne rat-race to hand-craft tiny quantities of superlative Pinot Noir which, at its finest, has no equal in Australia. Painstaking site selection, ultra-close vine spacing, and the very, very cool climate of south Gippsland are the keys to the magic of Bass Phillip and its eerily Burgundian Pinots. Exports to the UK and elsewhere.

### Caledonia Australis ☆☆☆☆☆

*PO Box 54, Abbotsford, Vic 3067, ☎ (03) 9416 4156, Ⓕ (03) 9416 4157; est NA; ⚗ NA; no visitors*

The reclusive Caledonia Australis is a Pinot Noir and Chardonnay specialist, with a total of eighteen hectares planted to Chardonnay and Pinot Noir in three separate vineyard locations. The Chardonnay is superb, with great texture and balance, with an eye cocked at Burgundy.

### Cannibal Creek Vineyard ☆☆☆☆

*260 Tynong North Road, Tynong North, Vic 3813, ☎ (03) 5942 8380, Ⓕ (03) 5942 8202; est 1997; ⚗ 1,600 cases; ⚐; A$; 7 days 11-5; local gourmet produce*

The Hardiker family began plantings in 1997, using organically based cultivation methods. A heritage shed built from locally milled timber has been converted into a winery and small cellar-door facility. Chardonnay, Sauvignon Blanc, Merlot, and Cabernet Sauvignon are all commendable.

### Chestnut Hill Vineyard ☆☆☆☆

*1280 Pakenham Road, Mount Burnett, Vic 3781, ☎ (03) 5942 7314, Ⓕ (03) 5942 7314; est 1995; ⚗ 1,200 cases; ⚐; A$; wkds & public hols 10.30-5.30, or by appt*

Charlie and Ivka Javor started Chestnut Hill in 1985 and have slowly increased the vineyards to their present total of a little over three hectares of Chardonnay, Sauvignon Blanc, and Pinot Noir. All three wines are fine-boned and elegant.

**Jinks Creek Winery** ☆☆☆☆⁴
*Tonimbuk Road, Tonimbuk, Vic 3815, ☎ (03) 5629 8502, Ⓕ (03) 5629 8551;*
*est 1981; ⬥ 1,000 cases; ⚑; A$; by appt*
The 2.5-hectare vineyard borders on the evocatively named Bunyip State
Park. Andrew Clarke completed the on-site winery in 1992: the eclectic
collection of wines is headed by Gippsland Shiraz, Gippsland Pinot Noir,
Heathcote Shiraz, and Yarra Valley Shiraz.

**Kouark Vineyard** ☆☆☆⁴
*300 Thompson Road, Drouhin South, Vic 3818, ☎ & Ⓕ (03) 5627 6337; est 1997;*
*⬥ 1,000 cases; ⚑; A$; wkds 12-5*
Dairy farmers Phil and Jane Gray have diversified into viticulture and
grape-growing, doing it all themselves via Charles Sturt University
courses. Both Pinot Noir and Shiraz hold much promise for the future.

**Lyre Bird Hill** ☆☆☆
*370 Inverloch Road, Koonwarra, Vic 3954, ☎ (03) 5664 3204, Ⓕ (03) 5664 3206;*
*est 1986; ⬥ 2,000 cases; ⚑; A$; wkds & public hols 10-5, or by appt; ⇥*
Former Melbourne professionals Owen and Robyn Schmidt run a
combined winemaking and bed-and-breakfast business. Pinot Noir has
been the most successful wine to date, with varietal character in a
sappy/tomato style that will appeal to some.

**Moondarra** ☆☆☆⁴
*Browns Road, Moondarra, Vic 3825, ☎ (03) 9598 3049, Ⓕ (03) 9598 0677;*
*est 1991; ⬥ NA; no visitors*
A Pinot Noir specialist using organic, estate-grown grapes from Gippsland
and also from Whitlands at the top of the King Valley, whence its Pinot Gris
also comes. Ambitious winemaking doesn't always pay off.

**Narkoojee** ☆☆☆☆ V
*170 Francis Road, Glengarry, Vic 3854, ☎ (03) 5192 4257, Ⓕ (03) 5192 4257;*
*est 1981; ⬥ 1,500 cases; ⚑; A$; 10-4 by appt*
The four-hectare vineyard is near the old gold-mining town of Walhalla.
Harry Friend was an amateur winemaker of note before turning to
commercial winemaking with Narkoojee. His skills show through in the
elegant, well-balanced Chardonnay, Merlot, and Cabernets. Exports to the
UK and elsewhere.

**Nicholson River** ☆☆☆☆
*Liddells Road, Nicholson, Vic 3882, ☎ (03) 5156 8241, Ⓕ (03) 5156 8433;*
*est 1978; ⬥ 3,000 cases; ⚑; A$; 7 days 10-4 by appt*
The fierce commitment to quality in the face of the temperamental
Gippsland climate and frustratingly small production has been repaid by
some massive Chardonnays. Ken Eckersley does not refer to these as
white wines, but as gold wines, and you understand why. Recent success
with Merlot and The Nicholson (Merlot/Shiraz).

**Phillip Island Vineyard** ☆☆☆☆⁴
*Berrys Beach Road, Phillip Island, Vic, ☎ (03) 5956 8465, Ⓕ (03) 5956 8465;*
*est 1993; ⬥ 3,500 cases; ⚑; A$; Nov-March 7 days 11-7, April-Oct 7 days 11-5;*
*lunch platters*
When the Lance family planted the first vines on Phillip Island, it was well
known for its penguins and motor-bike races. Now there is the remarkable
sight of a permanently enclosed 2.5-hectare vineyard. The netting provides
protection against both wind and birds. Sauvignon Blanc, Chardonnay,
Pinot Noir, Merlot, and Cabernet Sauvignon are all delicately refined but
impressive. Pinot Noir and Chardonnay are the pick.

**Sarsfield Estate** ☆☆☆½

*345 Duncan Road, Sarsfield, Vic 3875, ☏ (03) 5156 8962, Ⓕ (03) 5156 8970; est 1995; ❖ 1,000 cases; 🍷; A$; by appt*

Owned by Swiss-born Peter Albrecht and Suzanne Rutschmann, who has a PhD in chemistry, a diploma in horticulture, and a BSc (wine science) from Charles Sturt University. Deceptively light, savoury/foresty Pinot Noir is now the best.

**Tanjil** ☆☆☆☆

*11 Brigantine Court, Patterson Lakes, Vic 3197, ☏ & Ⓕ (03) 9773 0378; est 2001; ❖ 1,200 cases; no visitors*

Robert Hewet and Olga Garot planted three hectares of Pinot Noir and one hectare of Pinot Grigio on a north-facing slope at an altitude of 200 metres between the Latrobe and Tanjil valleys. The red-brown loam over clay has good water retention, and the vines have not been nor will be irrigated, with an expected yield of only five tonnes per hectare. The Pinot Noir promises much.

**Wild Dog** ☆☆☆

*South Road, Warragul, Vic 3820, ☏ (03) 5623 1117, Ⓕ (03) 5623 6402; est 1982; ❖ 3,000 cases; 🍷; A$; 7 days 9-5; music/theatre events*

An aptly named winery, which produces somewhat rustic wines from the 12 hectares of estate vineyards. Even winemaker John Farrington says that the Shiraz comes "with a bite", also pointing out that there is minimal handling, fining, and filtration. However, the Shiraz has considerable breed. Exports to the UK and elsewhere.

**Wyanga Park** ☆☆½

*Baades Road, Lakes Entrance, Vic 3909, ☏ (03) 5155 1508, Ⓕ (03) 5155 1443; est 1970; ❖ 3,000 cases; 🍷; A$; 7 days 9-5; boat cruises; art gallery*

Offers a broad range of wines of diverse provenance directed at the tourist trade; one of the Chardonnays and the Cabernet Sauvignon are estate-grown. Winery cruises are scheduled four days a week.

## Murray Darling and Swan Hill

The Murray River, Australia's answer to the Mississippi, is the umbilical cord that joins the largest vineyard plantings of New South Wales, Victoria, and South Australia in an area often called the Riverlands. The water of the Murray River has transformed the parched red sand and stunted growth of this region. Viticulture is an important, but by no means dominant, part of this miraculously transformed landscape.

The Murray Darling and Swan Hill regions together form a vast area extending from Mildura in the west and Swan Hill in the east. Together they are responsible for growing almost forty per cent of the annual Australian grape crush. This is the industrial face of winemaking, efficient and economical. The vineyards are vast, the wineries more like refineries; costs are kept under rigid control. As the new millennium unfolds, so does a major challenge to the economy of the Murray Darling, Swan Hill, and South Australia's Riverlands regions. Only seventeen years ago, two-thirds of the grapes used to make Australia's wine were multi-purpose – for winemaking, drying (sultanas), or fresh table grapes. Obviously, a large volume of the grapes then went to winemaking. However, there has been a continuing annual decrease in the tonnage of multi-purpose grapes used for winemaking. This is simply because of the avalanche of premium

Chardonnay, Shiraz, and Cabernet Sauvignon (and the other classic vinifera varieties) to come from the 80,000 hectares of new vineyard plantings in Australia between 1995 and 2003. It remains to be seen how the Riverlands adapts both its viticultural and agricultural means of income to this changing scene. There are twenty-nine wine producers in the region.

### Andrew Peace Wines ☆☆☆ V

*Murray Valley Highway, Piangil, Vic 3597, ☎ (03) 5030 5291, Ⓕ (03) 5030 5605; est 1995; ♦ 300,000 cases; ♀; A$; Mon-Fri 8-5, Sat 10-4, Sun by appt; Ⲕ*

The Peace family has been a major Swan Hill grape-grower since 1980 and moved into winemaking with a A$3 million winery in 1997. The modestly priced wines are aimed at the export market, including the UK. The quality of the wines is consistently good.

### Brumby Wines ☆☆☆♩

*Sandyanna, 24 Cannon Lane, Wood Wood, Vic 3596, ☎ 0438 305 364, Ⓕ (03) 5030 5366; est 2001; ♦ 3,500 cases; ♀; A$; Mon-Fri 9-5*

The derivation of the name is even more direct and simple than you might imagine: the owners are Stuart and Liz Brumby, who decided to plant grapes for supply to others before moving to having an increasing portion of their production from the fifteen hectares of Chardonnay, Cabernet Sauvignon, Shiraz, and Durif contract-made under their own label.

### Bullers Beverford ☆☆♩ V

*Murray Valley Highway, Beverford (Swan Hill), Vic 3590, ☎ (03) 5037 6305, Ⓕ (03) 5037 6803; est 1951; ♦ 50,000 cases; ♀; A$; Mon-Sat 9-5*

Traditional wines that, in the final analysis, reflect both their Riverlands origin and a fairly low-key approach to style in the winery. However, there can be no argument about the low prices. Exports to the UK and elsewhere.

### Deakin Estate ☆☆☆ V

*Kulkyne Way, via Red Cliffs (Murray Darling), Vic 3496, ☎ (03) 5029 1666, Ⓕ (03) 5024 3316; est 1980; ♦ 500,000 cases; no visitors*

This is the sharp end of the wine empire owned by the Yunghanns family, consistently producing excellent Chardonnay, Shiraz, and Merlot at two price and quality levels (Select is best). Both offer outstanding value. Worldwide distribution.

### Evans & Tate Salisbury ☆☆☆ V

*Campbell Avenue Irymple, Vic 3498, ☎ (03) 5024 6800, Ⓕ (03) 5024 6605; est 1977; ♦ NFP; ♀; A$; Mon-Sat 10-4.30, Sun 12-4*

This is the former Milburn Park winery. The positions of the Salisbury and Milburn brands have been reversed, with Salisbury now the senior, the re-launched Milburn Park label, sold at cellar door and export only, part of the Salisbury production. Exports to the UK and elsewhere.

### Lindemans (Karadoc) ☆☆☆ V

*Edey Road, Karadoc via Red Cliffs (Murray Darling), Vic 3496, ☎ (03) 5051 3333, Ⓕ (03) 5051 3390; est 1974; ♦ 8 million cases; ♀; A$; 7 days 10-4.30*

Now the centre for all of the Lindemans and Leo Buring wines, with the exception of some super-premiums. Bin 65 remains one of the world's leading Chardonnays in volume (and value) terms; Bin 50 Shiraz and Bin 45 Cabernet Sauvignon also good. Clever landscaping imparts a friendly welcome to visitors. Worldwide distribution.

### Nursery Ridge Estate ☆☆☆ V

*Calder Highway, Red Cliffs, Vic 3496, ☎ (03) 5024 3311, Ⓕ (03) 5024 3311; est 1999; ♦ 1,100 cases; ♀; A$; by appt*

The estate takes its name from the fact that it is situated on the site of the original vine nursery at Red Cliffs. It is a family-owned and -operated affair; the well-priced wines are usually well-made, with greater richness and depth of fruit flavour than most other wines from the region, the Petit Verdot in particular.

**Roberts Estate Wines** ☆☆☆
*Game Street, Merbein (Murray Darling), Vic 3505, ☎ (03) 5024 2944, Ⓕ (03) 5024 2877; est 1998; ♦ 100,000; no visitors*
A very large winery acting as a processing point for grapes grown up and down the Murray River. Over 10,000 tonnes are crushed each vintage. Much of the wine is sold in bulk to others, but some is exported under the Denbeigh and Commissioners Block labels. Exports to the UK and elsewhere.

**Robinvale** ☆☆☆
*Sea Lake Road, Robinvale (Murray Darling), Vic 3549, ☎ (03) 5026 3955, Ⓕ (03) 5026 1123; est 1976; ♦ 10,000 cases; ♗; A$; Mon-Fri 9-6, Sun 1-6; playground*
Was the first winery in Australia to be fully accredited with the Biodynamic Agricultural Association of Australia. Most, but not all, of the wines are produced from organically grown grapes, some are preservative-free. Production has increased dramatically, reflecting the interest in organic and biodynamic viticulture and winemaking. Exports to the UK and elsewhere.

**Tall Poppy** ☆☆☆
*PO Box 4147, Mildura, Vic 3502, ☎ (03) 5022 7255, Ⓕ (03) 5022 7250; est 1997; ♦ 20,000 cases; ♗; A$; 7 days 8.30-5*
In its infancy as a wine brand, but with lofty ambitions of an ultimate production level of up to 400,000 cases, drawn from 170 hectares of vineyards owned by its directors. Exports to the UK and elsewhere.

**Trentham Estate** ☆☆☆☆ V
*Sturt Highway, Trentham Cliffs, NSW 2738, ☎ (03) 5024 8888, Ⓕ (03) 5024 8800; est 1988; ♦ 65,000 cases; ♗; A$; 7 days 9.30-5; ⦿; ✗*
Consistent tasting notes across all wine styles since 1989 attest to the expertise of ex-Mildara winemaker Tony Murphy, now making the Trentham wines from his family vineyards. The quality/price ratio is exceptional; the restaurant is also recommended. Exports to the UK and elsewhere.

**Zilzie Wines** ☆☆☆☆ V
*Lot 66, Kulkyne Way, Karadoc via Red Cliffs, Vic 3496, ☎ (03) 5025 8100, Ⓕ (03) 5025 8116; est 1999; ♦ NFP; no visitors*
The Forbes family has been farming Zilzie Estate since 1911; the most recent diversification being 250 hectares of vines and a multi-function, 16,000-tonne winery. Branded wine production is projected to increase to 250,000 cases by 2006. New, trendy grape varieties are represented in a three-tiered portfolio, with Buloke Reserve at the bottom, Zilzie Estates in the middle, and Zilzie Show Reserve at the top. Exports to the UK and elsewhere.

# Central Victoria Zone

While the jigsaw map of Victoria may seem complete at first glance, there are gaps. In this instance, there is a substantial area to the north of the Bendigo region (and west of the Goulburn Valley) in which Gentle Annie and Tallis Wines are to be found. Pretty Sally Estate is in an enclave at the southern end, in a radically cooler climate, yet neither in Macedon nor Bendigo. There are five wine producers in the Zone.

**Gentle Annie** ☆☆☆☆✦

*455 Nalinga Road, Dookie, Vic 3646, ☎ 0408 028 201, Ⓕ (03) 9670 8085; est 1997; ✦ 8,000 cases; ⛉; A$; by appt*

This sixty-eight-hectare vineyard was established by Melbourne businessman Tony Cotter, together with wife Anne and five daughters assisting with sales and marketing. The name Gentle Annie was that of an early settler renowned for her beauty and gentle temperament. It is planted on old volcanic ferrosol soils, similar to the red Cambrian loam at Heathcote. It has hitherto sold the major part of its grape production, winning the Brown Brothers Grower of the Year title for the last two vintages. The increasing production of Gentle Annie wines has a substantial export component, likely to grow in the future.

**Pretty Sally Estate** ☆☆☆☆

*PO Box 549, Kilmore East, Vic 3764, ☎ +1 650 851 8662, Ⓕ +1 650 851 1868; est 1996; ✦ 900 cases; no visitors*

The McKay, Davies, and Cornew families have joined to create the Pretty Sally business. It is based on estate plantings of 11.7 hectares of Shiraz, 23.8 hectares of Cabernet Sauvignon, and a splash of Sauvignon Blanc. The vineyard is still coming into production, the first commercial vintage being made in 2001. The wines are made by industry veteran John Ellis and are chiefly exported to the US, where Pretty Sally has a permanent office.

**Tallis Wines** ☆☆☆☆✦

*PO Box 10, Dookie, Vic 3646, ☎ (03) 5823 5383, Ⓕ (03) 5828 6532; est 2000; ✦ 2,000 cases; no visitors*

Richard, Mark, and Alice Tallis have a substantial vineyard, with sixteen hectares of Shiraz, five hectares of Cabernet Sauvignon, two hectares of Viognier, and one hectare of Merlot. While most of the grapes are sold, they have embarked on winemaking with the aid of consultant Gary Baldwin, and have done so with considerable success.

# Port Phillip Zone

Centred as it is around Melbourne, and with five fully fledged regions falling within its boundaries, there are a surprising number of chinks, evidenced by the six producers which do not qualify for any of those five regions.

**Brunswick Hill Wines NR**

*34 Breese Street, Brunswick, Vic 3056, ☎ (03) 9383 4681, Ⓕ (03) 9386 5699; est 1999; ✦ NA; ⛉; A$; by appt*

Peter Atkins and Graeme Rojo are partners in the Brunswick Hill Wines venture, which is claimed to be Melbourne's only urban winery, fifteen minutes from the CBD. Studley Park Vineyard (q.v.) is even closer, but its grapes are sent to Granite Hills for winemaking. The ability to open the winery where it is doubtless reflects Peter Atkins' background as an environmental and urban planner, taking grapes from the Yarra Valley and elsewhere.

**Patterson Lakes Estate** ☆☆☆☆

*Riverend Road, Bangholme, Vic 3175, ☎ (03) 9773 1034, Ⓕ (03) 9772 5634; est 1998; ✦ NA; no visitors*

Former property developer James Bate has followed in the footsteps of the late Sid Hamilton (who established Leconfield in Coonawarra when he was eighty). The eight-hectare vineyard is a Joseph's Coat of many varieties, Pinot Noir and Shiraz leading the way. A small winery was completed for the 2004 vintage, with Bill Christophersen as consultant winemaker.

### Rojo Wines NR

*34 Breese Street, Brunswick, Vic 3056, ☎ (03) 9383 4681, Ⓕ (03) 9386 5699; est 1999; ♦ NA; ⚱; by appt*

Graeme Rojo is a biochemistry graduate who worked in the marketing area post-graduation, while home winemaking for over twenty years. In 1999 he finally moved to establish his own label while working as assistant winemaker at Brunswick Hill Wines. Here the focus is on Nebbiolo, Sangiovese, and Dolcetto.

### Studley Park Vineyard ☆☆☆☆

*5 Garden Terrace, Kew, Vic 3101, ☎ (03) 9254 2777, Ⓕ (03) 9254 2535; est 1994; ♦ 250 cases; no visitors*

Geoff Pryor's Studley Park Vineyard is one of Melbourne's best-kept secrets. It is situated on a bend of the Yarra River barely four kilometres from the Melbourne CBD on a half-hectare block once planted to vines, but for a century used for market gardening until replanted with Cabernet Sauvignon. A spectacular aerial photograph shows how immediately across the river, and looking directly to the CBD, is the epicentre of Melbourne's light industrial development, while on the northern and eastern boundaries are suburban residential blocks. Because of zoning restrictions most sales take place directly over the internet from the website (www.studleypark.com).

### Toomah Wines NR

*"Seven Oaks", 635 Toomuc Valley Road, Pakenham, Vic 3810, ☎ & Ⓕ (03) 5942 7583; est 1996; ♦ 2,000 cases; ⚱; A$; wkds 11-6, or by appt*

Toomah Wines is owned and managed by Matt and Michelle Robinson; the 6.5 hectares of vineyards have been planted on Matt's parents' historically important 226-hectare grazing property. Various historic buildings on the property are being restored, one serving as the winery, the other the cellar door.

### Woongarra Estate ☆☆☆☆

*95 Hayseys Road, Narre Warren East, Vic 3804, ☎ (03) 9796 8886, Ⓕ (03) 9796 8580; est 1992; ♦ 2,000 cases; ⚱; A$; Thurs-Sun by appt*

Dr Bruce Jones, and wife Mary, purchased their Narre Warren East sixteen-hectare property many years ago; it falls within the Yarra Ranges Shire Council's jurisdiction and is zoned "Landscape", but because nearby Cardinia Creek does not flow into the Yarra River, it is not within the Yarra Valley wine region. Sauvignon Blanc and – importantly – Pinot Noir (under the Three Wise Men label) are the wines to look for.

## Western Victoria Zone

The majority of the wineries are situated around the famous gold-mining city of Ballarat, one of the tourism showpieces of the state. It is also known as one of the coldest areas, frequently mentioned in the daily television weather reports for Victoria. Although there are ten wine producers (twice the number needed for registration as a GI), the area under vine is insufficient, and the challenges provided by the climate are such that any expansion in plantings will be slow. In addition, there are the two outlying producers – Empress Vineyard and Red Rock Winery – with no regional ascription.

### Chepstowe Vineyard ☆☆☆⅟

*Fitzpatricks Lane, Carngham, Vic 3351, ☎ (03) 5344 9412, Ⓕ (03) 5344 9403; est 1994; ⅌ 700 cases; ⚱; A$; 7 days 10-5; ⊨*

The ultra-cool climate means that Chardonnay and Pinot Noir can only produce table wine in the warmest vintages; otherwise they head towards sparkling-wine use.

### Dulcinea ☆☆☆⅟

*Jubilee Road, Sulky, Ballarat, Vic 3352, ☎ (03) 5334 6440, Ⓕ (03) 5334 6828; est 1983; ⅌ 3,000 cases; ⚱; A$; 7 days 10-6*

Rod Stott is a part-time but passionate grape-grower. With winemaking help from various sources, he has produced a series of very interesting and often complex wines.

### Eastern Peake NR

*Clunes Road, Coghills Creek, Vic 3364, ☎ (03) 5343 4245, Ⓕ (03) 5343 4365; est 1983; ⅌ 3,000 cases; ⚱; A$; 7 days 10-5*

Over fifteen years ago Norm Latta and Di Pym established 4.5 hectares of Chardonnay and Pinot Noir. They now make austere, cool-climate wines. Exports to the UK.

### Empress Vineyard ☆☆☆⅟

*Drapers Road, Irrewarra, Vic 3250 (postal Amberley House, 391 Sandy Bay Road, Hobart, Tas 7005), ☎ (03) 6225 1005, Ⓕ (03) 6225 0639; est 1998; ⅌ 1,000 cases; ⚱; A$; by appt*

If the address of Empress and its Zone seem schizophrenic, don't be alarmed. Allistair Lindsay is in the course of moving to Tasmania while seeking to re-establish both restaurant and vineyard/winemaking near Hobart. It is uncertain whether both vineyard operations will be kept going in tandem; the quality of the wines from the existing Empress Vineyard must tempt Lindsay to maintain the operation.

### Mount Beckworth ☆☆☆

*RMB 915 Learmonth Road, Tourello via Ballarat, Vic 3363, ☎ & Ⓕ (03) 5343 4207; est 1984; ⅌ 1,000 cases; ⚱; A$; wkds 10-6, or by appt*

This place has a near-identical history to Eastern Peake, moving from grape-growing to winemaking (at Best's) and, again like Eastern Peake, producing quite lean wines.

### Mount Coghill Vineyard ☆☆☆☆

*Clunes-Learmonth Road, Coghills Creek, Vic 3364, ☎ (03) 5343 4329; est 1993; ⅌ 200 cases; ⚱; A$; wkds 10-5*

Ian and Margaret Pym began the development of their tiny vineyard in 1995 with the planting of 1,280 Pinot Noir rootlings, adding 450 Chardonnay rootlings the next year. The first commercial vintage was 2001, followed by an excellent Chardonnay in 2002, a fine achievement given the particularly cool growing season that year.

### Norton Estate ☆☆☆⅟

*Plush Hannan Road, Lower Norton, Vic 3400, ☎ & Ⓕ (03) 5384 8235; est 1997; ⅌ 600 cases; ⚱; A$; 7 days 10-4*

Donald Spence worked for the Victorian Department of Forests for thirty-six years before retiring. In 1996 he and his family purchased a farm at Lower Norton, and instead of following the regional wool, meat, and wheat farming, trusted their instincts in planting vines on the lateritic buckshot soil. The vineyard is six kilometres northwest of the Grampians GI, and will have to be content with the Western Victoria Zone until a sufficient number of others follow suit and plant on the 1,000 or so hectares of suitable soil in the area. The quality of the wines is encouragement enough.

### Red Rock Winery NR

*Red Rock Reserve Road, Alvie, Vic 3249, ☎ & ⓕ (03) 5234 8382; est 1981; 5,000 cases; ⚑; A$; 7 days 10-5; ⧉*

The former Barongvale Estate, which has progressively established ten hectares of Sauvignon Blanc, Semillon, Pinot Noir, and Shiraz; a part-time occupation for Rohan Little, with wines sold under both the Red Rock and Otway Vineyards labels. It takes its new name from the now dormant Red Rock volcano, which created the lakes and craters of the Western Districts when it last erupted, eight thousand years ago. The winery café opened in early 2002.

### Yellowglen ☆☆☆⟡

*Whites Road, Smythesdale, Vic 3351, ☎ (03) 5342 8617, ⓕ (03) 5333 7102; est 1976; 420,000 cases; ⚑; A$; Mon-Fri 10-5, wkds 11-5*

Just as the overall quality of Australian sparkling wine has improved out of all recognition over the past fifteen years, so has that of Yellowglen. Initially the quality lift was apparent at the top end of the range but now extends right to the non-vintage commercial releases. Exports to the UK and elsewhere.

# South Australia

1994     27,447 hectares     40.93 per cent of total plantings
2003     66,654 hectares     42.32 per cent of total plantings
South Australia is re-asserting itself as the "Wine State"; and if grape tonnage for winemaking is the measure, it did in fact produce over forty-six per cent of the national grape crush in 2003.

## Barossa Valley

The Barossa Valley continues to be at the heart of Australia's wine industry. Past, present, and future are inextricably bound here. The essence of the valley is all around you. There are the patches of bush-pruned vines, many

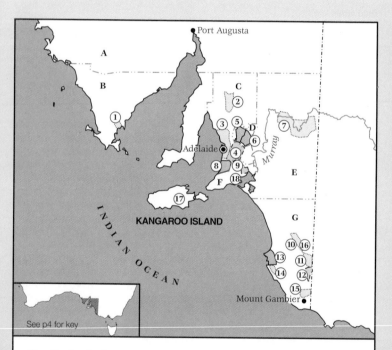

See p4 for key

## South Australia

| | | | | | |
|---|---|---|---|---|---|
| A | Far North | 1 | Port Lincoln | 10 | Padthaway |
| B | The Peninsulas | 2 | Clare Valley | 11 | Koppamurra |
| C | Mt Lofty Ranges | 3 | Adelaide Plains | 12 | Coonawarra |
| | and Adelaide | 4 | Adelaide Hills | 13 | Mount Benson |
| D | Barossa | 5 | Barossa Valley | 14 | Robe |
| E | Lower Murray | 6 | Eden Valley | 15 | Mount Gambier |
| F | Fleurieu | 7 | Riverland | 16 | Wrattonbully |
| G | Limestone Coast | 8 | McLaren Vale | 17 | Kangaroo Island |
| | | 9 | Langhorne Creek | 18 | Currency Creek |

over a hundred years old; the 140-year-old granite and bluestone buildings are as immovable as the day they were built (mid-nineteenth century). Then there are the wonderful smoked meats, sausages, and breads found nowhere else in Australia. And, of course, the wine.

More wine is now made in the Barossa each year than in any other single region. A large amount is certainly trucked in as grapes, must, or

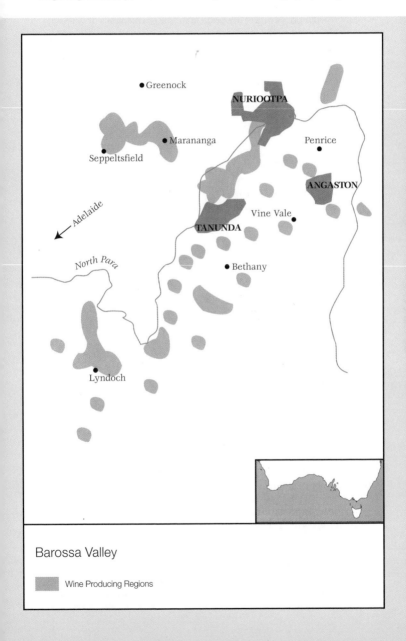

Barossa Valley

Wine Producing Regions

juice from elsewhere in South Australia, as many of Australia's largest wine companies have their headquarters here. (Only Hardys, based in McLaren Vale, is missing.)

As a viticultural region in its own right, the Barossa has more than recovered from the decline it suffered in the 1970s and early 1980s. It is first and foremost a red-wine region. Shiraz is its first grape; Cabernet Sauvignon, too, is an important part of the viticultural scene, and rapidly increasing prices reflect the demand for the old plantings of Grenache and Mourvèdre. The style of these red wines is unfailingly rich, ripe, and generous, and lends itself to the influence of vanilla-flavoured American oak.

Statistics tell you there is almost as much white wine as there is red made from Barossa Valley grapes. What they do not tell you is that, with the qualified exception of Riesling, the white wines are decidedly inferior to the red wines. If ever the criticism of clumsy, oaky, phenolic white wines is to be justly levelled, it is at Barossa Semillon and Chardonnay.

Little more than an hour's drive from Adelaide, the Barossa Valley is the first place wine tourists wish to visit. It's hardly surprising, given its rich viticultural history and the wineries, large and small, now to be visited. The Barossa also has an abundance of good restaurants and guest houses, including an ever-increasing number of bed-and-breakfast places that are by far the best in Australia. There are eighty-one wine producers in the region.

**Balthazar of the Barossa** ☆☆☆☆

*Lot 10, Stonewell Road, Marananga, SA 5355, ☏ & Ⓕ (08) 8562 2949; est 1999; 1,000 cases; no visitors*

In announcing her occupation as a "forty-something sex therapist with a seventeen-year involvement in the wine industry" Anita Bowen hides part of her light under a bushel, for she has a twenty-six-hectare vineyard on Stonewell Road, Marananga, and is a fully fledged winemaker. As for her Shiraz, she says, "Anyway, prepare a feast, pour yourself a glass (no chalices, please) of Balthazar and share it with your concubines. Who knows? It may help to lubricate thoughts, firm up ideas and get the creative juices flowing!" Exports to the UK and elsewhere.

**Barossa Ridge Wine Estate** ☆☆☆☆

*Light Pass Road, Tanunda, SA 5352, ☏ & Ⓕ (08) 8563 2811; est 1987; 2,000 cases; 🍷; A$; by appt*

A grape-grower-turned-winemaker with a small list of interesting red varietals, including the Valley of Vines blend of Merlot, Cabernet Franc, Cabernet Sauvignon, and Petit Verdot. All of its wines are built in an impressively heroic style.

**Barossa Valley Estate** ☆☆☆½

*Seppeltsfield Road, Marananga, SA 5355, ☏ (08) 8562 3599, Ⓕ (08) 8562 4255; est 1984; 100,000 cases; 7 days 10-4.30; 🍽*

In the wake of its acquisition by Hardys, the estate moved to the Barossa Valley. The E & E Black Pepper Shiraz and Ebenezer Shiraz are richly oaky flagships. Exports to the UK and elsewhere.

**Basedow** ☆☆☆½

*c/o James Estate, 951 Bylong Valley Way, Baerami via Denman, NSW 2333 ☏ 1300 887 966, Ⓕ (02) 6574 5164; est 1896; 75,000 cases; 🍷 no visitors*

An old, well-regarded winery which underwent several ownership changes in the 1990s, with another change likely. Full-bodied, oaky Semillon (once called White Burgundy) is its best-known, albeit slightly old-fashioned, wine.

### Bethany Wines ☆☆☆⚘

*Bethany Road, Bethany via Tanunda, SA 5352, ☎ (08) 8563 2086, Ⓕ (08) 8563 0046; est 1977; ⚘ 25,000 cases; ⚑; A$; Mon-Sat 10-5, Sun 1-5; ⚔*

The Schrapel family has been growing grapes for over 140 years, and making wine since 1977. The peacock packaging is a little strident, but the wine is good, especially the opulent Shiraz.

### Burge Family Winemakers ☆☆☆☆ V

*Barossa Way, Lyndoch, SA 5351, ☎ (08) 8524 4644, Ⓕ (08) 8524 4444; est 1928; ⚘ 3,000 cases; ⚑; A$; Thurs-Mon 10-5*

An arm of the Burge winemaking dynasty, with invaluable vineyards. Look out for the Rhône blends from old vines and Draycott Shiraz (especially the magnificent, voluptuous Reserve), built to last on a foundation of richly concentrated fruit.

### Charles Cimicky NR

*Gomersal Road, Lyndoch, SA 5351, ☎ (08) 8524 4025, Ⓕ (08) 8524 4772; est 1972; ⚘ 15,000 cases; ⚑; A$; Tues-Sat 10.30-4.30*

A quixotic combination of conservatism and adventure, this winery is best known within South Australia. Intense Sauvignon Blanc and richly flavoured, vanilla/cherry Signature Shiraz lead the way.

### Charles Melton ☆☆☆☆☆

*Krondorf Road, Tanunda, SA 5352, ☎ (08) 8563 3606, Ⓕ (08) 8563 3422; est 1984; ⚘ 15,000 cases; ⚑; A$; 7 days 11-5*

Diminutive dynamo Graeme (Charlie) Melton has taken his Nine Popes red (a blend of Shiraz, Grenache, and Mourvèdre from old vines) to icon status in short order. It, the Rosé of Virginia, the Shiraz, and Cabernet Sauvignon are all beautifully crafted and balanced. Exports to the UK and elsewhere.

### Craneford ☆☆☆☆

*Moorundie Street, Truro, SA 5356, ☎ (08) 8564 0003, Ⓕ (08) 8564 0008; ⚘ 25,000 cases; ⚑; A$; 7 days 10-5; ⚏*

The purchase of Craneford by owner/winemaker John Zilm has led to a new winery, far better grape supply, and a lift in both quality and consistency; crisp, citrus Riesling is good.

### Dutschke Wines ☆☆☆☆☆

*Lyndoch Valley Road, Lyndoch, SA 5351, ☎ (08) 8524 5485, Ⓕ (08) 8524 5489; est 1990; ⚘ 4,000 cases; no visitors*

The partnership of Wayne Dutschke, a ten-year flying winemaker veteran, and vineyard-owning uncle Ken Semmler has yielded rich rewards, with outstanding Shiraz and Shiraz/Merlot/Cabernet blends, powerful and concentrated but not jammy. Exports to the US and elsewhere.

### Elderton ☆☆☆☆⚘

*3 Tanunda Road, Nuriootpa, SA 5355, ☎ (08) 8568 7878, Ⓕ (08) 8568 7879; est 1984; ⚘ 32,000 cases; ⚑; A$; Mon-Fri 8.30-5, wkds & hols 11-4*

The core of this substantial business is old, high-quality vineyards on the valley floor. Shiraz, Cabernet Sauvignon, and blends are best, led by a fleshy, vanilla Command Shiraz much admired by the redoubtable Robert Parker. Exports to the UK and elsewhere.

**Gibson's BarossaVale Wines** ☆☆☆☆

*Willows Road, Light Pass, SA 5355, ☏ (08) 8562 3193, Ⓕ (08) 8562 4490; est 1996; ❖ 3,500 cases; 🍷; A$; Fri-Mon & public hols 11-5*

Former Penfolds senior viticulturist Rob Gibson was ideally positioned to find small parcels of very old vines when he struck out on his own, with Shiraz and Shiraz blends complemented by a single-varietal Merlot, all commendable. Exports to the UK.

**Glaetzer Wines** ☆☆☆☆

*34 Barossa Valley Way, Tanunda, SA 5352, ☏ (08) 8563 0288, Ⓕ (08) 8563 0218; est 1996; ❖ 5,000 cases ; 🍷; A$; Mon-Sat 10.30-4.30, public hols 1-4.30*

Colin and Ben Glaetzer come from a very well-known wine family. They purchase grapes from Barossa Valley growers, and make an impressive array of reds centred around Shiraz. Exports to the UK and elsewhere.

**Glen Eldon** ☆☆☆☆

*Glen Eldon, O'Herbig Road, Springton, SA 5235, ☏ (08) 8568 2996, Ⓕ (08) 8568 1833; ❖ 4,000 cases; no visitors*

The Sheedy family – brothers Richard and Andrew, and their wives Mary and Sue – has established its base at the Glen Eldon property, given its name over 100 years ago and which is today the home of Richard and Mary. It is here that the Riesling is planted, while the Shiraz and Cabernet Sauvignon come from their vineyards in the Barossa Valley. Exports to the UK and elsewhere.

**Grant Burge** ☆☆☆☆½

*Barossa Vines, Krondorf Road, Tanunda, SA 5352, ☏ (08) 8563 3700, Ⓕ (08) 8563 2807; est 1988; ❖ 200,000 cases; 🍷; A$; 7 days 10-5; light meals*

Astute, energetic winemaker-cum-marketer Grant Burge has amassed a vineyard empire and hugely successful winemaking enterprise. Meshach Shiraz, Shadrach Cabernet Sauvignon, and Holy Trinity (a Grenache/Shiraz/Mourvèdre blend) are as bold as Burge himself. Exports to the UK and elsewhere.

**Greenock Creek Wines NR**

*Radford Road, Seppeltsfield, SA 5360, ☏ (08) 8562 8103, Ⓕ (08) 8562 8259; est 1978; ❖ 2,500 cases; 🍷; A$; Wed-Mon 11-5; 🛏*

This is one of the first wineries you will see driving up to the Barossa Valley, where stonemason Michael Waugh and wife offer cult wines that sell rapidly at their cellar door if not already snapped up in the US at stratospheric prices.

**Haan Wines** ☆☆☆☆½

*Siegersdorf Road, Tanunda, SA 5352, ☏ & Ⓕ (08) 8562 4590; est 1993; ❖ 4,000 cases; no visitors*

Hans and Fransien Haan have a sixteen-hectare vineyard near Tanunda, successfully focusing on supple, chocolate-and-mulberry Merlot, specialty of contract winemaker James Irvine. Honeysuckle-rich Viognier, Shiraz, and red blend Wilhelmus are also very good. Exports to the UK and elsewhere.

**Hamilton's Ewell Vineyards** ☆☆☆½

*Siegersdorf Vineyard, Barossa Valley Way, Tanunda, SA 5352, ☏ (08) 8231 0088, Ⓕ (08) 8231 0355; est 1837; ❖ 13,000 cases; 🍷; A$; Mon-Fri 10-5, wkds 11-5*

Mark Hamilton, an Adelaide lawyer, is a sixth-generation direct descendant of Richard Hamilton. Since 1991, he has set about building yet another Hamilton wine business by a series of astute vineyard acquisitions, buying back the name Hamilton's Ewell from Beringer Blass, and making very good Shiraz. Exports to the UK and elsewhere.

**Hare's Chase** ☆☆☆☆⌐

*PO Box 46, Melrose Park, SA 5039, ☎ (08) 8277 3506, Ⓕ (08) 8277 3543; est 1998; ⬧ 2,500 cases; no visitors*

A joint venture between Penfolds' senior red winemaker Peter Taylor and two families with a 100-year-old Shiraz vineyard, and much younger Merlot plantings. Top-flight wines.

**Heritage Wines** ☆☆☆☆☆ **V**

*106a Seppeltsfield Road, Marananga, SA 5355, ☎ (08) 8562 2880, Ⓕ (08) 8562 2692; est 1984; ⬧ 6,000 cases; ⚕; A$; 7 days 11-5*

A little-known winery that deserves a far wider audience, for Stephen Hoff is apt to produce some startlingly good Shiraz and Cabernet Sauvignon., the 2002 wines superb. Exports to the UK and US.

**Jenke Vineyards** ☆☆☆⌐

*Barossa Valley Way, Rowland Flat, SA 5352, ☎ (08) 8524 4154, Ⓕ (08) 8524 5044; est 1989; ⬧ 8,000 cases; ⚕; A$; 7 days 11-5*

The Jenkes have been grape-growers since 1854, but only since 1989 have they made wines from a small part of their production. Shiraz and dark berry/bitter chocolate Old Vine Mourvèdre can be profoundly impressive.

**Kaesler** ☆☆☆☆☆

*Barossa Valley Way, Nuriootpa, SA 5355, ☎ (08) 8562 4488, Ⓕ (08) 8562 4499; est 1990; ⬧ 12,000 cases; ⚕; A$; Mon-Sat 10-5, Sun & public hols 11.30-4; ⦿; ⊨*

The farm dates back to 1893, when the Kaesler family planted the first vines, and which remain in production. Plantings of twelve hectares have doubled since the purchase of the next-door property. The Old Vine varieties and Rhône blends are outstanding.

**Kalleske Wines** ☆☆☆☆☆

*Vinegrove Road, Greenock, SA 5360, ☎ 0409 339 599, Ⓕ (08) 8562 8118; est 1999; ⬧ 2,000 cases; no visitors*

The Kalleske family have been vignerons for over 100 years, and the fifth generation finally took the plunge, established a small winery, and proceeded to make glorious Shiraz and Grenache from the best of their estate-grown grapes.

**Kellermeister/Trevor Jones** ☆☆☆⌐

*Barossa Valley Highway, Lyndoch, SA 5351, ☎ (08) 8524 4303, Ⓕ (08) 8524 4880; est 1996; ⬧ 25,000 cases; ⚕; A$; 7 days 9-6*

Industry veteran Trevor Jones has finally introduced his own label (itself strikingly designed), offering Riesling, Virgin Chardonnay, Dry Grown Shiraz, and Cabernet/Merlot. Yet another icon in the US market.

**Langmeil Winery** ☆☆☆☆

*Corner Para and Langmeil Roads, Tanunda, SA 5352, ☎ (08) 8563 2595, Ⓕ (08) 8563 3622; est 1996; ⬧ 15,000 cases; ⚕; A$; 7 days 11-4.30*

This winery has had a convoluted Barossa-Deutsch lineage since the 1840s, with various ownership and direction changes, the most recent in 1996. Langmeil now produces luscious red wines from two vineyards of Grenache, Shiraz, and Cabernet Sauvignon. Exports to the US and elsewhere.

**Leo Buring** ☆☆☆☆☆

*Tanunda Road, Nuriootpa, SA 5355, ☎ (08) 8560 9408, Ⓕ (08) 8563 2804; est 1931; ⬧ NFP; ⚕ no visitors*

An arm of the Southcorp octopus, with a great lineage of superb, long-lived Rieslings formerly made by genius John Vickery. Happily, now makes only Riesling, with Leonay the super-premium release, supported by a Clare and an Eden Valley Riesling from each vintage. Exports to the UK.

### Liebich Wein ☆☆☆☆⊰

*Steingarten Road, Rowland Flat, SA 5352, ☎ & Ⓕ (08) 8524 4543; est 1992; ⬥ 3,000 cases; ⚲; A$; 7 days 11-5, appts advisable*

Barossa-Deutsch for "I love wine," this is a small venture into winemaking by long-term grape-grower and local character Ron Liebich, who has been making wine for others since 1969. Leveret Shiraz, The Darkie Shiraz, and Crackerjack Cabernet can be outstanding (*e.g.* 2002). Exports to the UK and elsewhere.

### Orlando ☆☆☆☆⊰

*Jacob's Creek Visitor Centre, Barossa Valley Way, Rowland Flat, SA 5352, ☎ (08) 8521 3000, Ⓕ (08) 8521 3003; est 1847; ⬥ NFP; ⚲; A$; 7 days 10-5; gift shop*

Owned by Pernod-Ricard and known around the world for its mega-brand, Jacob's Creek. In recent times it has made a concerted effort to improve and expand its range of super-premium and premium wines. These include St Helga Riesling, Centenary Hill Shiraz, Lawson's Shiraz, Jacaranda Ridge Cabernet Sauvignon, and special-release Jacob's Creek wines. Exports to the UK and elsewhere.

### Penfolds ☆☆☆☆☆

*Tanunda Road, Nuriootpa, SA 5355, ☎ (08) 8568 9290, Ⓕ (08) 8568 9493; est 1844; ⬥ 1,400,00 cases; ⚲; A$; Mon-Fri 10-5, wkds & public hols 11-5*

Heads the Southcorp wine group, which now includes Rosemount and is Australia's largest vineyard owner. Justifiably famous for Grange, the peerless and (almost) ageless Shiraz created by the late Max Schubert, but also for a pyramid of red wines of great depth of flavour and structure, sold at all price points. Exports to the UK and elsewhere.

### Peter Lehmann ☆☆☆☆ V

*Para Road, Tanunda, SA 5352, ☎ (08) 8563 2100, Ⓕ (08) 8563 3402; est 1979; ⬥ 200,000 cases; ⚲; A$; Mon-Fri 9.30-5, wkds & public hols 10.30-4.30; lunch platter; children's books*

The godfather of the Barossa threw his lot in with the Swiss-owned Hess Group, warding off Allied Domecq in late 2003. Resolutely using only Barossa and Eden Valley grapes, the style is as honest as the day is long. The Mentor and Stonewell Shiraz, both marrying sweet vanilla oak with ripe and luscious fruit, are rather special, as is the Eden Valley Reserve Riesling. Exports to the UK and elsewhere.

### Richmond Grove ☆☆☆☆

*Para Road, Tanunda, SA 5352, ☎ (08) 8563 7300, Ⓕ (08) 8563 2804; est 1983; ⬥ 150,000 cases; ⚲; A$; 7 days 10.30-4.30; ✗; jazz concerts*

Once Chateau Leonay of Leo Buring, now renamed and owned by Orlando-Wyndham. In fairy-tale fashion, John Vickery (formerly of Leo Buring) became winemaker and produces glorious limey, minerally Rieslings, particularly from Clare Valley (Watervale) grapes.

### Rockford ☆☆☆☆⊰ V

*Krondorf Road, Tanunda, SA 5352, ☎ (08) 8563 2720, Ⓕ (08) 8563 3787; est 1984; ⬥ NFP; ⚲; A$; Mon-Sat 11-5*

Robert (Rocky) O'Callaghan is a richly bearded, larger-than-life, passionate defender of old-style, handmade wines from old, low-yielding vines.

Velvety sparkling Black Shiraz is diamond-scarce and Basket Press Shiraz almost as rare. All ooze character, and are reasonably priced. Exports to the UK and elsewhere.

**Rosenvale** ☆☆☆☆✓ **V**

*Lot 385, Railway Terrace, Nuriootpa, SA 5355, ☎ 0407 390 788, Ⓕ (08) 8565 7206; est 2000; ⬥ 2,000 cases; ♀; A$; by appt*

The Rosenzweig family has eighty hectares of vineyards, some old and some new; most of the grapes are sold to other producers, but since 2000 some of the best parcels have been made into very high-quality Shiraz, Cabernet Sauvignon, and handy Semillon and Chardonnay.

**Saltram** ☆☆☆☆✓

*Salters Gully, Nuriootpa, SA 5355, ☎ (08) 8564 3355, Ⓕ (08) 8564 2209; est 1859; ⬥ NFP; ♀; A$; 7 days 10-5; ⦿*

Now part of the Beringer Blass empire, but winemaker Nigel Dolan has breathed new life and credibility into Saltram as a true Barossa winery, with No. 1 Shiraz an outstanding leader of a series of lesser-priced wines, including Mamre Brook, principally red. Exports to the UK and elsewhere.

**Schild Estate Wines** ☆☆☆☆

*Corner Barossa Valley Way and Lyndoch Valley Road, Lyndoch, SA 5351, ☎ (08) 8524 5560, Ⓕ (08) 8524 4333; est 1998; ⬥ 10,000 cases; ♀; A$; 7 days 10-5; ⦿*

Ed Schild has steadily increased his vineyard holdings over the past forty years to 157 hectares. Currently only twelve per cent of the production produces the Schild Estate wines, but this percentage is increasing. The flagship wine will be made from 150-year-old Shiraz vines on the Moorooroo Block. Exports to the UK and elsewhere.

**Schubert Estate** ☆☆☆☆☆

*Roennfeldt Road, Marananga, SA 5355, ☎ (08) 8562 3375, Ⓕ (08) 8562 4338; est 2000; ⬥ 100 cases; ♀; A$; by appt*

Steve and Cecilia Schubert are primarily grape-growers, with fourteen hectares of Shiraz and little over one hectare of Semillon, and almost all the production is sold to Torbreck Vintners. However, a little wine is made on-site, with wild yeast, open fermentation, basket pressing, and bottling without filtration. The 2002 wine is utterly exceptional; the challenge will be to keep the quality in the years ahead.

**Seppelt** ☆☆☆☆☆

*1 Seppeltsfield Road, Seppeltsfield via Nuriootpa, SA 5355, ☎ (08) 8568 6217, Ⓕ (08) 8562 8333; est 1851; ⬥ NFP; ♀; A$; Mon-Fri 10-5, wkds & public hols 11-5*

This gloriously historic winery (with a recent A$1 million renovation and expansion) is the focal point for a dazzling array of fortified wines made by James Godfrey. The wines range from a fresh manzanilla sherry-style fino (exported as Palomino), to an unctuous 100-year-old Para Liqueur (port style) that is bottled each year on its centenary. A must-visit Barossa destination. Exports to the UK and elsewhere.

**St Hallett** ☆☆☆☆✓ **V**

*St Hallett's Road, Tanunda, SA 5352, ☎ (08) 8563 7000, Ⓕ (08) 8563 7001; est 1944; ⬥ 100,000 cases; ♀; A$; 7 days 10-5; ⫏*

The changes came thick and fast in 2001; first St Hallett became part of Banksia wines, which was in turn acquired by New Zealand's Lion Nathan. Old Block Shiraz remains the rock of ages, Eden Valley Riesling and the various Shiraz brands offer great value. Exports to the UK and elsewhere.

**Tait Wines NR**

*Yaldara Drive, Lyndoch, SA 5351, ☎ (08) 8524 5000, ⓕ (08) 8524 5220; est 1994; ⚘ 2,000 cases; ⚱; A$; wkds 11-5, or by appt*

The Tait family has been involved in the wine industry in the Barossa for over 100 years, making not wine but barrels. Their recent venture into winemaking was immediately successful, with Basket Press Shiraz and Cabernet Sauvignon to the fore.

**Thorn-Clarke Wines ☆☆☆☆ V**

*Milton Park, Gawler Park Road, Angaston, SA 5353, ☎ (08) 8564 3036, ⓕ (08) 8564 3255; est 1997; ⚘ 20,000 cases; ⚱; A$; Mon-Fri 9-5*

An ambitious newcomer with 240 hectares of estate plantings, the pick going to make a thoroughly impressive array of Riesling, Pinot Gris, Chardonnay, Shiraz, Cabernet Sauvignon, and blends; all deliver excellent value, the Shiraz especially. Exports to the UK and elsewhere.

**Tollana ☆☆☆☆**

*Tanunda Road, Nuriootpa, SA 5355, ☎ (08) 8560 9408, ⓕ (08) 8562 2494; est 1888; ⚘ NFP; ⚱; no visitors*

Part of Southcorp, drawing most of its grapes from its long-established Eden Valley Woodbury Vineyard. Makes citrus Riesling, stylish Chardonnay, and smooth but substantial Bin TR16 Shiraz and Bin TR222 Cabernet Sauvignon. Exports to the UK and elsewhere.

**Torbreck Vintners ☆☆☆☆☆**

*Roenfeldt Road, Marananga, SA 5352, ☎ (08) 8562 4155, ⓕ (08) 8562 4195; est 1994; ⚘ 40,000 cases; 7 days 10-6*

Behind the scenes shareholding changes have not impacted on quality but rather funded expansion. The Steading (Grenache/Shiraz), The RunRig (Shiraz), and The Struie (Shiraz) are crammed full with luscious fruit and supported by great structure. Woodcutter's is the economy version. US demand has pulled price rises.

**Turkey Flat ☆☆☆☆⚘ V**

*Bethany Road, Tanunda, SA 5352, ☎ (08) 8563 2851, ⓕ (08) 8563 3610; est 1990; ⚘ 16,000 cases; ⚱; A$; 7 days 11-5*

Another Barossa dynasty (since 1870) of grape-growers-turned-winemakers. Peter Schulz makes delectable Rosé and highly regarded Shiraz from a precious patch of 145-year-old vines, still priced within the reach of mortals. Exports to the UK and elsewhere.

**Veritas ☆☆☆☆**

*Corner Seppeltsfield and Stelzer Roads, Tanunda, SA 5352, ☎ (08) 8562 3300, ⓕ (08) 8562 1177; est 1955; ⚘ 22,000 cases; ⚱; A$; Mon-Fri 10-4.30, wkds 11-5; ⛺; ⚔*

Rolf Binder celebrates his Hungarian heritage with Binder's Bull's Blood, but also (with partner Christa Deans) makes an array of neatly turned, conventional white and red wines. Development of export markets, including the UK, has seen a significant increase in production.

**Viking Wines ☆☆☆☆⚘**

*RSD 108 Seppeltsfield Road, Marananga, SA 5355, ☎ (08) 8562 3842, ⓕ (08) 8562 4266; est 1995; ⚘ 1,000 cases; 7 days 11-5*

Based upon fifty-year-old, dry-grown, and near-organic vineyards with a yield of only 1–1.5 tonnes per hectare, Viking Wines has been discovered by Robert Parker with inevitable consequences for the price of its top red wines, notably Odin's Honour, Grand Shiraz, and blends. Exports to the US.

**Whistler Wines** ☆☆☆☆↻
*Seppeltsfield Road, Marananga, SA 5355, ☎ (08) 8562 4942, Ⓕ (08) 8562 4943;*
*est 1999; ♦ 3,000 cases; ☗; A$; 7 days 10.30-5; ☝*

Fourteen hectares of estate plantings (some still young) and contract
winemaking by Rolf Binder and Christa Deans have resulted in high-quality
Cabernet/Merlot, Cabernet Sauvignon, Shiraz, and Merlot, the increased
production still not meeting demand, particularly with the prices
held in check.

**The Willows Vineyard** ☆☆☆☆↻
*Light Pass Road, Light Pass, Barossa Valley, SA 5355, ☎ (08) 8562 1080,*
*Ⓕ (08) 8562 3447; est 1989; ♦ 6,000 cases; ☗; A$; 7 days 10.30-4.30*

Successive generations of the Scholz family have grown grapes. Now Peter
and Michael Scholz are making smooth, balanced, and flavourful wines.
Shiraz and Cabernet Sauvignon are best, super-premium Bonesetter
Shiraz outstanding. Exports to the UK.

**Wolf Blass** ☆☆☆☆☆ V
*Bilyara Vineyards, Sturt Highway, Nuriootpa, SA 5355, ☎ (08) 8562 1955, Ⓕ (08)*
*8562 2156; est 1966; ♦ NFP; ☗; A$; Mon-Fri 9.15-4.30, wkds 10-4.30; wine museum*

The Australian arm of Beringer Blass, performing very much better than its
US counterpart, led by an outstanding team of Chris Hatcher, John Glaetzer,
and Caroline Dunn. Gloriously silky fruit-driven reds led by Platinum label,
then Black, Gold, Red, etc. Great Riesling, too. Worldwide distribution.

**Yalumba** ☆☆☆☆↻
*Eden Valley Road, Angaston, SA 5353, ☎ (08) 8561 3200, Ⓕ (08) 8561 3393;*
*est 1849; ♦ 900,000 cases; ☗; A$; Mon-Fri 8.30-5, Sat 10-5, Sun 12-5; ☝*

The surviving Anglo-Australian aristocracy lorded over by actor Jeremy
Irons' alter ego Robert Hill Smith. Languidly changing hats with just a
ghost of a crooked smile, Hill Smith runs the very complex winemaking,
importing, and exporting business of the Yalumba stable and other
producers. Committed to quality, Yalumba is a particularly serious player
with a kaleidoscopic array of varietals, exotic (Viognier, Nebbiolo, etc.)
and mainstream (Riesling, Octavius Shiraz and Shiraz/Cabernet).
Worldwide exports.

# Eden Valley

The Eden Valley is a windswept series of often bare hills, more an elevated
plateau than anything else. There are magic spots – none more so than the
150-year-old Hill of Grace Vineyard, with its stone church directly across
the road, and the groves of white-trunked gums. Eden Valley is primarily a
grape-growing region. It is the mirror reverse, if you like, of the Barossa
Valley. Here, just two producers represent Eden Valley's major winery
action. They are Henschke, the most highly regarded family winery in
Australia, and the well-known Mountadam estate.

Eden Valley produces Shiraz of outstanding quality, but its chief claim to
fame is its great Rieslings. These are wines that literally blossom with ten to
fifteen years' bottle age, and have a lime-citrus character and caressing texture
that give them greater appeal in their youth than those of the Clare Valley.

It was the quality of Eden Valley's Riesling that led Yalumba progressively
to establish its Pewsey Vale, Heggies, and Hill Smith vineyards (and brands)

here, and to forsake its sources of Barossa Valley Riesling. There are fifteen wine producers in the region.

### Glen Eldon Wines ☆☆☆☆

*Glen Eldon, O'Herbig Road, Springton, SA 5235, ☎ (08) 8568 2996, Ⓕ (08) 8568 1833; est 1997; ♦ 4,000 cases; no visitors*

The Sheedy family has established its base at the Glen Eldon property, which is today the source of the outstanding lime-juice Riesling; the Dry Bore Shiraz and Cabernet Sauvignon come from the Barossa Valley. Exports to the UK and elsewhere.

### Heathvale ☆☆☆⅟

*Saw Pit Gully Road, via Keyneton, SA 5353, ☎ & Ⓕ (08) 8564 8248; est 1987; ♦ 1,250 cases; ▼; A$; by appt*

Trevor March is completing his studies for a Master of Viticulture degree at the Waite campus of the University of Adelaide, and runs Heathvale with wife Faye. Son James March is perhaps best known for the *Winemaker's Essential Phrase Book,* also published by Mitchell Beazley. Chardonnay and Shiraz are both good. Exports to the UK and elsewhere.

### Heggies Vineyard ☆☆☆☆

*Heggies Range Road, Eden Valley, SA 5235, ☎ (08) 8565 3203, Ⓕ (08) 8565 3380; est 1971; ♦ 13,000 cases; ▼; A$; 7 days at Yalumba*

Heggie was the horseman pictured on the striking label – a classic after twenty years. The vineyard, established in 1973, lies at 570 metres. While owned by Yalumba, Heggies strives to keep its identity quite separate. Overall, the Riesling (soft toast, lime, and kerosene flavours with a few years' bottle age) is best, Viognier the most interesting.

### Henschke ☆☆☆☆☆

*Henschke Road, Keyneton, SA 5353, ☎ (08) 8564 8223, Ⓕ (08) 8564 8294; est 1868; ♦ 40,000 cases; ▼; A$; Mon-Fri 9-4.30, Sat 9-12, public hols 10-3*

Winemaker Stephen Henschke and viticulturist wife Prue have taken Henschke to the pinnacle of small(ish) Australian wineries since 1978. The 140-year-old Shiraz vines at the Hill of Grace Vineyard produce a wine second only to Penfolds' Grange in price, and equally sought after. Mount Edelstone is another great classic Shiraz. A scintillating array of white (chiefly from the Adelaide Hills) and red wines of diverse styles but consistent quality makes up the portfolio of wines. Exports to the UK and elsewhere.

### Hill Smith Estate ☆☆☆☆

*Flaxmans Valley Road, Eden Valley, SA 5235, ☎ (08) 8561 3200, Ⓕ (08) 8561 3393; est 1973; ♦ 5,000 cases; ▼; A$; 7 days at Yalumba*

Also part of the Yalumba Estate, with twenty-three hectares of Chardonnay and Sauvignon Blanc yielding two estate wines. Quality varies considerably with vintage; the rating is a compromise between best and least. Exports to the UK and elsewhere.

### Irvine ☆☆☆☆

*PO Box 308, Angaston, SA 5353, ☎ (08) 8564 1046, Ⓕ (08) 8564 1314; est 1980; ♦ 6,000 cases; no visitors*

Industry veteran Jim Irvine successfully guided the destiny of several substantial South Australian wineries while quietly setting up his own vineyard and brand, which has focused on producing silky, cedary Merlot (known as Grand Merlot) that is chiefly sold abroad. Exports to the UK and elsewhere.

**Karl Seppelt** ☆☆☆✤

*Ross Dewells Road, Springton, SA 5235, ☎ (08) 8568 2378, Ⓕ (08) 8568 2799; est 1981; ✤ 5,000 cases; ⛾; A$; 7 days 10-5*

The squeaky Australian twang in Karl Seppelt's voice should not deceive you; this former marketing director of B Seppelt & Sons made the major decisions leading to the pioneering of the Drumborg (Western Victoria) and Padthaway regions. His own vineyard virtually straddles the Adelaide Hills-Eden Valley boundary, and (with contract winemaking) produces solidly flavoured, ultra-consistent sparkling, white, and red wines.

**Mountadam** ☆☆☆✤

*High Eden Road, High Eden Ridge, SA 5235, ☎ (08) 8564 1900, Ⓕ (08) 8564 1999; est 1972; ✤ 25,000 cases; ⛾; A$; 7 days 11-4*

Established by the late David Wynn (of Wynns Coonawarra fame) but, in a mildly surprising move, acquired by Cape Mentelle (effectively LVMH) in 2000. Quality has wandered around in recent years; Shiraz and Riesling have been the most reliable. Exports to the UK and elsewhere.

**Pewsey Vale** ☆☆☆☆

*PO Box 10, Angaston, SA 5353, ☎ (08) 8561 3200, Ⓕ (08) 8561 3393; est 1961; ✤ 18,000 cases; ⛾; A$; at Yalumba*

The first of the Hill Smith/Yalumba ventures into the hills of the Eden Valley, overnight proving that this indeed was a superior region for producing Riesling. Museum releases of The Contour Riesling at five to six years of age, sealed with Stelvin screwcaps, have lifted the profile of the winery to the highest level. These are, quite simply, great wines. Exports to the UK and elsewhere.

**Tin Shed Wines** ☆☆☆☆

*PO Box 504, Tanunda, SA 5352, ☎ & Ⓕ (08) 8563 3669; est 1998; ✤ 3,000 cases; no visitors*

Proprietors Andrew Wardlaw and Peter Clarke weave all sorts of mystique in producing and marketing the Tin Shed wines. However, when you look behind the palaver to the Riesling, Shiraz, and Three Vines Mourvèdre/Shiraz/Grenache the quality is there. Exports to the UK and elsewhere.

# Clare Valley

It was Mick Knappstein who once observed, "There are only two kinds of people: those who were born in Clare, and those who wish they had been." I fall unashamedly in the latter category. The topography of the Clare Valley has seemingly acted as a bulwark against the intrusion of the twentieth century. This illusion is heightened by the abundance of stone buildings and wineries as precious as the Jesuit-run Sevenhill and Wendouree, to name but two among many. Most of the wineries are small, family-owned and -run, which adds to the feeling of intimacy. And once you have set up shop here, it is hard not to make wines with equally strongly defined character.

Clare Rieslings, shy and minerally/chalky in their youth, slowly and majestically reveal their core of honey, lightly browned toast, and balancing twist of lemony acidity as they age sometimes for thirty years or more. The Shiraz, Cabernet Sauvignon, and Malbec are awesome. Some makers quite legitimately choose to tame them partially; others are content to give them free play, while yet others encourage and build on that power with new oak and prolonged fermentations. And how wonderful it is to find that the Clare Valley is one of the few places on this planet not to have welcomed Chardonnay. There are forty-three wine producers in the region.

### Annie's Lane ☆☆☆☆☆ V

*Quelltaler Road, Watervale, SA 5452, ☎ (08) 8843 0003, Ⓕ (08) 8843 0096; est 1856; ◈ 120,000 cases; ☐; A$; Mon-Fri 8.30-5, wkds 11-4*

The Clare Valley portfolio of Beringer Blass, formerly made at the Quelltaler Winery, is now sold under the Annie's Lane label, the name coming from turn-of-the-twentieth-century local identity Annie Weyman. The wines are crammed with flavour and character, and (other than the super-premium Cooper Trail releases) are seriously under-priced. Exports to the UK and elsewhere.

### Brian Barry Wines ☆☆☆

*PO Box 128, Stepney, SA 5069, ☎ (08) 8363 6211, Ⓕ (08) 8362 0498; est 1977; ◈ 6,000 cases*

Brian Barry is an industry veteran with a wealth of winemaking and show-judging experience. He sells a substantial part of the production from this vineyard-only enterprise, and contract-makes some wine (under his supervision) at various wineries. On the market at the time of writing.

### Cardinham Estate ☆☆☆☆✓

*Main North Road, Stanley Flat, SA 5453, ☎ (08) 8842 1944, Ⓕ (08) 8842 1955; est 1980; ◈ 3,000 cases; ☐; A$; 7 days 10-5*

A joint venture between the Smith family, with sixty hectares of vines, and veteran winemaker Stephen John. A range of winemaking services and bulk wines stands alongside the limited production of excellent Riesling, Shiraz, and Cabernet/Merlot under the Cardinham Estate label.

### Claymore Wines ☆☆☆☆

*Leasingham Road, Leasingham, SA 5452, ☎ 0412 822 250, Ⓕ (08) 8284 2899; est 1998; ◈ 3,000 cases; ☐; A$; wkds & public hols 10-5*

Draws on various vineyards, some situated in the Clare Valley, others in McLaren Vale. The Clare Valley Joshua Tree Riesling has been the pick of the releases. The contract winemaker is Adelaide cardiologist Justin Ardill, owner of Reilly's Wines.

### Clos Clare ☆☆☆☆

*Old Road, Watervale, SA 5452, ☎ & Ⓕ (08) 8843 0161; est 1993; ◈ 1,200 cases; ☐; A$; wkds & public hols 10-5*

Clos Clare is based on a small (two hectares), unirrigated section of the original Florita Vineyard once owned by Leo Buring. It produces Riesling of impressive concentration and power, and a Shiraz of equal quality.

### Crabtree of Watervale ☆☆☆☆ V

*North Terrace, Watervale, SA 5452, ☎ (08) 8843 0069, Ⓕ (08) 8843 0144; est 1979; ◈ 5,000 cases; ☐; A$; 7 days 11-5; ✗*

The gently eccentric Robert Crabtree and wife Elizabeth are once again very much part of the Watervale business, making full-flavoured, classic Clare wines, with Riesling (in particular), Shiraz, and Cabernet Sauvignon to the fore, Tempranillo promising.

### Eldredge ☆☆☆☆

*Spring Gully Road, Clare, SA 5453, ☎ & Ⓕ (08) 8842 3086; est 1993; ◈ 7,000 cases; ☐; A$; 7 days 11-5; ⦿*

Leigh and Karen Eldredge have established their cellar-door facility at an altitude of 500 metres in the Sevenhill Ranges. Riesling, Shiraz, and

Cabernet Sauvignon variously excel, with a nicely focused Sangiovese adding interest. Exports to the UK and elsewhere.

**Grosset** ☆☆☆☆☆

*King Street, Auburn, SA 5451, ☎ (08) 8849 2175, Ⓕ (08) 8849 2292; est 1981; ⚘ 9,000 cases; ⚑; A$; Wed-Sun 10-5 from first week of Sept for approx 6 weeks*

Jeffrey Grosset is best known for his supremely elegant Rieslings from the Watervale and Polish Hill River areas, but his Bordeaux blend, Gaia, is equally superb. His winemaking skills do not stop there: he also makes a brilliant Semillon/Sauvignon Blanc (Clare Semillon and Adelaide Hills Sauvignon Blanc), and an even better Adelaide Hills Chardonnay (intense but harmonious), and a Reserve Pinot Noir (in minuscule quantities but of awesome quality).

**Jeanneret Wines** ☆☆☆☆♪

*Jeanneret Road, Sevenhill, SA 5453, ☎ (08) 8843 4308, Ⓕ (08) 8843 4251; est 1992; ⚘ 8,000 cases; ⚑; A$; Mon-Fri 11-5, wkds & public hols 10-5; ✗*

The Jeanneret winery has a most attractive outdoor tasting area and equally charming picnic facilities on the edge of a small lake, surrounded by bushland. The wines have already established a loyal following; Riesling, Shiraz, and Cabernets all very good. Exports to the UK and elsewhere.

**Jim Barry Wines** ☆☆☆☆♪

*Craig's Hill Road, Clare, SA 5453, ☎ (08) 8842 2261, Ⓕ (08) 8842 3752; est 1959; ⚘ 60,000 cases; ⚑; A$; Mon-Fri 9-5, wkds & hols 9-4*

The irrepressibly Irish Barry family owns 160 hectares of mature vineyards, including most of the great Florita Riesling vineyard. Another provides the superlative Shiraz for The Armagh, a pretender to the Grange throne, and the McRae Wood duo of Shiraz and Cabernet/Malbec. Exports to the UK and elsewhere.

**Kilikanoon** ☆☆☆☆☆

*Penna Lane, Penwortham, SA 5453, ☎ & Ⓕ (08) 8843 4377; est 1997; ⚘ 15,000 cases; ⚑; A$; wkds & public hols 11-5; ❢⦿❢; ✗*

Kilikanoon has twenty hectares of estate at Leasingham and Penwortham. It also has a restaurant that was set up in a restored 1880s cottage. Has had an outstanding run of success in recent years with Morts Block Riesling, Oracle Shiraz, Covenant Shiraz, and Blocks Road Cabernet Sauvignon. Exports to the UK and elsewhere.

**Kirrihill Estates** ☆☆☆☆ **V**

*Wendouree Road, Clare, SA 5453, ☎ (08) 8842 4087, Ⓕ (08) 8842 4089; est 1998; ⚘ 25,000 cases; ⚑; A$; 7 days 10-4; ❢⦿❢; ✗*

A large, investor-funded business with a new A$10 million winery and management of 1,300 hectares of vineyards through the Clare Valley, Adelaide Hills, and Langhorne Creek. Riesling, Shiraz, and Cabernet Sauvignon are all excellent value.

**Knappstein Wines** ☆☆☆☆

*2 Pioneer Avenue, Clare, SA 5453, ☎ (08) 8842 2600, Ⓕ (08) 8842 3831; est 1976; ⚘ 45,000 cases; ⚑; A$; Mon-Fri 9-5, Sat 11-5, Sun & public hols 11-4*

Very much part of the Petaluma empire, with winemaker Andrew Hardy now a veteran of the region. The ninety hectares of mature estate vineyards in prime locations supply grapes both for the Knappstein brand and for wider Petaluma use. Riesling, Enterprise Shiraz, and Cabernet Sauvignon are best. Exports to the UK and elsewhere.

**Leasingham** ☆☆☆☆⚘ **V**

*7 Dominic Street, Clare, SA 5453, ☎ (08) 8842 2555, Ⓕ (08) 8842 3293; est 1893;*
*⚘ 70,000 cases; ☗; A$; Mon-Fri 8.30-5.30, wkds 10-4*

Successive big-company ownerships and peregrinations in labelling have
not caused any permanent loss of identity or quality. With a core of high-
quality vineyards planted with old vines to draw on, Leasingham is going
from strength to strength under Hardys' direction. Superb Bin 7 Riesling
and the stentorian red wines take no prisoners, compacting densely rich
fruit and layer upon layer of oak into every long-lived bottle.

**Mintaro Wines** ☆☆☆⚘

*Leasingham Road, Mintaro, SA 5415, ☎ (08) 8843 9046, Ⓕ (08) 8843 9050;*
*est 1984; ⚘ 5,000 cases; ☗; A$; 7 days 10-4.30*

Peter Houldsworth has produced some impressive Riesling over the years,
that develops particularly well in bottle. The red wines are formidable,
massive in body and extract, and built for the long haul.

**Mitchell** ☆☆☆☆ **V**

*Hughes Park Road, Sevenhill, SA 5453, ☎ (08) 8843 4258, Ⓕ (08) 8843 4340;*
*est 1975; ⚘ 30,000 cases; ☗; A$; 7 days 10-4*

One of the stalwarts of Clare for many years now, producing long-lived
Rieslings and Cabernet Sauvignons in classic regional style but having
extended the range with very creditable Semillon and Shiraz. A lovely old
stone apple shed provides the cellar door and upper section of the
compact winery. Exports to the US.

**Mount Horrocks** ☆☆☆☆⚘

*The Old Railway Station, Curling Street, Auburn, SA 5451, ☎ (08) 8849 2243,*
*Ⓕ (08) 8849 2265; est 1982; ⚘ 4,500 cases; ☗; A$; wkds & public hols 10-5;*
*wkd lunches*

Under the ownership of the feisty Stephanie Toole, this winemaking estate
has well and truly established its own identity, with finely honed Riesling,
Semillon, Shiraz, and Cabernet/Merlot all impressive. Exports to the UK
and elsewhere.

**Neagles Rock Vineyards** ☆☆☆☆⚘ **V**

*Lot 1 & 2, Main North Road, Clare, SA 5453, ☎ (08) 8843 4020, Ⓕ (08) 8843*
*4021; est 1997; ⚘ 6,000 cases; ☗; A$; 7 days 10-5; ℿ*

Owner-partners Jane Willson and Steve Wiblin bring thirty-five years of
industry experience to Neagles Rock, resuscitating two old vineyards, and –
for good measure – stripping a dilapidated house to the barest of bones
and turning it into a first-rate, airy restaurant-cum-cellar door. Shiraz,
Cabernet Sauvignon, and Grenache/Shiraz, all fruit-driven and supple, are
especially good.

**O'Leary Walker Wines** ☆☆☆☆☆ **V**

*PO Box 49, Watervale, SA 5452, ☎ (08) 8343 0022, Ⓕ (08) 8343 0156; est 2001;*
*⚘ 14,000 cases; no visitors*

David O'Leary and Nick Walker have more than thirty years' combined
experience as winemakers working for some of the biggest Australian wine
groups. They have backed themselves to establish their own winery and
brand. Delicious, well-priced wines from the Adelaide Hills and Clare Valley
have brought just rewards. Exports to the UK and elsewhere.

**Old Station Vineyard** ☆☆☆⚘

*St Vincent Street, Watervale, SA 5452, ☎ 0414 441 925, Ⓕ (02) 9144 1925;*
*est 1926; ⚘ 2,000 cases; no visitors*

Former leading Sydney wine retailers Bill and Noel Ireland purchased a six-hectare vineyard planted with seven-year-old vines in 1995, and, with skilled contract winemaking, hauled in a bag full of medals, continuing on in much the same vein.

### Paulett ☆☆☆☆ V
*Polish Hill Road, Polish Hill River, SA 5453, ☎ (08) 8843 4328, ⓕ (08) 8843 4202; est 1983; ⚑ 12,500 cases; ⚐; A$; 7 days 10-5*

Former Hunter Valley winemaker Neil Paulett and wife Alison purchased their forty-seven-hectare property in 1982. The next summer their patch of old vines and the house in a grove of old trees were destroyed in the terrible bushfires of 1983. Undeterred, they have gone on to build a beautifully situated winery and to craft Rieslings and Shirazes (especially) that are never less than good, and sometimes quite brilliant. Exports to the UK.

### Penna Lane ☆☆☆☆�‎⚋ V
*Lot 51, Penna Lane, Penwortham via Clare, SA 5453, ☎ (08) 8843 4364, ⓕ (08) 8843 4349; est 1998; ⚑ 3,000 cases; ⚐; A$; Thurs-Sun & public hols 11-5, or by appt*

Ray and Lynette Klavin, together with Stephen Stafford-Brookes, have built up Penna Lane Wines the hard way, with unrelenting work substituting for capital, and deserve the success which has come their way with Riesling, Shiraz, The Willsmore Shiraz, and Cabernet Sauvignon.

### Pikes ☆☆☆☆
*Polish Hill River Road, Sevenhill, SA 5453, ☎ (08) 8843 4370, ⓕ (08) 8843 4353; est 1984; ⚑ 35,000 cases; ⚐; A$; 7 days 10-4*

Owned by the energetic Pike brothers. Until 1998, Andrew was chief viticulturist for Southcorp, while Neil was the winemaker at Mitchell. Both are now focused on this thriving business, producing powerful, complex wines (especially Riesling, Shiraz, and Cabernet Sauvignon) in mainstream Clare style. Exports to the UK and elsewhere.

### Pycnantha Hill Estate ☆☆☆☆
*Benbournie Road, Clare, SA 5453, ☎ & ⓕ (08) 8842 2137; est 1997; ⚑ 1,000 cases; no visitors*

The Howarth family has established 2.4 hectares of vineyards since 1987, making its first commercial vintage ten years thereafter. It seemed a natural choice to name their vineyard after *Acacia pycnantha* (a golden wattle growing wild over the farm). I'm not so sure, but the Riesling and Shiraz are sufficiently appealing to carry the day.

### Reilly's Wines ☆☆☆☆
*Corner Hill and Burra Streets, Mintaro, SA 5415, ☎ & ⓕ (08) 8843 9013; est 1994; ⚑ 10,000 cases; ⚐; A$; 7 days 10-5; ⋔; ⊨*

Adelaide cardiologist Justin Ardill and his wife Julie are relative newcomers to the Clare Valley, but their wine quality is improving year by year. An interesting sideline is the production of olive oil made from wild olive trees scattered around Mintaro. An on-site restaurant adds appeal.

### Sevenhill Cellars ☆☆☆☆⚋ V
*College Road, Sevenhill, SA 5453, ☎ (08) 8843 4222, ⓕ (08) 8843 4382; est 1851; ⚑ 35,000 cases; ⚐; A$; Mon-Fri 9-5, wkds & public hols 10-5; ⋔; cycle hire*

Sevenhill is one of the historical treasures of Australia, whose oft-photographed stone wine cellars are the oldest in the Clare Valley. Winemaking is still carried out under the direction of the Jesuitical Manresa Society; quality is very good, particularly that of the Riesling and powerful

Shiraz, but all the wines reflect the character of the estate-grown old-vine grapes. Exports to the UK and elsewhere.

### Skillogalee ☆☆☆♦

*Off Hughes Park Road, Sevenhill via Clare, SA 5453, ☎ (08) 8843 4311, Ⓕ (08) 8843 4343; est 1970; ♦ 7,000 cases; ☗; A$; 7 days 10-5; ⦿*

Owned by the Palmers since the late 1980s. The thirty-year-old terraced vines produce intensely rich, lime-juice Riesling, and opulently structured Shiraz (black cherry and mint) and Cabernets (succulent blackberry and vanilla). Exports to the UK and elsewhere.

### Stephen John Wines ☆☆☆☆

*Government Road, Watervale, SA 5452, ☎ & Ⓕ (08) 8843 0105; est 1994; ♦ 7,500 cases; ☗; A$; 7 days 11-5*

The John family has been at the heart of winemaking (and barrel-making) in the Barossa and Clare valleys for over a hundred years. Former Quelltaler chief winemaker Stephen John (and wife Rita) now run a family business with the cellar door housed in an old converted stone stable. Riesling and the various versions of Shiraz are very good indeed. Exports to the UK and elsewhere.

### Taylors ☆☆☆☆♦

*Taylors Road, Auburn, SA 5451, ☎ (08) 8849 2008, Ⓕ (08) 8849 2240; est 1969; ♦ 250,000 cases; ☗; A$; Mon-Fri 9-5, Sat & public hols 10-5, Sun 10-4*

With 500 hectares of estate vineyards, this is by far the largest producer in the Clare Valley. After building a very successful business based primarily on low prices and modest but reliable wine styles, Taylors has lifted quality spectacularly, particularly with the premium St Andrew's Range. Exports to the UK and elsewhere.

### Tim Adams ☆☆☆☆♦

*Warenda Road, Clare, SA 5453, ☎ (08) 8842 2429, Ⓕ (08) 8842 3550; est 1986; ♦ 35,000 cases; ☗; A$; Mon-Fri 10.30-5, wkds 11-5*

Former Leasingham winemaker Tim Adams runs a thriving contract winemaking business alongside that of his own wines. These are invariably full-bodied and full-flavoured, the reds (especially Aberfeldy Shiraz) crammed with ripe cherry, mulberry, and plum fruit. Exports to the UK and elsewhere.

### Tim Gramp ☆☆☆☆

*Mintaro/Leasingham Road, Watervale, SA 5452, ☎ (08) 8344 4079, Ⓕ (08) 8342 1379; est 1990; ♦ 6,000 cases; ☗; A$; wkds & hols 10.30-4.30*

Tim Gramp has built a solid reputation and business, buying grapes from others in the Clare Valley and McLaren Vale. Watervale Riesling (powerful lemon/citrus and mineral) and McLaren Vale Shiraz (dark chocolate and black cherry) are best. Exports to the UK and elsewhere.

### Wendouree ☆☆☆☆☆ V

*Wendouree Road, Clare, SA 5453, ☎ (08) 8842 2896; est 1895; ♦ 2,500 cases; ☗; A$; by appt*

An "iron fist in a velvet glove" is the best description for these extraordinary and ultra-long-lived wines. They are fashioned with passion and yet precision from a very old vineyard, with a unique terroir, by Tony and Lita Brady, who rightly see themselves as custodians of a priceless treasure. The hundred-year-old stone winery is virtually unchanged from the day it was built.

### Wilson Vineyard ☆☆☆☆♦

*Polish Hill River, Sevenhill via Clare, SA 5453, ☎ (08) 8843 4310; est 1974; ♦ 4,000 cases; ☗; A$; wkds 10-4*

Dr John Wilson is a tireless ambassador for the Clare Valley and for wine, and its beneficial effect on health. When still in charge of winemaking (the mantle has now passed to his son Daniel) he created wines that could occasionally be idiosyncratic, but in recent years have been most impressive, especially Riesling. Exports to the US.

# Adelaide Hills

Visitors to the Adelaide Hills, particularly in the autumn season, could be forgiven for thinking they were in England, with the blaze of orange, golden, and red leaves on the exotic deciduous trees and the little towns and hamlets. Although only thirty minutes' drive from the centre of Adelaide, the climate in the Hills is radically different. The 400- to 500-metre altitude is one of the principal factors, and often leads to a 10°C temperature differential at noon on a summer's day. Site selection (aspect, degree of slope, location) is critical. South, between Lenswood and Piccadilly, only Chardonnay and Pinot Noir can be relied upon to ripen fully, although Riesling and Sauvignon Blanc usually make racy, elegant wines. Shiraz and Cabernet have really only flourished in the north, on west-facing slopes, but some recent plantings of Shiraz in the south have resulted in striking Rhône-style wines.

The Adelaide Hills region is an ultra-sensitive water-catchment area for the city, and there are consequently exceptionally stringent controls on the building of wineries. As a result, there is much contract winemaking in shared facilities, which has aided rather than impaired wine quality. Petaluma and Glenara were the first and, for a long time, the only wineries. Nepenthe is a recent arrival, investing considerable capital and high-tech, expensive waste-removal systems. Bridgewater Mill (of Petaluma) is a Mecca in a beautiful and easily accessible region. There are fifty-six wine producers in the region.

### Annvers Wines ☆☆☆☆✦
*Lot 10, Razorback Road, Kangarilla, SA 5157, ☎ (08) 8374 1787, Ⓕ (08) 8374 2102; est 1998; ✧ 5,000 cases; no visitors*
Myriam and Wayne Keoghan source their grapes from vineyards in Langhorne Creek, McLaren Vale, and their own Annvers Vineyard in the Adelaide Hills. The focus is on superbly textured Shiraz and Cabernet Sauvignon. Exports to the UK and elsewhere.

### Ashton Hills ☆☆☆☆☆
*Tregarthen Road, Ashton, SA 5137, ☎ & Ⓕ (08) 8390 1243; est 1982; ✧ 1,500 cases; ♈; A$; wkds 11-5.30*
Stephen George is a modern-day renaissance man. He seems to effortlessly produce fragrant lime-and-mineral Riesling, slow-developing Chardonnay, and intense yet delicate Pinot Noir at this, his family-owned vineyard. He also makes the brooding, dark Wendouree Clare Valley red wines. Exports to the UK and US.

### Barratt ☆☆☆☆☆
*Uley Vineyard, Cornish Road, Summertown, SA 5141, ☎ & Ⓕ (08) 8390 1788; est 1993; ✧ 1,200 cases; ♈; A$; wkds & public hols 11.30-5, or by appt; small wine and food events*
Lindsay and Carolyn Barratt own this excellent 8.4-hectare vineyard, which they share-farm with Jeffrey Grosset. Grosset takes part of the production, and makes the remainder for the Barratt label. Ultra-complex,

Burgundian-accented Chardonnay and silky, plummy Pinot Noir are the result. Exports to the UK and US.

## Bird in Hand ☆☆☆☆✓

*Bird in Hand Road, Woodside, SA 5244, ☎ (08) 8232 9033, Ⓕ (08) 8232 9066; est 1997; ✦ 8,000 cases; no visitors*

Typically elegant and intense Sauvignon Blanc/Semillon, Sauvignon Blanc, and Merlot lead an impressive portfolio, the winery named after a nineteenth-century gold mine. Exports to the UK and elsewhere.

## Bridgewater Mill ☆☆☆☆

*Mount Barker Road, Bridgewater, SA 5155, ☎ (08) 8339 3422, Ⓕ (08) 8339 5311; est 1986; ✦ 50,000 cases; ⚑; A$; Mon-Fri 9.30-5, wkds 10-5; ⵏ*

Petaluma's second label, which sometimes lives in the shadow of its parent. Immaculately crafted Sauvignon Blanc, Chardonnay, Shiraz, and Cabernet/Malbec sourced from several regions. Superlative restaurant. Exports to the UK and elsewhere.

## Cawdor Wines ☆☆☆☆✓

*Old Mount Barker Road, Echunga, SA 5153, ☎ (08) 8388 8456, Ⓕ (08) 8388 8807; est 1999; ✦ 350 cases; ⚑; A$; by appt*

Jock Calder and family have established eighteen hectares of vines, selling the lion's share to Nepenthe, which in turn makes a small quantity of superb Sauvignon Blanc for Cawdor.

## Chain of Ponds ☆☆☆☆

*Adelaide Road, Gumeracha, SA 5233, ☎ (08) 8389 1415, Ⓕ (08) 8389 1877; est 1993; ✦ 17,500 cases; ⚑; A$; Mon-Fri 11-4, wkds & public hols 10.30-4.30; ⛺; ⵏ*

The largest grape-grower in the Adelaide Hills, owned by Caj and Genny Amadio. One hundred hectares of vineyards produce 1,000 tonnes of grapes a year; most is sold to Penfolds, increasing amounts skilfully made for Chain of Ponds by former Penfolds winemaker Neville Falkenberg. Riesling, Sauvignon Blanc, Semillon, Chardonnay, and Cabernet Sauvignon are all powerful and impressive. Exports to the UK and elsewhere.

## Geoff Hardy Wines ☆☆☆☆✓

*c/o Pertaringa Wines, Corner Hunt and Rifle Range Roads, McLaren Vale, SA 5171, ☎ (08) 8323 8125, Ⓕ (08) 8323 7766; est 1996; ✦ 3,000 cases; ⚑; A$; Mon-Fri 9-5, wkds & public hols 11-5*

Geoff Hardy is a member of the Hardy family who has gone his own way over the past two decades as a successful viticulturist. The K1 premium range introduced in late 2003 is truly excellent.

## Geoff Weaver ☆☆☆☆☆

*2 Gilpin Lane, Mitcham, SA 5062, ☎ (08) 8272 2105, Ⓕ (08) 8271 0177; est 1982; ✦ 3,500 cases; no visitors*

Former Hardy chief winemaker Geoff Weaver fastidiously crafts classic estate-grown lime-and-mineral Riesling, fragrant gooseberry/passion-fruit Sauvignon Blanc, and a truly classic, long-lived grapefruit, apple, and melon Chardonnay. All are packaged with the most beautiful labels in Australia. Exports to the UK and elsewhere.

## Hillstowe ☆☆☆☆

*104 Main Road, Hahndorf, SA 5245, ☎ (08) 8388 1400, Ⓕ (08) 8388 1411; est 1980; ✦ 12,000 cases; ⚑; A$; 7 days 10-5; café; gallery*

Hillstowe had no sooner been acquired by Banksia Wines (joining St Hallett and Tatachilla) than Banksia was taken over by Lion Nathan of New Zealand. Wine style has not suffered. Exports to the UK and elsewhere.

**Johnston Oakbank** ☆☆☆☆✓

*18 Oakwood Road, Oakbank, SA 5243, ☎ (08) 8388 4263, Ⓕ (08) 8388 4278; est 1843; ♦ 4,000 cases; ♥; A$; Mon-Fri 8-5*

The origins of this business, owned by the Johnston Group, date back to 1839, making it the oldest known family-owned producer in South Australia. Twenty-nine hectares of estate plantings provide lovely herb and gooseberry Sauvignon Blanc, all-spice, plum, and forest Pinot Noir, and raspberry/cherry Shiraz.

**Knappstein Lenswood Vineyards** ☆☆☆☆✓

*Crofts Road, Lenswood, SA 5240, ☎ (08) 8389 8111, Ⓕ (08) 8389 8555; est 1981; ♦ 10,000 cases; ♥; A$; by appt*

This is Tim Knappstein's third winemaking venture. Together with wife Annie, he makes complex, richly flavoured, barrel-fermented Chardonnay, intense Sauvignon Blanc and Semillon, and broodingly powerful Pinot Noir. Exports to the UK and elsewhere.

**The Lane** ☆☆☆☆✓

*Ravenswood Lane, Hahndorf, SA 5245, ☎ (08) 8388 1250, Ⓕ (08) 8388 7233; est 1993; ♦ 35,000 cases; no visitors*

Formerly known as Ravenswood Lane, a highly successful business owned by John and Helen Edwards which has profited from its close relationship with Hardys. Chardonnay, Cabernet Sauvignon, Merlot, Sauvignon Blanc, and the sparkling wine are all excellent. Exports to the UK and elsewhere.

**Leabrook Estate** ☆☆☆☆☆

*24 Tusmore Avenue, Leabrook, SA 5068, ☎ (08) 8331 7150, Ⓕ (08) 8364 1520; est 1998; ♦ 4,500 cases; ♥; A$; by appt*

Colin Best planted his substantial vineyard with an ultra-close 1.2 × 1.2 metre spacing, which has been an unqualified success. A glorious Cabernet Franc, reminiscent of Chinon, leads the way, with Cabernet/Merlot, Pinot Noir and Shiraz in close attendance.

**Longview Vineyard** ☆☆☆☆✓

*Pound Road, Macclesfield, SA 5153, ☎ (08) 8388 9694, Ⓕ (08) 8388 9693; est 1995; ♦ 5,300 cases; ♥; A$; Sun 11-5, or by appt*

Duncan MacGillivray made a small fortune from a lemon-based alcohol pop drink, and has invested it in fifty hectares of vineyards, and A$1.2 million worth of barrel storage, cellar-door, and function facilities. The diverse, high-quality range of wines has different contract winemakers.

**Malcolm Creek Vineyard** ☆☆☆☆

*Bonython Road, Kersbrook, SA 5231, ☎ & Ⓕ (08) 8389 3235; est 1982; ♦ 700 cases; ♥; A$; wkds & public hols 11-5, or by appt*

This is the low-profile retirement venture of Reg Tolley. The two wines (Chardonnay and Cabernet Sauvignon) are invariably well-made and age gracefully; worth seeking out.

**Mount Lofty Ranges Vineyard** ☆☆☆☆

*Harris Road, Lenswood, SA 5240, ☎ (08) 8389 8339, Ⓕ (08) 8389 8349; est 1992; ♦ 1,000 cases; ♥; A$; wkds 11-5, or by appt; ⚓*

Owned by Alan Herath and Jan Reed, who have been involved from the outset in establishing the 4.5-hectare vineyard. Both have professional careers but are intending to become full-time vignerons. Skilled winemaking by Peter Leske at Nepenthe has already brought rewards and recognition.

**Murdoch Hill** ☆☆☆⚐
   *Mappinga Road, Woodside, SA 5244, ☎ (08) 8389 7081, ⓕ (08) 8389 7991;*
   *est 1998; ⚶ 1,500 cases; ⚱; A$; by appt*
   A little over twenty-one hectares of vines have been planted on the
   undulating, gum-studded countryside of the Erinka property, owned by
   the Downer family, four kilometres (2.5 miles) east of Oakbank. Passion-
   fruit-accented Sauvignon Blanc and Cabernet Sauvignon are contract-
   made by Brian Light.

**Nepenthe Vineyards** ☆☆☆☆☆
   *Jones Road, Balhannah, SA 5240, ☎ (08) 8431 7588, ⓕ (08) 8431 7688;*
   *est 1994; ⚶ 60,000 cases; ⚱; A$; 7 days 10-4*
   The Tweddell family investment in 160 hectares of vineyards, a
   state-of-the-art winery, and skilled winemaking by Peter Leske has
   propelled Nepenthe into the first rank with a kaleidoscopic array of
   high-quality wines produced in substantial quantities. Exports to the
   UK and elsewhere.

**Normans** ☆☆☆⚐
   *Grant's Gully Road, Clarendon, SA 5157, ☎ (08) 8383 5555, ⓕ (08) 8383 5551;*
   *est 1853; ⚶ 80,000 cases; ⚱; A$; Mon-Sat 9-4*
   Now owned by Xanadu Normans, but with the Normans brands, especially
   estate-based Chais Clarendon, retained with a separate identity.

**Paracombe Wines** ☆☆☆☆⚐
   *Main Road, Paracombe, SA 5132, ☎ (08) 8380 5058, ⓕ (03) 8380 5488;*
   *est 1983; ⚶ 4,500 cases; no visitors*
   The twelve-hectare vineyard of the Drogemuller family has been
   progressively established since 1983. Part of the production is sold, but
   limited amounts of crisp Sauvignon Blanc, supple Chardonnay, spicy/berry
   Shiraz, and Reuben, a fragrant Bordeaux blend, lead the way. Exports to
   the UK and elsewhere.

**Petaluma** ☆☆☆☆☆
   *Spring Gully Road, Piccadilly, SA 5151, ☎ (08) 8339 4122, ⓕ (08) 8339 5253;*
   *est 1976; ⚶ 30,000 cases; (see Bridgewater Mill)*
   Universally recognized as one of Australia's finest wineries, founded and
   driven by the fearsome intellect and boundless energy of Brian Croser. It
   (together with its various group wineries) was acquired by Lion Nathan
   late in 2001, but Croser continues to ferociously protect the Petaluma name
   and quality. Exports to the UK and elsewhere.

**Pfitzner** ☆☆☆☆
   *PO Box 1098, North Adelaide, SA 5006, ☎ & ⓕ (08) 8390 0188; est 1996;*
   *⚶ 1,500 cases; no visitors*
   The subtitle to the Pfitzner name is Eric's Vineyard. The late Eric Pfitzner
   purchased and aggregated a number of small, subdivided farmlets to
   protect the beauty of the Piccadilly Valley from ugly rural development.
   Half of the twelve-hectare property has been planted, the remainder
   preserving the natural eucalyptus forest. The wines are made by Petaluma,
   with exports to the UK. The Pinot Noir is best.

**Piccadilly Fields** NR
   *185 Piccadilly Road, Piccadilly, SA 5151, ☎ (08) 8370 8800, ⓕ (08) 8232 5395;*
   *est 1989; ⚶ 2,000 cases; no visitors*
   Piccadilly Fields has only a passing resemblance to its original state. The
   Virgara family has joined with a syndicate of investors which jointly own

176 hectares of vineyards through various parts of the Adelaide Hills, producing up to 1,000 tonnes per year. The lion's share is sold as grapes to other winemakers, a token thirty or so tonnes held for the Piccadilly Fields label.

### Pike & Joyce ☆☆☆☆♪

*Mawson Road, Lenswood, SA 5240, ☎ (08) 8843 4370, ⓕ (08) 8843 4353; est 1998; ♦ 2,500 cases; no visitors*

A joint venture between the Pike family (of Clare Valley fame) and their relatives, the Joyce family, orchardists at Lenswood for over 100 years, recently diversifying with the planting of 18.5 hectares of vines. Chardonnay and Pinot Noir excel. Exports to the UK and elsewhere.

### Setanta Wines ☆☆☆☆

*RSD 43 Williamstown Road, Forreston, SA 5233, ☎ & ⓕ (08) 8380 5516; est 1997; ♦ 1,800 cases; no visitors*

A family-owned operation of the Irish-descended Sullivan family which burst onto the scene with strikingly imaginative packaging and super-premium-quality Riesling, Chardonnay, Shiraz, and Cabernet Sauvignon released in 2002–3. Exports to Ireland.

### Shaw & Smith ☆☆☆☆

*Lot 4, Jones Road, Balhannah, SA 5242, (08) 8398 0500, (08) 8398 0600; est 1989; ♦ 30,000 cases; ⟨glass⟩; A$; wkds 10-4*

Martin Shaw, one of the pioneering Australian flying winemakers, and Michael Hill Smith, Australia's first MW, make a formidable team. Immaculate Sauvignon Blanc and subtle yet powerful and textured Reserve Chardonnay have been joined by equally impressive Shiraz and Merlot. Exports to the UK and elsewhere.

# Adelaide Plains

This is one of the least appealing and most infrequently visited regions in Australia. It is laser-flat, searingly hot in summer, and not far to the east of the blue-collar industrial suburb of Elizabeth. However, with irrigation the region becomes an efficient grape producer. The very dry summer weather reduces the incidence of disease to the point where protective sprays are rarely needed; yields are high, and good sugar levels are routinely reached. Most of the production disappears into the anonymity of wine casks. There are nine producers in the region.

### Ceravolo Wines ☆☆☆♪

*Suite 16, Tranmere Village, 172 Glynburn Road, Tranmere, SA 5073, ☎ (08) 8336 4522, ⓕ (08) 8365 0538; est 1995; ♦ 10,000 cases; no visitors*

The Ceravolo family has established a substantial business in the Adelaide Plains region, moving from contract grape-growing to winemaking. In 1999 the label was launched, centred around Shiraz, but with Chardonnay and Merlot in support. Conspicuous success at the London International Wine Challenge led to exports to the UK.

### Diloreto Wines ☆☆☆☆

*45 Wilpena Terrace, Kilkenny, SA 5009, ☎ (08) 8345 0123; est 2001; ♦ 250 cases; no visitors*

The Diloreto family has been growing grapes since the 1960s, with eight hectares of Shiraz, Cabernet Sauvignon, Mourvèdre, and Grenache. Son

Tony decided to do some home winemaking, and in 2001 entered two Shirazes in the Australian Amateur Wine Show, competing against 700 vignerons from around Australia. Both won gold medals, and the judges strongly recommended that the wines be sold commercially. Great oaks from little acorns indeed.

**Primo Estate** ☆☆☆☆↙
*Old Port Wakefield Road, Virginia, SA 5120, ☎ (08) 8380 9442, Ⓕ (08) 8380 9696; est 1979; ♦ 20,000 cases; ⏱; A$; June-Aug Mon-Sat 10-4, Sept-May Mon-Fri 10-4*
Joe Grilli is little short of a magician, producing Colombard that tastes like a zesty young Sauvignon Blanc, an elegant Shiraz, a trendy Shiraz/Sangiovese, and a masterly Amarone-influenced Cabernet/Merlot made from partially dried Coonawarra and McLaren Vale grapes. Exports to the UK and elsewhere.

# Coonawarra

After litigation which dragged on for almost ten years, cost millions of dollars in legal and expert witness fees, and in the end extended the boundaries further than the initial adversaries ever contemplated, the region can now focus on what it does best – providing grapes and wine of the highest quality. Highest, that is, when proper viticultural methods are used to match variety with soil, to control yield, and to maximize the potential quality. Here the news is good: led by Southcorp, hundreds of thousands of dollars are being spent annually to reverse the low-cost minimal pruning techniques developed in the late 1970s and early 1980s, as well as introducing sophisticated systems measuring the vines' need for water. There is no question this is Australia's foremost region for Cabernet Sauvignon (a quick look at wine-show results around the country stifles any argument to the contrary) and provides high-quality Shiraz and Merlot.

Riesling, Sauvignon Blanc, and Chardonnay are all made, but it is easy to wonder why, unless the vines are planted on the lighter, sandy soils or the black clays. It is here the chickens come home to roost in the wake of the enlarged boundary lines, for these soils are vastly inferior to the terra rossa which is the key to Coonawarra's greatness.

There are thirty-one wine producers in the region.

**Balnaves of Coonawarra** ☆☆☆☆☆ V
*Main Road, Coonawarra, SA 5263, ☎ (08) 8737 2946, Ⓕ (08) 8737 2945; est 1975; ♦ 10,000 cases; ⏱; A$; Mon-Fri 9-5, wkds 10-5*
Viticultural consultant-cum-grape-grower Doug Balnaves built his striking 300-tonne winery in 1996. Under the direction of former Wynns winemaker Peter Bissell all of the wines have risen to the very top of the Coonawarra tree. Exports to the UK and elsewhere.

**Bowen Estate** ☆☆☆☆
*Riddoch Highway, Coonawarra, SA 5263, ☎ (08) 8737 2229, Ⓕ (08) 8737 2173; est 1972; ♦ 12,000 cases; ⏱; A$; 7 days 10-5*
The ruddy cheeks and ready smile of Doug Bowen match the temperament and visage of his golden Labrador and the generous, welcoming style of his wines. He favours late picking, producing rich wines in intermediate vintages where others seem to struggle. Exports to the UK and elsewhere.

### Brand's of Coonawarra ☆☆☆☆☆

*Riddoch Highway, Coonawarra, SA 5263, ☎ (08) 8736 3260, Ⓕ (08) 8736 3208; est 1966; ⬧ NFP; ⚑; A$; Mon-Fri 8-5, wkds 10-4; Ⅳ*

Now fully owned by McWilliam's, but with continued Brand family involvement, Brand's achieved its full potential in the latter part of the 1990s. Its icon reds (Stentiford's Reserve Shiraz and Patron's Reserve Cabernet blend) are outstanding – as is its Riesling with bottle age.

### DiGiorgio Family Wines ☆☆☆☆

*Riddoch Highway, Coonawarra, SA 5263, ☎ (08) 8736 3222, Ⓕ (08) 8736 3233; est 1998; ⬧ 10,000 cases; ⚑; A$; 7 days 10-5*

Stefano DiGiorgio emigrated from Abruzzi, Italy, arriving in Australia in July 1952. His business interests flourished, and in 1989 he ventured into grape-growing. The family now has 140 hectares of vines in the Limestone Coast Zone, and in 2002 purchased the Rouge Homme winery from Southcorp. Wine production under the DiGiorgio brand is but a small part of a multifaceted wine business.

### Hollick ☆☆☆☆

*Riddoch Highway, Coonawarra, SA 5263, ☎ (08) 8737 2318, Ⓕ (08) 8737 2952; est 1983; ⬧ 50,000 cases; ⚑; A$; 7 days 9-5; ⦿*

Ian Hollick has been the winner of many wine trophies (including the most famous of all, the Jimmy Watson). His elegant wines are well-crafted and competitively priced, albeit light-bodied. A luxury cellar door and restaurant opened in June 2002. Exports to the UK and elsewhere.

### Jamiesons Run Winery ☆☆☆☆☆ V

*Penola-Naracoorte Road, Coonawarra, SA 5263, ☎ (08) 8736 3380, Ⓕ (08) 8736 3307; est 1955; ⬧ 160,000 cases; ⚑; A$; Mon-Fri 9-4.30, wkds 10-4*

Once the prized possession of a stand-alone Mildara, which spawned a child called Jamiesons Run to fill the need for a cost-effective second label. Now the name Mildara is very nearly part of ancient wine history, and the child has usurped the parent. Worldwide distribution of its large range via Beringer Blass.

### Katnook Estate ☆☆☆☆☆

*Riddoch Highway, Coonawarra, SA 5263, ☎ (08) 8737 2394, Ⓕ (08) 8737 2397; est 1979; ⬧ 100,000 cases; ⚑; A$; Mon-Fri 9-4.30, Sat 10-4.30, Sun 12-4.30*

Not only a major contract grape-grower in Coonawarra but going from strength to strength as a winemaker. Fragrant, Germanic-styled Riesling, long-lived, elegantly tangy Chardonnay, crisp Sauvignon Blanc, berryish, cedary Merlot, subtly oaked, cassis-driven Cabernet Sauvignon, and the intense flagships Odyssey (Reserve Cabernet) and Prodigy (Reserve Shiraz) are all impressive. Exports to the UK and elsewhere.

### Ladbroke Grove ☆☆☆☆☆

*Riddoch Highway, Coonawarra, SA 5263, ☎ (08) 8737 3777, Ⓕ (08) 8737 3268; est 1982; ⬧ 5,000 cases; ⚑; A$; Wed-Sun 10-5*

Born again under the (new) ownership of John Cox and Marie Valenzuela, Ladbroke Grove is producing stunning cassis and blackberry Cabernet Sauvignon and supple, smooth black-cherry Shiraz.

### Leconfield ☆☆☆☆☆

*Riddoch Highway, Coonawarra, SA 5263, ☎ (08) 8737 2326, Ⓕ (08) 8737 2285; est 1974; ⬧ 15,000 cases; ⚑; A$; 7 days 10-5*

A distinguished estate with a proud, even if relatively short, history. Long renowned for its Cabernet Sauvignon, the overall style is fruit- rather than oak-driven. The advent of Paul Gordon (ex Rouge Homme) has seen a significant lift in quality. Exports to the UK and elsewhere.

### Lindemans (Coonawarra) ☆☆☆☆↓

*Main Penola-Naracoorte Road, Coonawarra, SA 5263, ☎ (02) 4998 7684, Ⓕ (02) 4998 7682; est 1908; ⚘ NFP; ⚑; A$; no visitors*

Part of the Southcorp group, and one of the major brands in Coonawarra. Its trio of St George Vineyard Cabernet Sauvignon, Limestone Ridge Shiraz/Cabernet, and Pyrus (a Cabernet-dominant Bordeaux blend) routinely amass gold and silver medals; they all have elegant fruit, obvious oak, and soft, silky tannins in a user-friendly style. Worldwide distribution.

### Majella ☆☆☆☆☆

*Lynn Road, Coonawarra, SA 5263, ☎ (08) 8736 3055, Ⓕ (08) 8736 3057; est 1969; ⚘ 12,000 cases; ⚑; A$; 7 days 10-4.30*

Brian (the Prof) Lynn was a highly successful grape-grower before deciding he would keep part of the production from his sixty-one-hectare vineyard to make high-quality Shiraz and Cabernet Sauvignon. He subsequently released a super-premium red called The Malleea, consistently of exceptional quality.

### Murdock ☆☆☆☆

*Riddoch Highway, Coonawarra, SA 5263, ☎ (08) 8737 3700, Ⓕ (08) 8737 2107; est 1998; ⚘ 2,000 cases; no visitors*

The Murdock family has established fifteen hectares of Cabernet Sauvignon, Shiraz, Merlot, Chardonnay, and Riesling, and produces small quantities of an outstanding Cabernet Sauvignon, contract-made by Peter Bissell at Balnaves.

### Parker Coonawarra Estate ☆☆☆☆☆

*Penola Road, Coonawarra, SA 5263, ☎ (02) 8737 3525, Ⓕ (02) 8737 3527; est 1985; ⚘ 5,000 cases; 7 days 10-4*

The name of the flagship Terra Rossa First Growth may grate, but the quality is undoubted. The winemaking skills of Peter Bissell and the surprise appointment of Andrew Pirie as chief executive underwrite the quality and focus of the wines, but its acquisition by Yering Station (*q.v.*) in May 2004 may lead to changes. Exports to the UK and elsewhere.

### Penley Estate ☆☆☆☆↓

*McLeans Road, Coonawarra, SA 5263, ☎ (08) 8736 3211, Ⓕ (08) 8736 3124; est 1988; ⚘ 30,000 cases; ⚑; A$; 7 days 10-4*

Kym Tolley was bred in the vinous "purple" via the Penfold and Tolley families, but spent seventeen years making wine for others before establishing Penley Estate (get it?). The Reserve Cabernet Sauvignon is tops, culled from eighty-one hectares of estate vineyards. Exports to the UK and elsewhere.

### Punters Corner ☆☆☆☆↓

*Corner Riddoch Highway and Racecourse Road, Coonawarra, SA 5263, ☎ (08) 8737 2007, Ⓕ (08) 8737 3138; est 1988; ⚘ 8,500 cases; ⚑; A$; 7 days 10-5; ⊨*

Started life as James Haselgrove in 1975, and was acquired in 1992 by a group of investors with a sense of humour. Innovative packaging and the skills of contract winemaker Peter Bissell (at Balnaves) have turned this into a past-the-post favourite. Exports to the UK and elsewhere.

**Redman** ☆☆☆

*Riddoch Highway, Coonawarra, SA 5253, ☎ (08) 8736 3331; Ⓕ (08) 8736 3013; est 1966; ⚘ 11,000 cases; ⚑; A$; Mon-Fri 9-5, wkds 10-4*

After a prolonged period of mediocrity, the Redman wines are showing sporadic signs of improvement, partly through the introduction of modest amounts of new oak, even if principally American. It would be nice to say the wines now reflect the full potential of the vineyard, but there is still some way to go.

**Reschke Wines** ☆☆☆☆

*Level 1, 43 The Parade, Norwood, SA 5067, ☎ (08) 8363 3343, Ⓕ (08) 8363 3378; est 1998; ⚘ 6,000 cases; no visitors*

It's not often that the first release from a new winery is priced at A$100 a bottle, but that is precisely what Reschke Wines Empyrean Cabernet Sauvignon has achieved. The family has been a landholder in the Coonawarra region for almost a hundred years with (inter alia) 105 hectares of Cabernet Sauvignon in production.

**Rymill** ☆☆☆☆

*The Riddoch Run Vineyards, Coonawarra, SA 5263, ☎ (08) 8736 5001, Ⓕ (08) 8736 5040; est 1970; ⚘ 50,000 cases; ⚑; A$; 7 days 10-5; ⚔*

The Rymills are descendants of John Riddoch, founding father of the region, and have long owned some of the finest Coonawarra soil, on which they have grown grapes since 1970. Present plantings cover 170 hectares. A handsome winery was built in 1991, marking a major entry into winemaking. Exports to the UK and elsewhere.

**S Kidman Wines** ☆☆☆☆⚘

*Riddoch Highway, Coonawarra, SA 5263, ☎ (08) 8736 5071, Ⓕ (08) 8736 5070; est 1984; ⚘ 8,000 cases; ⚑; A$; 7 days 9-5*

Sid Kidman is one of the pioneers with a fully mature sixteen-hectare estate vineyard. Quality has been decidedly variable; quite why, I am not sure.

**Wynns Coonawarra Estate** ☆☆☆☆☆⚘ V

*Memorial Drive, Coonawarra, SA 5263, ☎ (08) 8736 2225, Ⓕ (08) 8736 2228; est 1891; ⚘ NFP; ⚑; A$; 7 days 10-5; platters; tutored tastings*

The most important winery in Coonawarra and surely its best. Part of Southcorp, its two flagships are the awesomely rich and concentrated John Riddoch Cabernet and Michael Shiraz (approach with extreme caution when less than ten years old). Supported by a spread of perfectly crafted wines comprising a floral, crisp Riesling and a subtle, barrel-fermented Chardonnay (both ludicrously cheap), Shiraz, a Cabernet/Shiraz/Merlot blend, and Cabernet Sauvignon (great value). Worldwide exports.

**Yalumba The Menzies** ☆☆☆☆⚘

*Riddoch Highway, Coonawarra, SA 5263, ☎ (08) 8737 3603, Ⓕ (08) 8737 3604; est 2002; ⚘ 5,000 cases; ⚑; A$; 7 days 10-4.30*

For decades an active grape buyer and thereafter landholder in the Limestone Coast Zone, Yalumba has established a physical presence in Coonawarra via a striking rammed-earth tasting and function centre supporting its range of Coonawarra and Smith & Hooper Wrattonbully wines.

**Zema Estate** ☆☆☆☆☆ V

*Riddoch Highway, Coonawarra, SA 5263, ☎ (08) 8736 3219, Ⓕ (08) 8736 3280; est 1982; ⚘ 10,000 cases; ⚑; A$; 7 days 9-5*

One of the last outposts of hand-pruning in Coonawarra; winemaking practices are straightforward. If ever there were an example of great wines being made in the vineyard, this is it. Beautifully proportioned, fruit-driven Shiraz and Cabernet Sauvignon stand out. Exports to the UK and elsewhere.

# Padthaway

Once called Keppoch, this region shares a number of things in common with Coonawarra, not least its unremarkable topography and relative isolation. It has similar patches of terra rossa soil, although not so restricted or regular in its distribution, and it also has underground water for irrigation and spring frost control. Its points of difference are the somewhat warmer climate and the gentle undulations of the land, which are associated with significant changes in soil type. The suitability of the best soil was recognized by government studies back in 1944, but it was not until 1963 that Seppelt acquired land for planting. It was followed by BRL Hardy and Lindemans in 1968, but it was not until 1998 that the first large winery was built in the region, Hardys Stonehaven Estate, with a particularly attractive cellar door.

It has since become startlingly clear that, properly managed, Padthaway is capable of far, far more. The last five to ten years have seen the region gain a reputation as one of Australia's premium white-wine regions. That said, it produces outstanding wines across the full spectrum, from Riesling, Sauvignon Blanc, and Chardonnay to Shiraz, Merlot, and Cabernet Sauvignon. Tangy Chardonnay and succulent, dark-hued Shiraz are the best. There are six wine producers in the region.

**Browns of Padthaway** ☆☆☆⁄
*Keith Road, Padthaway, SA 5271, ☎ (08) 8765 6063, Ⓕ (08) 8765 6083; est 1993; ◈ 35,000 cases; ▾; A$; at Padthaway Estate*
After many years as major contract grape-growers, the Brown family entered the winemaking scene in 1993. The early results were disappointing, but have improved greatly since 1998.

**Henry's Drive** ☆☆☆☆
*PMB 182 Naracoorte, SA 5271, ☎ (08) 8765 6057, Ⓕ (08) 8765 6090; est 1998; ◈ 8,000 cases; ▾; no visitors*
This substantial vineyard has 130 hectares of Cabernet Sauvignon, Shiraz, Chardonnay, and Merlot. The excellent red wines are made by Sparky and Sarah Marquis, for many years the winemaking duo at Fox Creek Wines. Exports to the UK and elsewhere.

**Lindemans (Padthaway)** ☆☆☆☆ V
*Naracoorte Road, Padthaway, SA 5271, ☎ (02) 4998 7684, Ⓕ (02) 4998 7682; est 1908; ◈ NFP; no visitors*
A revamped product range offers Reserve Padthaway Chardonnay, Shiraz, and Cabernet/Merlot, and a keenly priced Limestone Coast varietal range at half the price of the Reserves. Chardonnay is especially commendable. Exports to the UK and elsewhere.

**Padthaway Estate** ☆☆☆☆
*Riddoch Highway, Padthaway, SA 5271, ☎ (08) 8734 3148, Ⓕ (08) 8734 3188; est 1980; ◈ 6,000 cases; ▾; A$; 7 days 10-4; ▮◉▮; ⊨; tennis; winter golf*
Established in a gracious old stone wool shed, this was until 1998 the only resident winery (specializing in sparkling wines). In association with a Relais et Châteaux Homestead, it also offers luxurious

accommodation, fine food, and a tasting centre for regional wines. Exports to the UK.

**Stonehaven** ☆☆☆☆ **V**

*Riddoch Highway, Padthaway, SA 5271,* ☎ *(08) 8765 6140,* Ⓕ *(08) 8765 6137; est 1998;* ❧ *NFP; 7 days 10-4;* 🍴

Hardys' A$20 million Stonehaven winery opened in March 1998, the largest single winery to be built in the previous twenty years. Padthaway fruit has been an important contributor to the Eileen Hardy Chardonnay and Shiraz flagships, as well as a range of good, regionally branded varietal wines under the Stonehaven label. Exports to the UK and elsewhere.

# Mount Benson and Robe

Mount Benson has its own Geographic Indication registration; Robe has (apparently) decided it does not need one, nor does it seem disposed to join Mount Benson! Yet both regions have undulating countryside (Mount Benson is a complete misnomer, incidentally) and terra rossa over limestone interspersed with siliceous sands on the ridges and hillside slopes.

Given the proximity of the ocean (and numerous large, shallow lakes), it is hard to imagine that frost poses a threat, but it can do so. In fact, these two regions are by far the coolest in the Limestone Coast Zone (which also includes Coonawarra and Padthaway), yet rather unexpectedly have proved capable of producing excellent Cabernet Sauvignon and Shiraz. In the longer term, yield may prove the most important factor, as the potential is unquestionably there. The driving force in the establishment of Robe has been Southcorp, which now has 150 hectares planted. Over in Mount Benson, M Chapoutier & Co (of Rhône Valley fame) moved in during 1998 to produce wines for the Asian market, followed by the striking (and large) Kreglinger winery. There are twelve wine producers in the region.

**Anthony Dale** ☆☆☆☆⁄

*Lot 202, Robe Road, Bray, SA 5276,* ☎ & Ⓕ *(08) 8735 7255; est 1994;* ❧ *1,750 cases; no visitors*

A single wine, a blend of Shiraz and Cabernet Sauvignon, is made for Anthony Dale by former Penfolds winemaker John Bird. The very low yield (2.5 tonnes per hectare) nonetheless results in a light-bodied, elegant wine reflecting the sand and limestone terroir.

**Cape Jaffa Wines** ☆☆☆☆

*Limestone Coast Road, Cape Jaffa, SA 5276,* ☎ *(08) 8768 5053,* Ⓕ *(08) 8768 5040; est 1993;* ❧ *18,000 cases;* 🍷 *A$; 7 days 10-5*

The first Mount Benson winery, producing a range of very elegant wines with various appellations, increasingly from Mount Benson, but still venturing elsewhere. Sauvignon Blanc, Semillon/Sauvignon Blanc (Mount Benson and Padthaway), and Mount Benson are the picks. Exports to the UK and elsewhere.

**Frog Island** ☆☆☆☆ **V**

*PO Box 423, Kingston SE, SA 5275,* ☎ *(08) 8768 5000,* Ⓕ *(08) 8768 5008; est 2003;* ❧ *3,500 cases; no visitors*

Sarah Squire (daughter of Ralph Fowler) is producing delicious Chardonnay and Shiraz from Robe and Mount Benson sources.

### Guichen Bay Vineyards ☆☆☆↗

*PO Box 582, Newport, NSW 2106, ☎ (02) 9997 6677, ℉ (02) 9997 6177; est 2003; ♦ 200 cases; no visitors*

Three adjacent vineyards, with 120 hectares of vines, have decided to vinify part of their production, starting with a token amount of aromatic Sauvignon Blanc and elegant Shiraz, but with an increasing range of varietals planned for the future.

### Kreglinger Estate NR

*Limestone Coast Road, Mount Benson, SA 5265, ☎ (08) 8768 5080, ℉ (08) 8768 5083; est 2000; ♦ 85,000 cases; no visitors*

By far the largest Mount Benson development, with a 2,000-tonne winery and 160-hectare vineyard owned by the Belgian company G & C Kreglinger, which also owns Pipers Brook Vineyard (and, in Pomerol, Vieux Château Certan). No wines available at the time of going to print.

### M Chapoutier Australia ☆☆☆↗

*PO Box 437, Robe, SA 5276, ☎ (08) 8768 5076, ℉ (08) 8768 5073; est 1998; ♦ 4,000 cases; no visitors*

A thirty-six-hectare biodynamically farmed vineyard of Shiraz, Cabernet Sauvignon, Marsanne, Viognier, and Sauvignon Blanc has had its problems (mainly frost) but exotic, slightly funky Shiraz does reflect the cool climate. Exports to the UK and elsewhere.

### Ralph Fowler Wines ☆☆☆↗

*Limestone Coast Road, Mount Benson, SA 5275, ☎ (08) 8768 5000, ℉ (08) 8768 5008; est 1999; ♦ 6,000 cases; ☗; A$; 7 days 10-5*

Veteran winemaker Ralph Fowler helped design the Kreglinger winery and has a consulting role there; his home patch is headed by complex liquorice, spice, and blackberry Shiraz/Viognier and a blackcurrant and cedar Limestone Coast Cabernet Sauvignon, both excellent.

### Stoney Rise ☆☆☆↗

*PO Box 12, Kings Meadows, Tas 7249, ☎ 0419 540 770, ℉ (03) 6243 2076; est 2000; ♦ 2,500 cases; no visitors*

Joe Holyman (who also works at Cape Jaffa) makes Sauvignon Blanc, Hey Hey Rosé and Cotes du Robe Shiraz, all with great personality. Exports to the US.

### Wangolina Station ☆☆☆☆

*Corner Southern Ports Highway/Limestone Coast Road, Kingston SE, SA 5275; ☎ (08) 8768 6187, ℉ (08) 8768 6149; ♦ 1,500 cases; ☗; A$; 7 days 10-5*

Four generations of the Goode family have been graziers at Wangolina Station; fifth-generation Anita Goode has nibbled off a corner to plant eight hectares of Shiraz, Cabernet Sauvignon, Sauvignon Blanc, and Semillon. The fragrant Cabernet and fresh, clear Sauvignon Blanc amply justify the decision.

### Wehl's Mount Benson Vineyards ☆☆☆☆☆

*Wrights Bay Road, Mount Benson, SA 5275, ☎ & ℉ (08) 8768 6251; est 1989; ♦ 1,000 cases; ☗; A$; 7 days 10-4*

Peter and Leah Wehl were the first to plant vines in the Mount Benson area, with twenty-four hectares dating back to 1989. An array of glorious red wines was produced in 2002, underlining the ability of the Mount Benson region to produce joyously fruity, intensely elegant wines.

# Wrattonbully

Another region in the Limestone Coast Zone chosen for viticulture because of its abundance of terra rossa soil and the ample non-saline underground water. After a slow start in the 1970s, the region has developed dramatically. Hardys, Beringer Blass, and Yalumba have been in the vanguard of the vineyard growth, and are responsible for a significant part of the 1,000-plus hectares planted so far. Its climate is poised between neighbours Coonawarra and Padthaway, warmer than the former and cooler than the latter, although there is surprising variation across what is a basically flat region. The bottom line, as it were, is a temperate region ideally suited to the production of medium- to full-bodied wines based primarily on Cabernet, Merlot, and Shiraz. The announcement of the formation of Tapanappa in 2004 has given the region an unexpected (but thoroughly justified) boost. There are four wine producers in the region.

**Kopparossa Estate** ☆☆☆
*PO Box 922, Naracoorte, SA 5271, ☎ 1800 620 936, Ⓕ (08) 8762 0937; est 1996; ⚭ 5,000 cases; no visitors*
Industry veteran winemakers Mike Press and Gavin Hogg formed a partnership to establish an eighty-hectare vineyard, but put it on the market for sale in March 2002, having already produced stylish wines.

**Russet Ridge** ☆☆☆⸱
*Corner Caves Road and Riddoch Highway, Naracoorte, SA 5271, ☎ (08) 8762 0114, Ⓕ (08) 8762 0341; est 2000; ⚭ 35,000 cases; ⚱; A$; Thurs-Mon 11-4.30; ⚐*
This is the former Heathfield Ridge winery, built in 1998 as a contract crush and winemaking facility for multiple clients, but purchased by Orlando in 2000. It is the only winery in the large Wrattonbully region, and also receives Orlando's Coonawarra and Padthaway grapes, and other Limestone Coast fruit.

**Stone Coast** ☆☆☆☆
*18 North Terrace, Adelaide, SA 5000, ☎ (08) 8212 1801, Ⓕ (08) 8212 4022; est 1997; ⚭ 900 cases; no visitors*
The development of the thirty-three hectares of Cabernet Sauvignon and eleven hectares of Shiraz which constitute the vineyard was exceptionally difficult. It is situated on a terra rossa ridge top, but had unusually thick limestone slabs running through it. A ninety-five-tonne bulldozer did the job; the immensely experienced Steve Maglieri is now making The Struggle Shiraz and The Commitment Cabernet Sauvignon.

**Tapanappa NR**
*PO Box 174, Crafers, SA 5152, ☎ 0418 818 223, Ⓕ (08) 8370 8374; est 2003; ⚭ NFP; no visitors*
Arguably the most interesting of all new wineries to be announced in Australia over the past few years. Its partners are Brian Croser of Petaluma, Jean-Michel Cazes of Château Lynch-Bages in Pauillac, and Société Jacques Bollinger, the parent company of Champagne Bollinger.

The core of the business is the Koppamurra vineyard acquired from Koppamurra Wines prior to the 2003 vintage. Obviously, no wines yet released.

# McLaren Vale

The development of viticulture in the Southern Vales, an area stretching from Reynella to McLaren Vale to Langhorne Creek, was due almost exclusively to the efforts of three Englishmen – John Reynell, Thomas Hardy, and Dr AC Kelly – with a lesser contribution from George Manning at Hope Farm. John Reynell laid the foundations for Chateau Reynella in 1838. As in the Clare Valley, the fertility of the soil was soon exhausted, and by the mid-1870s the once-thriving township of McLaren Vale was all but deserted. Thanks to the success of Thomas Hardy, by 1903 the nineteen wine producers in the region were producing over 3,000,000 litres of wine. Much of it was deeply coloured, high-alcohol, tannic, dry red exported to the UK. The Emu Wine Company continued this business until well into the 1950s, before being acquired by Thomas Hardy (now Hardys).

At the height of the white-wine boom, it became apparent that McLaren Vale could produce excellent Chardonnay, and good Sauvignon Blanc and Semillon. This discovery temporarily diverted attention from the outstanding quality of its old-vine Shiraz and Grenache, and its more than useful Cabernet. It is clear that there is enough maritime influence to invest the red wines with elegance, yet sufficient warmth to guarantee a lush, velvety texture and a recurrent taste theme of fine, dark chocolate.

Over all, McLaren Vale is vying with Coonawarra and the Clare Valley to be South Australia's best red-wine region (with profuse apologies to the Barossa Valley). There are eighty-nine wine producers in the region.

## Andrew Garrett ☆☆☆☆ V
*Ingoldby Road, McLaren Flat, SA 5171, ☎ (08) 8383 0005, Ⓕ (08) 8383 0790; est 1983; ◈ 170,000 cases; ℟; A$; 7 days 10-4*
This estate bears the name of its founder, who has long since moved on. It is now a brand in the Beringer Blass empire, but thanks to the skill of winemaker Charles Hargrave produces luscious, peachy Chardonnay and a scented cherry, chocolate, and vanilla Shiraz with impressive regularity.

## Arakoon ☆☆☆☆↓
*229 Main Road, McLaren Vale, SA 5171, ☎ (08) 8323 7339, Ⓕ (02) 6566 6288; est 1999; ◈; ℟; A$; Fri-Sun, or by appt*
After an irreverent start, Arakoon has become altogether serious with a string of excellent Shiraz and Shiraz blends closed with screwcaps, all abounding in black fruits and regional chocolate. Exports to the UK and elsewhere.

## Bent Creek Vineyards ☆☆☆☆
*Lot 10, Blewitt Springs Road, McLaren Flat, SA 5171, ☎ (08) 8383 0414, Ⓕ (08) 8239 1538; est 2001; ◈ 5,000 cases; ℟; A$; Sun & public hols 11-5*
Loretta and Peter Polson became wine drinkers and collectors a decade before they acquired a small patch of forty-year-old dry-grown Chardonnay and Shiraz at McLaren Flat, followed by another small vineyard. Michael Scarpantoni makes the wines, with powerful blackberry and chocolate Shiraz to the fore.

**Bosworth** ☆☆☆☆
*Edgehill Vineyards, Gaffney Road, Willunga, SA 5172, ☏ (08) 8556 2441, Ⓕ (08) 8556 4881; est 1996; ⚘ 1,000 cases; ☖; A$; by appt*
Produced from 6.5 hectares of certified A-grade organic Shiraz and Cabernet Sauvignon, the wines branded Battle of Bosworth to signify the viticultural challenge the organic approach poses. The wines are quite elegant, a rarity these days in the region.

**Cape Barren Wines** ☆☆☆☆⚘
*Lot 20, Little Road, Willunga, SA 5172, ☏ (08) 8556 4374, Ⓕ (08) 8556 4364; est 1999; ⚘ 1,600 cases; ☖; A$; by appt*
A single wine made from four hectares of seventy-year-old Shiraz vines at Blewitt Springs in archetypal McLaren Vale style, with lashings of dark chocolate wrapped around a core of blackberry fruit, the oak barely evident.

**Cascabel** ☆☆☆☆
*Rogers Road, Willunga, SA 5172, ☏ (08) 8557 4434, Ⓕ (08) 8557 4435; est 1997; ⚘ 2,500 cases; ☖; no visitors*
Proprietors Susana Fernandez and Duncan Ferguson, although young, have made wine in seven countries. The focus here is to produce red wines with a mix of Rhône Valley and Rioja influences, using estate-grown Tempranillo, Graciano, Monastrell, Grenache, Shiraz, and Viognier. Exports to the UK and elsewhere.

**Chalk Hill** ☆☆☆☆⚘
*PO Box 205, McLaren Vale, SA 5171, ☏ (08) 8556 2121, Ⓕ (08) 8556 2221; est 1973; ⚘ 2,500 cases; no visitors*
Chalk Hill is in full flight again, drawing upon the 12.5 hectares of vineyards for grape-growing owners John and Di Harvey, who acquired Chalk Hill in 1996. Dark-chocolate-accented Shiraz and blackberry Cabernet lead the way, now joined by very impressive Barbera and Sangiovese.

**Chapel Hill** ☆☆☆☆
*Chapel Hill Road, McLaren Vale, SA 5171, ☏ (08) 8323 8429, Ⓕ (08) 8323 9245; est 1979; ⚘ 45,000 cases; ☖; A$; 7 days 12-5*
In the second half of 2000, Chapel Hill was sold to the diversified Swiss group Thomas Schmidheiny, which owns the respected Cuvaison Winery in California. It is in safe hands, with elegant Chardonnay and Cabernet Sauvignon leading the way. Exports to the UK and elsewhere.

**Clarendon Hills Winery** ☆☆☆☆⚘
*Brookmans Road, Blewitt Springs, SA 5171, ☏ & Ⓕ (08) 8364 1484; est 1989; ⚘ 12,000 cases; ☖; A$; by appt*
Roman Bratasiuk is a larger-than-life figure who makes larger-than-life wines: immense, brooding reds from small patches of old, low-yielding vines. Shiraz and Grenache are the best, much headed to the US market. Exports to the UK and elsewhere.

**Classic McLaren Wines** ☆☆☆☆
*Lot B, Coppermine Road, McLaren Vale, SA 5171, ☏ & Ⓕ (08) 8323 9551; est 1996; ⚘ 7,000 cases; ☖; A$; by appt*
Tony and Krystina De Lisio have established a substantial business in a relatively short period of time. They have planted forty-five hectares of Shiraz, Merlot, Cabernet Sauvignon, Semillon, and Chardonnay, and are currently building a new winery and underground cellar. Exports to the UK and elsewhere.

### Coriole ☆☆☆☆⁄

*Chaffeys Road, McLaren Vale, SA 5171, ☎ (08) 8323 8305, Ⓕ (08) 8323 9136;*
*est 1967; ♦ 34,000 cases; ⴲ; A$; Mon-Fri 10-5; wkds & public hols 11-5; wkd lunches*

Coriole neatly balances the traditional virtues of Shiraz (Lloyd Reserve from
seventy-year-old vines at the pinnacle) and the trendy appeal of Sangiovese.
Also offers impeccable, fragrant, lemony Semillon and luscious, blackberry-
and-plum Grenache/Shiraz. Exports to the UK and elsewhere.

### d'Arenberg ☆☆☆☆☆

*Osborn Road, McLaren Vale, SA 5171, ☎ (08) 8323 8206, Ⓕ (08) 8323 8423;*
*est 1912; ♦ 180,000 cases; ⴲ; A$; 7 days 10-5; ⴵ*

The garrulous labels (front and back) should not deceive or distract you.
This historic winery is doing everything right these days, with a dazzling
array of richly robed reds, many based on Shiraz (here and there with a
dash of Viognier) and Grenache, that exude berry, dark chocolate, and
balanced oak flavours. Worldwide exports.

### Dowie Doole ☆☆☆⁄

*Tatachilla Road, McLaren Vale, SA 5171, ☎ (08) 8323 7428, Ⓕ (08) 8323 7305;*
*est 1996; ♦ 7,000 cases; at Ingleburne, Willunga Road; Mon-Fri 10-5, wkds &*
*public hols 11-5*

McLaren Vale grape-growers Drew Dowie (an architect) and Norm Doole
(former international banker) have forty hectares of vines. They sell most
of the grapes, but have three imaginatively packaged white wines (Chenin
Blanc, Semillon/Sauvignon Blanc, and Chardonnay) and a Merlot made
under contract.

### Dyson Wines ☆☆☆☆

*Sherriff Road, Maslin Beach, SA 5170, ☎ (08) 8386 1092, Ⓕ (08) 8327 0066;*
*est 1976; ♦ 2,000 cases; ⴲ; A$; 7 days 10-5*

Allan Dyson, who describes himself as "a young man of fifty-odd years",
has recently added 1.5 hectares of Viognier to his Chardonnay and
Cabernet plantings, and has no intention to retire. Lush Clarice Cabernet
Sauvignon laden with blackcurrant fruit and dark chocolate is best.

### The Fleurieu ☆☆☆☆

*Main Road, McLaren Vale, SA 5171, ☎ (08) 8323 8999, Ⓕ (08) 8323 9332;*
*est 1994; ♦ 3,500 cases; ⴲ; A$; 7 days 9-5; ⴵ; ⴿ; wine bar*

A specialist Shiraz producer, with 6.5 hectares of estate vineyards and
contract winemaking by the former long-serving Seaview/Edwards &
Chaffey winemaker Mike Farmilo. Stump Hill Shiraz leads the band.
Exports to the UK and elsewhere.

### Fox Creek Wines ☆☆☆☆

*Malpas Road, Willunga, SA 5172, ☎ (08) 8556 2403, Ⓕ (08) 8556 2104; est 1995;*
*♦ 35,000 cases; ⴲ; A$; 7 days 11-5; ⴿ*

Has made a major impact since coming on-stream in 1995, making bold,
full-bodied reds with a rich reservoir of black-cherry, plum, dark-chocolate,
and earthy fruit flavours, supported by lots of oak and tannins. The
Reserve wines (Shiraz and Cabernet Sauvignon) thoroughly deserve their
label status. Exports to the UK and elsewhere.

### Gemtree Vineyards ☆☆☆☆⁄

*PO Box 164, McLaren Vale, SA 5171, ☎ (08) 8323 8199, Ⓕ (08) 8323 7889;*
*est 1992; ♦ 6,000 cases; no visitors*

The Buttery family owns a little over 130 hectares of vines, the oldest block
of twenty-five hectares on Tatachilla Road at McLaren Vale, planted in 1970.

The flag bearer is Paragon Shiraz with slurpy, lush dark fruits; other reds (including Bloodstone Tempranillo) also commendable. Exports to the UK and elsewhere.

**Geoff Merrill** ☆☆☆☆⁄

*291 Pimpala Road, Woodcroft, SA 5162, ☎ (08) 8381 6877, ⓕ (08) 8322 2244; est 1980; ◈ 70,000 cases; ♗; A$; Mon-Fri 10-5, Sun 12-5; ⚹*

The luxuriant moustache, the raucous laugh, and the endless stream of jokes and bonhomie are as well-known in England as in Australia, for Geoff Merrill is a tireless promoter of his wines. Over the years he has also accumulated an amazing number of trophies and gold medals for his wines, most of which are released with several years' bottle age. Ultra-premium Henley Shiraz underlines his skill with this variety; Cabernet Sauvignon also good. Exports to the UK and elsewhere.

**Hardys Reynella** ☆☆☆☆☆

*Reynell Road, Reynella, SA 5161, ☎ (08) 8392 2222, ⓕ (08) 8392 2202; est 1853; ◈ NFP; ♗; A$; Mon-Fri 10-4, Sat 10-3.30, Sun 11-3.30; ⚹; café*

McLaren Vale is the headquarters of Hardys, now married to the US Constellation group, the largest wine company in the world. Willowy Eileen Hardy Chardonnay and potent, berryish, minty Shiraz are unambiguously great wines, as is the glossy Thomas Hardy Cabernet Sauvignon. Quality is maintained at all price points in the empire. Worldwide distribution.

**Haselgrove** ☆☆☆☆

*Sand Road, McLaren Vale, SA 5171, ☎ (08) 8323 8706, ⓕ (08) 8323 8049; est 1981; ◈ 60,000 cases; ♗; A$; Mon-Fri 9-5, wkds 10-5*

A turbulent but brief ownership by Barrington Estates (now departed) has led to a decrease in volume, but has not affected the quality of the 'H' series of varietals from McLaren Vale (Shiraz), Adelaide Hills (Chardonnay and Viognier), and Wrattonbully (Cabernet Sauvignon). Exports to the UK and elsewhere.

**Hastwell & Lightfoot** ☆☆☆☆ V

*Foggo Road, McLaren Vale, SA 5171, ☎ (08) 8323 8692, ⓕ (08) 8323 8098; est 1990; ◈ 2,000 cases; no visitors*

An offshoot of a fifteen-hectare grape-growing business, with small amounts of Chardonnay and Cabernet Sauvignon contract-made. Wine quality is good, the labels fun, Tempranillo an impressive newcomer.

**Hills View Vineyards** ☆☆☆⁄

*11 Main Avenue, Frewville, SA 5063, ☎ & ⓕ (08) 8338 0666; est 1998; ◈ 12,000 cases; no visitors*

District veteran Brett Howard, with twenty years' winemaking experience, is now the winemaker for Hills View Vineyards, the Blewitt Springs range (Chardonnay and Shiraz both stylish), and the Howard label. The latter is a Coonawarra Shiraz released only in the best vintages.

**Hugh Hamilton** ☆☆☆☆⁄

*McMurtrie Road, McLaren Vale, SA 5171, ☎ (08) 8323 8689, ⓕ (08) 8323 9488; est 1991; ◈ 6,000 cases; ♗; A$; Mon-Fri 10-5, wkds & public hols 11-5*

After a quiet start, has picked up the pace dramatically with The Rascal Shiraz (inky but not jammy), The Villain Cabernet Sauvignon (cassis; good depth and tannins), and The Loose Cannon Viognier (strongly varietal but not phenolic).

**Hugo** ☆☆☆⁄

*Elliott Road, McLaren Flat, SA 5171, ☎ (08) 8383 0098, ⓕ (08) 8383 0446; est 1982; ◈ 12,000 cases; ♗; A$; Mon-Fri 9.30-5, Sat 12-5, Sun 10.30-5*

John Hugo burst on the scene in the 1980s with the extravagantly flavoured and oaked style that was then de rigueur. Less exotic and challenging wines are now the order of the day; Shiraz and Cabernet Sauvignon are good, however. Exports to the UK and elsewhere.

### Kangarilla Road Vineyard & Winery ☆☆☆
*Kangarilla Road, McLaren Vale, SA 5171, ☎ (08) 8383 0533, Ⓕ (08) 8383 0044; est 1975; ♦ 25,000 cases; ⚲; A$; Mon-Fri 9-5, wkds 11-5*

A new direction for wine-industry executive Kevin O'Brien (and wife Helen), who purchased Stevens Cambrai vineyard and winery. They renamed it, and have now released five varietal wines, including one of Australia's few Zinfandels, full of spice, cigar box, plum, and blackberry flavours. Exports to the UK and elsewhere.

### Kay Bros Amery ☆☆☆☆ V
*Kay Road, McLaren Vale, SA 5171, ☎ (08) 8323 8211, Ⓕ (08) 8323 9199; est 1890; ♦ 10,000 cases; ⚲; A$; Mon-Fri 9-5, wkds & public hols 12-5; ⋈*

A priceless piece of history with 100-year-old estate vineyards and a winery to match. Now concentrating on red wines, with excellent results for Shiraz (several versions) and Cabernet Sauvignon.

### Maglieri of McLaren Vale ☆☆☆☆
*Douglas Gully Road, McLaren Flat, SA 5171, ☎ (08) 8383 0177, Ⓕ (08) 8383 0735; est 1972; ♦ 14,000 cases; ⚲; A$; Mon-Sat 9-4, Sun 12-4*

Since its acquisition by Mildara Blass in 1999, all becomes academic: whether it's the vast production of red and white wines in the style of Italy's Lambrusco, or the much smaller output of glorious Shiraz. One can only hope the velvety, rich Shiraz – the epitome of everything great about McLaren Vale Shiraz – does not disappear into the Beringer Blass maw. So far so good.

### Maxwell Wines ☆☆☆☆☆
*Olivers Road, McLaren Vale, SA 5171, ☎ (08) 8323 8200, Ⓕ (08) 8323 8900; est 1979; ♦ 10,000 cases; ⚲; A$; 7 days 10-5; maze*

This family business has come a long way since 1979, moving from cramped makeshift premises to a state-of-the-art winery in 1997. Reserve Lime Cave Cabernet Sauvignon superb; varietal Lime Cave Cabernet Sauvignon and Ellen Street Shiraz excellent examples of McLaren Vale terroir. Exports to the UK and elsewhere.

### McLaren Vale III Associates ☆☆☆☆
*130 Main Road, McLaren Vale, SA 5171, ☎ 1800 501 513, Ⓕ (08) 8323 7422; est 1999; ♦ 14,000 cases; ⚲; A$; Mon-Fri 9-5, tasting by appt*

The type of name which gives editors and indexers nightmares. The three associates – Mary Greer, Reginald Wymond, and Christopher Fox – all have a decade of wine industry experience. The partnership owns twenty-five hectares spanning two vineyards planted chiefly to mainstream red varieties, with Shiraz leading the way.

### Mitolo Wines ☆☆☆☆☆
*34 Barossa Valley Way, Tanunda, SA 5352, ☎ (08) 8282 9000, Ⓕ (08) 8380 8312; est 1999; ♦ 4,000 cases; no visitors*

Imaginative packaging and branding, impeccable old vineyard grape sources, an innate understanding of wine, and the choice of highly skilled contract winemakers have brought rich rewards to Frank Mitolo in a very short space of time. Exports to the UK and elsewhere.

### Mr Riggs Wine Company ☆☆☆☆☆
*PO Box 584, McLaren Vale, SA 5171, ☎ (08) 8556 4460, Ⓕ (08) 8556 4462; est 2001; ♦ 1,000 cases; no visitors*

Long-serving Wirra Wirra winemaker Ben Riggs has struck out on his own as a consultant and own-brand winemaker. Small parcels of Shiraz, Tempranillo, and Viognier, part McLaren Vale, part Adelaide Hills, represent a cautious but impressive debut. Exports to the UK and elsewhere.

**Paxton Wines** ☆☆☆☆
*Sand Road, McLaren Vale, SA 5171, ☎ (08) 8323 8645, Ⓕ (08) 8323 8903; est 1997; ☸ 1,500 cases; no visitors*
David Paxton is one of Australia's best-known viticulturists and consultants, founding Paxton Vineyards in McLaren Vale in 1997. As a means of promoting the quality of the grapes produced by the vineyards, Paxton Wines has ventured into small-scale winemaking (via contract) with Shiraz and Chardonnay. Exports to the US and elsewhere.

**Penny's Hill Vineyards** ☆☆☆☆
*Main Road, McLaren Vale, SA 5171, ☎ (08) 8556 4460, Ⓕ (08) 8556 4462; est 1988; ☸ 7,000 cases; ⚏; A$; 7 days 10-5; ℻; gallery*
Tony Parkinson's advertising agency background shows in the innovative red-dot labelling, mimicking the red "sold" dot stuck on pictures at an art gallery sale. Contract winemaking by Ben Riggs has guaranteed the quality of the Chardonnay, Shiraz, and Shiraz blend. Exports to the UK and elsewhere.

**Pertaringa** ☆☆☆☆ V
*Corner Hunt and Rifle Range Roads, McLaren Vale, SA 5171, ☎ (08) 8323 8125, Ⓕ (08) 8323 7766; est 1980; ☸ 10,000 cases; ⚏; A$; Mon-Fri 9-5, wkds & public hols 11-5*
The Pertaringa label wines are made from grapes grown by leading viticulturists Geoff Hardy and Ian Leask on the Pertaringa Vineyard, acquired as a run-down thirty-three-hectare vineyard in 1980 and since rejuvenated. The Shiraz is a classic: plum, dark cherry, and chocolate abound.

**Pirramimma** ☆☆☆☆ẏ V
*Johnston Road, McLaren Vale, SA 5171, ☎ (08) 8323 8205, Ⓕ (08) 8323 9224; est 1892; ☸ 40,000 cases; ⚏; A$; Mon-Fri 9-5, Sat 11-5, Sun & public hols 11.30-4*
Pirramimma has vineyard holdings second to none in McLaren Vale. Some are old, others of more recent origin under long-term contract to Beringer Blass. Wine quality has always been good, but conservative marketing has under-priced the wines. Chardonnay, Shiraz, Grenache, and Petit Verdot (a specialty) all shine. Exports to the UK and elsewhere.

**Possums Vineyard** ☆☆☆☆ẏ V
*31 Thornbest Street, Unley Park, SA 5061, ☎ & Ⓕ (08) 8272 3406; est 2000; ☸ 3,000 cases; no visitors*
Owned by the very distinguished wine scientist and researcher Dr John Possingham and Carol Summers. With forty-seven hectares and two vineyards, they are grape-growers rather than winemakers, but have a portion of excellent Shiraz and Cabernet Sauvignon contract-made. Exports to the UK and elsewhere.

**Reynell** ☆☆☆☆
*Reynell Road, Reynella, SA 5161, ☎ (08) 8392 2222, Ⓕ (08) 8392 2202; est 1838; ☸ 16,000 cases; ⚏; A$; 7 days 10-4 except public hols*
The fashionably shortened name of the beautiful and historic Chateau Reynella, and headquarters for Hardys. Its three basket-pressed red wines (Shiraz, Merlot, and Cabernet) are richly opulent and consistently excellent.

**Richard Hamilton** ☆☆☆☆◊

*Main Road, Willunga, SA 5172,* ☎ *(08) 8556 2288,* Ⓕ *(08) 8556 2868; est 1972;*
⚐ *20,000 cases;* ⚑; *A$; 7 days 10-5*

Richard Hamilton has outstanding estate vineyards, some of great age, all
fully mature. The arrival (in 2002) of former Rouge Homme winemaker
Paul Gordon has allowed the full potential of those vineyards to be
expressed. Exports to the UK and elsewhere.

**RockBare Wines** ☆☆☆☆

*PO Box 63, Mt Torrens, SA 5244,* ☎ *(08) 8389 9584,* Ⓕ *(08) 8389 9587; est 2000;*
⚐ *20,000 cases; no visitors*

Honours graduate and former Penfolds winemaker Tim Burvill has struck
out on his own to make wines under lend-lease arrangements with other
wineries. Shiraz heads a reliable, sensibly limited range of wines.

**Rosemount Estate** ☆☆☆☆☆

*Ingoldby Road, McLaren Vale, SA 5171,* ☎ *(08) 8383 0001,* Ⓕ *(08) 8383 0456;*
*est 1888;* ⚐ *NFP;* ⚑; *A$; Mon-Sat 10-5, Sun & public hols 11-4*

A physically distinct and distant winery that is part of the Rosemount
empire. It produces four outstanding red wines, led by the exceptionally
lush and bountiful Balmoral Syrah, packed with black cherry and
blackberry fruit. Show Reserve Shiraz, GSM (a Rhône blend), and
Traditional (a Bordeaux blend) are also impressive. Exports to the UK
and elsewhere.

**Scarpantoni Estate** ☆☆☆☆

*Scarpantoni Drive, McLaren Flat, SA 5171,* ☎ *(08) 8383 0186,* Ⓕ *(08) 8383 0490;*
*est 1979;* ⚐ *30,000 cases;* ⚑; *A$; Mon-Fri 9-5, wkds 11-5; pottery*

An Italian family-owned business with a range of wines, none better
than the sensually rich, bitter-chocolate, red-berry, and vanilla-oak
Block 3 Shiraz, unless it be the Reserve Shiraz/Cabernet. Exports to the
UK and elsewhere.

**Serafino Wines** ☆☆☆☆◊

*McLarens on the Lake, Kangarilla Road, McLaren Vale, SA 5171,* ☎ *(08) 8323*
*0157,* Ⓕ *(08) 8323 0158; est 2000;* ⚐ *17,000 cases;* ⚑; *A$; Mon-Fri 10-5, wkds &*
*public hols 10-4.30;* ⦿; ⇔

In the wake of the sale of Maglieri Wines to Beringer Blass in 1998, Maglieri
founder Steve Maglieri acquired the McLarens on the Lake complex
originally established by Andrew Garrett. The accommodation has been
upgraded and a larger winery was commissioned prior to the 2002 vintage.
Exports to the UK and elsewhere.

**Shingleback** ☆☆☆☆

*Corner Little and California Roads, McLaren Vale, SA 5171,* ☎ *(08) 8370 3299,*
Ⓕ *(08) 8370 0088; est 1995;* ⚐ *40,000 cases;* ⚑; *A$; by appt*

An export-oriented business with eighty hectares of vineyards. D Block
Reserve Shiraz and Cabernet Sauvignon are the pick of the crop.

**Shottesbrooke** ☆☆☆☆

*Bagshaws Road, McLaren Flat, SA 5171,* ☎ *(08) 8383 0002,* Ⓕ *(08) 8383 0222;*
*est 1984;* ⚐ *10,000 cases;* ⚑; *A$; Mon-Fri 10-4.30, wkds & public hols 11-5*

Winemaker/owner Nick Holmes handcrafts subtly oaked and invariably
elegant wines, combining his own philosophy and his long experience
with the grapes (and wines) of the region. Newly introduced Punch
Cabernet Sauvignon and Eliza Shiraz are altogether superior. Exports to
the UK and elsewhere.

**Simon Hackett** ☆☆☆↙
*Budgens Road, McLaren Vale, SA 5171, ☎ (08) 8323 7712, Ⓕ (08) 8323 7713;*
*est 1981; ♦ 20,000 cases; ♈; A$; Wed-Sun 11-5*
In 1998, Simon Hackett acquired the former Taranga winery in McLaren
Vale, which has made his winemaking life a great deal easier. He also has
eight hectares of estate vines and has contract growers in McLaren Vale,
the Adelaide Hills and the Barossa Valley, with another thirty-two hectares
of vines.

**Tapestry** ☆☆☆☆
*Olivers Road, McLaren Vale, SA 5171, ☎ (08) 8323 9196, Ⓕ (08) 8323 9746;*
*est 1971; ♦ 10,000 cases; ♈; A$; 7 days 11-5; art & crafts*
After a relatively brief period of ownership by Brian Light, the former
Merrivale Winery was then acquired by the Gerard family in 1997,
previously owners of Chapel Hill. It has forty hectares of thirty-year-old
vineyards; less than half the grapes are used for the Tapestry label. Fifteen
Barrels Cabernet Sauvignon and The Vincent Shiraz are the best.

**Tatachilla** ☆☆☆☆ V
*151 Main Road, McLaren Vale, SA 5171, ☎ (08) 8323 8656, Ⓕ (08) 8323 9096;*
*est 1901; ♦ 250,000 cases; ♈; A$; Mon-Sat 10-5, Sun & public hols 11-5*
Briefly the head of Banksia Wines, now owned by Lion Nathan. Since then,
the management and winemaking teams have made every post a winner.
Best are the spicy, juicy, berry-filled Keystone (Grenache, Shiraz) and
Foundation Shiraz, bursting with glossy cherry fruit and high-quality oak.
Exports to the UK and elsewhere.

**Twelve Staves Wine Company** ☆☆☆↙
*Box 620, McLaren Vale, SA 5171, ☎ & Ⓕ 8178 0900; est 1997; ♦ 600 cases;*
*no visitors*
Twelve Staves has a single vineyard block of five hectares of seventy-year-old,
bush-pruned Grenache vines. The highly experienced team of Peter Dennis
and Brian Light (in a consulting role) produce an appealing wine in a
lighter mode which has an eclectic range of retail outlets and limited
exports. Exports to the UK and elsewhere.

**Ulithorne** ☆☆☆☆☆
*PO Box 487, McLaren Vale, SA 5171, ☎ & Ⓕ (08) 8382 5528; est 1971; ♦ 1,000*
*cases; no visitors*
An outstanding producer of Shiraz named Frux Frugis, coming from the
estate vineyard planted in 1971, the first vintage arriving exactly thirty
years later. Expansion is underway.

**Wirra Wirra** ☆☆☆☆☆
*McMurtie Road, McLaren Vale, SA 5171, ☎ (08) 8323 8414, Ⓕ (08) 8323 8596;*
*est 1969; ♦ 110,000 cases; ♈; A$; Mon-Sat 10-5, Sun 11-5; ✗*
One of the leading wineries of the region, established by Greg Trott and
family, with Tim James (of Hardys) as the very capable chief executive. All
the wines, white and red, are excellent, with a sophisticated polish that
enhances their strong varietal character. RSW Shiraz and The Angelus
Cabernet Sauvignon are simply brilliant. Exports to the UK and elsewhere.

**Woodstock** ☆☆☆↙
*Douglas Gully Road, McLaren Flat, SA 5171, ☎ (08) 8383 0156, Ⓕ (08) 8383*
*0437; est 1974; ♦ 30,000 cases; ♈; A$; Mon-Fri 9-5, wkds & hols 12-5; ❖; ⛵*
One of the stalwarts of McLaren Vale, producing archetypal, invariably
reliable full-bodied red wines and showing versatility with spectacular

botrytis sweet wines. Also offers a charming restaurant-cum-reception centre. Exports to the UK and elsewhere.

**Yangarra Estate** ☆☆☆☆⁄

*Kangarilla Road, McLaren Vale, SA 5171, ☎ (08) 8383 7459, (08) 8383 7518; est 2000; ◈ 100,000 cases; ♀; A$; by appt*

Owned by Kendall-Jackson of California, and based on the ninety-seven-hectare Eringa Park Vineyard, with vines dating back to 1923. The excellent 2002 vintage wines mark a retreat back to an estate-grown portfolio, with Shiraz, Grenache, and Mourvèdre in varying configurations the best. Exports to the UK, US, and Europe.

# Langhorne Creek

Cooled by the lake and nearby sea and easily able to ripen fifteen tonnes of grapes to the hectare, producing several million cases of wine a year, this is the modern face of Langhorne Creek, a paradigm of the advantages Australia has over so many of its New (and Old) World competitors. Vines were first planted here around 1860 by Frank Potts of Bleasdale, and five generations later, the Potts family is better than ever. It was only in the late 1960s that the big boys took notice of Langhorne Creek. While Lindemans had begun to buy grapes from the region, it was Wolf Blass who most influenced attitudes; Orlando-Wyndham arrived in 1995. It is significant that the prime function of this booming area is to grow grapes of good to very good quality with a low cost base, which go on to contribute to mega-brands like Jacob's Creek. There are fifteen wine producers in the region.

**Bleasdale Vineyards** ☆☆☆☆ V

*Wellington Road, Langhorne Creek, SA 5255, ☎ (08) 8537 3001, Ⓕ (08) 8537 3224; est 1850; ◈ 100,000 cases; ♀; A$; Mon-Sat 9-5, Sun 11-5; ⊬*

One of Australia's most historic wineries, drawing upon vineyards that are flooded every winter by diversion of the Bremer River to provide moisture throughout the dry, cool growing season (a scheme devised by founder Frank Potts in the 1860s). The red wines offer excellent value for money, all showing the particular softness that is the hallmark of the Langhorne Creek region. Exports to the UK and elsewhere.

**Bremerton Wines** ☆☆☆☆

*Strathalbyn Road, Langhorne Creek, SA 5255, ☎ (08) 8537 3093, Ⓕ (08) 8537 3109; est 1988; ◈ 22,500 cases; ♀; A$; 7 days 10-5; wkd lunches*

Initially grape-growers, the Willsons now run a complex business, both buying and selling grapes and making some delicious wines, particularly Old Adam and Selkirk Shiraz; Walter's Cabernet Sauvignon also good. Exports to the UK and elsewhere.

**Brothers in Arms** ☆☆☆⁄

*PO Box 840, Langhorne Creek, SA 5255, ☎ (08) 8537 3070, Ⓕ (08) 8537 3415; est 1998; ◈ 18,000 cases; no visitors*

The Adams family has been growing grapes in Langhorne Creek since 1891, but it was not until 1998 that they had part of the Shiraz from the forty-hectare vineyard contract-made by David Freschi. Exports to the UK and elsewhere.

**Casa Freschi** ☆☆☆⁄

*30 Jackson Avenue, Strathalbyn, SA 5255, ☎ & Ⓕ (08) 8536 4569; est 1998; ◈ 1,000 cases; no visitors*

David Freschi graduated with a degree in oenology from Roseworthy in 1991, and spent most of the decade working overseas. In 1998, he and his wife decided to trade in the corporate world for a small, family-owned business, with a core of 2.5 hectares of vines established by Freschi's parents in 1972.

**Lake Breeze Wines** ☆☆☆⚐
  *Step Road, Langhorne Creek, SA 5255, ☎ (08) 8537 3017, Ⓕ (08) 8537 3267;*
  *est 1987; ⚐ 12,000 cases; ⚑; A$; 7 days 10-5*
The Follett family has farmed at Langhorne Creek since 1880, been grape-growers since the 1930s, wine producers since 1987, and opened a cellar-door facility in 1991. The quality of their wines has been exemplary, especially the rich, dense Winemaker's Selection range of red wines. Exports to the UK and elsewhere.

**Temple Bruer** ☆☆☆☆
  *Milang Road, Strathalbyn, SA 5255, ☎ (08) 8537 0203, Ⓕ (08) 8537 0131;*
  *est 1980; ⚐ 14,000 cases; ⚑; A$; Mon-Fri 9.30-4.30*
Known for its eclectic range of wines, Temple Bruer (which also runs a substantial business as a vine-propagation nursery) has seen a sharp lift in quality. Clean, modern, redesigned labels add to the appeal of its stimulatingly different range of red wines. Bin 621 Mataro/Shiraz/Grenache (delicious raspberry and redcurrant fruit) is a stand-out.

# Riverland

The engine room of the Australian wine industry, producing almost sixty per cent of South Australia's grapes and hence more than a quarter of the national grape crush. Originally developed by the Californian-born and -trained Chaffey brothers (George and William), who provided the expertise for the construction of the irrigation channels that turned near desert into ideal horticultural and viticultural land, the Riverland's hundred-year existence has seen the emphasis on production of the maximum possible tonnages at the minimum possible cost, an approach which served it (and Australia) well. But increasing attention is now being paid to raising quality. This is reflected in better viticultural practices, better water usage, and better grape varieties and clones.

The challenge for Australia is to make characterful wines with quality. Commercially, success or failure will be determined right here. There are thirteen wine producers in the region.

**Angove's** ☆☆☆⚐ V
  *Bookmark Avenue, Renmark, SA 5341, ☎ (08) 8580 3100, Ⓕ (08) 8580 3155;*
  *est 1886; ⚐ 1,300,000 cases; ⚑; A$; Mon-Fri 9-5; 𝒓*
Exemplifies the economies of scale achievable in the Riverland. Wines are never poor and often exceed their theoretical station in life. The white varietals are normally best, but all please in vintages such as 2002. Worldwide distribution.

**Banrock Station** ☆☆☆⚐ V
  *Holmes Road, off Sturt Highway, Kingston-on-Murray, SA 5331, ☎ (08) 8583 0299, Ⓕ (08) 8583 0288; est 1994; ⚐ 1.9 million cases; ⚑; A$; 7 days 10-4, closed public hols; 𝒓; conference centre, wetland conservation/interpretive centre; café*

Owned by Hardys, the property covers over 1,700 hectares. There are 230 hectares of vineyard, while the rest is a wildlife and wetland preservation area. A A\$1 million visitor centre was opened in October 1998. All of the varietal wines offer excellent value. Worldwide distribution.

### Kingston Estate ☆☆☆☆

*Sturt Highway, Kingston-on-Murray, SA 5331, ☎ (08) 8583 4500, Ⓕ (08) 8583 4511; est 1979; ♦ NFP; ♟; A\$; by appt*

A substantial and successful Riverland winery, crushing 10,000 tonnes each vintage. It has also set up long-term purchase contracts with growers in the Clare Valley, Adelaide Hills, Langhorne Creek, and Mount Benson, adding to the range and quality of its releases. It is also successfully exploring varietal wines such as Arneis, Petit Verdot, Viognier, Tempranillo, etc. Worldwide distribution.

### Salena Estate NR

*Bookpurnong Road, Loxton, SA 5343, ☎ (08) 8584 1333, Ⓕ (08) 8584 1388; est 1998; ♦ 130,000 cases; ♟; A\$; Mon-Fri 8.30-5*

This business, established in 1998 by Bob and Sylvia Franchitto, encapsulates the hectic rate of growth across the entire Australian wine industry. Its 1998 crush was 300 tonnes, and by 2001 it was processing 7,000 tonnes, with 200 hectares of estate vineyards. Exports to the UK and elsewhere.

# Adelaide Zone

This is a so-called Super Zone, which includes the Mount Lofty Ranges, Fleurieu and Barossa Zones, as well as capturing the regions within those Zones. Its purpose is to pick up those wineries that fall outside regional boundaries, or that are virtual wineries.

### Heartland Wines ☆☆☆☆ V

*Level 1, 205 Greenhill Road, Eastwood, SA 5063, ☎ (08) 8357 9344, Ⓕ (08) 8357 9388; est 2001; ♦ 36,000 cases; no visitors*

A virtual winery joint venture between four wine industry veterans taking grapes grown in the Limestone Coast, Barossa Valley, and McLaren Vale, chiefly owned by the participants. It has been a runaway success, sales far exceeding forecasts, not surprising given the quality and pricing of the wines, led by Shiraz and Cabernet Sauvignon. Exports to the UK and elsewhere.

### Hewitson ☆☆☆☆☆

*The Old Dairy Cold Stores, 66 London Road, Mile End, SA 5031, ☎ (08) 8443 6466, Ⓕ (08) 8443 6866; est 1996; ♦ 15,000 cases; ♟; A\$; by appt*

Dean Hewitson was a Petaluma winemaker for ten years, and during that time managed to do three vintages in France and one in Oregon, as well as undertaking his master's degree at UC Davis, California. His background ensured high-level technical skills, now complemented by superbly sourced old vine grapes from vines up to 145 years old. Ned & Henry's Barossa Shiraz, L'Oizeau McLaren Vale Shiraz, Old Garden Mourvèdre, Eden Valley Riesling, and Miss Harry Dry Grown and Ancient are all wonderful wines. Exports to the UK and elsewhere.

### Journeys End Vineyards ☆☆☆☆♪

*248 Flinders Street, Adelaide, SA 5000, ☎ 0409 011 633; est 2001; ♦ 3,000 cases; no visitors*

Another highly successful virtual winery, primarily focused on four levels of McLaren Vale Shiraz, but also sourcing other varieties from the Adelaide Hills and Langhorne Creek. The skills of winemaker Ben Riggs are obvious in the Shiraz. Exports to the UK and elsewhere.

**Lashmar** ☆☆☆☆
*24 Lindsay Terrace, Belair, SA 5052, ☎ (08) 8278 3669, Ⓕ (08) 8278 3998; est 1996; ⚘ 1,000 cases; no visitors*
A citizen of the wine world, the grapes coming from McLaren Vale, the Clare and Eden Valleys, and Kangaroo Island. Shiraz, Shiraz blends, and Viognier are all recommended.

**Lengs & Cooter** ☆☆☆☆⚘
*24 Lindsay Terrace, Belair, SA 5042, ☎ & Ⓕ (08) 8278 3998; est 1993; ⚘ 8,000 cases; no visitors*
A sister but separate operation to Lashmar, in this instance sourcing Riesling and Semillon from the Clare Valley, Pinot Noir from the Adelaide Hills, and lusciously ripe Shiraz from McLaren Vale and old vines in the Clare Valley. Exports to the UK and elsewhere.

**Patritti Wines** ☆☆⚘ **V**
*13-23 Clacton Road, Dover Gardens, SA 5048, ☎ (08) 8296 8261, Ⓕ (08) 8296 5088; est 1926; ⚘ 100,000 cases; ⚑; A$; Mon-Sat 9-6; ⚔*
The Patrittis run a traditional family business offering wines at yesterday's prices, from substantial vineyard holdings in Blewitt Springs and Aldinga.

**Penfolds Magill Estate** ☆☆☆☆⚘
*78 Penfold Road, Magill, SA 5072, ☎ (08) 8301 5569, Ⓕ (08) 8301 5588; est 1844; ⚘ NFP; ⚑; A$; 7 days 10.30-4.30*
The birthplace of Penfolds, established by Dr Christopher Rawson Penfold in 1844, his house still part of the immaculately maintained property. It includes six hectares of precious Shiraz used to make Magill Estate; the original and subsequent winery buildings, most still in operation or in museum condition; and the much-acclaimed Magill Restaurant, with panoramic views back to the city, a great wine list, and fine dining. All this a twenty-minute drive from Adelaide's CBD. Worldwide distribution.

**Rumball Sparkling Wines NR**
*55 Charles Street, Norwood, SA 5067, ☎ (08) 8332 2761, Ⓕ (08) 8364 0188; est 1988; ⚘ 10,000 cases; ⚑; A$; Mon-Fri 9-5*
Peter Rumball has been making and selling sparkling wine for as long as I can remember. He now makes Sparkling Shiraz from Coonawarra, Barossa Valley, and McLaren Vale at various wineries.

**Two Hands Wines** ☆☆☆☆☆
*Neldner Road, Marananga, SA 5355, ☎ (08) 8562 4566, Ⓕ (08) 8562 4744; est 2000; ⚘ 10,000 cases; ⚑; A$; Wed-Fri 11-5, wkds & public hols 10-5*
Yet another virtual winery created by winemakers Michael Twelftree and Richard Mintz. Bella's Garden, Samantha's Garden, and Lily's Garden Shiraz provide the proverbial gobfuls of fruit, the Bull and Bear Shiraz/Cabernet and Bad Impersonator Shiraz are in close attendance. Exports to the UK and elsewhere.

**Uleybury Wines** ☆☆☆☆⚘
*Uley Road, Uleybury, SA 5114, ☎ (08) 8280 7335, Ⓕ (08) 8280 7925; est 1995; ⚘ 10,000 cases; ⚑; A$; 7 days 10-4*
The Pipicella family – headed by Italian-born Tony – has established nearly forty-five hectares of vineyard near the township of One Tree Hill in the

Mount Lofty Ranges. The wines are currently being made off-site under the direction of Tony Pipicella. A cellar door opened in June 2002; an on-site winery will follow.

**Will Taylor Wines** ☆☆☆☆☆

*1B Victoria Ave, Unley Park, SA 5061, ☎ & Ⓕ (08) 8271 6122; est 1997; ✦ 1,500 cases; ☧; A$; by appt*

Will Taylor is a partner in the leading Adelaide law firm Finlaysons and specializes in wine law. Together with Suzanne Taylor, he matches region and variety, having Clare Valley Riesling, Coonawarra Cabernet Sauvignon, Adelaide Hills Sauvignon Blanc, Yarra Valley/Geelong Pinot Noir, and Hunter Valley Semillon all contract-made. The quality of the wines is uniformly high.

# Currency Creek

One of the newer regions in the state, encompassing the mouth of the Murray River, the old trading town of Goolwa, and Hindmarsh Island. Like Langhorne Creek to its west, it fronts Lake Alexandrina, and, like Langhorne Creek, has a strongly maritime-influenced cool climate. There are five wine producers in the region.

**Angus Wines** ☆☆☆☆☆

*Captain Sturt Road, Hindmarsh Island, SA 5214, ☎ (08) 8555 2320, Ⓕ (08) 8555 2323; est 1995; ✦ 2,000 cases; ☧; A$; wkds & public hols 10-5*

Susan and Alistair Angus were the pioneer viticulturists on Hindmarsh Island, connected to the Fleurieu Peninsula by a bridge ultimately built in highly controversial circumstances. Right from the first vintage in 1998, the aromatic, lemony Semillon has been outstanding; the rich plum, prune, and dark-chocolate Shiraz not far behind. Exports to the UK.

**Ballast Stone Estate Wines** ☆☆☆☆

*Myrtle Grove Road, Currency Creek, SA 5214, ☎ (08) 8555 4215, Ⓕ (08) 8555 4216; est 2001; ✦ 15,000 cases; ☧; A$; 7 days 10.30-4.30*

The Shaw family had been grape-growers in McLaren Vale for twenty-five years before deciding to establish a large vineyard in Currency Creek in 1994. Two hundred and fifty hectares have been planted, and a large on-site winery has been built.

**Currency Creek Estate** ☆☆☆

*Winery Road, Currency Creek, SA 5214, ☎ (08) 8555 4069, Ⓕ (08) 8555 4100; est 1969; ✦ 7,000 cases; ☧; A$; 7 days 10-5; ▯; ▭; art exhibitions*

Owned by the Tonkin family. Constant name changes have not helped the quest for identity, but the winery has nonetheless produced some outstanding wood-matured whites and pleasant soft reds that sell at attractive prices.

**Middleton Wines** ☆☆☆

*Flagstaff Hill Road, Middleton, SA 5213, ☎ (08) 8555 4136, Ⓕ (08) 8555 4108; est 1979; ✦ 3,000 cases; ☧; A$; Fri-Sun 11-5; ▯*

The Bland family has acquired Middleton Wines and has changed the entire focus of the business. Previously, all of the production from the twenty hectares of estate plantings was sold either as grapes or as bulk wine; now much is made into wine at the on-site winery.

**Salomon Estates** ☆☆☆☆

*PO Box 621, McLaren Vale, SA 5171, ☎ 0419 864 155, Ⓕ (08) 8323 7726; est 1997; ✦ NA; no visitors*

Bert Salomon, formerly head of the Austrian Wine Marketing Board, is Austria's flying winemaker, simultaneously running the long-established family winery in Kremstal (not far from Vienna) and Salomon Estates in South Australia, and overseeing the making of the wines (chiefly under the Finniss River label) at Mike Farmilo's Boar's Rock winery. The Cabernet/Merlot, Shiraz, and Shiraz/Petit Verdot are all very good.

# Southern Fleurieu

A beautiful part of the world, with gentle rolling hills, abundant old gum trees, and native flora, and the ocean ever in the foreground. Its climate is inevitably strongly maritime, and shares many things in common with that of Kangaroo Island, Currency Creek, and Langhorne Creek. There are nine wine producers in the region.

**Allusion Wines NR**

*Smith Hill Road, Yankalilla, SA 5203, ☏ & Ⓕ (08) 8558 3333; est 1996; ⚬ 750 cases; ⚐; A$; Thurs-Sun 11-5*

Steve and Wendy Taylor purchased the property on which Allusion Wines is established in 1980, since planting four hectares of vineyard with 3,000 vines. Steve Taylor's twenty years as a chef has strongly influenced both the varietal plantings and the wine styles made, designed to be consumed with good food.

**Trafford Hill Vineyard NR**

*Lot 1, Bower Road, Normanville, SA 5204, ☏ (08) 8558 3595; est 1996; ⚬ 500 cases; ⚐; A$; Thurs-Mon & hols 10.30-5*

Irene and John Sanderson have established 1.25 hectares of vineyard at Normanville, near the southern extremity of the Fleurieu Peninsula. Irene tends the vineyards and John makes the wine, with help from district veteran Allan Dyson.

**Twin Bays NR**

*Lot 1, Martin Road, Yankalilla, SA 5203, ☏ (08) 8267 2844, Ⓕ (08) 8239 0877; est 1989; ⚬ 1,000 cases; ⚐; A$; wkds & hols; ⚑; playground*

Adelaide doctor Bruno Giorgio and his wife Ginny were the first to plant vines in the Yankalilla district of the Fleurieu Peninsula, with spectacular views from the sloping hillside vineyard. Planting began in 1989, but they have elected to keep the operation small. The focus is on Riesling, Shiraz, Grenache, and Cabernet Sauvignon.

# Kangaroo Island

Kangaroo Island is strongly reminiscent of Margaret River, which may seem strange given the fact that they are (more or less) on opposite sides of the continent. The similarity comes from the Australian bush, with wild flowers and spear-grass blackboys growing in abundance on the red soil. Native life, too, is everywhere, from penguins and seals to wallabies and small kangaroos. The climate is, as one might expect, strongly maritime-influenced and much cooler than McLaren Vale; it is closer to its neighbour, the Southern Fleurieu Peninsula. There are five producers with the addition of Lashmar (*q.v.*), which makes wine from Kangaroo Island along with wines from other regions.

**Kangaroo Island Vines** ☆☆☆☆

*c/o 413 Payneham Road, Felixstow, SA 5070, ☎ (08) 8365 3411, ⓕ (08) 8336 2462; est 1990; ⚱ 600 cases; no visitors*

Kangaroo Island is an utterly magical part of Australia, and the Special Reserve Cabernet/Merlot (when available) is a beautifully balanced and elegant wine. Production should increase.

# The Peninsulas Zone

Takes in the Eyre Peninsula to the west and the Yorke Peninsula to the east, which together straddle the Spencer Gulf. Here, too, the maritime influence is the factor which determines climate, amplified by those sites facing the sea.

**Boston Bay Wines** ☆☆☆ V

*Lincoln Highway, Port Lincoln, SA 5606, ☎ (08) 8684 3600, ⓕ (08) 8684 3637; est 1984; ⚱ 3,000 cases; ⚐; A$; wkds, school/public hols 11.30-4.30*

Situated on the southern tip of the Eyre Peninsula, the vineyards offer frequent sightings of whales at play. Contract-made Riesling and Cabernet/Merlot have been consistently good.

**Delacolline Estate NR**

*Whillas Road, Port Lincoln, SA 5606, ☎ (08) 8682 5277, ⓕ (08) 8682 4455; est 1984; ⚱ 650 cases; ⚐; A$; wkds 9-5*

Tony Bassett has three hectares of Riesling, Sauvignon Blanc, and Cabernet Sauvignon. The wine style reflects the cool, maritime influence, with ocean currents sweeping up from the Antarctic.

# Western Australia

1994   2,713 hectares   4.05 per cent of total plantings
2003   11,736 hectares   7.45 per cent of total plantings

Obviously enough, this state is a relatively small contributor to the national grape crush. The most vocal of all wine regions (the Margaret River) accounted for less than one per cent of the 2003 crush, but would (justifiably) assert that size doesn't matter.

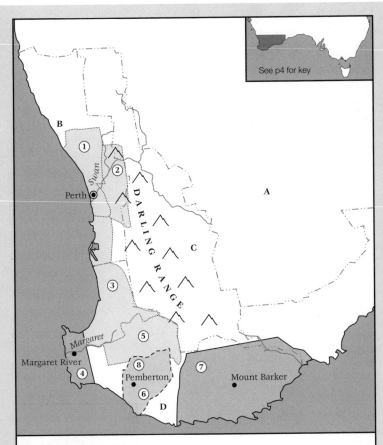

See p4 for key

Perth

Margaret River

Pemberton

Mount Barker

## Western Australia

| | | | |
|---|---|---|---|
| A | Eastern Plains, Inland and North of Western Australia | 1 | Swan District |
| | | 2 | Perth Hills |
| | | 3 | Geographe |
| B | Greater Perth | 4 | Margaret River |
| C | Central Western Australia | 5 | Blackwood Valley |
| D | Southwest Australia | 6 | Pemberton |
| E | West Australian Southeast Coastal | 7 | Great Southern |

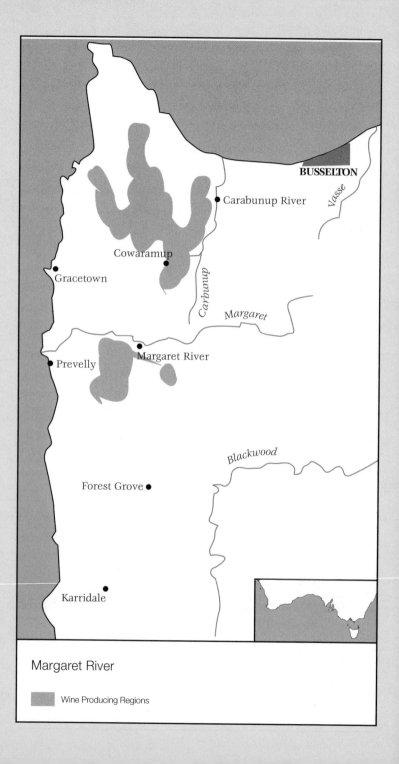

BUSSELTON

Vasse

● Carabunup River

Carabunup

Cowaramup ●

Margaret

● Gracetown

● Margaret River

● Prevelly

Blackwood

Forest Grove ●

Karridale ●

Margaret River

Wine Producing Regions

# Margaret River

Whether it is in part due to the subliminal sound of the name, I do not know, but I have always felt there is a feminine quality to the soft beauty of the Margaret River region. Yet at the same time it is uncompromisingly Australian. The doctors-cum-winemakers who, for some strange reason, dominated the early development of viticulture here (and still have a strong presence), were unusually sensitive to the environment. Their wineries tend to merge into the countryside rather than stand superimposed on it, with the conspicuous exception of Palandri.

Margaret River is now one of Australia's best-regarded regions, with intensely rich but long-lived Chardonnay, and textured Cabernet Sauvignon and Merlot second to none. Yet a cloud now hangs over the Margaret River. Between 1996 and 2003, vineyard plantings more than trebled, and of the new areas now under vine, some are apparently not suited to quality wine production. One of the more controversial areas is Jindong, at the northern end of the region. On the face of it, Jindong will produce pleasant, light-bodied, fast-maturing wines at a relatively low cost. This is not what the Margaret River is, or should be, about. The wineries established between 1970 and 1995, with the best vineyard sites, however, will justly retain their reputation. There are 108 wine producers in the region.

### Abbey Vale NR
*392 Wildwood Road, Yallingup, WA 6282, ☎ & Ⓕ (08) 9755 2121; est 1986; ♦ 10,000 cases; ♥; A$; 7 days 10-5*

A subtle name change hints at the major underlying restructure headed by former Pemberton viticulturist Philip May. Most of the twenty-five-hectare grape production is sold, part vinified for a three-tiered product portfolio. Exports to the UK and elsewhere.

### Alexandra Bridge Estate ☆☆☆☆
*Brockman Highway, Karridale, WA 6288, ☎ (08) 9758 5000, Ⓕ (08) 9384 4811; est 1994; ♦ 12,000 cases; 7 days 10-4.30; gallery*

Much corporate reconstruction has left Alexandra Bridge with an 800-tonne winery built in February 2000, a thirty-hectare estate vineyard, and external grower contracts. Luscious Cabernet and rich Semillon are best.

### Amberley Estate ☆☆☆☆
*Thornton Road, Yallingup, WA 6282, ☎ (08) 9755 2288, Ⓕ (08) 9755 2171; est 1986; ♦ 90,000 cases; ♥; A$; 7 days 10-4.30; ▮*

Eddie Price is the winemaker at this highly successful and substantial enterprise. Slightly sweet Chenin Blanc provides the cash flow, excellent tangy, herbal Semillon/Sauvignon Blanc and powerful, inky Shiraz the sex appeal. Acquired by Canadian company Vincor in 2004. Exports to the UK and elsewhere.

### Arlewood Estate ☆☆☆☆
*Harmans Road South, Wilyabrup, WA 6284, ☎ & Ⓕ (08) 9755 6267; est 1988; ♦ 6,000 cases; ♥; A$; wkds 11-5*

A premier address, between Ashbrook and Vasse Felix, and contract winemaking at Voyager Estate underwrites the quality, led by zesty, citrus Semillon. Exports to the UK and elsewhere.

### Ashbrook Estate ☆☆☆☆ V

*Harmans Road South, Wilyabrup, WA 6284, ☏ (08) 9755 6262, ℱ (08) 9755 6290;*
*est 1975; ✦ 8,000 cases; ⚱; A$; 7 days 11-5*

This estate is one of the quietest and highest achievers in Australia, maintaining excellent viticulture and fastidious winemaking. It is hard to choose between the complex, herby, tropical Semillon, subtly oaked, long Chardonnay, the crisp Sauvignon Blanc, or powerful briar and cassis Cabernet. Exports to the UK and elsewhere.

### Beckett's Flat ☆☆☆☆

*Beckett Road, Metricup, WA 6280, ☏ (08) 9755 7402, ℱ (08) 9755 7344;*
*est 1992; ✦ 6,000 cases; ⚱; A$; 7 days 10-6; ⊨*

One of the northern outriders of the region; clean, medium-bodied wines are "easy on the gums" (using Sir James Hardy's memorable expression). Since 1998 they have been made (well) on site.

### Bettenay's ☆☆☆☆

*Lot 1685, Corner Harmans South and Miamup Roads, Wilyabrup, WA 6284,*
*☏ & ℱ (08) 9755 5539; est 1989; ✦ 1,500 cases; ⚱; A$; 7 days 10-5; ⊨; gallery*

Greg Bettenay began the development of ten hectares of vineyards in 1989, and the development now includes a luxury tree-top spa apartment known as The Leafy Loft. Merlot, Shiraz, and Chardonnay all good.

### Briarose Estate ☆☆☆☆

*Bussell Highway, Augusta, WA 6290, ☏ (08) 9758 4160, ℱ (08) 9758 4161;*
*est 1998; ✦ 12,000 cases; ⚱; A$; 7 days 10-4.30*

A substantial and impressive estate at the southern end of the region, the cooler climate reflected in the crisp wine style.

### Brookland Valley ☆☆☆☆

*Caves Road, Wilyabrup, WA 6284, ☏ (08) 9755 6250, ℱ (08) 9755 6214;*
*est 1984; ✦ 2,800 cases; ⚱; A$; 7 days 10-5; ⊘; gallery*

Has an idyllic setting, with Flutes Café one of the best winery restaurants in the region. In 1997, Hardys acquired a fifty-per-cent interest and took responsibility for viticulture and winemaking. The move towards richer and more complex red wines has continued; the white wines have an extra degree of finesse. Worldwide distribution.

### Brookwood Estate ☆☆☆

*Treeton Road, Cowaramup, WA 6284, ☏ (08) 9755 5604, ℱ (08) 9755 5870;*
*est 1999; ✦ 2,500 cases; ⚱; A$; 7 days 10-6*

Trevor and Lyn Mann began the development of their fifty-hectare property in 1996, and now have 1.3 hectares each of Shiraz, Cabernet Sauvignon, Semillon, Sauvignon Blanc, and Chenin Blanc planted. An on-site winery was constructed in 1999 to accommodate the first vintage.

### Brown Hill Estate ☆☆☆☆ V

*Corner Rosa Brook Road and Barrett Road, Rosa Brook, WA 6285, ☏ (08) 9757*
*4003, ℱ (08) 9757 4004; est 1995; ✦ 3,000 cases; ⚱; A$; 7 days 10-5; ⚘*

The Bailey family's stated aim is to produce top-quality wines at affordable prices, tending their twenty-two-hectare vineyard without outside help. Nathan Bailey produces succulent blackcurrant Cabernet and fragrant, spicy black-cherry Shiraz.

### Cape Grace ☆☆☆☆✓

*Fifty One Road, Cowaramup, WA 6284, ☏ (08) 9755 5669, ℱ (08) 9755 5668;*
*est 1996; ✦ 1,500 cases; ⚱; A$; 7 days 10-5; gallery*

A highly successful newcomer, producing excellent Shiraz and Cabernet Sauvignon, and very good Chardonnay from estate plantings.

**Cape Mentelle** ☆☆☆☆

*Off Wallcliffe Road, Margaret River, WA 6285, ☎ (08) 9757 0888, Ⓕ (08) 9757 3233; est 1970; ⚘ 55,000 cases; ☙; A$; 7 days 10-4.30*

One of the top four regional wineries, with an international reputation that must please its owner, Champagne Veuve Clicquot. Quite marvellous, seductively fruity, subtly oaked Semillon/Sauvignon Blanc; glorious figgy, melon and cashew Chardonnay; spicy, dark-plum, liquorice, and game Shiraz; and Australia's only serious Zinfandel, a powerful, turbo-charged V8. Worldwide distribution.

**Carbunup Crest Vineyard** ☆☆☆☆ V

*PO Box 235, Busselton, WA 6280, ☎ & Ⓕ (08) 9754 2618; est 1998; ⚘ 2,000 cases; no visitors*

The brand name (Cella Rage) is pure kitsch, but the Shiraz, Cabernet/ Merlot, and Cabernet Sauvignon overflow with juicy berry fruit, and sell for the proverbial song.

**Casa Wines** ☆☆☆☆

*RMB 236D Rosa Brook Road, Margaret River, WA 6285, ☎ (08) 9757 4542, Ⓕ (08) 9757 4006; est 1992; ⚘ 2,000 cases; ☙; A$; by appt*

A highly regarded producer, with skilled contract winemaking by Janice McDonald producing excellent Cabernet and Shiraz. Exports to the UK and US.

**Chalice Bridge Estate** ☆☆☆☆ V

*Rosa Glen Road, Margaret River, WA 6285, ☎ (08) 9388 6088, Ⓕ (08) 9382 1887; est 1998; ⚘ 12,000 cases; ☙; A$; by appt*

Important newcomer with 121 hectares of vines producing precise Sauvignon Blanc, Semillon/Sauvignon Blanc, Shiraz, and Shiraz/Cabernet, the latter with delicious raspberry/redcurrant fruit and subtle oak.

**Clairault** ☆☆☆☆

*Caves Road, Wilyabrup, WA 6280, ☎ (08) 9755 6225, Ⓕ (08) 9755 6229; est 1976; ⚘ 40,000 cases; ☙; A$; 7 days 10-5; ❖*

The Martin family has dramatically increased the size of the renamed Clairault since acquiring it. The lively, bracing style of the wines is largely unchanged. The wines are served at the restaurant, which is open seven days. Exports to the UK and elsewhere.

**Cullen Wines** ☆☆☆☆☆

*Caves Road, Cowaramup, WA 6284, ☎ (08) 9755 5277, Ⓕ (08) 9755 5550; est 1971; ⚘ 20,000 cases; ☙; A$; 7 days 10-4; ❖*

Vanya Cullen presides over one of Australia's best small wineries. Concentrated, complex, flavour-packed, fig, and peach-flavoured Chardonnay and powerful, minerally Sauvignon Blanc yield only to the imperious Cabernet/Merlot, surely Australia's best, replete with luscious cassis and fine, balanced tannins. Exports to the UK.

**Deep Woods Estate** ☆☆☆☆

*Lot 10, Commonage Road, Yallingup, WA 6282, ☎ (08) 9756 6066, Ⓕ (08) 9756 6066; est 1987; ⚘ 20,000 cases; ☙; A$; Tues-Sun 11-5, 7 days during hols*

The Gould family has owned and run Deep Woods since 1991. Fifteen hectares of estate plantings and an on-site winery erected in 1998 produce stylish, barrel-fermented Semillon and Semillon/Sauvignon Blanc; spicy, small berry/cherry Shiraz is also good.

**Devil's Lair** ☆☆☆☆☆

*Rocky Road, Forest Grove via Margaret River, WA 6285, ☎ (08) 9757 7573,*
*Ⓕ (08) 9757 7533; est 1985; ⬧ 40,000 cases; ⚲; no visitors*

Highly regarded for stylish, structured Chardonnay, a classic red Bordeaux
blend with lingering tannins, and the jazzy second label, Fifth Leg White
and Red. Striking label designs. Part of Southcorp; exports to the UK
and elsewhere.

**Driftwood Estate** ☆☆☆⟋ **V**

*Lot 13, Caves Road, Yallingup, WA 6282, ☎ (08) 9755 6323, Ⓕ (08) 9755 6343;*
*est 1989; ⬧ 15,000 cases; ⚲; A$; 7 days 11-4.30; ⧆; amphitheatre*

Baroque-look Greek architecture is perhaps an appropriate backdrop for
the fleshy Semillon and Battlestar Galactica Chardonnay, armed with
masses of toasty/nutmeg oak and peachy/buttery fruit. The cheaper
varietals offer good value for money in the context of the region.

**Eagle Vale** ☆☆☆☆☆

*51 Caves Road, Margaret River, WA 6285, ☎ (08) 9757 6477, Ⓕ (08) 9757 6199;*
*est 1997; ⬧ 5,000 cases; ⚲; A$; 7 days 10-5; gallery*

A joint venture involving the US, Indonesia, and the Loire Valley, via the
Jacobs and Gallienne families. French-born, Adelaide-University-qualified
winemaker Guy Gallienne is producing a suite of totally delicious varietal
wines. Exports to the UK and elsewhere.

**Edwards Vineyard** ☆☆☆☆

*Corner Caves Road and Ellensbrook Road, Cowaramup, WA 6284, ☎ (08) 9755*
*5999, Ⓕ (08) 9755 5988; est 1994; ⬧ 2,000 cases; ⚲; A$; 7 days 10.30-5.30*

Very much a family affair for the Edwards clan, who have a twenty-hectare
vineyard. Sauvignon Blanc (gooseberry, a hint of oak), Semillon/Sauvignon
Blanc (outstanding), Shiraz (spicy/cedary), and blackberry Cabernet
Sauvignon all appeal greatly. Exports to the UK and elsewhere.

**Evans & Tate** ☆☆☆☆

*Metricup Road, Wilyabrup, WA 6280, ☎ (08) 9755 6244, Ⓕ (08) 9755 6346;*
*est 1970; ⬧ NFP; ⚲; A$; 7 days 10.30-5; café*

Growing like an overcharged Topsy, with the acquisition of Cranswick Estate
and Oakridge (*q.v.*), making the group Australia's eighth-largest producer.
Sophisticated winemaking shines through all the Margaret River wines, but
you sometimes "wonder where the yellow went" in white wines that are
elegant but lack the expected regional richness. Worldwide distribution.

**Fermoy Estate** ☆☆☆☆

*Metricup Road, Wilyabrup, WA 6280, ☎ (08) 9755 6285, Ⓕ (08) 9755 6251;*
*est 1985; ⬧ 25,000 cases; ⚲; A$; 7 days 11-4.30; ⊨*

Changes in ownership and philosophy have brought the sharp-edged
wine style back into the mainstream and allow the naturally soft fruit of the
region to express itself more fully, especially Chardonnay. Exports to the
UK and elsewhere.

**Fire Gully** ☆☆☆⟋

*Metricup Road, Wilyabrup, WA 6280, ☎ (08) 9755 6220, Ⓕ (08) 9755 6308;*
*est 1988; ⬧ 5,000 cases; ⚲; A$; by appt*

In 1998, Mike Peterkin of Pierro purchased the property and regards the
Fire Gully wines as entirely separate to those of Pierro, being estate-
grown, with just under nine hectares planted with Cabernet Sauvignon,
Merlot, Shiraz, Semillon, Sauvignon Blanc, Chardonnay, Viognier, and
Chenin Blanc.

**Flinders Bay** ☆☆☆☆⬗

*Davis Road, Witchcliffe, WA 6286, ☎ (08) 9757 6281, Ⓕ (08) 9757 6353;
est 1995; ⬗ 10,000 cases; no visitors*

A joint venture between the Margaret River Gillespie family and the
Ireland family (*q.v.* Old Station). There have been fifty hectares planted and
the wines are contract-made and sold through the cellar door at Vasse
Felix under the Flinders Bay label. Exports to the UK and elsewhere.

**Flying Fish Cove** ☆☆☆☆☆

*Lot 125, Caves Road, Wilyabrup, WA 6284 (postal), ☎ (08) 9755 6688,
Ⓕ (08) 9755 6788; est 2001; ⬗ 10,000 cases; ☘; A$; 7 days 11-5*

Flying Fish Cove's major activity is that of a large contract winemaking
facility for Margaret River (and other) vignerons. A skilled winemaking
team and a high-tech winery are producing a stream of excellent wines
(chiefly red) across a range of price points, both for its own label and
for others.

**Forester Estate** ☆☆☆☆⬗ **V**

*Lot 11, Wildwood Road, Yallingup, WA 6282, ☎ (08) 9755 2788, Ⓕ (08) 9755
2766; est 2001; ⬗ 7,000 cases; ☘; A$; by appt*

Another newcomer, but with an ultra-qualified team producing
outstanding, zesty Sauvignon Blanc, fragrant, cassis-accented Cabernet
Sauvignon, and high-toned, black-cherry Shiraz.

**Gralyn Cellars** ☆☆☆☆⬗

*Caves Road, Wilyabrup, WA 6280, ☎ (08) 9755 6245, Ⓕ (08) 9755 6136;
est 1975; ⬗ 2,500 cases; ☘; A$; 7 days 10.30-4.30*

A substantial thirty-year-old vineyard is the rock upon which the Hutton
family bases its full-bodied, full-blooded Cabernet and Shiraz-based reds
(with a touch of vanilla-tinged American oak). Unusually for the region, the
Huttons also produce port-style fortified wines.

**Green Valley Vineyard** ☆☆☆☆

*3137 Sebbes Road, Forest Grove, WA 6286, ☎ & Ⓕ (08) 9757 7510; est 1980;
⬗ 3,500 cases; ☘; A$; 7 days 10-6*

Ed and Eleanore Green have the luxury of Moss Wood as contract
winemaker, with predictably very good, complex Chardonnay and
Cabernet Sauvignon.

**Hamelin Bay** ☆☆☆☆

*McDonald Road, Karridale, WA 6288, ☎ & Ⓕ (08) 9758 6779; est 1992;
⬗ 10,000 cases; ☘; A$; 7 days 10-5*

Made its mark with elegant, fragrant, lemony/grassy/gooseberryish
Semillon, Sauvignon Blanc, and blends thereof, coming from twenty-five
hectares of estate plantings. Cabernet Sauvignon is also good. Exports to
the UK and elsewhere.

**Happs** ☆☆☆

*571 Commonage Road, Dunsborough, WA 6281, ☎ (08) 9755 3300, Ⓕ (08) 9755
3846; est 1978; ⬗ 18,000 cases; ☘; A$; 7 days 10-5; ⚲; pottery*

Erl Happ suffers fools (and critics) badly, yet is an iconoclastic and
compulsive experimenter, sticking only with the Merlot which has been
the winery specialty for more than a decade. The Cabernet/Merlot can
also impress.

**Hay Shed Hill Wines** ☆☆☆☆

*RMB 398, Harmans Mill Road, Wilyabrup, WA 6280, ☎ (08) 9755 6234,
Ⓕ (08) 9755 6305; est 1987; ⬗ 17,000 cases; ☘; A$; 7 days 10.30-5*

After a quick ownership double shuffle, is now part of the Alexandra Bridge group. Shiraz (at two levels) is impressive, as is the cheap Pitchfork Shiraz/Cabernet.

## Howard Park ☆☆☆☆☆ V

*Miamup Road, Cowaramup, WA 6284, ☎ (08) 9848 2345, ⓕ (08) 9848 2064; est 1986; ◈ 100,000 cases; ☟; A$; 7 days 10-5*

The splendid winery (incorporating feng shui principles) and a catchment of 230 hectares of estate and contract vineyards are producing a stream of utterly immaculate wines, second label MadFish providing unbeatable value. Worldwide distribution.

## Island Brook Estate ☆☆☆☆

*817 Bussell Highway, Metricup, WA 6280, ☎ (08) 9755 7501, ⓕ (08) 9755 7008; est 1985; ◈ 2,000 cases; ☟; A$; 7 days 10-5; ⇛*

Linda and Peter Jenkins purchased Island Brook from Ken and Judy Brook in early 2001, re-trellising the vineyard, opening a new cellar door, followed by luxurious accommodation set among forty-five acres of forest.

## Juniper Estate ☆☆☆☆☆

*Harmans Road South, Cowaramup, WA 6284, ☎ (08) 9755 9000, ⓕ (08) 9755 9100; est 1973; ◈ 10,000 cases; ☟; A$; 7 days 10-5*

Based on a ten-hectare, thirty-year-old vineyard purchased by the Junipers in 1998. In February 2000, a new 250-tonne capacity winery, barrel hall, and cellar-door facility were completed. The Juniper family is a famous one in the region, its strong artistic bent evident in the immaculate packaging and background material. Exports to the UK and elsewhere.

## Leeuwin Estate ☆☆☆☆☆

*Stevens Road, Margaret River, WA 6285, ☎ (08) 9759 0000, ⓕ (08) 9759 0001; est 1974; ◈ 60,000 cases; ☟; A$; 7 days 10.30-4.30; ❦; ⚸; annual concert; charter flights*

Produces Australia's best Chardonnay, immensely complex and long-lived, developing Burgundian characters with age. The second-label Prelude Chardonnay is also better than most. Shiraz is an interesting newcomer. Worldwide distribution.

## Lenton Brae Estate ☆☆☆☆⟋

*Wilyabrup Valley, Margaret River, WA 6285, ☎ (08) 9755 6255, ⓕ (08) 9755 6268; est 1983; ◈; NFP; ☟; A$; 7 days 10-6*

Edward Tomlinson has responsibility for winemaking, with fine results for Chardonnay, Semillon/Sauvignon Blanc, Sauvignon Blanc, and a beautifully balanced Cabernet blend simply called Margaret River. Exports to the UK and elsewhere.

## Maiolo Wines ☆☆☆⟋

*Bussell Highway, Carbunup River, WA 6282, ☎ & ⓕ (08) 9755 1060; est 1999; ◈ 3,000 cases; ☟; A$; 7 days 10-5; wood-turning gallery*

Charles Maiolo has established a twenty-eight-hectare vineyard planted with Semillon, Sauvignon Blanc, Chardonnay, Pinot Noir, Shiraz, Merlot, and Cabernet Sauvignon. He has a wine-science degree and presides over a winery with a capacity of 250-300 tonnes. Shiraz and Cabernet Sauvignon are the pick.

## Moss Brothers ☆☆☆☆

*Caves Road, Wilyabrup, WA 6280, ☎ (08) 9755 6270, ⓕ (08) 9755 6298; est 1984; ◈ 20,000 cases; ☟; A$; 7 days 10-5*

Established by long-term viticulturist Jeff Moss and his family. A 100-tonne rammed-earth winery was built in 1992, and wine quality is consistently good, especially intense, long, mineral, and gooseberry Semillon/Sauvignon Blanc. Exports to the UK and elsewhere.

**Moss Wood** ☆☆☆☆☆

*Metricup Road, Wilyabrup, WA 6280, ☎ (08) 9755 6266, Ⓕ (08) 9755 6303; est 1969; ⚭ 11,000 cases; ⚱; A$; by appt*

One of the Margaret River icons. Keith Mugford produces immaculate estate-grown wines of distinctive style: rich, tropical Semillon; deep, peachy honey and fig Chardonnay; and uniquely soft, multi-layered Cabernet Sauvignon. Lefroy Brook and Ribbon Vale are additional estate-based varietals. Exports to the UK and elsewhere.

**Palandri Wines** ☆☆☆

*Bussell Highway, Cowaramup, WA 6284, ☎ (08) 9755 5711, Ⓕ (08) 9755 5722; est 1999; ⚭ 240,000 cases; ⚱; A$; 7 days 10-5; ⓘ; ✗*

After extensive public fundraising in Australia, Palandri has turned to London to raise yet more capital, but remains the subject of much local discussion and speculation. Apart from anything else, its extensive vineyards are in the Great Southern, although it does buy grapes from Margaret River and elsewhere. It is driven by relentless marketing, the wines adequate. Exports to the UK and elsewhere.

**Palmer Wines** ☆☆☆☆

*Caves Road, Wilyabrup, WA 6280, ☎ (08) 9756 7388, Ⓕ (08) 9756 7399; est 1977; ⚭ 6,000 cases; ⚱; A$; 7 days 10-5*

Stephen and Helen Palmer had to deal with natural hindrances such as cyclones and grasshopper plagues before ultimately bringing their fifty-five-hectare vineyard into production. The spotlessly clean Sauvignon Blanc/Semillon, glossy, oaky Chardonnay, and powerful Merlot and Cabernet Sauvignon make it all worthwhile. A new cellar door opened in April 2002.

**Pierro** ☆☆☆☆☆

*Caves Road, Wilyabrup via Cowaramup, WA 6284, ☎ (08) 9755 6220, Ⓕ (08) 9755 6308; est 1979; ⚭ 7,500 cases; ⚱; A$; 7 days 10-5*

Dr Michael Peterkin makes wines in his own image: complex and concentrated (he is a doctor of medicine as well as a qualified winemaker) with towering, multi-flavoured creamy/nutty/toasty/figgy Chardonnay and a commensurately complex LTC Semillon/Sauvignon Blanc (LTC for Les Trois Cuvées or a little touch of Chardonnay . . . take your pick). Exports to the UK and elsewhere.

**Preveli Wines** ☆☆☆☆☆

*Bessell Road, Rosa Brook, Margaret River, WA 6285, ☎ (08) 9757 2374, Ⓕ (08) 9757 2790; est 1995; ⚭ 8,000 cases; ⚱; A$; Mon-Sat 10.30-8.30, Sun 12-6*

Andrew and Greg Home have quickly developed a substantial, high-quality business based on fifteen hectares of vineyards at Rosabrook plus external grape sources, employing a series of skilled contract winemakers for excellent Chardonnay, Semillon, Merlot, and Cabernet Sauvignon.

**Redgate** ☆☆☆☆

*Boodjidup Road, Margaret River, WA 6285, ☎ (08) 9757 6488, Ⓕ (08) 9757 6308; est 1977; ⚭ 14,000 cases; ⚱; A$; 7 days 10-5*

Draws upon twenty hectares of mature vineyards to make a wide range, including various Semillon/Sauvignon Blanc combinations, Chardonnay, the occasional surprising Cabernet Franc, and Bordeaux-style reds. Exports to the UK and elsewhere.

**Rivendell** ☆☆☆✠

*Lot 328, Wildwood Road, Yallingup, WA 6282, ☎ (08) 9755 2235, Ⓕ (08) 9755 2301; est 1987; ✿ 3,000 cases; ☗; A$; 7 days 10-5; ⑩*

Doubtlessly named in honour of JRR Tolkien, Rivendell is a producer of wines such as Honeysuckle Late Harvest Semillon that would delight any hobbit. Exports to the UK and elsewhere.

**Rockfield Estate Vineyard** ☆☆☆☆

*Rosa Glen Road, Margaret River, WA 6285, ☎ & Ⓕ (08) 9757 5006; est 1997; ✿ 8,000 cases; ☗; A$; 7 days 10.30-5; ⑩; ✗*

Five members of Dr Andrew Gaman's family are involved in one capacity or another, with an on-site winery producing both excellent estate-based wines (Reserve Cabernet Sauvignon and Reserve Chardonnay both gloriously complex) and contract winemaking for others. Exports to the UK and elsewhere.

**Rosabrook Estate** ☆☆☆☆✠

*Rosa Brook Road, Margaret River, WA 6285, ☎ (08) 9757 2286, Ⓕ (08) 9757 3634; est 1980; ✿ 4,000 cases; ☗; A$; 7 days 10-4*

Several quick-fire changes of ownership have not dimmed the ability of this mature fourteen-hectare vineyard to produce excellent Semillon/ Sauvignon Blanc, Shiraz, and Cabernet/Merlot. Exports to the UK and elsewhere.

**Rosily Vineyard** ☆☆☆☆ V

*Yelveton Road, Wilyabrup, WA 6284, ☎ (08) 9755 6336, Ⓕ (08) 9221 3309; est 1994; ✿ 7,000 cases; ☗; A$; by appt*

The Scott and Allan families acquired the site in 1994; under the direction of consultant Dan Pannell (of the Pannell family), twelve hectares of vineyard were planted, followed in 1999 by a 120-tonne winery. Sauvignon Blanc, Semillon/Sauvignon Blanc, Cabernet Sauvignon, and Shiraz are all consistently impressive.

**Suckfizzle & Stella Bella** ☆☆☆☆☆

*PO Box 536, Margaret River, WA 6288, ☎ (08) 9757 6377, Ⓕ (08) 9757 6022; est 1997; ✿ 20,000 cases; no visitors*

The wildly improbable Suckfizzle name comes from Rabelais, companion Stella Bella I know not where. Janice McDonald, previously an unseen hand, emerges as a winemaker of truly exceptional Cabernet Sauvignon, Sauvignon Blanc, Sauvignon Blanc/Semillon, Shiraz, Chardonnay, and Tempranillo (among others). Exports to the UK and elsewhere.

**Thompson Estate** ☆☆☆☆

*Harmans Road South, Wilyabrup, WA 6280, ☎ (08) 9386 1751, Ⓕ (08) 9386 1708; est 1998; ✿ 2,000 cases; no visitors*

Cardiologist Peter Thompson has established twelve hectares of estate vineyards, using no less than four different contract winemaking facilities for the very good stone-fruit, cashew, and oak Chardonnay; cassis, earth, and olive Cabernet Sauvignon; and complex mineral, herb, and spice Semillon/Sauvignon Blanc.

**Vasse Felix** ☆☆☆☆☆

*Corner Caves Road and Harmans Road South, Wilyabrup, WA 6284, ☎ (08) 9756 5000, Ⓕ (08) 9755 5425; est 1967; ✿ 150,000 cases; ☗; A$; 7 days 10-5; ⑩*

The most senior winery in the region, established by Dr Tom Cullitty but now owned by Janet Holmes à Court's Heytesbury Holdings. A new winery and expanded vineyards have capitalized on the strength of the brand; the flagship Heytesbury Bordeaux blend is superb. Exports to the UK and elsewhere.

**Voyager Estate** ☆☆☆☆☆

*Lot 1, Stevens Road, Margaret River, WA 6285, ☎ (08) 9757 6354, ⓕ (08) 9757 6494; est 1978; ⅋ 30,000 cases; ☙; A$; 7 days 10-5; ¶○¶; Ⲕ*

The flamboyant venture of mining magnate Michael Wright, with manicured rose gardens and a Cape Dutch cellar-door-sales mansion. Tucked away in the back, Cliff Royle makes wonderfully rich and skilfully oaked Semillon and Chardonnay, and powerful Reserve Cabernet/Merlot. Exports to the UK and elsewhere.

**Watershed Wines** ☆☆☆☆☆

*Corner Bussell Highway and Darch Road, Margaret River, WA 6285, ☎ (08) 9758 8633, ⓕ (08) 9757 3999; est 1999; ⅋ 40,000 cases; ☙; A$; 7 days 10-5*

Established by a syndicate of investors, seemingly without regard to cost, including a striking cellar-door sales area and a 200-seat café and restaurant. The outstanding quality of the Sauvignon Blanc, Chardonnay, Shiraz, and Cabernet/Merlot has led to significant show success with the first and subsequent releases. Exports to the UK and elsewhere.

**We're Wines** ☆☆☆☆☆

*Corner Wildberry and Johnson Roads, Wilyabrup, WA 6280, ☎ (08) 9755 6273, ⓕ (08) 9389 9166; est 1998; ⅋ 3,600 cases; ☙; A$; Wed-Sun & public hols 10.30-5*

One look at the front and back labels of the wines bears out Diane and Gordon Davies's statement "we're original, we're bold, we're innovative . . ." All the fandango should not detract from the elegant, cedary, blackcurrant Cabernet Sauvignon, nor the gooseberry, passion-fruit, and herb Semillon/Sauvignon Blanc.

**Wildwood of Yallingup** ☆☆☆☆

*Caves Road, Yallingup, WA 6282, ☎ (08) 9755 2066, ⓕ (08) 9754 1389; est 1984; ⅋ 3,000 cases; ☙; A$; 7 days 10-5; ¶○¶; ⊨; gallery*

The 5.5-hectare vineyard, planted in the mid-1980s and established (and maintained) without irrigation, produces richly robed Chardonnay, Cabernet/Merlot, Semillon, and (against the odds) Pinot Noir.

**Windance Wines** ☆☆☆☆

*Lot 12, Loc 589, Caves Road, Yallingup, WA 6282, ☎ & ⓕ (08) 9755 2293; est 1998; ⅋ 3,000 cases; ☙; A$; Sept-May 7 days 10-5, June-Aug Fri-Mon 10-5*

Drew and Rosemary Brent-White have established 6.5 hectares of Sauvignon Blanc, Shiraz, Merlot, and Cabernet Sauvignon using sustainable/organic viticultural practices. Highly skilled winemaking has produced a trophy-winning 2002 Shiraz and very good Cabernet/Merlot.

**Wise Wine** ☆☆☆☆

*Lot 4, Eagle Bay Road, Dunsborough, WA 6281, ☎ (08) 9756 8627, ⓕ (08) 9756 8770; est 1986; ⅋ 40,000 cases; ☙; A$; 7 days 10-5; ¶○¶; ⊨*

Wise Vineyards, headed by Perth entrepreneur Ron Wise, brings together three substantial estate vineyards in Geographe, Pemberton, and Margaret River, forty hectares in all. The on-site restaurant is open daily, and there are five chalets, variously sleeping two to ten people, all within ten minutes' walk from the restaurant. Quality has lifted sharply, led (of all things) by its exceptional Single Vineyard Verdelho. Exports to the UK and elsewhere.

**Woodlands** ☆☆☆☆↓

*Corner Caves and Metricup Roads, Wilyabrup via Cowaramup, WA 6284, ☎ (08) 9755 6226, ⓕ (08) 9481 1700; est 1973; ⅋ 2,500 cases; ☙; A$; wkds by appt*

A long-established winery and estate vineyard, with quality rising and falling over the years; currently going through a purple patch with an unusual array of small-batch Cabernet/Merlot, Cabernet Sauvignon, Malbec, and Cabernet Franc.

**Woody Nook** ☆☆☆☆ **V**

*Metricup Road, Busselton, WA 6280, ☎ (08) 9755 7547, ⓕ (08) 9755 7007; est 1982; ⚘ 5,000 cases; ⚑; A$; 7 days 10-4.30; ▮◖▮*

This improbably named and not terribly fashionable winery has produced some truly excellent wines over the years, with its zesty Classic Dry White, Sauvignon Blanc and blackberry/blackcurrant Cabernet Sauvignon both starring at a number of wine competitions and shows. Exports to the UK and elsewhere.

**Xanadu Normans Wines** ☆☆☆☆☆

*Boodjidup Road, Margaret River, WA 6285, ☎ (08) 9757 2581, ⓕ (08) 9757 3389; est 1977; ⚘ 100,000 cases; ⚑; A$; 7 days 10-5*

Xanadu, once a somewhat quirky, small family winery, has entered the lists of the Stock Exchange, raising substantial capital and spreading its empire from west to east with major acquisitions, including that of Normans. Perhaps surprisingly, wine quality has risen, with outstanding Semillon/Sauvignon Blanc, Cabernet Sauvignon, Merlot, and Chardonnay leading the way. Worldwide distribution.

# Great Southern

Even by the standards of Australia, Great Southern is a large region, forming a rectangle 150 kilometres (ninety-three miles) long and 100 kilometres (sixty-two miles) wide. It embraces climates that range from strongly maritime-influenced to moderately Continental, and has an ever-changing topography. The suitability of the region for premium-quality table wine was pinpointed in 1955 by the distinguished Californian viticulturist Professor Harold Olmo.

It was another ten years before the first experimental vineyard was planted at Forest Hill (now owned by Janet Holmes à Court as an adjunct to Vasse Felix in the Margaret River). Vineyards spread slowly between 1965 and 1985. Most were small. The only large planting was the 100-hectare Frankland River Estate, leased by Houghton in 1981 and ultimately acquired by it. Then, in the second half of the 1980s, Goundrey Wines appeared, and the originally small Alkoomi and Plantagenet wineries flourished and grew. Howard Park, too, acquired near-icon status. All was set for the boom of the 1990s.

The two greatest wines of the region are Riesling (a serious challenge to the primacy of the Clare and Eden valleys) and Cabernet Sauvignon. Shiraz, too, can be superb, with intense spicy, cherry flavours. Indeed, with suitable site selection, every one of the classic varieties can produce top-class wine somewhere in Great Southern. It now has five sub-regions: Albany, Denmark, Frankland River, Mount Barker, and Porongurup. There are fifty-two wine producers in the region.

**Alkoomi** ☆☆☆☆☆ **V**

*Wingeballup Road, Frankland, WA 6396, ☎ (08) 9855 2229, ⓕ (08) 9855 2284; est 1971; ⚘ 80,000 cases; ⚑; A$; 7 days 10.30-5; ▰▰*

Through sheer hard work and experience, Merv and Judy Lange – and their children – have built a significant wine business in a remote part of the Great Southern. Racy Riesling, tangy Sauvignon Blanc, sophisticated Wandoo Semillon, fruit-driven melon/citrus Chardonnay, peppery Shiraz/Viognier, and finely crafted, cedary Blackbutt (Bordeaux blend) are all consistently excellent. Exports to the UK and elsewhere.

### Castle Rock Estate ☆☆☆☆

*Porongurup Road, Porongurup, WA 6324, ☎ (08) 9853 1035, Ⓕ (08) 9853 1010; est 1983; ◈ 5,000 cases; ⚑; A$; Mon-Fri 10-4, wkds & public hols 10-5; picnic lunches*
One of the more beautifully situated vineyards in Australia, with sweeping vistas from its hillside location in the Porongurups. Initially delicate Riesling blossoms with age, as does Chardonnay; the light-bodied reds are less convincing. Exports to the UK.

### Chatsfield ☆☆☆☆ᶲ V

*O'Neil Road, Mount Barker, WA 6324, ☎ & Ⓕ (08) 9851 1704; est 1976; ◈ 7,000 cases; ⚑; A$; Tues-Sun, public hols 10.30-4.30*
Mature, low-yielding vineyards are the cornerstone of this producer. The crisp, minerally Riesling, elegant Chardonnay, and spice and cherry Shiraz are complemented by an excellent, early-release, unoaked Cabernet Franc, as lively a red wine as you could wish for. Exports to the UK and elsewhere.

### Ferngrove Vineyards ☆☆☆☆☆

*Ferngrove Road, Frankland, WA 6396, ☎ (08) 9855 2378, Ⓕ (08) 9855 2368; est 1997; ◈ 20,000 cases; ⚑; A$; 7 days 10-4; ⊨*
After ninety years of cattle-farming heritage, Murray Burton ventured into premium grape-growing and winemaking in 1997, establishing 414 hectares on three vineyards in the Frankland River sub-region, and a fourth at Mount Barker. A large, rammed-earth winery was built in early 2000, making both highly regarded estate Riesling and a panoply of reds, as well as contract-making for others. Exports to the UK and elsewhere.

### Forest Hill Vineyard ☆☆☆ᶲ

*South Coast Highway, Denmark, WA 6333, ☎ (08) 9381 2911, Ⓕ (08) 9381 2955; est 1966; ◈ 20,000 cases; ⚑; A$; 7 days 10-5*
This is one of the oldest "new" vineyards in West Australia, the site for the first grape plantings for the Great Southern region in 1966. In 1997, the property was acquired by Perth stockbroker Tim Lyons, and a programme of renovation and expansion of the now eighty-hectare vineyards commenced, followed by a new winery in 2003 and new cellar door in September. Exports to the UK and US.

### Frankland Estate ☆☆☆☆

*Frankland Road, Frankland, WA 6396, ☎ (08) 9855 1544, Ⓕ (08) 9855 1549; est 1988; ◈ 15,000 cases; ⚑; A$; by appt*
Established on the gently rolling hills of a large sheep property by Barrie Smith and Judi Cullam. A Riesling specialist, with a number of individual vineyard Rieslings on offer. Exports to the UK and elsewhere.

### Garlands ☆☆☆☆ V

*Marmion Street off Mount Barker Hill Road, Mount Barker, WA 6324, ☎ (08) 9851 2737, Ⓕ (08) 9851 2686; est 1996; ◈ 3,500 cases; ⚑; A$; Thurs-Sun & public hols 10-4, or by appt; ✗*
Garlands is a partnership between Michael and Julie Garland and Craig and Caroline Drummond. A 150-tonne winery was erected in early 2000,

contract making for other small producers in the region as well as making the wine from the six hectares of estate vineyards; Cabernet Franc is a specialty, Chardonnay and Merlot also very good. Exports to the UK and elsewhere.

### Gilberts ☆☆☆☆☆ V

*RMB 438 Albany Highway, Kendenup via Mount Barker, WA 6323, ☎ (08) 9851 4028, Ⓕ (08) 9851 4021; est 1980; ♦ 4,000 cases; ♟; A$; 7 days 10-5; café*

A part-time occupation and diversification for sheep and beef farmers Jim and Beverley Gilbert. The wines are made at Plantagenet, the intense, limey, lingering Riesling often winning trophies, with a luscious black-cherry and blackberry Shiraz in company. Exports to the UK and elsewhere.

### Goundrey ☆☆☆☆

*Muir Highway, Mount Barker, WA 6324, ☎ (08) 9851 1777, Ⓕ (08) 9851 1997; est 1976; ♦ 300,000 cases; ♟; A$; 7 days 10-4.30*

Acquired by Canadian wine giant Vincor in 2003; a large portfolio of wines of differing price and quality. Reserve Riesling and Reserve Chardonnay fully live up to their name. Exports to the UK and elsewhere.

### Harewood Estate ☆☆☆☆

*Scotsdale Road, Denmark, WA 6333, ☎ (08) 9840 9078, Ⓕ (08) 9840 9053; est 1988; ♦ 4,000 cases; ♟; A$; 7 days 10-4*

Former Howard Park winemaker James Kellie, in partnership with his father and sister, is now the owner of Harewood Estate and has lifted both quality and quantity, Chardonnay and Pinot Noir leading the way.

### Howard Park ☆☆☆☆☆⸘

*Scotsdale Road, Denmark, WA 6333, ☎ (08) 9848 2345, Ⓕ (08) 9848 2064; est 1986; ♦ 100,000 cases; 7 days 10-4*

Began a major metamorphosis in 1999, with founder John Wade departing and owner Jeff Burch establishing a second new winery in the Margaret River region. The Denmark winery continues, producing sublime Riesling and exceptional Scotsdale Shiraz. Worldwide distribution.

### Marribrook ☆☆☆☆⸘

*Albany Highway, Kendenup, WA 6323, ☎ (08) 9851 4651, Ⓕ (08) 9851 4652; est 1990; ♦ 2,000 cases; ♟; A$; Wed-Sun & public hols 10.30-4.30; café; gallery*

An interesting range of varietal wines including Marsanne (both oaked and unoaked) and an excellent blackcurrant, blackberry, and liquorice Cabernet/Malbec/Merlot blend.

### Matilda's Estate ☆☆☆⸘

*RMB 654 Hamilton Road, Denmark, WA 6333, ☎ (08) 9848 1951, Ⓕ (08) 9848 1957; est 1990; ♦ 5,000 cases; ♟; A$; 7 days 10-5; ⑩*

Purchased by former citizen of the world Steve Hall in late 2002, this six-hectare vineyard produces a wide range of wines; Cabernet/Merlot is the pick. The restaurant is open Tuesday to Sunday.

### Montgomery's Hill ☆☆☆☆⸘

*Hassell Highway, Upper Kalgan, Albany, WA 6330, ☎ (08) 9844 3715, Ⓕ (08) 9844 1104; est 1996; ♦ 2,000 cases; ♟; A$; 7 days 11-5*

Situated on a north-facing slope on the banks of the Kalgan River, this is a diversification for the third generation of the Montgomery family. Since 1999, the wine has been made at the new Porongurup winery. A newly constructed cellar door opened in May 2001. Stylish grapefruit and melon Chardonnay outstanding. Exports to the UK.

**Mount Trio Vineyard** ☆☆☆☆♦
*Corner Castle Rock and Porongurup Roads, Porongurup, WA 6324, ☎ (08) 9853 1136, ⓕ (08) 9853 1120; est 1989; ♦ 5,000 cases; ♟; A$; by appt*
Established by Gavin Berry and Gill Graham after they moved to the district in 1988. Gavin is now senior winemaker and managing director of Plantagenet, and Gill is the mother of their two young children. In the meantime they have slowly but surely built up the Mount Trio business.

**Old Kent River** ☆☆☆☆♦
*Turpin Road, Rocky Gully, WA 6397, ☎ (08) 9855 1589, ⓕ (08) 9855 1660; est 1985; ♦ 3,000 cases; ♟; A$; at South Coast Highway, Kent River Wed-Sun 9-5 (extended hours during tourist season); crafts & local produce*
Mark and Debbie Noack had it tough but earned respect from their neighbours and from the other producers to whom they sell more than half the production of Pinot and Chardonnay from the 16.5-hectare vineyard established on their sheep property. "Grapes," they used to say, "saved us from bankruptcy." Pinot Noir excellent. Exports to the UK and elsewhere.

**Plantagenet** ☆☆☆☆☆ V
*Albany Highway, Mount Barker, WA 6324, ☎ (08) 9851 2150, ⓕ (08) 9851 1839; est 1974; ♦ 130,000 cases; ♟; A$; 7 days 9-5; ⑩*
One of the oldest and most important wineries in the region, Plantagenet has played a dual role as maker of its own consistently excellent wines (Riesling, Chardonnay, Shiraz, and Cabernet Sauvignon to the fore, all combining flavour with elegance) and as a contract winemaker for numerous small grape-growers scattered throughout the Great Southern region. Going from strength to strength; exports to the UK and elsewhere.

**Tingle-Wood** ☆☆☆☆♦ V
*Glenrowan Road, Denmark, WA 6333, ☎ & ⓕ (08) 9840 9218; est 1976; ♦ 1,000 cases; ♟; A$; Thurs-Mon 9-5, 7 days during hols; ✗; tea rooms; sheepskin products*
An intermittent producer of Riesling of extraordinary quality, although birds and other disasters do intervene and prevent production in some years. A personal favourite. Exports to the UK.

**Trevelen Farm** ☆☆☆☆ V
*Weir Road, Cranbrook, WA 6321, ☎ (08) 9826 1052, ⓕ (08) 9826 1209; est 1993; ♦ 3,000 cases; ♟; A$; Thurs-Mon 10-4.30, or by appt; garden & bush walks*
John and Katie Sprigg operate a 1,300-hectare farm, with sustainable agriculture at its heart. As a minor diversification, they established five hectares of Sauvignon Blanc, Riesling, Chardonnay, Cabernet Sauvignon, and Merlot in 1993. The quality of the wines is as consistent as the prices are modest. Exports to the UK and elsewhere.

**West Cape Howe Wines** ☆☆☆☆☆ V
*Lot 42, South Coast Highway, Denmark, WA 6333, ☎ (08) 9848 2959, ⓕ (08) 9848 2903; est 1997; ♦ 42,000 cases; ♟; A$; 7 days 10-5*
Brenden Smith was winemaker at Goundrey before opening his own contract winemaking business in 1998. Spectacular success followed with high-quality wines across a range of varietals. Sold to Gavin Berry and others in 2004. Exports to the UK and elsewhere.

**Wignalls Wines** ☆☆☆☆
*Chester Pass Road (Highway 1), Albany, WA 6330, ☎ (08) 9841 2848, ⓕ (08) 9842 9003; est 1982; ♦ 7,000 cases; ♟; A$; 7 days 12-4*
One of the best-known labels in the Great Southern, thanks to its early success with fragrant Pinot Noir. The mantle has slipped a little (ageing

problems), but some lovely citrus, melon-like Chardonnay and fragrant Shiraz have helped redress the balance. Exports to the UK and elsewhere.

**Yilgarnia** ☆☆☆☆⁄

*6634 Redmond West Road, Redmond, WA 6327, ☎ & Ⓕ (08) 9845 3031; ⬥ 1,500 cases; no visitors*

Peter Buxton combines commercial propagation of Australian wild flowers, viticulture and winemaking, farming and grazing with great success, using his tertiary education and experience with the Western Australian Department of Agriculture to full effect. Shiraz, Cabernet Sauvignon, and Merlot all rich and strongly varietal.

**Zarephath Wines** ☆☆☆⁄

*Moorialup Road, East Porongurup, WA 6324, ☎ (08) 9853 1152, Ⓕ (08) 9841 8124; est 1994; ⬥ 3,000 cases; ⚱; A$; Mon-Sat 10-5, Sun 12-4*

The Zarephath vineyard is owned and operated by the Brothers and Sisters of The Christ Circle, a Benedictine community. They say the most outstanding feature of the location is the feeling of peace and tranquillity that permeates the site, something I can well believe on the basis of numerous visits to the Porongurups. Exports to the UK and elsewhere.

# Manjimup

After a good deal of debate, the greater Warren Valley area has been divided into two regions, Manjimup and Pemberton. What they have in common is great beauty, with lush forest and plant growth encouraged by the usually ideal soils (for growth), mild temperatures, and generous rainfall. Both before and after the separation of Manjimup and Pemberton, there has been ongoing vigorous debate on the suitability of the region for the Burgundy varieties (Chardonnay and Pinot Noir) on the one hand, and the Bordeaux varieties (Sauvignon Blanc and Merlot) on the other, with Shiraz an interested bystander. Site (and hence soil) selection will be critical in answering at least some of the questions, as will vine maturity. As with Pemberton, large areas are heavily forested, and, on average, only twenty-five per cent of the region is available for, and suitable for, viticulture. There are ten wine producers in the region.

**Chestnut Grove** ☆☆☆☆

*Chestnut Grove Road, Manjimup, WA 6258, ☎ (08) 9772 4345, Ⓕ (08) 9772 4543; est 1988; ⬥ 12,000 cases; ⚱; A$; 7 days 10-4*

Yet another to produce Merlots of the highest quality in this region, and set itself up as one of the serious makers of this variety in Australia. Its other wines are more than adequate. Exports to the UK and elsewhere.

**Peos Estate** ☆☆☆

*Graphite Road, Manjimup, WA 6258, ☎ (08) 9772 1378, Ⓕ (08) 9772 1372; est 1996; ⬥ 3,000 cases; ⚱; A$; 7 days 10-4*

The Peos family has farmed in the west Manjimup district for fifty years, the third generation of four brothers planting a thirty-three-hectare vineyard in 1996. Fragrant, spicy Shiraz impresses most.

**Smithbrook** ☆☆☆☆

*Smith Brook Road, Middlesex via Manjimup, WA 6258, ☎ (08) 9772 3557, Ⓕ (08) 9772 3579; est 1988; ⬥ 15,000 cases; ⚱; A$; by appt*

A major player in the Pemberton region, with sixty hectares of vines in production. Although majority interest was acquired by Petaluma in 1997, it will continue its role as a contract grower for other companies, as well as supplying Petaluma's needs and making relatively small amounts of wine under its own label. Perhaps the most significant change has been the removal of Pinot Noir from the current list, and the introduction of spice and olive Merlot to carry the flag. Exports to the UK and elsewhere.

### Stone Bridge Estate NR

*RMB 189 Holleys Road, Manjimup, WA 6258, ☎ (08) 9773 1371, ⓕ (08) 9773 1309; est 1991; ◈ 3,000 cases; ⚱; A$; by appt*

Syd and Sue Hooker purchased the estate in 1990, and progressively planted eight hectares. The Pinot Noir and Chardonnay go to provide the *méthode champenoise*, made (on-site, like all the other wines) by daughter Kate, a graduate winemaker and viticulturist from the Lycée Viticole d'Avize in Champagne.

# Pemberton

Situated in the lower southwest of Western Australia, west of the Great Southern region and southeast of the Margaret River, the area is centred around the town of Pemberton. This richly timbered region was first planted experimentally in 1977, with commercial vineyards following in 1982, and has enjoyed rapid growth in the 1990s.

Pemberton has a somewhat cooler climate than neighbouring Manjimup, with slightly lower temperatures, fewer sunshine hours, more rainfall (except in January and February), and greater relative humidity – although temperature variability remains about the same. The high annual rainfall means that a number of vineyards do not use irrigation, but the very pronounced winter/spring dominance can lead to stress late in the growing season if subsoil moisture diminishes. While Manjimup is seen as more suited to the Bordeaux varieties, at Pemberton the Burgundian varieties intermingle with others.There are twenty-one wine producers in the region.

### Channybearup Vineyard ☆☆☆☆

*Lot 4, Channybearup Road, Pemberton, WA 6260 (postal), ☎ (08) 9776 0042, ⓕ (08) 9776 0043; est 1999; ◈ 11,000 cases; no visitors*

A small group of Perth businessmen has provided the funds to develop sixty-two hectares of vineyards, and to secure the services of high-profile ex-Houghton winemaker Larry Cherubino. Part of the crop is sold to other winemakers, part expertly vinified by Cherubino under the Channybearup Vineyard label, with Merlot, Cabernet Sauvignon, and Shiraz to the fore. Exports to the UK and elsewhere.

### Donnelly River Wines NR

*Lot 159, Vasse Highway, Pemberton, WA 6260, ☎ (08) 9776 2052, ⓕ (08) 9776 2053; est 1986; ◈ 15,000 cases; ⚱; A$; 7 days 9.30-4.30; cheese platters*

Blair Meiklejohn planted sixteen hectares of estate vineyards in 1986, and produced the first wines in 1990. The Chardonnay has been the pick of the bunch, the Cabernet Sauvignon good in warmer vintages. Exports to the UK and elsewhere.

### Fonty's Pool Vineyards ☆☆☆☆⚬

*Seven Day Road, Manjimup, WA 6258, ☎ (08) 9777 0777, ⓕ (08) 9777 0788; est 1998; ◈ 20,000 cases; ⚱; A$; 7 days 10-4.30*

The first grapes were planted in 1989, and the 110-hectare vineyard is now one of the region's largest, supplying grapes to a number of leading Western Australian wineries. Part of the production is used for Fonty's Pool; the wines are made at Cape Mentelle by Eloise Jarvis. Splendid Viognier and Merlot lead the way. Exports to the UK and elsewhere.

### Gloucester Ridge Vineyard ☆☆☆☆

*Lot 7489, Burma Road, Pemberton, WA 6260, ☎ (08) 9776 1035, Ⓕ (08) 9776 1390; est 1985; ◊ 6,000 cases; ⛾; A$; 7 days 10-5, later on Sat; café*

Owned and operated by Don and Sue Hancock, this is the only vineyard located within the Pemberton town boundary, making it an easy walk from the centre. Sauvignon Blanc, Chardonnay, and Cabernet Sauvignon are contract-made by Brenden Smith. Exports to the UK and elsewhere.

### Merum ☆☆☆☆☆

*Hillbrook Road, Quinninup, WA 6258, ☎ (08) 9776 6011, Ⓕ (08) 9776 6022; est 1996; ◊ 1,000 cases; ⛾; A$; by appt*

Michael Melsom is continuing Merum, notwithstanding the accidental death of his winemaker-wife Maria, producing strikingly aromatic Semillon and superbly textured plum and cherry Shiraz. Exports to the UK and elsewhere.

### Mountford ☆☆☆☆

*Bamess Road, West Pemberton, WA 6260, ☎ & Ⓕ (08) 9776 1345; est 1987; ◊ 3,000 cases; ⛾; A$; Mon-Fri 10-4, wkds 10-5; ✗; fine art gallery; light lunches*

English-born and trained Andrew Mountford and wife Sue migrated to Australia in 1983. They first endeavoured to set up a winery at Mudgee, thereafter moving to Pemberton with far greater success. Their strikingly packaged wines (complete with beeswax and paper seals) have been well-received on eastern Australian markets, being produced from six hectares of permanently netted, dry-grown vineyards.

### Phillips Estate ☆☆☆

*Lot 964a, Channybearup Road, Pemberton, WA 6230, ☎ & Ⓕ (08) 9776 0381; est 1996; ◊ 5,000 cases; ⛾; A$; 7 days 10.30-4*

Phillip Wilkinson has developed 4.5 hectares of vines framed by an old-growth Karri forest on one side and a large lake on the other. Sophisticated winemaking techniques are used at the fermentation stage, but fining and filtration are either not used at all, or employed to a minimum degree. Exports to the UK.

### Picardy ☆☆☆☆☆

*Corner Vasse Highway and Eastbrook Road, Manjimup, WA 6260, ☎ (08) 9776 0036, Ⓕ (08) 9776 0245; est 1993; ◊ 5,000 cases; ⛾; A$; by appt*

Owned by Dr Bill Pannell and his wife Sandra, the founders of Moss Wood winery in the Margaret River region (in 1969). It is one of the relatively few wineries in Pemberton to consistently shine, with excellent Chardonnay, Pinot Noir, Shiraz, and Merlot/Cabernet, all with rich and clearly articulated varietal character. Exports to the UK and elsewhere.

### Salitage ☆☆☆⚐

*Vasse Highway, Pemberton, WA 6260, ☎ (08) 9776 1771, Ⓕ (08) 9776 1772; est 1989; ◊ 20,000 cases; ⛾; A$; 7 days 10-4; ⇤; ✗*

One of the highest-profile wineries in the region, with marked vintage variation impacting on the Chardonnay and Pinot Noir, excellent some years but not always. Exports to the UK and elsewhere.

**Wine & Truffle Company** ☆☆☆☆√
*PO Box 611, Mt Hawthorn, WA 6915, ☎ (08) 9228 0328; est 1996; ♦ NFP; no visitors*
Exactly as its name suggests, a producer of excellent Riesling and Merlot, but also with 13,000 truffle-inoculated hazelnut and oak trees under the supervision of former CSIRO scientist Dr Nicholas Malajcsuk, who cares for the trees as well as the management of the dog-training and truffle-hunting programme. The ultra-fragrant Riesling is most impressive.

# Geographe

The newly created Geographe region is a far more compact and logical area than the sprawling Southwest Coastal Plain from which it has been divided. Its centre is Bunbury, its southern (or, more properly, southeastern) corner is Busselton, while many rivers create valleys from the hills with distinctive climates.

Geographe is an area of considerable beauty and great variation in its topography and scenery. Although not yet officially demarcated, three distinct sub-regions are strongly suggested by the topographic and climatic factors: Capel, on the coast; the Donnybrook area, cut off from the maritime influence and once famous for its apple orchards; and the Bunbury Hills, which include the scenic Ferguson Valley.

The dominant varieties are familiar enough: Chardonnay, Shiraz, and Cabernet Sauvignon, with clear-cut varietal flavour in the wines. As the Margaret River continues to grow, it is expected that Geographe will, too. There are eighteen wine producers in the region.

**Brookhampton Estate** ☆☆☆√
*South West Highway, Donnybrook, WA 6239, ☎ (08) 9731 0400, Ⓕ (08) 0731 0500; est 1998; ♦ 4,000 cases; ⚱; A$; Wed-Sun 10-4*
A major new player, with 112 hectares of Cabernet Sauvignon, Shiraz, and Merlot, plus a touch of Tempranillo and Grenache. The whites are Chardonnay, Sauvignon Blanc, and Semillon. Exports to the UK and US.

**Capel Vale** ☆☆☆☆☆
*Lot 5, Stirling Estate, Mallokup Road, Capel, WA 6271, ☎ (08) 9727 1986, Ⓕ (08) 9727 1904; est 1979; ♦ 100,000 cases; ⚱; A$; 7 days 10-4; ▮●▮*
The seemingly ever-expanding Capel Vale empire extends from Geographe to the Margaret River and to the Great Southern. A long-time producer of finely honed Riesling and tangy Chardonnay, it has added super-premium Shiraz and Cabernet/Merlot at the head of a dauntingly long list of products. Worldwide distribution.

**Hackersley** ☆☆☆☆√
*Ferguson Road, Dardanup, WA 6236, ☎ (08) 9384 6247, Ⓕ (08) 9383 3364; est 1997; ♦ 1,000 cases; ⚱; A$; Fri-Sun 10-4; ▮●▮*
A partnership between the Ovens, Stacey, and Hewitt families, with (they say) the misguided belief that growing their own wine would be cheaper than buying it. Most of the grapes go to Houghton; however, small quantities of excellent wines, most recently Merlot and Sauvignon Blanc, are contract-made for Hackersley.

**St Aidan** ☆☆☆√
*RMB 205 Ferguson Road, Dardanup, WA 6236, ☎ (08) 9728 3007, Ⓕ (08) 9728 3006; est 1996; ♦ 1,000 cases; ⚱; A$; wkds & public hols 10-5, or by appt*

A part-time business for Phil and Mary Smith, but one they have taken seriously. The estate-grown Chardonnay and Cabernet Sauvignon are contract-made, showing commendable elegance.

**Willow Bridge Estate** ☆☆☆☆✓

*Gardin Court Drive, Dardanup, WA 6236, ☎ (08) 9728 0055, ⓕ (08) 9728 0066; est 1997; ◈ 25,000 cases; ⚑; A$; 7 days 11-5; ✗*

The Dewar family has followed a fast track in developing the estate since acquiring their spectacular 180-hectare hillside property in the Ferguson Valley. Over sixty hectares have already been planted, and a 1,200-tonne winery erected. The Winemaker's Reserve range is excellent, with Sauvignon Blanc, Semillon/Sauvignon Blanc, and Shiraz leading an impressive portfolio. Exports to the UK and elsewhere.

# Blackwood Valley

This is the least-known and one of the newest of West Australia's wine regions. The first vineyard and winery was Blackwood Crest, established in 1976 in the northeastern corner of the region. The region's boundaries are in large part self-defining; in the south it abuts Pemberton, to the west and north Geographe, and on the southeast it meets the northern limits of Great Southern. It is situated on the same latitude as Margaret River, and shares many of the same basic climatic characters, most notably wet and relatively warm winters and relatively cool, dry summers. Over fifty vineyards support eight wine producers in the region.

**Blackwood Crest Wines NR**

*RMB 404A Boyup Brook, WA 6244, ☎ & ⓕ (08) 9767 3029; est 1976; ◈ 1,500 cases; ⚑; A$; 7 days 10-6*

Max Fairbrass runs a remote and small winery that has produced one or two striking red wines full of flavour and character, likewise Riesling and Sauvignon Blanc. Quality is, however, variable.

**Blackwood Wines** ☆☆✓ V

*Kearney Street, Nannup, WA 6275, ☎ (08) 9756 0088, ⓕ (08) 9756 0089; est 1998; ◈ 5,000 cases; ⚑; A$; Thurs-Tues 10-4; ⑩*

A comprehensive range of wines is made from both estate-grown and contract-grown grapes. They do not aspire to greatness, but the Fishbone series in particular offers good value. The restaurant is open every day except Wednesday. Exports to the UK and elsewhere.

**Hillbillé** ☆☆☆☆ V

*Blackwood Valley Estate, Balingup Road, Nannup, WA 6275, ☎ (08) 9218 8199, ⓕ (08) 9218 8099; est 1998; ◈ 2,500 cases; ⚑; A$; wkds & hols 10-4*

Gary Bettridge has planted nineteen hectares in a very attractive location. Most of the grapes are sold to leading regional wineries, but a limited amount is made by the Watsons at Woodlands Wines, including a slightly unusual but very good Merlot/Shiraz blend.

**Wattle Ridge Vineyard** ☆☆☆☆

*Loc 11950, Boyup-Greenbushes Road, Greenbushes, WA 6254, ☎ & ⓕ (08) 9764 3594; est 1997; ◈ 1,000 cases; ⚑; A$; 7 days 10-5*

James and Vicky Henderson have established 6.5 hectares of vines at their Nelson vineyard, planted to Riesling, Verdelho, Merlot, and Cabernet

Sauvignon. The contract-made wines are sold by mail order and through the cellar door, which offers light meals, crafts, and local produce.

# Swan District and Swan Valley

The Geographic Indications procedures have created the Swan District region, the Swan Valley as a sub-region; all but eight of the forty-five producers are in the Swan Valley, so I have elected to combine both. Two waves of immigration by Yugoslavs, the first at the turn of the century (principally from Dalmatia) and the second after the WWII, brought with them two claims to fame for the Swan Valley. The first, and most surprising, is that for a time it had more wineries in operation than either NSW or Victoria; the second, and more obvious, is that it joined the Barossa Valley (German) and Riverland (Italian) as a significant ethnically driven wine-producing region.

It is basically a flat, alluvial river plain, bisected by the Swan River, and without much visual attraction other than the historic oasis of the Houghton winery. Its summer temperatures are fierce, often around (or above) 40°C for days on end, and vintage is underway in earnest by the end of January. Chenin Blanc and Verdelho have long been specialties, now joined by Chardonnay.

Swan District's importance as a grape-growing region has declined dramatically over the past twenty years, from fifty-eight per cent down to ten per cent of Western Australian production. It is a trend that will continue, simply as a reflection of the explosive growth in the Great Southern, Margaret River, and Pemberton plantings. The anchors that keep the Swan District from drifting are Houghton and Sandalford, and, to a lesser extent, the small wineries serving the ever-growing wine-tourism trade. There are forty-five wine producers in the region.

**Aquila Estate** ☆☆☆✓
*85 Carabooda Road, Carabooda, WA 6033 (Swan District), ☎ (08) 9561 8166, Ⓕ (08) 9561 8177; est 1993; ⚱ 20,000 cases; Mon-Fri by appt, wkds & public hols 11-5; light meals*
As Aquila Estate has matured, so have its grape sources, centred on the Margaret River (principally) and Blackwood Valley. Chardonnay and Cabernet Sauvignon are made in pleasant, soft styles. Exports to the UK and elsewhere.

**Carabooda Estate NR**
*297 Carabooda Road, Carabooda, WA 6033 (Swan District), ☎ & Ⓕ (08) 9407 5283; est 1989; ⚱ 1,500 cases; ⚱; A$; 7 days 10-6*
Terry Ord made his first wine in 1979, and planted the first estate vines in 1981. His first commercial vintage was 1989. The slowly, slowly approach is reflected in the range of back vintages available at the cellar door.

**Carilley Estate** ☆☆☆✓
*Lot 2, Hyem Road, Herne Hill, WA 6056 (Swan Valley), ☎ & Ⓕ (08) 9296 6190; est 1985; ⚱ 2,000 cases; ⚱; A$; 7 days 10.30-5; ⑩*
Doctors Laura and Isavel Carija have two hectares each of Chenin Blanc, Shiraz, and Chardonnay, and a hectare of Merlot. Most of the grapes are sold, with an increasing amount made under the Carilley Estate label.

**Faber Vineyard** ☆☆☆⚐

*233 Hadrill Road, Baskerville, WA 6056 (Swan Valley), ☎ (08) 9296 0619,*
*Ⓕ (08) 9296 0681; est 1997; ⚐1,000 cases; no visitors*

Former Houghton winemaker and now university lecturer and consultant
John Griffiths has teamed up with his wife Jane Micallef to found Faber
Vineyard. Possessed of an excellent palate, and with an impeccable
winemaking background, he makes sumptuous, quality Shiraz.

**Garbin Estate** ☆☆☆⚐

*209 Toodyay Road, Middle Swan, WA 6056 (Swan Valley), ☎ & Ⓕ (08) 9274 1747;*
*est 1956; ⚐ 4,000 cases; ⚑; A$; 7 days 10.30-5.30*

Peter Garbin, winemaker by weekend and design draughtsman by week,
decided in 1990 to substantially upgrade the family business. The
vineyards have been replanted, the winery re-equipped, and some
consistently attractive Shiraz and Merlot have been the result.

**Houghton** ☆☆☆☆☆ V

*Dale Road, Middle Swan, WA 6056 (Swan Valley), ☎ (08) 9274 5100,*
*Ⓕ (08) 9274 5372; est 1836; ⚐ 280,000 cases; ⚑; A$; 7 days 10-5; ⦿; café; museum*

The five-star rating may seem extreme, but rests partly upon Houghton
White Burgundy (aka Supreme), almost entirely consumed within days of
purchase, but superlative with seven or so years' bottle age, and on the
Jack Mann and John Gladstones ultra-premium red wines sourced from
the Frankland and Margaret rivers. The Moondah Brook brand is
excellent quality and value, with a multi-regional base for its red wines.
Worldwide distribution.

**Jane Brook Estate** ☆☆☆⚐

*229 Toodyay Road, Middle Swan, WA 6056 (Swan Valley), ☎ (08) 9274 1432,*
*Ⓕ (08) 9274 1211; est 1972; ⚐ 20,000 cases; ⚑; A$; Mon-Fri 10-5, wkds & public*
*hols 12-5; ⦿; overseas gift service*

An attractive winery, which relies in part on substantial cellar-door trade
and in part on varying export markets. It has established a vineyard in the
Margaret River and is now also sourcing fruit from Pemberton, Ferguson
Valley, and Arthur River. Exports to the UK and elsewhere.

**John Kosovich** ☆☆☆☆

*Corner Memorial Avenue and Great Northern Highway, Baskerville, WA 6056*
*(Swan Valley), ☎ & Ⓕ (08) 9296 4356; est 1922; ⚐ 11,000 cases; ⚑; A$; 7 days 10-5.30*

John Kosovich is a consistent producer of a surprisingly elegant and
complex Chardonnay; the other wines are more variable, but from time to
time attractive Verdelho and excellent Cabernet Sauvignon have appeared.
A family-owned vineyard at Pemberton now broadens the blend choice.
(Formerly Westfield.)

**Lamont Wines** ☆☆☆☆⚐ V

*85 Bisdee Road, Millendon, WA 6056 (Swan Valley), ☎ (08) 9296 4485,*
*Ⓕ (08) 9296 1663; est 1978; ⚐ 12,000 cases; ⚑; A$; Wed-Sun 10-5; ⦿; gallery*

Corin Lamont is the daughter of the late Jack Mann, and makes her wines
in the image of those made by her father, resplendent in their generosity
but with a touch of true finesse. Lamont also boasts a superb restaurant
with a gallery for the sale and promotion of local arts. Exports to the UK
and elsewhere.

**LedaSwan** ☆☆☆

*179 Memorial Avenue, Baskerville, WA 6065 (Swan Valley), ☎ (08) 9296 0216;*
*est 1998; ⚐ 250 cases; ⚑; A$; 7 days 11-4.30; 𝒦*

LedaSwan claims to be the smallest winery in the Swan Valley using organically grown grapes, moving to 100 per cent estate-grown in the future, utilizing the two hectares of estate vineyards. Duncan Harris retired from engineering in 2001 to become a full-time vintner, winning several awards. Unpretentious Shiraz is best.

**Lilac Hill Estate** ☆☆☆ **V**

*55 Benara Road, Caversham, WA 6055 (Swan Valley), ☏ (08) 9378 9945, Ⓕ (08) 9378 9946; est 1998; ❖ 15,000 cases; 🍷; A$; Tues-Sun 10.30-5; art & crafts*

Part of the renaissance which is sweeping the Swan Valley, based on wine tourism. Thus Lilac Hill Estate, drawing in part upon four hectares of estate vineyards, has already built a substantial business, relying on cellar-door trade and limited retail distribution in Perth.

**Mann NR**

*105 Memorial Avenue, Baskerville, WA 6056 (Swan Valley), ☏ & Ⓕ (08) 9296 4348; est 1988; ❖ 600 cases; 🍷; A$; wkds 10-5, or by appt*

Industry veteran Dorham Mann has established a label solely for what must be Australia's most unusual wine: a dry, only faintly inky sparkling wine made exclusively from Cabernet Sauvignon grown on the 2.4-hectare estate surrounding the cellar door.

**The Natural Wine Company** ☆☆☆

*217 Copley Road, Upper Swan, WA 6069 (Swan Valley), ☏ & Ⓕ (08) 9296 1436; est 1998; ❖ 1,500 cases; 🍷; A$; Wed-Sun & public hols 10-5*

Owners Colin and Sandra Evans say the name of the business is intended to emphasize that no herbicides or systemic pesticides are used in the vineyard, situated on the western slopes of the Darling Range. The vineyard is within a short walk of the Bells Rapids and close to the Walunga National Park.

**Oakover Estate** ☆☆☆½

*14 Yukich Close, Middle Swan, WA 6056 (Swan Valley), ☏ (08) 9274 0777, Ⓕ (08) 9274 0788; est 1990; ❖ 3,500 cases; 🍷; A$; 7 days 11-5; 🍽; 🚶*

Part of the new wave in the Swan Valley, with a large vineyard of sixty-four hectares. Much of the production is sold to others, with Julie White as contract winemaker for the 3,500 cases sold through the cellar door and the large café/restaurant and function centre situated in the heart of the vineyard.

**Olive Farm NR**

*77 Great Eastern Highway, South Guildford, WA 6055 (Swan Valley), ☏ (08) 9277 2989, Ⓕ (08) 9277 6828; est 1829; ❖ 3,500 cases; 🍷; A$; Wed-Sun 10-5.30 cellar sales; 11.30-2.30 café*

The oldest winery in Australia in use today, and arguably the least communicative. The ultra-low profile tends to disguise the fact that wine quality is, by and large, good. The wines come from twelve hectares of estate plantings of eleven different varieties.

**Paul Conti** ☆☆☆½

*529 Wanneroo Road, Woodvale, WA 6026 (Greater Perth Zone), ☏ (08) 9409 9160, Ⓕ (08) 9309 1634; est 1948; ❖ 7,000 cases; 🍷; A$; Mon-Sat 9.30-5.30, Sun by appt; 🍽*

The gently mannered Paul Conti has made some quite lovely wines in his time, the hallmarks being softness, freshness, and balance. Supple Carabooda Chardonnay and chewy, cherry Marijiniup Shiraz have been the best. Son Jason is now taking the reins. Exports to the UK and elsewhere.

### Pinelli ☆☆☆
*30 Bennett Street, Caversham, WA 6055 (Swan Valley),* ☎ *(08) 9279 6818,*
Ⓕ *(08) 9377 4259; est 1979;* ◊ *10,000 cases;* ⚏; *A$; Mon-Fri 9-5.30, wkds 10-5*
Dominic Pinelli and son Robert, the latter a Roseworthy College graduate,
sell seventy-five per cent of their production in flagons, but are seeking to
place more emphasis on bottled wine sales in the wake of recent show
success with Chenin Blanc and a pleasant unwooded Chardonnay.

### Platypus Lane Wines ☆☆☆
*PO Box 1140, Midland, WA 6936 (Swan District),* ☎ *(08) 9250 1655,*
Ⓕ *(08) 9274 3045; est 1996;* ◊ *NA; no visitors*
Platypus Lane, with a small core of 2.5 hectares of Chardonnay, Shiraz, and
Muscat, gained considerable publicity for owner Ian Gibson when its
Shiraz won the inaugural John Gladstones Trophy at the Qantas Western
Australian Wines Show for the wine showing greatest regional and varietal
typicity. Much of the credit can no doubt go to then contract winemaker
Brenden Smith. Exports to the UK and elsewhere.

### RiverBank Estate ☆☆☆
*126 Hamersley Road, Caversham, WA 6055 (Swan Valley),* ☎ *(08) 9377 1805,*
Ⓕ *(08) 9377 2168; est 1993;* ◊ *5,000 cases;* ⚏; *A$; 7 days 10-5*
Robert Bond, a graduate of Charles Sturt University and Swan Valley
viticulturist for twenty years, established RiverBank Estate in 1993. He
draws upon eleven hectares of estate plantings, and, in his words, "The
wines are unashamedly full-bodied, produced from ripe grapes." Exports
to the UK and elsewhere.

### Sandalford ☆☆☆☆⚏
*West Swan Road, Caversham, WA 6055 (Swan Valley),* ☎ *(08) 9374 9343,*
Ⓕ *(08) 9274 2154; est 1840;* ◊ *100,000 cases;* ⚏; *A$; 7 days 10-5;* 🍴; ⛴; *river
cruises*
The arrival of a new winemaking team, coupled with the refurbishment of
the winery, has heralded major changes at Sandalford. Wine quality has
improved year on year, with Riesling, Margaret River Cabernet Sauvignon,
and Frankland/Margaret River Shiraz leading the way, but not alone.

### Sittella Wines ☆☆☆
*100 Barrett Road, Herne Hill, WA 6056 (Swan Valley),* ☎ & Ⓕ *(08) 9296 2600;
est 1998;* ◊ *5,000 cases;* ⚏; *A$; Tues-Sun & public hols 11-4;* 🍴
Perth couple Simon and Maaike Berns acquired a seven-hectare block at
Herne Hill, producing the first wine in 1998 and opening the most
attractive winery and cellar-door facility later that year. They also own a
ten-hectare vineyard in the Margaret River. The wines are elegant.

### Swan Valley Wines ☆☆☆
*261 Haddrill Road, Baskerville, WA 6065 (Swan Valley),* ☎ *(08) 9296 1501,*
Ⓕ *(08) 9296 1733; est 1999;* ◊ *3,000 cases;* ⚏; *A$; Fri-Sun & public hols 10-5*
The Hoffmans acquired their six-hectare property in 1989. In 1999 the
family built a new winery to handle estate-grown Chenin Blanc, Grenache,
Semillon, Malbec, Cabernet Sauvignon, and Shiraz. The latter is their best
wine, powerful and robust.

### Swanbrook Estate Wines ☆☆☆☆⚏
*38 Swan Street, Henley Brook, WA 6055 (Swan Valley),* ☎ *(08) 9296 3100,*
Ⓕ *(08) 9296 3099; est 1998;* ◊ *10,000 cases;* ⚏; *A$; 7 days 10-5;* 🍴
The reincarnation of Evans & Tate's Gnangara Winery. Owner John
Andreou has invested A$2 million in upgrading and expanding the

facilities, and former Evans & Tate winemaker Rob Marshall has continued
at Swanbrook, providing an appealing array of white wines plus richly
fruited Shiraz. Exports to the UK and elsewhere.

**Talijancich NR**

*26 Hyem Road, Herne Hill, WA 6056 (Swan Valley), ☎ (08) 9296 4289,
Ⓕ (08) 9296 1762; est 1932; ⚱ 10,000 cases; ₹; A$; Sun-Fri 11-5*

A former fortified wine specialist (a 1969 Liqueur Tokay was released in
July 1999) now making a broad range of table wines, with particular
emphasis on Verdelho. Exports to the UK and elsewhere.

**Upper Reach Vineyard** ☆☆☆✦ **V**

*77 Memorial Avenue, Baskerville, WA 6056 (Swan Valley), ☎ (08) 9296 0078,
Ⓕ (08) 9296 0278; est 1996; ⚱ 5,000 cases; ₹; A$; Thurs-Mon 11-5; ⏚*

The ten-hectare property, on the banks of the upper reaches of the Swan
River, was purchased by Laura Rowe and Derek Pearse in 1996. Four
hectares of twelve-year-old Chardonnay made up the original vineyard,
expanded with 2.5 hectares of Shiraz and Cabernet Sauvignon. Wine
quality across the board is good. Exports to the UK.

# Peel

The registration of Peel as a wine region by the Geographic Indications
Committee put in place the last significant piece in the West Australian
wine map, and in a sense was long overdue. It is an exercise in
pragmatism, for it takes in the sandy, coastal region from which it takes its
name, but extends far inland to the west (to the townships of Wandering
and Williams), taking in country with a very different climate but which
would otherwise have been orphaned. And so it is that Peel has filled in
the gap with the Swan District and Perth Hills to its north, and Geographe
to its south. The European settlement of Peel dates back to 1829, when a
visionary, Thomas Peel, brought three ships of migrants from England for
the Peel Settlement Scheme.

The first commercial vineyard was started by Will Nairn at Peel Estate
in 1974 with a planting of Shiraz, and while most other varieties have since
been established, Shiraz remains the flagship variety for the region, Peel
Estate its flagship producer. There are six wine producers in the region.

**Peel Estate** ☆☆☆☆

*Fletcher Road, Baldivis, WA 6171, ☎ (08) 9524 1221, Ⓕ (08) 9524 1625;
est 1974; ⚱ 7,000 cases; ₹; A$; 7 days 10-5*

The winery rating is given for its Shiraz, a wine of considerable finesse and
with a remarkably consistent track record. Every year Will Nairn holds a
Great Shiraz tasting for six-year-old Australian Shirazes (in a blind tasting
attended by sixty or so people), and pits Peel Estate against Australia's
best; it is never disgraced. Exports to the UK and elsewhere.

**Wandering Brook Estate NR**

*North Wandering Road, Wandering, WA 6308, ☎ (08) 9884 1084, Ⓕ (08) 9884 1064;
est 1989; ⚱ 1,400 cases; ₹; A$; wkds 9.30-6; ⏚*

In a move to diversify, Laurie and Margaret White have planted ten
hectares of vines on their 130-year-old family property. The contract-made
wines include such exotic offerings as Sparkling Verdelho and a
port-style wine.

# Perth Hills

The Perth Hills is a pretty region, with constantly changing vistas, and a rich profusion of exotic and native vegetation. Viticulture has been carried on intermittently in the picturesque area for over a century, but on a generally tiny scale. The longest-established of the present wineries, Hainault, dates back only to 1980. Following an ownership change, it has been significantly expanded and is the only winery crushing more than 100 tonnes, processing grapes both on its own account and as a contract maker for others.

The region has a cooler climate than the nearby Swan District, thanks to its altitude of up to 400 metres. But it could not be described as cool by any stretch of the imagination; Chardonnay, Shiraz, and Cabernet Sauvignon are the most successful varieties, all showing warm-climate generosity of flavour. The arrival of Millbrook and Western Range wineries has brought a degree of sophistication and winemaking skill hitherto altogether lacking, and has already led to a much higher profile for the region. There are twenty-three wine producers in the region.

**Carosa** ☆☆☆½

*310 Houston Street, Mount Helena, WA 6082, ☎ (08) 9572 1603, Ⓕ (08) 9572 1604; est 1984; ❖ 800 cases; 🍷; A$; wkds & hols 11-5, or by appt; 🍽*

Winemaker/owner Jim Elson worked at wineries over in the eastern states before coming to the Perth Hills and setting up his own small business, with generous blackberry/plum Cabernet Sauvignon.

**Cosham** ☆☆☆

*101 Union Road, Carmel via Kalamunda, WA 6076, ☎ (08) 9293 5424, Ⓕ (08) 9293 5062; est 1989; ❖ 1,000 cases; 🍷; A$; wkds & public hols 10-5*

Contract winemaking by Jane Brook Estate has lifted the quality of the wines, led by nicely balanced Chardonnay and workmanlike Cabernet/Merlot.

**Darlington Estate** ☆☆☆

*Lot 39, Nelson Road, Darlington, WA 6070, ☎ (08) 9299 6268, Ⓕ (08) 9299 7107; est 1983; ❖ 3,000 cases; 🍷; A$; Thurs-Sun & hols 12-5; 🍽; music events*

A substantial track record across a wide range of white and red wines, but no longer the dominant player it once was.

**François Jacquard** ☆☆☆½

*14 Neil Street, Osborne Park, WA 6017, ☎ & Ⓕ (08) 9380 9199; est 1997; ❖ 2,000 cases; no visitors*

François (Franky) Jacquard graduated from Dijon University in 1983. A ten-year career as a flying winemaker in Oregon, Australia, and France followed before he became winemaker at Chittering Estate in 1992. In 1997 he established his own business, making his wines at Sittella Estate's winery in the Swan Valley.

**Hainault** ☆☆☆

*255 Walnut Road, Bickley, WA 6076, ☎ (08) 9293 8339; est 1980; ❖ 1,800 cases; 🍷; A$; wkds & public hols 11-5, or by appt*

Lyn and Michael Sykes became the owners of Hainault in 2002, after Bill Mackey and wife Vicki headed off elsewhere. The eleven hectares of close-planted vines are hand-pruned and hand-picked, and the Pinot Noir is very sensibly used to make a sparkling wine, rather than a table wine. The plans are to open a restaurant when the necessary bureaucratic regulations have been dealt with.

### Hartley Estate ☆☆☆
*260 Chittering Valley Road, Lower Chittering, WA 6084, ☎ (08) 9481 4288,*
*Ⓕ (08) 9481 4291; est 1999; ⏁ 1,700 cases; ⏁; A$; by appt*
Planting of seventeen hectares of vines began soon after the Hartley family
purchased the property in 1999, and after a tiny initial vintage in 2002,
Cabernet/Merlot, Cabernet Sauvignon, and Shiraz were made in
commercial quantities in 2003. The major part of the crop goes to Western
Range Wines, the remainder under the Hartley Estate label, made at
Western Range.

### Millbrook Winery ☆☆☆☆⚮
*Old Chestnut Lane, Jarrahdale, WA 6124, ☎ (08) 9525 5796, Ⓕ (08) 9525 5672;*
*est 1996; ⏁ 10,000 cases; ⏁; A$; 7 days 10-5; light meals*
Highly successful new winery drawing in part on 7.5 hectares of estate
vineyards in the Perth Hills, supplemented by contract-grown grapes in
the Perth Hills and Geographe regions. Barking Owl is the second label;
Chardonnay, Cabernet/Merlot, Shiraz, and Semillon/Sauvignon Blanc lead
the high-quality range of wines. Exports to the UK and elsewhere.

### Piesse Brook ☆☆☆
*226 Aldersyde Road, Bickley, WA 6076, ☎ & Ⓕ (08) 9293 3309; est 1974; ⏁ 1,200*
*cases; ⏁; A$; Sat 1-5, Sun & public hols 10-5, or by appt*
The winemaking team of Di Bray, Ray Boyanich, and consultant Michael
Davies has consistently produced good wines from the four hectares
of Chardonnay, Shiraz, Merlot, and Cabernet Sauvignon produced on
this estate.

### Western Range Wines ☆☆☆☆
*Lot 88, Chittering Road, Lower Chittering, WA 6084, ☎ (08) 9571 8800,*
*Ⓕ (08) 9571 8844; est 2001; ⏁ 42,000 cases; ⏁; A$; Wed-Sun 10-5; light meals; tapas*
Between the mid-1990s and 2001 several prominent West Australians
established 125 hectares of vines (under separate ownership), with a
kaleidoscopic range of varietals. The next step was to join forces to build a
substantial winery which is a separate venture to the growers' individual
vineyards, but which takes the grapes and then markets the wine under
the Western Range brand. All in all, an impressive combination. Exports to
the UK and elsewhere.

# Western Australia: Rest of State

A quick glance at a map clearly shows that the official wine regions and
relevant zones of Western Australia are congregated in the southeastern
corner of the state. Nevertheless, there is a handful of wineries that have
found themselves outside this section of the map, including Dalyup River,
at Esperance. Time will tell whether some of these wineries are the
harbingers of new regions, or merely quixotic choices by their founders.
What is certain is that the viticultural map of Western Australia will
continue to expand over the early years of this millennium.

### Dalyup River Estate NR
*Murrays Road, Esperance, WA 6450, ☎ & Ⓕ (08) 9076 5027; est 1987; ⏁ 1,000*
*cases; ⏁; A$; wkds 10-4 Oct-May*
Tom Murray runs what is arguably the most remote winery in Australia
other than Chateau Hornsby in Alice Springs. The quantities are as small

as the cellar-door prices are modest. Came from out of the clouds to win the trophy for Best Wine of Show at the West Australian Show in 1999 with its Shiraz.

**WJ Walker Wines/Lake Grace** ☆☆☆☆☆
*Burns Road, Lake Grace, WA 6353, ☎ (08) 9865 1969; est NA; ⊕ 1,000 cases; no visitors*

Lake Grace is 300 kilometres due east of Bunbury, one of those isolated viticultural outposts which are appearing in many parts of Australia these days. There are 1.5 hectares of Shiraz and half a hectare of Chardonnay; the 2002 Shiraz mimicked Dalyup River Estate by winning the Shiraz trophy at the 2003 Western Australian Wine Show.

# Tasmania

| 1994 | 362 hectares | 0.054 per cent of total plantings |
| 2003 | 1,144 hectares | 0.072 per cent of total plantings |

## Northern Tasmania

As in previous editions, I have arbitrarily divided Tasmania into two parts, North and South. It has so far elected not to seek registration of any regions, even though there are at least three areas in the North and four in the South which could satisfy the requirements for recognition. For the time being, this focuses attention on "Brand Tasmania" (and the frequent "Taste of Tasmania" promotions) and serves the state well. But the time will come when increasing awareness of the complexity and richness of the offering will demand greater individual recognition.

The development of viticulture in Northern Tasmania has come a long way since French-born Jean Miguet founded La Provence – now Providence – in 1956. There is a world of difference between the climate and terroir of the Pipers River and Tamar River regions respectively, while the far northeastern corner of the state is another thing again. The distinguished viticulturist Dr Richard Smart is to orchestrate the planting of 100 hectares a year for the next five years for the new owner of Tamar Ridge in what he (Dr Smart) describes as the warmest and driest part of the state. The level of attention to detail in canopy management, the correct selection of site and matching of variety, and the limitation of yield are all of crucial importance in meeting the challenges of late vintages triggered by cooler and/or wetter summers. When the weather gods smite, the result is wines of exceptional finesse, length, and varietal character. There are thirty-nine wine producers in the region.

### Andrew Pirie NR
*17 High Street, Launceston, Tas 7250, ☎ (03) 6334 7772, Ⓕ (03) 6334 0751; est 2004; ◈ 5,000 cases; no visitors*
In the wash-up of Pipers Brook, Andrew Pirie has retained his eponymous brand; he has leased the Rosevears Winery, where he will produce the wines for the Rosevears group, for himself, and for others, on a contract basis. For the time being, he is relying on contract-grown grapes.

### Barringwood Park ☆☆☆☆
*60 Gillams Road, Lower Brighton, Tas 7306, ☎ (03) 6492 3140, Ⓕ (03) 6492 3360; est 1993; ◈ 1,200 cases; ♀; A$; Wed-Sun & public hols 10-5; light food*
Judy and Ian Robinson planted a few vines in 1993 for some home winemaking; one thing led to another, and they now have four hectares of vineyards, having built their own cellar door and tasting room with skills learnt from their continuing sawmilling business. Chardonnay, Pinot Noir, Pinot Gris, and sparkling are the pick.

### Bay of Fires ☆☆☆☆
*40 Baxters Road, Pipers River, Tas 7252, ☎ (03) 6382 7622, Ⓕ (03) 6382 7225; est 2001; ◈ 3,000 cases; ♀; A$; 7 days 10-5*
Hardys' Tasmanian winemaking base, established in what was originally

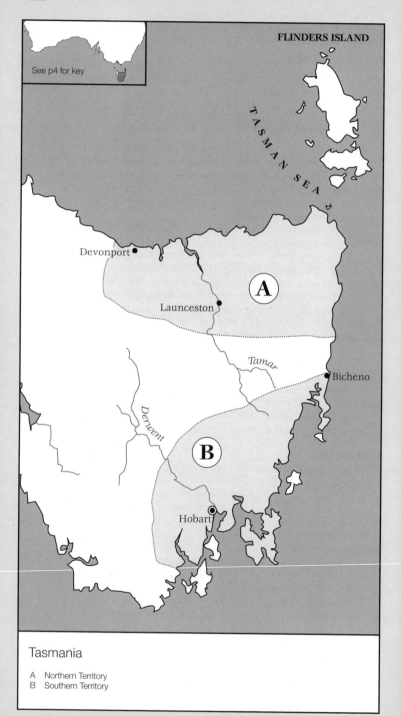

FLINDERS ISLAND

TASMAN SEA

Devonport

Launceston

A

Tamar

Bicheno

Derwent

B

Hobart

Tasmania

A  Northern Territory
B  Southern Territory

Rochecombe, then Ninth Island, and now Bay of Fires. Fine, elegant, and aromatic white wines, Pinot Noir, and sparkling are all made here.

**Bundaleera Vineyard** ☆☆☆✠

*449 Glenwood Road, Relbia, Tas 7258, ☎ (03) 6343 1231, Ⓕ (03) 6343 1250; est 1996; ⚘ 1,000 cases; no visitors*

David and Jan Jenkinson have 2.5 hectares of Riesling, Chardonnay, and Pinot Noir on a sunny, sheltered north slope of the Esk Valley; Jan is the full-time viticulturist and gardener for this immaculate property.

**Clover Hill** ☆☆☆☆☆

*Clover Hill Road, Lebrina, Tas 7254, ☎ (03) 6395 6114, Ⓕ (03) 6395 6257; est 1986; ⚘ 4,000 cases; ☕; A$; 7 days 10-5; by appt in winter*

Established by Taltarni in 1986 with the sole purpose of making a premium sparkling wine, drawing on twenty hectares of Chardonnay, Pinot Noir, and Pinot Meunier. Wine quality is excellent, combining finesse with power and length.

**Dalrymple** ☆☆☆☆

*1337 Pipers Brook Road, Pipers Brook, Tas 7254, ☎ (03) 6382 7222, Ⓕ (03) 6382 7222; est 1987; ⚘ 4,500 cases; ☕; A$; 7 days 10-5*

Former Melbourne radio executive Jill Mitchell and her sister and brother-in-law Anne and Bert Sundstrup have patiently built up Dalrymple. Potent Sauvignon Blanc is one of Tasmania's best, with strong support from fragrant, tangy Chardonnay and plummy, foresty Pinot Noir.

**Delamere** ☆☆☆✠

*Bridport Road, Pipers Brook, Tas 7254, ☎ (03) 6382 7190, Ⓕ (03) 6382 7250; est 1983; ⚘ 2,500 cases; ☕; A$; 7 days 10-5; gallery*

Richie Richardson produces elegant, rather light-bodied wines that have a strong following. Textured, creamy sparkling is the pick, while the pale and wan food-loving Pinot Noir is Richardson's favourite.

**East Arm Vineyard** ☆☆☆☆

*111 Archers Road, Hillwood, Tas 7250, ☎ (03) 6334 0266, Ⓕ (03) 6334 1405; est 1993; ⚘ 1,200 cases; ☕; A$; wkds & public hols, or by appt*

Gastroenterologist Dr John Wettenhall and partner Anita James, who has a wine-science degree, have a glorious, historic site sloping down to the Tamar River. They immediately struck gold with Riesling (contract-made by Andrew Hood) and have done so consistently since.

**Golders Vineyard** ☆☆☆✠

*Bridport Road, Pipers Brook, Tas 7254, ☎ & Ⓕ (03) 6395 4142; est 1991; ⚘ 450 cases; ☕; A$; by appt*

Richard Crabtree's Pinot Noirs have gone from strength to strength since 1995. The 1.5 hectares of Pinot Noir have been followed by a hectare of Chardonnay. Worth the following.

**Grey Sands** ☆☆☆☆

*Corner Kerrisons Road and Frankford Highway, Glengarry, Tas 7275, ☎ (03) 6396 1167, Ⓕ (03) 6396 1153; est 1989; ⚘ 450 cases; ☕; A$; last Sunday of month 10-5, or by appt*

Bob and Rita Richter have very slowly established 2.5 hectares of ultra-high-density vineyards. The mouthfeel of their Pinot Gris is first-class, the texture and tannins of their Merlot likewise.

**Hawley Vineyard** ☆☆☆☆

*Hawley Beach, Hawley, Tas 7307, ☎ (03) 6428 6221, Ⓕ (03) 6428 6844; est 1988; ⚘ 1,000 cases; ☕; A$; 7 days; ⦿; ⨳; gardens*

Hawley Vineyard has a seaside location overlooking Hawley Beach and the Bass Strait to the northeast. Good, unoaked Chardonnay, spicy/plummy/foresty Pinot Noir.

### Holm Oak ☆☆☆☆

*RSD 256 Rowella, West Tamar, Tas 7270, ☎ (03) 6394 7577, Ⓕ (03) 6394 7350; est 1983; ⚱ 3,000 cases; ⚐; A$; 7 days 10-5*

Nick Butler is Tasmania's own flying winemaker, making prodigiously rich and strongly flavoured wines on the banks of the Tamar River. Depending on the vintage, any one or more of Riesling, Chardonnay, Pinot Noir, or Cabernet Sauvignon will shine.

### Iron Pot Bay Wines ☆☆☆⚹

*766 Deviot Road, Deviot, Tas 7275, ☎ (03) 6394 7320, Ⓕ (03) 6394 7346; est 1988; ⚱ 2,600 cases; ⚐; A$; Sept-May Thurs-Sun 11-5, June-Aug by appt*

Now part of the Rosevears Estate (q.v.) syndicate; the name comes from a bay on the Tamar River. Delicate but intensely flavoured unoaked Chardonnay, Sauvignon Blanc, and Pinot Grigio are produced. The last has a great reputation.

### Jansz ☆☆☆☆☆

*1216b Pipers Brook Road, Pipers Brook, Tas 7254, ☎ (03) 6382 7066, Ⓕ (03) 6382 7088; est 1985; ⚱ 15,000 cases; ⚐; A$; 7 days 10-5; cheese tastings*

Part of the Yalumba group; its fifteen hectares of Chardonnay, twelve hectares of Pinot Noir, and three hectares of Pinot Meunier correspond almost exactly to the blend composition of the Jansz wines. It is the only Tasmanian winery entirely devoted to the production of sparkling wine, which is of the highest quality.

### Kelly's Creek ☆☆☆☆

*RSD 226a Lower Whitehills Road, Relbia, Tas 7258, ☎ (03) 6234 9696, Ⓕ (03) 6231 6222; est 1992; ⚱ 650 cases; no visitors*

One hectare of Riesling, and a dash of Chardonnay, Pinot Noir, and Cabernet Sauvignon are tended by majority owner Darryl Johnson. The Riesling has striking, tropical fruit-salad flavours, gathering many gold medals.

### Lake Barrington Estate ☆☆☆⚹

*1133-1136 West Kentish Road, West Kentish, Tas 7306, ☎ (03) 6491 1249, Ⓕ (03) 6334 2892; est 1986; ⚱ 500 cases; ⚐; A$; Wed-Sun 10-5 (Nov-Apr)*

A former sparkling-wine specialist owned by vivacious Maree Taylor, now also making Riesling, Chardonnay, and Pinot Noir. The eponymous lake on the Tasmanian north coast makes a beautiful site for a picnic.

### Pipers Brook Vineyard ☆☆☆☆☆

*1216 Pipers Brook Road, Pipers Brook, Tas 7254, ☎ (03) 6382 7527, Ⓕ (03) 6382 7226; est 1974; ⚱ 90,000 cases; ⚐; A$; 7 days 10-5; café*

Acquired by Belgian-owned Kreglinger (q.v.) in 2001, the empire has continued to grow apace, with an astonishing 220 hectares of vineyard to support the Pipers Brook, Heemskerk Ninth Island, and Rochecombe labels. All the wines bear the stamp of founder Andrew Pirie: finesse and elegance. The Riesling seldom, if ever, misses the bull's-eye. Exports to the UK and elsewhere.

### Providence Vineyards ☆☆☆☆☆

*236 Lalla Road, Lalla, Tas 7267, ☎ (03) 6395 1290, Ⓕ (03) 6395 2088; est 1956; ⚱ 800 cases; ⚐; A$; 7 days 10-5; ⚔*

Provençal Jean Miguet pioneered viticulture in Northern Tasmania while working for the Hydroelectric Commission. Forty years later, the EU forced a change of name from Provence to Providence Vineyards. Mature vines produce great wines, none better than the Miguet Reserve Pinot Noir, unless it be the Miguet Reserve Chardonnay.

**Rosevears Estate** ☆☆☆↓

*1a Waldhorn Drive, Rosevears, Tas 7277, ☎ (03) 6330 1800, Ⓕ (03) 6330 1810; est 1999; ◈ 8,000 cases; ℗; A$; 7 days 10-4; ⚔*

The multi-million dollar Rosevears Estate winery, restaurant complex, and luxury accommodation units were opened by the Tasmanian premier in November 1999. Built on a steep hillside overlooking the Tamar River, it is certain to make a lasting and important contribution to the Tasmanian wine industry. It incorporates both Notley Gorge and Ironpot Bay brands, and is leased by Andrew Pirie, who will also make his own wines there.

**Sharmans** ☆☆☆↓ V

*Glenbothy, 175 Glenwood Road, Relbia, Tas 7258, ☎ (03) 6343 0773, Ⓕ (03) 6343 0773; est 1987; ◈ 1,000 cases; ℗; A$; Thurs-Sun 10-5, closed during winter*

Mike Sharman has pioneered a very promising region that is situated not far south of Launceston but with a warmer climate than Pipers Brook. Three hectares of Riesling, Sauvignon Blanc, Chardonnay, Pinot Noir, and Cabernet are all producing quality wines at modest prices.

**Silk Hill** ☆☆☆☆

*324 Motor Road, Deviot, Tas 7275, ☎ (03) 6394 7385, Ⓕ (03) 6394 7392; est 1990; ◈ 300 cases; ℗; A$; Thurs-Sun 9-5*

Long-term pharmacist-cum-viticulturist Gavin Scott is producing excellent Pinot Noir from a 1.5-hectare vineyard planted in 1989 (by others).

**St Matthias** ☆☆☆

*113 Rosevears Drive, Rosevears, Tas 7277, ☎ (03) 6330 1700, Ⓕ (03) 6330 1975; est 1983; ◈ 16,000 cases; ℗; A$; 7 days 10-5*

After an uncomfortable period in the wilderness following the sale of the vineyard to Moorilla Estate, and the disposal of the wine made by the previous owners under the St Matthias label, Moorilla has re-introduced the label, and markets a full range of competitively priced wines.

**Tamar Ridge** ☆☆☆☆☆

*Auburn Road, Kayena, Tas 7270, ☎ (03) 6394 1111, Ⓕ (03) 6394 1126; est 1994; ◈ 35,000 cases; 7 days 10-5; ⚔*

Acquired by large Tasmanian forestry company Gunns Limited in April 2003, with consultant viticulturist Dr Richard Smart orchestrating the development of a very large vineyard in the far northeast corner of Tasmania, which will be the state's largest planting when completed. In the meantime, truly excellent wines continue to come from Tamar Ridge, spanning all the major varieties.

## Southern Tasmania

The birthplace of Tasmania's wine industry is the Derwent Valley. Here, in 1827, Tasmania's first (Australia's second) commercial winemaker, Bartholemew Broughton, offered his first wine for sale. When Claudio Alcorso (of Moorilla Estate) arrived 110 years later and planted vines on the unique Derwent River isthmus, the official view of the Department of Agriculture was that viticulture was not feasible in Tasmania. Broughton and Alcorso were right; the department embarrassingly wrong. Southern

Tasmania alone boasts four quite distinct (albeit unofficial) regions where grapes now flourish. The four areas are the Derwent Valley, where the Derwent River has a significant influence on vineyard siting, the hills and valleys of the beautiful Huon Valley, the rapidly expanding Coal River/Richmond region, and the East Coast.

A pattern quickly emerges that is repeated across the regions – the best-suited varieties are Riesling, Gewurztraminer, Chardonnay, and Pinot Noir (the latter two for both still and sparkling wines). On the east coast, Pinot Noir is hotly pursued by Chardonnay; Cabernet Sauvignon and Merlot are also successfully grown. The Coal River/Richmond grows virtually all varieties, with site selection (as ever) the key. And Andrew Hood, an extraordinary winemaker, makes wines for literally dozens of producers in quantities that would elsewhere be regarded as ludicrously small and uneconomic. This has allowed many grape-growers to experiment, but also to enjoy (and sell) wines – of a quality they alone could probably not achieve – that would otherwise never see the light of day. There are sixty-one wine producers in the region.

### Apsley Gorge Vineyard ☆☆☆☆⚘
*The Gulch, Bicheno, Tas 7215, ☎ (03) 6375 1221, Ⓕ (03) 6375 1589; est 1988;*
*⚘ 3,000 cases; ⚱; A$; by appt*
Situated inland from Bicheno, but sharing with the other wineries of the east coast region the capacity to produce Chardonnay and Pinot Noir of excellent richness and quality.

### Bream Creek Vineyard ☆☆☆ V
*Marion Bay Road, Bream Creek, Tas 7175, ☎ (03) 6231 4646, Ⓕ (03) 6231 4646;*
*est 1975; ⚘ 3,500 cases; ⚱; A$; at Potters Croft, Dunally, ☎ (03) 6253 5469;*
*🖼; arts & crafts*
Legendary viticulturist Fred Peacock has managed to coax this temperamental coastal vineyard into reliable production, and has been rewarded with Riesling, Chardonnay, and a spicy, dark-plum Pinot Noir skilfully contract-made by Steve Lubiana and/or Julian Alcorso.

### Broadview Estate ☆☆☆⚘
*Rowbottoms Road, Granton, Tas 7030, ☎ (03) 6263 6882, Ⓕ (03) 6263 6840;*
*est 1996; ⚘ 250 cases; ⚱; A$; Tues-Sun 10-5; 🍴*
David and Kaye O'Neil planted their micro vineyard in the spring of 1996. Chardonnay (minerally, fine) and Riesling (toasty, herbaceous) have appeal.

### Casa Fontana NR
*4 Cook Street, Lutana, Tas 7009, ☎ (03) 6272 3180; est 1994; ⚘ 250 cases;*
*no visitors*
Metallurgist Mark Fontana and Japanese wife Shige planted their first Pinot Noir in 1994, and over the following two years expanded the vineyard to its present level of 2.6 hectares, with melon/citrus Chardonnay and lush, plummy Pinot Noir.

### Clemens Hill ☆☆☆⚘
*686 Richmond Road, Cambridge, Tas 7170, ☎ (03) 6248 5985, Ⓕ (03) 6248 5985; est 1994; ⚘ 650 cases; ⚱; A$; by appt*
The Shepherd family acquired Clemens Hill in June 2001 after selling Rosabrook in Margaret River. They also have a shareholding in Winemaking Tasmania, the newly established contract winemaking facility run by Julian Alcorso, who will henceforth make Clemens Hill wines.

### Coal Valley Vineyard ☆☆☆↓

*257 Richmond Road, Cambridge, Tas 7170, ☎ (03) 6248 5367, ⓕ (03) 6248 4175; est 1991; ⚭ 500 cases; ⚑; A$; 7 days 10-4, Fri tapas 4-8; ⦿; cheese platters*

Coal Valley Vineyard is the new name for Treehouse Vineyard and Wine Centre, the change brought about by the fact that Treehouse had been trademarked by the Pemberton winery, Salitage. The vineyard was purchased by Todd Goebel and wife Gillian Christian in 1999. They have set about doubling the size of the existing Riesling vineyard and establishing 1.5 hectares of another vineyard planted to Pinot Noir.

### Coombend Estate ☆☆☆☆

*Coombend via Swansea, Tas 7190, ☎ (03) 6257 8881, ⓕ (03) 6257 8484; est 1985; ⚭ 2,000 cases; ⚑; A$; 7 days 9-6; ⛾; olive oil*

Being graziers by background, the Fenn Smiths calculate their vineyard holdings not by area but by vine numbers. This whimsy to one side, Andrew Hood contract-makes crisp, herbal/mineral Riesling, fresh, gooseberry Sauvignon Blanc, and one of Tasmania's most reliable and best Cabernet Sauvignons, oozing cedar, cigar-box, and sweet, dark-berry fruit. Exports to the UK.

### Craigie Knowe NR

*80 Glen Gala Road, Cranbrook, Tas 7190, ☎ & ⓕ (03) 6259 8252; est 1979; ⚭ 500 cases; ⚑; A$; 7 days by appt*

John Austwick makes a small quantity of full-flavoured, robust Cabernet Sauvignon in a tiny winery as a relief from a metropolitan dental practice. The Pinot Noir is made in a style which will appeal to confirmed Cabernet Sauvignon drinkers.

### Craigow ☆☆☆☆☆

*528 Richmond Road, Cambridge, Tas 7170, ☎ (03) 6248 5379, ⓕ (03) 6248 5482; est 1989; ⚭ 2,000 cases; 7 days Christmas to Easter (except public hols), or by appt*

Barry and Cathy Edwards have moved from the nominal production of one wine from ten hectares of vineyards to a balance between grape-growing and winemaking (via contract). Botrytis Riesling and Gewurztraminer are outstanding; Riesling very good; Chardonnay and Pinot Noir adequate.

### Crosswinds Vineyard ☆☆☆↓

*10 Vineyard Drive, Tea Tree, Tas 7017, ☎ (03) 6268 1091, ⓕ (03) 6268 1091; est 1990; ⚭ 650 cases; ⚑; A$; Mon-Fri 10-5*

Andrew Vasiljuk makes Chardonnay, Pinot Noir, and sparkling wines from two one-hectare vineyards. An unoaked Pinot Noir can be surprisingly good. To prevent boredom, he also works as a consultant in Queensland each vintage. Small UK exports.

### Darlington Vineyard ☆☆☆↓

*Holkam Court, Orford, Tas 7190, ☎ & ⓕ (03) 6257 1630; est 1993; ⚭ 450 cases; ⚑; A$; Thurs-Mon 10-5*

Peter and Margaret Hyland planted a little under two hectares of vineyard in 1993. The first wines were made from the 1999 vintage, forcing retired builder Peter Hyland to complete their home so the small building in which they had been living could be converted to a cellar door.

### Derwent Estate ☆☆☆☆

*329 Lyell Highway, Granton, Tas 7070, ☎ & ⓕ (03) 6248 5073; est 1993; ⚭ 300 cases; no visitors*

The Hanigan family has a 400-hectare mixed farming property, diversifying with five hectares of vineyard planted with Pinot Noir,

Chardonnay, and Riesling. Most of the grapes are sold to Stefano Lubiana, who contract-makes the three wines for Derwent Estate. The Riesling is always excellent.

**Domaine A** ☆☆☆☆☆
*Campania, Tas 7026, ☎ (03) 6260 4174, ⓕ (03) 6260 4390; est 1973; ♦ 5,000 cases; ⚐; A$; Mon-Fri 9-4, wkds by appt; reception centre*

Swiss businessman Peter Althaus has quite literally transformed the former Stoney Vineyard, investing millions with a long-term view. Domaine A Cabernet Sauvignon (typically with ten per cent Merlot, Cabernet Franc, and Petit Verdot blended in) is Tasmania's best, the Lady A Fumé Blanc likewise, heading a two-tier range of the classic white and red varietals.

**Elsewhere Vineyard** ☆☆☆☆☆
*42 Dillons Hill Road, Glaziers Bay, Tas 7109, ☎ (03) 6295 1228, ⓕ (03) 6295 1591; est 1984; ♦ 4,000 cases; no visitors*

Kylie and Andrew Cameron's evocatively named Elsewhere Vineyard used to jostle for space with a commercial flower farm. The estate-produced range comes from six hectares of Pinot Noir, three hectares of Chardonnay, and two hectares of Riesling on their immaculately tended vineyard. Concentrated, long-lived Pinot Noir and explosively intense Riesling lead the way.

**ese Vineyards** ☆☆☆☆
*1013 Tea Tree Road, Tea Tree, Tas 7017, ☎ 0417 319 875, ⓕ (03) 6225 1989; est 1994; ♦ 2,600 cases; ⚐; A$; 7 days 10-5*

Elvio and Natalie Brianese are an architect and graphic designer couple, who have 2.5 hectares of vineyard and got off to a flying start with a gold and silver medal for their 1997 Pinot Noir, the 2002 a return to glory. A further four hectares of Pinot Noir and Chardonnay were planted in 2004.

**572 Richmond Road** ☆☆☆☆
*572 Richmond Road, Cambridge, Tas 7170, ☎ 0419 878 023, ⓕ (07) 3391 4565; est 1994; ♦ 450 cases; no visitors*

It hardly needs to be said that 572 Richmond Road is both the address and the name of the vineyard, owned by John and Sue Carney, medical professionals. The Riesling and light, spicy Gewurztraminer are best.

**Freycinet** ☆☆☆☆☆
*15919 Tasman Highway via Bicheno, Tas 7215, ☎ (03) 6257 8574, ⓕ (03) 6257 8454; est 1980; ♦ 5,000 cases; ⚐; A$; 7 days 9.30-4.30; ⚑; cheese & paté platters*

The nine-hectare Freycinet vineyards are beautifully situated on the sloping hillsides of a small valley. The combination of aspect, slope, soil, and heat summation produce red grapes of unusual depth of colour and ripe flavours. One of Australia's foremost producers of Pinot Noir, with a wholly enviable track record of consistency – rare with such a temperamental variety. The other wines in the portfolio are also top-class.

**Frogmore Creek** ☆☆☆☆☆
*Brinktop Road, Penna, Tas 7171, ☎ (03) 6224 6788, ⓕ (03) 6224 6788; est 1997; ♦ NA; no visitors*

This is a Pacific Rim joint venture between Tony Scherer of Tasmania and Jack Kidwiler of California. They are establishing the only organically certified commercial vineyard in Tasmania, with plans to take the vineyards to eighty hectares. A large on-site winery is being constructed, with Andrew Hood as winemaker. (Frogmore Creek now owns Wellington Wines [*q.v.*].) Frogmore Creek made a spectacular debut with its magnificent 2002 Reserve Pinot Noir.

**GlenAyr** ☆☆☆✠

*Back Tea Tree Road, Richmond, Tas 7025, ☎ (03) 6260 2388, Ⓕ (03) 6260 2691; est 1975; ◊ 500 cases; ⚱; A$; Mon-Fri 8-5*

The Tolpuddle Vineyard, which provides the grapes for the GlenAyr wines, is managed by viticulturist Warren Schasser. Most of the grapes are sold to Domaine Chandon and Hardys, a small amount under contract made by Andrew Hood. Tolpuddle Vineyards Pinot Noir is the pick.

**Grandview Vineyard** ☆☆☆✠

*59 Devlyns Road, Birchs Bay, Tas 7162, ☎ (03) 6267 4749, Ⓕ (03) 6267 4779; est 1996; ◊ 350 cases; ⚱; A$; 7 days 10-5; sheep, cheesery*

Ryan Hartshorn has acquired the vineyard formerly burdened by the impossible name 2 Bud Spur. Hartshorn is moving the vineyard towards organic, and it is anticipated that in 2005 it will be in the conversion phase. Elegant Pinot Noir and funky Chardonnay are best.

**Home Hill** ☆☆☆✠

*38 Nairn Street, Ranelagh, Tas 7109, ☎ (03) 6264 1200, Ⓕ (03) 6264 1069; est 1994; ◊ 2,500 cases; 7 days 10-5; ⦿; ✗*

Terry and Rosemary Bennett began the development of their 4.5-hectare Chardonnay and Pinot Noir vineyard on gentle slopes in the beautiful Huon Valley in 1994. An on-site restaurant serves the supple Kelly's Reserve Chardonnay and surprisingly good Sylvaner.

**Laurel Bank** ☆☆☆

*130 Black Snake Lane, Granton, Tas 7030, ☎ (03) 6263 5977, Ⓕ (03) 6263 3117; est 1987; ◊ 1,200 cases; ⚱; A$; by appt*

Laurel (hence Laurel Bank) and Kerry Carland planted their two-hectare vineyard in 1986. The wines are released with some years' bottle age, and have far more weight than many of their counterparts, particularly the powerful plum and spice Pinot Noir, and chocolate, vanilla, and berry Cabernet/Merlot. Riesling, too, is good.

**Meadowbank Estate** ☆☆☆☆

*699 Richmond Road, Cambridge, Tas 7170, ☎ (03) 6248 4484, Ⓕ (03) 6248 4485; est 1974; ◊ 7,000 cases; ⚱; A$; 7 days 10-5; S; ✗; gallery*

Now an important part of the Ellis family business on what was once (but no more) a large grazing property on the banks of the Derwent. A large new winery and a combined function centre-cum-restaurant-cum-cellar door opened in 2001, capable of handling up to 1,000 people. All the usual varieties are made and are consistently good.

**Milford Vineyard** ☆☆☆☆☆

*Tasman Highway, Cambridge, Tas 7170, ☎ (03) 6248 5029, Ⓕ (03) 6248 5076; est 1984; ◊ 200 cases; no visitors*

A single hectare of Pinot Noir grows on the largest Southdown sheep stud in Australia, which has been in Charlie Lewis's family since 1830. It is only fifteen minutes from Hobart to the very banks of the Coal River, a magical spot. The wine, made by Andrew Hood, is truly excellent.

**Moorilla Estate** ☆☆☆☆☆

*655 Main Road, Berriedale, Tas 7011, ☎ (03) 6277 9900, Ⓕ (03) 6249 4093; est 1958; ◊ 16,000 cases; ⚱; A$; 7 days 10-5; ⦿; ⊨; ✗; shop; museum*

This estate is once more a glittering star. Skilled on-site winemaking transformed the quality of the Pinot Noir and Merlot, and continued that of the Riesling, Gewurztraminer, and Chardonnay, although deciphering the label system is daunting. The world-class museum of eastern and African art in the former homestead designed by Sir Roy Grounds, self-contained luxury chalets, and a top restaurant complete a dazzling picture.

### Morningside Wines ☆☆☆

*711 Middle Tea Tree Road, Tea Tree, Tas 7017, ☎ & ⓕ (03) 6268 1748; est 1980; ❧ 500 cases; ☺; A$; by appt*

The name "Morningside" was given to the old property on which the vineyard stands, as it gets the morning sun first. The Chardonnay and Pinot Noir have good varietal flavour and length.

### No Regrets Vineyard NR

*40 Dillons Hill Road, Glaziers Bay, Tas 7109, ☎ (03) 6295 1509, ⓕ (03) 6295 1509; est 2,000; ❧ 160 cases; ☺; A$; by appt, also at Salamanca Market, Hobart most Saturdays*

Having sold Elsewhere Vineyard, Eric and Jette Phillips have turned around and planted another vineyard almost next door, called No Regrets. The first vintage came in 2003, and there is a hiatus in the meantime.

### Palmara ☆☆☆☆ V

*1314 Richmond Road, Richmond, Tas 7025, ☎ (03) 6260 2462, ⓕ (03) 6260 2462; est 1985; ❧ 300 cases; ☺; A$; Sept-May 7 days 12-6; playground*

Allan Bird makes tiny quantities of Chardonnay, Semillon, Ehrenfeltzer, Montage (blend), Exotica (Siegerrebe), Pinot Noir, and Cabernet Sauvignon. The Exotica is well-named.

### Panorama ☆☆☆☆

*1848 Cygnet Coast Road, Cradoc, Tas 7109, ☎ (03) 6266 3409, ⓕ (03) 6266 3482; est 1974; ❧ 2,250 cases; ☺; A$; Wed-Mon 10-5*

Michael and Sharon Vishacki purchased Panorama in 1997, and have since spent considerable sums in building a brand-new winery and an attractive cellar-door sales outlet, and trebling the vineyard size. They produce worthwhile Chardonnay, Sauvignon Blanc, Pinot Noir, and Cabernet Sauvignon.

### Pooley Wines ☆☆☆☆

*Cooinda Vale Vineyard, Barton Vale Road, Campania, Tas 7026, ☎ (03) 6224 3591, ⓕ (03) 6224 3591; est 1985; ❧ 1,500 cases; ☺; A$; Tues-Sun 10-5; �𝄞*

Three generations of the Pooley family have been involved in the development of the Cooinda Vale Estate; it was indeed under the Cooinda Vale label that the winery was previously known. Plantings have now reached eight hectares of Riesling, Chardonnay, and Pinot Noir. Exports to the UK and US.

### Spring Vale Vineyards ☆☆☆☆

*130 Spring Vale Road, Cranbrook, Tas 7190, ☎ (03) 6257 8208, ⓕ (03) 6257 8598; est 1986; ❧ 3,000 cases; ☺; A$; Mon-Fri 10-5, or by appt*

Rodney Lyne's east-coast vineyard produces rich, Burgundian-accented Chardonnay; stylish, sappy, Pinot Noir; and amiable Gewurztraminer. Exports to the UK.

### Stefano Lubiana ☆☆☆☆

*60 Rowbottoms Road, Granton, Tas 7030, ☎ (03) 6263 7457, ⓕ (03) 6263 7430; est 1990; ❧ 8,000 cases; ☺; A$; Sun-Thurs 11-3, closed some public hols*

Former Riverland grower and winemaker Stefano Lubiana moved from one extreme to the other in setting up a substantial sparkling- and table-wine business on the banks of the Derwent River. His Riesling, Chardonnay, Pinot Noir, Pinot Gris, and Vintage Brut are all immaculately crafted.

**Tinderbox** ☆☆☆☆✐

*Tinderbox, Tas 7054, ☎ & Ⓕ (03) 6229 2994; est 1994; ⚘ 185 cases; ⚐; A$; by appt; beach and marine park; salmon fish farm*

Liz McGown is a Hobart nurse who has established her Pinot Noir vineyard on the slope beneath her house, overlooking the entrance to the Derwent River and the D'Entrecasteaux Channel, doubling the size from one to two hectares in 2003. The Pinot Noir has all the length and finesse one could wish for.

**Wellington** ☆☆☆☆☆ V

*Corner Richmond and Denholms Roads, Cambridge, Tas 7170, ☎ (03) 6248 5844, Ⓕ (03) 6248 5855; est 1990; ⚘ 5,000 cases; ⚐; A$; first Sun of month 12-4, or by appt*

In late 2003 Wellington was acquired by the Frogmore Creek partners (*q.v.*). The Wellington winery will continue to operate as previously, under the direction of Andrew Hood, making both its own-label wines and those for contract customers. The Wellington wines are always beautifully poised and balanced.

**Winstead** ☆☆☆☆✐ V

*75 Winstead Road, Bagdad, Tas 7030, ☎ (03) 6268 6417, Ⓕ (03) 6268 6417; est 1989; ⚘ 350 cases; ⚐; A$; by appt*

The good news about Winstead is the outstanding quality of its intensely flinty Riesling and extremely generous and rich Pinot Noirs. The bad news is that production is so limited, with only 0.5 hectares of each variety being tended by fly-fishing devotee Neil Snare and wife Julieanne.

**Yaxley Estate** ☆☆☆☆

*31 Dransfield Road, Copping, Tas 7174, ☎ & Ⓕ (03) 6253 5222; est 1991; ⚘ 330 cases; ⚐; A$; 7 days 10-6.30*

While Yaxley Estate was established back in 1991, it was not until 1998 that it offered each of the four wines from its vineyard plantings, which total just under two hectares. Once again, the small-batch handling skills (and patience) of contract winemaker Andrew Hood have made the venture possible, with Pinot Gris and Chardonnay to the fore.

# Queensland

1994    1,154 hectares      1.75 per cent of total plantings
2003    2,186 hectares      1.38 per cent of total plantings
These figures, in fact, flatter Queensland, for a significant part of the plantings are of table grapes. Its wine-grape crush in 2003 was one quarter of one per cent of the total.

## Granite Belt

Although a few kilometres inside the border of Queensland, the Granite Belt looks south to NSW. It relies on the New England Highway to bring the all-important tourist traffic north across the state boundary. It is striking country, particularly in the south, where streams have deserted the granite bedrock, leaving boulder-strewn landscapes where patches of vineyard peep around the boulders and gum trees.

Lying on the western side of the Great Dividing Range, the climate is Continental yet counterbalanced by the altitude of around 800 metres. This creates moderate temperatures during the growing season and a late vintage. However, the Granite Belt is, like the Hunter Valley to its south, not a "natural" wine-growing region. The sting in the tail is the ever-present risk of spring frosts, followed by periods of drought that are often broken by rain falling at the most inconvenient time.

But that hasn't stopped the wine boom that is sweeping Australia from taking hold here, too. A significant part of the population in the Granite Belt has always been of Italian descent: growers of orchard fruits and table grapes. In 1965, the Ricci family planted the first wine grapes – amounting to one acre of Shiraz. It then fell to Angelo Puglisi to establish Ballandean Estate, the first Granite Belt winery to secure national distribution through a fine-wine wholesaler. Others followed, and the Granite Belt has shown itself capable of great things, notably with Shiraz, Cabernet Sauvignon, and Semillon. Its challenge is how to build on this for the future. There are thirty-eight wine producers in the region.

**Bald Mountain** ☆☆☆
*Hickling Lane, Wallangarra, Qld 4383, ☎ (07) 4684 3186, Ⓕ (07) 4684 3433; est 1985; ♦ 5,000 cases; ⚲; A$; 7 days 10-5*
One of the early movers in lifting the standards in the Granite Belt, but has lost a little focus, perhaps due to Denis Parsons' involvement in the large vineyard development at Tenterfield, just south of the Queensland border.

**Ballandean Estate** ☆☆☆⚘
*Sundown Road, Ballandean, Qld 4382, ☎ (07) 4684 1226, Ⓕ (07) 4684 1288; est 1970; ♦ 18,000 cases; ⚲; A$; 7 days 9-5; ⚭, ⚑, ⚐; concerts*
The eldest and largest winery in the Granite Belt. White wines are diverse but interesting, the red wines smooth and usually well-made. The estate specialty is Sylvaner Late Harvest, a particularly interesting wine of good flavour. Exports to the UK and US.

**Boireann** ☆☆☆☆⚘
*Donnellys Castle Road, The Summit, Qld 4377, ☎ (07) 4683 2194; est 1998; ♦ 500 cases; ⚲; A$; 7 days 10-4.30*

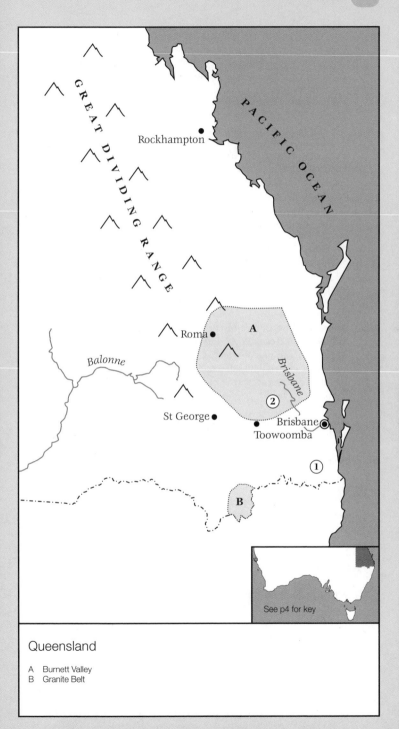

GREAT DIVIDING RANGE

PACIFIC OCEAN

Rockhampton

Roma

Balonne

A

Brisbane

2

St George

Toowoomba

Brisbane

1

B

See p4 for key

Queensland

A   Burnett Valley
B   Granite Belt

Peter and Therese Stark have a ten-hectare property strewn with granite boulders and one hectare of a mix of Bordeaux and Rhône varieties, now producing outstanding red wines, including a world-class Shiraz/Viognier in 2002. If only there were a little more of it.

**Felsberg Winery** ☆☆☆
*116 Townsends Road, Glen Aplin, Qld 4381, ☎ (07) 4683 4332, Ⓕ (07) 4683 4377; est 1983; ♦ 2,000 cases; ♀; A$; 7 days 9-5; ◉; Ⲕ*
Has a spectacular site, high on a rocky slope, the winery itself built on a single huge boulder. Former brewer Otto Haag makes powerful, somewhat rustic red wines.

**Golden Grove Estate** ☆☆☆ V
*Sundown Road, Ballandean, Qld 4382, ☎ (07) 4684 1291, Ⓕ (07) 4684 1247; est 1993; ♦ 10,000 cases; ♀; A$; 7 days 9-5; lunches; garden*
Sam Costanzo has taken a family business focused on table grapes and propelled it to success, with a sweetly tangy Classic White and potent, barrel-fermented Chardonnay.

**Granite Ridge Wines** ☆☆☆
*Sundown Road, Ballandean, Qld 4382, ☎ (07) 4684 1263, Ⓕ (07) 4684 1250; est 1995; ♦ 2,000 cases; ♀; A$; 7 days 9-5; ⇆; Ⲕ*
Over the years has had considerable success with its wines, notably with its unwooded Goldies Chardonnay and Cabernet Sauvignon.

**Heritage Estate** ☆☆☆☆
*Granite Belt Drive, Cottonvale, Qld 4375, ☎ (07) 4685 2197, Ⓕ (07) 4685 2112; est 1992; ♦ 5,000 cases; ♀; A$; 7 days 9-5; ⇆; coffee shop*
While inevitably tourist-oriented, produces wines which stand on their own merit, most notably an estate-grown Merlot, a quirky but striking Botrytis Chardonnay, and a Chardonnay/Semillon blend. Among the Granite Belt's better wineries.

**Hidden Creek NR**
*Eukey Road, Ballandean, Qld 4382, ☎ (07) 4684 1383, Ⓕ (07) 4684 1355; est 1997; ♦ 1,400 cases; ♀; A$; Mon-Fri 11-3, wkds 10-4; ◉*
A beautifully located vineyard and winery on a ridge overlooking the Ballandean township and the Severn River valley. The boulder-strewn hills of this seventy-hectare property provide only a little over six hectares of vineyard.

**Kominos NR**
*New England Highway, Severnlea, Qld 4352, ☎ (07) 4683 4311, Ⓕ (07) 4683 4291; est 1976; ♦ 4,000 cases; ♀; A$; 7 days 9-5*
Tony Comino is a dedicated viticulturist and winemaker, selling all his wine by cellar door and mail order. A district veteran, he prefers to keep a (frustratingly) low profile.

**Preston Peak** ☆☆☆
*31 Preston Peak Lane, Toowoomba, Qld 4352, ☎ & Ⓕ (07) 4630 9499; est 1994; ♦ 3,000 cases; ♀; A$; Wed-Sun 10-5; café; Ⲕ*
Dentist owners Ashley Smith and Kym Thumpkin have a substantial tourism business. The quality of the wines is certainly adequate.

**Robert Channon Wines** ☆☆☆☆☆
*Bradley Lane, Stanthorpe, Qld 4380, ☎ (07) 4683 3260, Ⓕ (07) 4683 3109; est 1998; ♦ 3,500 cases; ♀; A$; 7 days 10-5*
Peggy and English-trained former lawyer Robert Channon, aided by South-African-trained winemaker Mark Ravenscroft, have swept all before them. A clear-span, permanently netted, eight-hectare vineyard produces grapes of exceptional quality, which are then skilfully vinified by Ravenscroft.

The Verdelho is one of Australia's best, the Reserve Merlot, Reserve Cabernet, and Reserve Chardonnay all of unimpeachable quality.

**Robinsons Family Vineyards** ☆☆☆

*Curtin Road, Ballandean, Qld 4382, ☎ & Ⓕ (07) 4684 1216; est 1969; ⬥ 3,000 cases; ⛾; A$; 7 days 9-5*

The conjunction of a picture of a hibiscus and the prominently placed words "cool climate" on the labels was a strange one, but then this has always been the nature of Robinsons Family Vineyards. The red wines can be very good, particularly when not overly extracted and tannic.

**Severn Brae Estate NR**

*Lot 2, Back Creek Road (Mount Tully Road), Severnlea, Qld 4352, ☎ (07) 4683 5292, Ⓕ (07) 3391 3821; est 1987; ⬥ 1,400 cases; ⛾; A$; Mon-Fri 12-3, wkds 10-5, or by appt; café*

This is the home estate of energetic contract winemaker Bruce Humphery-Smith. He has established 5.5 hectares of Chardonnay, relatively closely spaced and trained on a high two-tier trellis. Two-thirds of the production is sold, one-third used for the Severn Brae label.

**Stone Ridge NR**

*35 Limberlost Road, Glen Aplin, Qld 4381, ☎ & Ⓕ (07) 4683 4211; est 1981; ⬥ 2,100 cases; ⛾; A$; 7 days 10-5*

Another early mover with quality Shiraz, now adding Viognier, Marsanne, and Malbec to more mainstream varieties. However, Jim Lawrie and Anne Kennedy these days seem content to rely on word of mouth, eschewing journalistic praise.

**Symphony Hill Wines NR**

*2017 Eukey Road, Ballandean, Qld 4382, ☎ (07) 4684 1388, Ⓕ (07) 4684 1399; est 1999; ⬥ 13,000 cases; ⛾; A$; 7 days 10-5; ⇤; ⚹; light meals, gallery*

Has come from the clouds since the Macpherson family secured the services of former Southcorp winemaker Blair Duncan as winemaker and Mike Hayes (a third-generation resident of the Granite Belt with a degree in viticulture) as viticulturist. A gold-medal-winning Reserve Cabernet Sauvignon from 2002 was an immediate reward. The trial vineyard of 50 varieties (including Picpoul, Tannat, and Mondeuse) adds interest.

**Wild Soul** ☆☆☆

*Horans Gorge Road, Glen Aplin, Qld 4381, ☎ & Ⓕ (07) 4683 4201; est 1995; ⬥ 400 cases; ⛾; A$; wkds & public hols 10-4*

Andy and Beth Boullier have established a hectare of vines, split between Cabernet Sauvignon and Shiraz. They use organic principles in growing the fruit, and a small winery enables Andy Boullier to make the wine on-site. Worth a visit.

**Winewood NR**

*Sundown Road, Ballandean, Qld 4382, ☎ & Ⓕ (07) 4684 1187; est 1984; ⬥ 1,000 cases; ⛾; A$; wkds & public hols 9-5*

A weekend and holiday activity for schoolteacher Ian Davis and town-planner wife Jeanette. The tiny winery is a model of neatness and precision planning. The three-hectare vineyard provides some interesting wines, including Chardonnay, Marsanne, and Shiraz/Marsanne.

# Queensland Coastal

Largely in response to the ever-growing wine-tourism market in Australia, wineries have mushroomed along the southern Queensland coast and adjacent ranges with bewildering speed. Those on the edge of the coast brave a climate as challenging, if not more, than any other part of Australia, with high summer humidity and rainfall part and parcel of the environment. In some instances this is met by securing grapes (or even bulk wine) from other parts of Queensland and/or southern Australia, but there is no doubting the seriousness of the commitment of the ventures such as Sirromet Wines (which in fact has ninety-five per cent of its vineyards in the Granite Belt). Moreover, some of the wineries have been established on the western (inland) slopes of the coastal ranges, where humidity and rainfall are lower, but the tourist potential remains high. As yet, there is no application for registration under the Geographic Indications legislation, and, when there is, it may well take a different shape to the marriage of convenience which I have arranged for the purposes of this book. There are thirty wine producers in the region.

**Albert River Wines** ☆☆☆

*1-117 Mundoolun Connection Road, Tamborine, Qld 4270, ☏ (07) 5543 6622, Ⓕ (07) 5543 6627; est 1998; ❖ 5,000 cases; 🍷; A$; 7 days 10-4; 🍽; wedding chapel; woodshop*

Tourism veterans David and Janette Bladin have moved historic buildings onto the site, including Auchenflower House, to house cellar-door sales, ballroom, and verandah restaurant. A highly professional operation. Shiraz and Shiraz blends do well, and Verdelho is handy.

**Canungra Valley Vineyards NR**

*Lamington National Park Road, Canungra Valley, Qld 4275, ☏ (07) 5543 4011, Ⓕ (07) 5543 4162; est 1997; ❖ 5,000 cases; 🍷; A$; 7 days 10-5; 🍽; ✗; tutored tastings; wine dinners*

Established in the hinterland of the Gold Coast, with a clear focus on broad-based tourism. Two hectares of vines have been established around the nineteenth-century homestead; in deference to the climate, seventy per cent is Chambourcin, the remainder Semillon.

**Cedar Creek Estate** ☆☆½

*104-144 Hartley Road, Mt Tamborine, Qld 4272, ☏ (07) 5545 1666, Ⓕ (07) 5545 4762; est 2000; ❖ 1,500 cases; 🍷; A$; 7 days 10-5; 🍽*

Takes its name from the creek which flows through the property at an altitude of 550 metres on the scenic Tamborine Mountain. A 3.7-hectare vineyard has been planted to Chambourcin and Verdelho, supplemented by grapes grown elsewhere. The wines are adequate.

**Delaney's Creek Winery NR**

*70 Hennessey Road, Delaneys Creek, Qld 4514, ☏ (07) 5496 4925, Ⓕ (07) 5496 4926; est 1997; ❖ 3,000 cases; 🍷; A$; Mon-Fri 10-4, wkds & public hols 10-5*

Barry and Judy Leverett have planted an exotic mix of one hectare each of Shiraz, Chardonnay, Sangiovese, Touriga Nacional, and Verdelho, supplemented by contract-grown grapes including the Cabernet family and Marsanne. A Joseph's Coat indeed.

**Dingo Creek Vineyard** ☆☆½

*265 Tandur-Traveston Road, Traveston, Qld 4570, ☏ (07) 5485 1731, Ⓕ (07) 5485 0041; est 1997; ❖ NA; 🍷; A$; wkds 10-4, or by appt*

Marg and David Gillespie were long-term wine industry professionals before moving to Queensland and planting Chardonnay, Cabernet

Sauvignon, Merlot, and Sauvignon Blanc, throwing in a six-metre by eighteen-metre aviary for good measure. The Cabernet/Merlot is a decent wine.

### Eumundi Winery NR
*2 Bruce Highway, Eumundi, Qld 4562, ☎ (07) 5442 7444, Ⓕ (07) 5442 7455; est 1996; ⚄ 2,500 cases; ⚐; A$; 7 days 10-6; ⭐; wine education evenings*

Set on twenty-one hectares of river-front land in the beautiful Eumundi Valley. The climate is hot, wet, humid, and maritime, and Robyn and Gerry Humphrey have trialled Tempranillo, Shiraz, Chambourcin, Petit Verdot, Durif, Mourvèdre, Tannat, and Verdelho, and three different trellis systems.

### Gecko Valley NR
*Bailiff Road, via 700 Glenlyon Road, Gladstone, Qld 4680, ☎ (07) 4979 0400, Ⓕ (07) 4979 0500; est 1997; ⚄ 1,000 cases; ⚐; A$; 7 days 10-5; ⭐; gift shop*

Extends the viticultural map of Queensland yet further, situated little more than fifty kilometres off the Tropic of Capricorn. The three-hectare vineyard of Chardonnay, Verdelho, and Shiraz provides the usually off-dry table wines, plus a range of ports made several thousand kilometres south; strongly tourist-oriented.

### Glastonbury ☆☆☆
*Shop 4, 104 Memorial Drive, Eumundi, Qld 4562, ☎ (07) 5442 8557, Ⓕ (07) 5442 8745; est 2001; ⚄ 4,000 cases; ⚐; A$; Tues 12-5, Wed 9-8, Thurs 12-8, Fri 12-5, Sat 9-8, Sun 12-5; ⛟*

Situated high in the hills of Glastonbury, eighty kilometres from Noosa on the coast. Steve Davoren has established 6.5 hectares of Chardonnay, Merlot, and Cabernet Sauvignon on terraces, and Peter Scudamore-Smith MW is the contract winemaker. The gaudy labels set the scene for Emotions Cabernet Sauvignon (and Beach Series Tickled Pink Rosé) which are modestly pleasant.

### Kenilworth Bluff Wines ☆☆⚄
*Lot 13, Bluff Road, Kenilworth, Qld 4574, ☎ (07) 5472 3723; est 1993; ⚄ NA; ⚐; A$; Fri-Sun 10-4, or by appt*

Brian and Colleen Marsh began planting the vineyards in 1993 in a hidden valley at the foot of Kenilworth Bluff, and now have four hectares coming into bearing; presently the wines are made off-site. The Bluff Semillon is the pick.

### Lilyvale Wines ☆☆⚄
*Riverton Road, via Texas, Qld 4385, ☎ (07) 4653 5280, Ⓕ (07) 4653 5287; est 1997; ⚄ 4,000 cases; ⚐; A$; 7 days 10-4 by appt*

A substantial and growing business (twenty hectares, 200 tonnes) situated just north of the border between New South Wales and Queensland. Has had particular success with its Semillon. Cabernet Sauvignon and Merlot are also pleasant.

### Settlers Rise Montville ☆☆☆⚄
*249 Western Avenue, Montville, Qld 4560, ☎ (07) 5478 5558, Ⓕ (07) 5478 5655; est 1998; ⚄ 3,000 cases; ⚐; A$; 7 days 10-5; food platters; local produce*

Located in the beautiful highlands of the Blackall Range, seventy-five minutes' drive north of Brisbane. First settled in 1887, Montville has become a tourist destination. Peter Scudamore-Smith MW is the contract winemaker, producing impressive Reserve Chardonnay, Reserve Shiraz, and Queensland Classic White. Deserves to be taken seriously.

**Sirromet Wines** ☆☆☆☆☆ **V**

*850-938 Mount Cotton Road, Mount Cotton, Qld 4165, ☎ (07) 3206 2999, Ⓕ (07) 3206 0900; est 1998; ◈ 60,000 cases; ♟; A$; 7 days 10-5; ¶; eco tours*

Unambiguously ambitious, with the aim of creating Queensland's premier winery, and succeeding. A leading architect designed the striking 80,000-case winery; the state's foremost viticultural consultant oversaw the 100-hectare Granite Belt vine plantings; and the most skilled winemaking team in Queensland, Adam Chapman and Alain Rousseau, make the wines. Outstanding Chardonnay, Cabernet Sauvignon, and Semillon are joined by Shiraz/Cabernet, Merlot, Cabernet/Merlot, and Petit Verdot in strong support. There is also a 200-seat restaurant offering genuinely fine dining. Exports to the UK and elsewhere.

**Tamborine Estate Wines NR**

*32 Hartley Road, North Tamborine, Qld 4272, ☎ (07) 5545 1711, Ⓕ (07) 5545 3522; est 1990; ◈ 3,000 cases; ♟; A$; 7 days 10-4; ✗*

Recently acquired by a joint venture between John Cassegrain (of Cassegrain Wines [q.v.]) and French-born entrepreneur Bernard Forey (owner of the large Richfield Vineyard at Tenterfield in northern NSW). Early days, but the expectations are high.

**Thumm Estate Wines NR**

*87 Kriedeman Road, Upper Coomera, Qld 4209, ☎ (07) 5573 6990, Ⓕ (07) 5573 4099; est 2000; ◈ 3,000 cases; ♟; A$; 7 days 9.30-5; ¶; ✗*

Geisenheim-trained Robert Thumm spent twenty-five years with the family wine business in the Barossa Valley before moving north (with wife Janet) to a new winery and vineyard below the Tamborine Mountain Tourist Centre.

**Warrego Wines** ☆☆☆

*9 Seminary Road, Marburg, Qld 4306, ☎ (07) 5464 4400, Ⓕ (07) 5464 4800; est 2000; ◈ 24,000 cases; ♟; A$; 7 days 10-4; ¶; ✗*

A mix of government and Chinese investment has transformed the small business started by Cathy and Kevin Watson, with a large new winery erected for both contract winemaking and the Warrego brand wines. Kevin Watson competently makes a wide range of wines, including a Pinot Noir utilizing grapes grown in Tasmania's Tamar Valley and Victoria's Strathbogie Ranges. The local wines have been well put together, too.

# South Burnett

While the modern history of the South Burnett region dates back only to 1993, vines were first planted in the early 1900s, and wine for home consumption was made from some of these vines. As in the Granite Belt, table grapes were used both for winemaking and eating, and a small table-grape industry has continued in existence since that time. The town of Kingaroy is the geographical centre of the region, which is basically defined by the Blackbutt, Brisbane, and Coast Ranges in the east, the Great Divide to the southwest and west, and gently declines to the Central Burnett and Burnett River to the north. The Stuart and Booie Ranges run south to north through the centre of the South Burnett, with undulating rolling landscape to the Stuart and Boyne River plain in the west and Barkers Creek in the east. It is the second Queensland region to gain full registration under the Geographic Indications legislation. There are twelve wine producers in the region.

### Barambah Ridge ☆☆☆↓

*79 Goschnicks Road, Redgate via Murgon, Qld 4605, ☎ (07) 4168 4766, Ⓕ (07) 4168 4770; est 1997; ♦ 10,000 cases; ⚑; A$; 7 days 10-5; ⬥; Ⲕ*

Since its inception, this unlisted public company has established itself as one of the major players in the Queensland wine industry, crushing 500 tonnes of grapes a year, much of it as a contract winemaker for many other Queensland wineries. The wines made under the Barambah Ridge label are reliably good, led by Reserve Shiraz, Semillon, Reserve Merlot, and Reserve Chardonnay.

### Captain's Paddock NR

*18 Millers Road, Kingaroy, Qld 4610, ☎ (07) 4162 4534, Ⓕ (07) 4162 4502; est 1995; ♦ 2,000 cases; ⚑; A$; 7 days 10-5; ⬥; ⇔; Ⲕ*

The artistic McCallum family runs this cellar door-cum-art gallery-cum-restaurant with views over the Booie Ranges. Chardonnay, Captain's White, Shiraz, and Shiraz/Cabernet/Merlot are contract-made.

### Clovely Estate ☆☆☆

*Steinhardts Road, Moffatdale via Murgon, Qld 4605, ☎ (07) 3216 1088, Ⓕ (07) 3216 1050; est 1998; ♦ 63,000 cases; ⚑; A$; Fri-Sun 10-5; ⇔*

Although new-born, Clovely Estate has the largest vineyards in Queensland, with 174 hectares at two locations near Murgon. Reserve Chardonnay and Reserve Shiraz/Cabernet (both good wines) come at the top of the pack; then Left Field varietals; then Fifth Row; and finally the Queensland varietal range for export. The wines are contract-made, much at Mudgee in NSW.

### Crane Winery NR

*Haydens Road, Kingaroy, Qld 4610, ☎ (07) 4162 7647, Ⓕ (07) 4162 8381; est 1996; ♦ 4,000 cases; ⚑; A$; 7 days 10-4; gourmet platters*

Sue Crane's grandfather planted Shiraz way back in 1898, so wine is in the blood. She and John Crane have four hectares of vineyard, but also purchase grapes from other growers in the burgeoning Kingaroy district.

### Dusty Hill Vineyard ☆☆☆↓

*Barambah Road, Moffatdale via Murgon, Qld 4605, ☎ (07) 4168 4700, Ⓕ (07) 4168 4888; est 1996; ♦ 3,000 cases; ⚑; A$; 7 days 10-5; ⬥; ⇔*

Joe Prendergast and family have established eight hectares of vineyards. The winery's specialty is the Dusty Rose, continuing a long tradition of Rosé/Beaujolais-style wines from Queensland.

### Hunting Lodge Estate ☆☆↓

*703 Mt Kilcoy Road, Mount Kilcoy, Qld 4515, ☎ & Ⓕ (07) 5498 1243; est 1999; ♦ 3,300 cases; ⚑; A$; 7 days 10-5; ⇔; ⬥; Ⲕ; coffee shop*

Yet another new player in the rapidly expanding Queensland wine industry, offering a range of wines, including "our famous Nairobi Port". A pleasant Verdelho is the pick.

### Kingsley Grove NR

*49 Stuart Valley Drive, Kingaroy, Qld 4610, ☎ (07) 4163 6433, Ⓕ (07) 4162 2201; est 1998; ♦ NA; no visitors*

A newcomer but with good credentials; Michael Berry has undertaken viticulture studies at Melbourne University, and he and Patricia Berry have established nine hectares of Verdelho, Chardonnay, Semillon, Shiraz, Merlot, Sangiovese, Chambourcin, and Cabernet Sauvignon. The wines are made by Michael Berry at an on-site winery. Sales by mail order and the internet (www.kingsleygrove.com).

### Rodericks NR

*90 Goshnicks Road, Murgon, Qld 4605; ☎ & Ⓕ (07) 4168 4768; est 1996; ✾ NA; ⓟ; A$; 7 days 10-5; 🛏; light meals; tutored tastings*

The Roderick family (Wendy, Colin, and Robert) have a substantial twenty-two-hectare vineyard planted to eleven varieties and make the wine on-site.

### Stuart Range Estates ☆☆☆ V

*67 William Street, Kingaroy, Qld 4610, ☎ (07) 4162 3711, Ⓕ (07) 4162 4811; est 1997; ✾ 15,000 cases; ⓟ; A$; 7 days 9-5; ✗; cheese platters; cheese factory*

Yet another flyer, with seven growers in the South Burnett Valley, fifty-two hectares, and a state-of-the-art winery in an old butter factory building. Chardonnay, Shiraz, and Cabernet Sauvignon/Shiraz/Merlot are the well-made pick of a substantial range of wines.

## Queensland Zone

The wine boom of the second half of the 1990s led to changes in the viticultural map of Queensland on a scale unimaginable at the start of the decade. Whether all the new ventures will succeed remains to be seen. Much will depend on wine tourism, and the extent to which the owners work their way around the hazards of grape-growing in the vicinity of their wineries. The one, long-standing winery so rich in history is Romavilla, way to the west.

### Governor's Choice Winery NR

*Berghofer Road, Westbrook via Toowoomba, Qld 4350, ☎ & Ⓕ (07) 4630 6101; est 1999; ✾ 1,500 cases; ⓟ; A$; 7 days 9-5; 🛏; ❑*

A part winery, part premium guest-house accommodation venture situated eighteen kilometres from Toowoomba. Three hectares of estate plantings produce Chardonnay, Shiraz, Verdelho, Cabernet Sauvignon, and Malbec, made on-site and sold through cellar door on weekends or to guests using the accommodation.

### Jimbour Wines ☆☆☆☆⟋

*Jimbour Station, Jimbour, Qld 4406, ☎ (07) 4663 6221, Ⓕ (07) 4663 6194; est 2000; ✾ 7,000 cases; ⓟ; A$; 7 days 10-4.30*

Jimbour Station was one of the first properties opened in the Darling Downs, the heritage-listed homestead built in 1876. The property has been owned by the Russell family since 1923, which has diversified by establishing a twenty-hectare vineyard and opening a cellar door on the property. Its excellent range of wines is contract-made by Peter Scudamore-Smith MW. The Reserve Merlot and Reserve Chardonnay are outstanding, supported by an impeccable range of other varietal wines. Sophisticated packaging is also a plus, with exports to many countries.

### Kooroomba Vineyards ☆☆☆

*168 FM Bells Road, Mount Alford via Boonah, Qld 4310, ☎ (07) 5463 0022, Ⓕ (07) 5463 0441; est 1998; ✾ 2,000 cases; ⓟ; A$; Wed-Sun & public hols 10-5*

Kooroomba Vineyards is little more than one hour's drive from the Brisbane CBD, offering cellar-door wine tasting and sales, a vineyard restaurant, and a lavender farm. The seven-and-a-half-hectare vineyard is planted to Verdelho, Marsanne, Merlot, Shiraz, and Cabernet Sauvignon, with Chardonnay purchased from contract growers.

### Normanby Wines ☆☆☆

*Rose-Lea Vineyard, Dunns Avenue, Harrisville, Qld 4307, ☎ (07) 5467 1214; est 1999; ❧ 800 cases; ⚊; A$; 7 days winter 10-5, summer 10-7*

Normanby Wines fills in more of the Queensland viticultural jigsaw puzzle, situated approximately fifty kilometres due south of Ipswich. The vineyard comprises one hectare each of Verdelho and Shiraz, and 0.2 hectares each of Chambourcin, Durif, and Grenache. A neatly turned Rosé, Verdelho, and Country Shiraz are all pleasant, well-made wines.

### Rimfire Vineyards ☆☆☆

*Bismarck Street, MacLagan, Qld 4352, ☎ (07) 4692 1129, Ⓕ (07) 4692 1260; est 1991; ❧ 6,000 cases; ⚊; A$; 7 days 10-5; café*

The Connellan family has planted twelve hectares of fourteen varieties on its 1,500-hectare cattle stud in the foothills of the Bunya Mountains, forty-five minutes' drive northeast of Toowoomba. They produce a kaleidoscopic array of wines; the Black Bull Café is open daily.

### Riversands Vineyards NR

*Whytes Road, St George, Qld 4487, ☎ (07) 4625 3643, Ⓕ (07) 4625 5043; est 1990; ❧ 3,500 cases; ⚊; A$; Mon-Sat 8-6, Sun 9-4*

Situated on the banks of the Balonne River near St George in the southwest corner of Queensland. The wines are very competently made under contract at Ballandean Estate and have already accumulated a number of silver and bronze medals. The Chardonnay is particularly meritorious.

### Romavilla NR

*Northern Road, Roma, Qld 4455, ☎ & Ⓕ (07) 4622 1822; est 1863; ❧ 3,000 cases; ⚊; A$; Mon-Fri 8-5, Sat 9-12, 2-4*

An amazing historic relic, seemingly untouched since its nineteenth-century heyday. The table wines are ordinary but there are some extraordinary fortifieds, including a truly elegant madeira-style wine, made from Riesling and Syrian.

### Stanton Estate NR

*135 North Isis Road, Childers, Qld 4660, ☎ (07) 4126 1255, Ⓕ (07) 4126 1823; est 2000; ❧ 500 cases; ⚊; A$; wkds 10-5, or by appt*

Keith and Joy Stanton have established two hectares of Verdelho, Marsanne, Cabernet Sauvignon, and Merlot using organic growing methods, and having the wines contract-made according to organic principles.

### Three Moon Creek ☆☆☆

*Waratah Vineyard, Gladstone Road, Mungungo via Monto, Qld 4630, ☎ (07) 4166 5100, Ⓕ (07) 4166 5200; est 1998; ❧ 1,500 cases; ⚊; A$; Tues-Sun & public hols 10–5*

A group including doyen Queensland wine journalist David Bray has banded together three hectares of vines at the Waratah Vineyard at the extreme northern end of the Burnett Valley (and well outside the South Burnett GI). The wines are contract-made by Peter Scudamore-Smith MW and sold under the Gentle Annie brand (not to be confused with Gentle Annie wines of Victoria). Shiraz, Verdelho, and Cabernet Sauvignon are all pleasant.

**Villacoola Vineyard & Winery NR**

*Carnarvon Highway, Surat, Qld 4417, ☎ (07) 4626 5103, ℗ (07) 4626 5516;*
*est 1992; ❧ NA; ♟; A$; 7 days 10-5; light meals*

Ron Ritchie has pushed the viticultural envelope yet further by establishing his vineyard seventy-eight kilometres to the north of Roma (and Romavilla Winery [*q.v.*]). Sauvignon Blanc, Semillon, Chardonnay, Merlot, Shiraz, and Muscat have been planted; the cellar door offers light meals.

# INDEX